High School DEBUT

Contents

Story Thus Far...

High school freshman Haruna was a sporty girl and an ace player for her softball team back in junior high. Now that she's in high school, she wants to give her all to finding true love instead! She gets Yoh, a guy who knows how to be popular, to be her "love coach" and soon begins to fall in love with him.

Haruna poses a hypothetical question to Yoh: "What would you do if you fell in love with someone you shouldn't?" Yoh tells her that she should just confess her feelings, so she summons up the courage to tell him how she feels. And they start dating! They're really happy, but neither of them is used to dating. Plus Haruna is more than a little distressed...

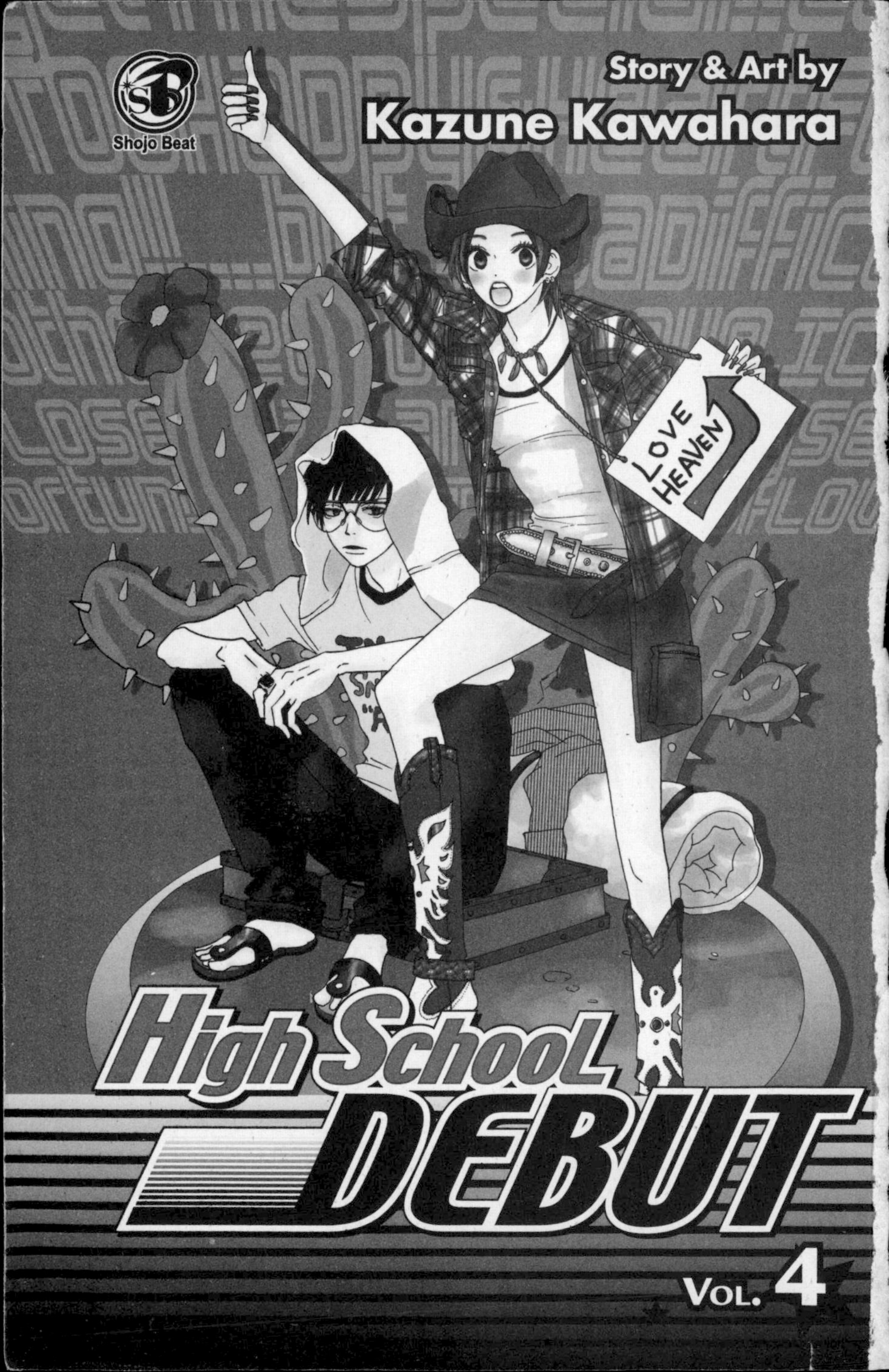
Shojo Beat
Story & Art by
Kazune Kawahara
LOVE HEAVEN
High School
DEBUT
VOL. 4

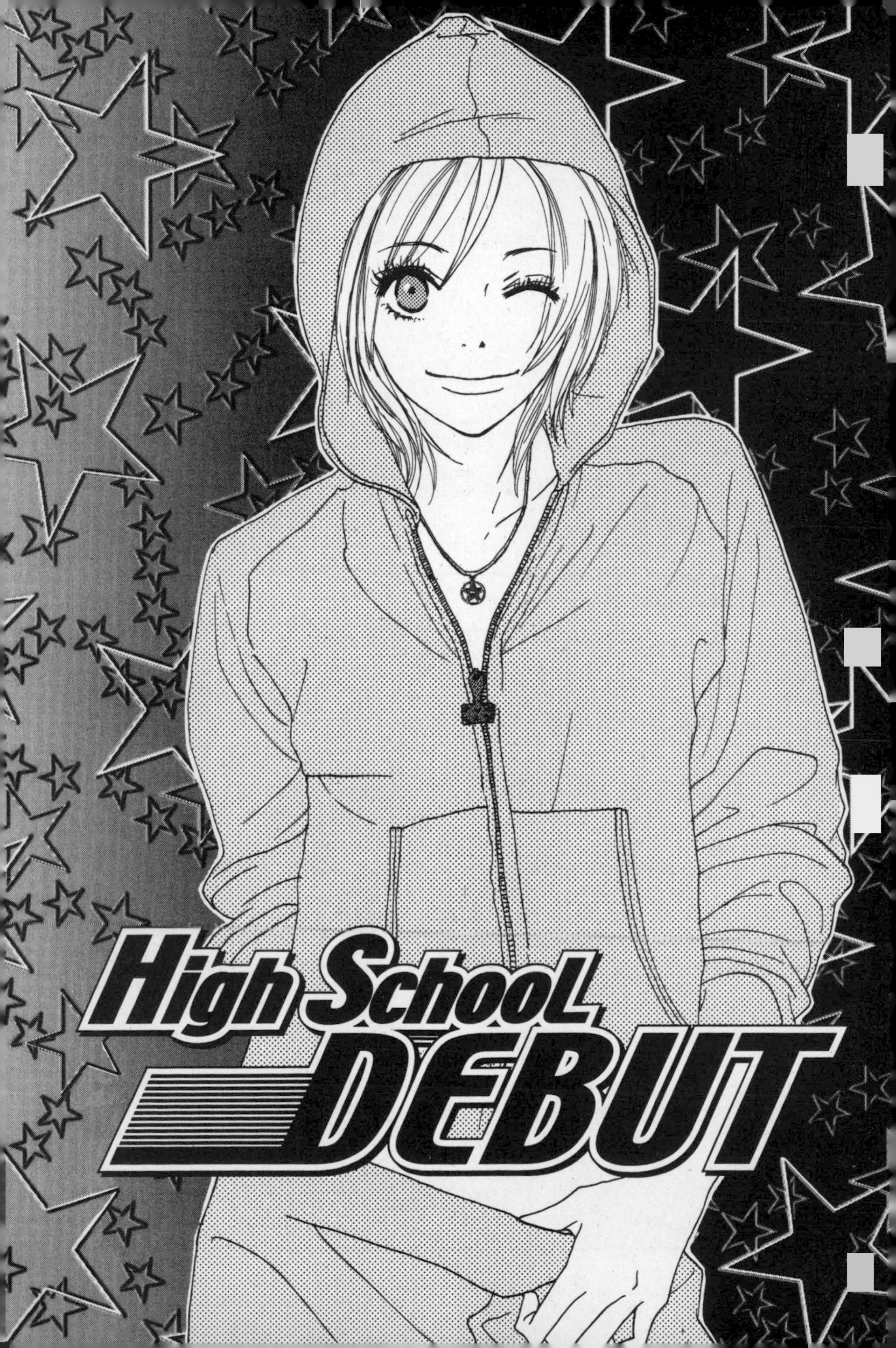
High School
DEBUT

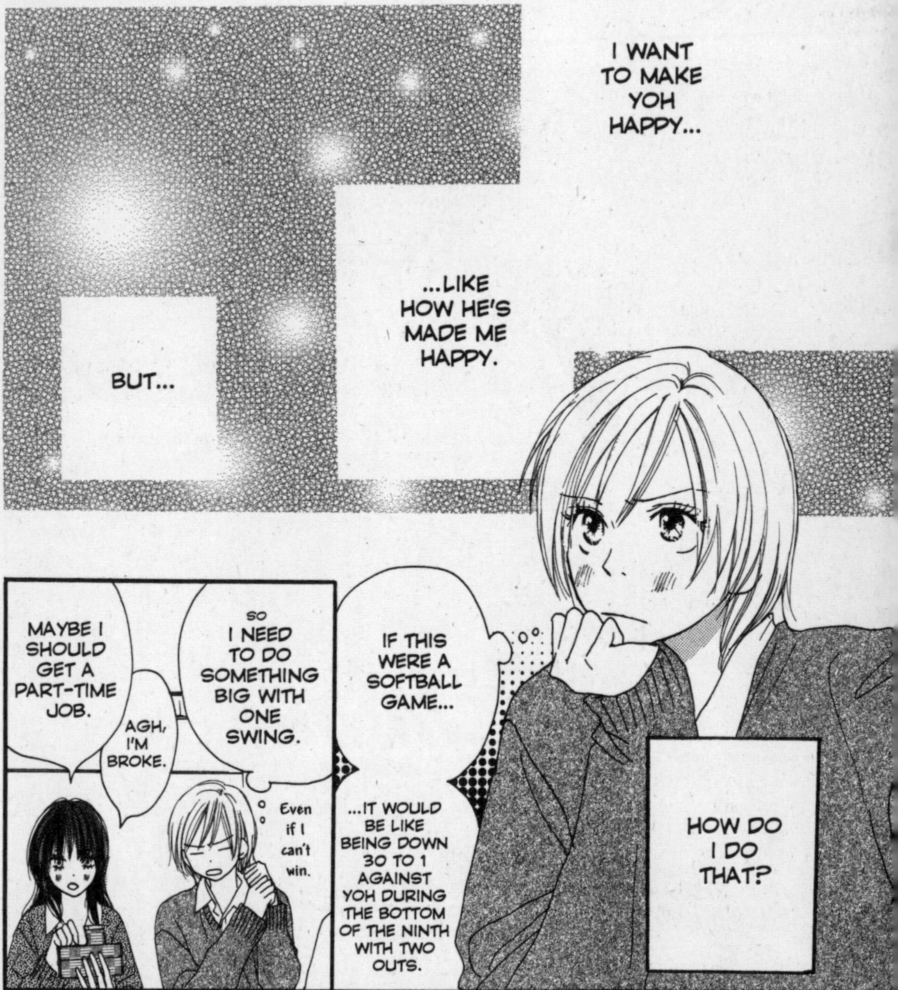
I WANT TO MAKE YOH HAPPY...
...LIKE HOW HE'S MADE ME HAPPY.
BUT...
HOW DO I DO THAT?
IF THIS WERE A SOFTBALL GAME...
...IT WOULD BE LIKE BEING DOWN 30 TO 1 AGAINST YOH DURING THE BOTTOM OF THE NINTH WITH TWO OUTS.
SO I NEED TO DO SOMETHING BIG WITH ONE SWING.
Even if I can't win.
MAYBE I SHOULD GET A PART-TIME JOB.
AGH, I'M BROKE.

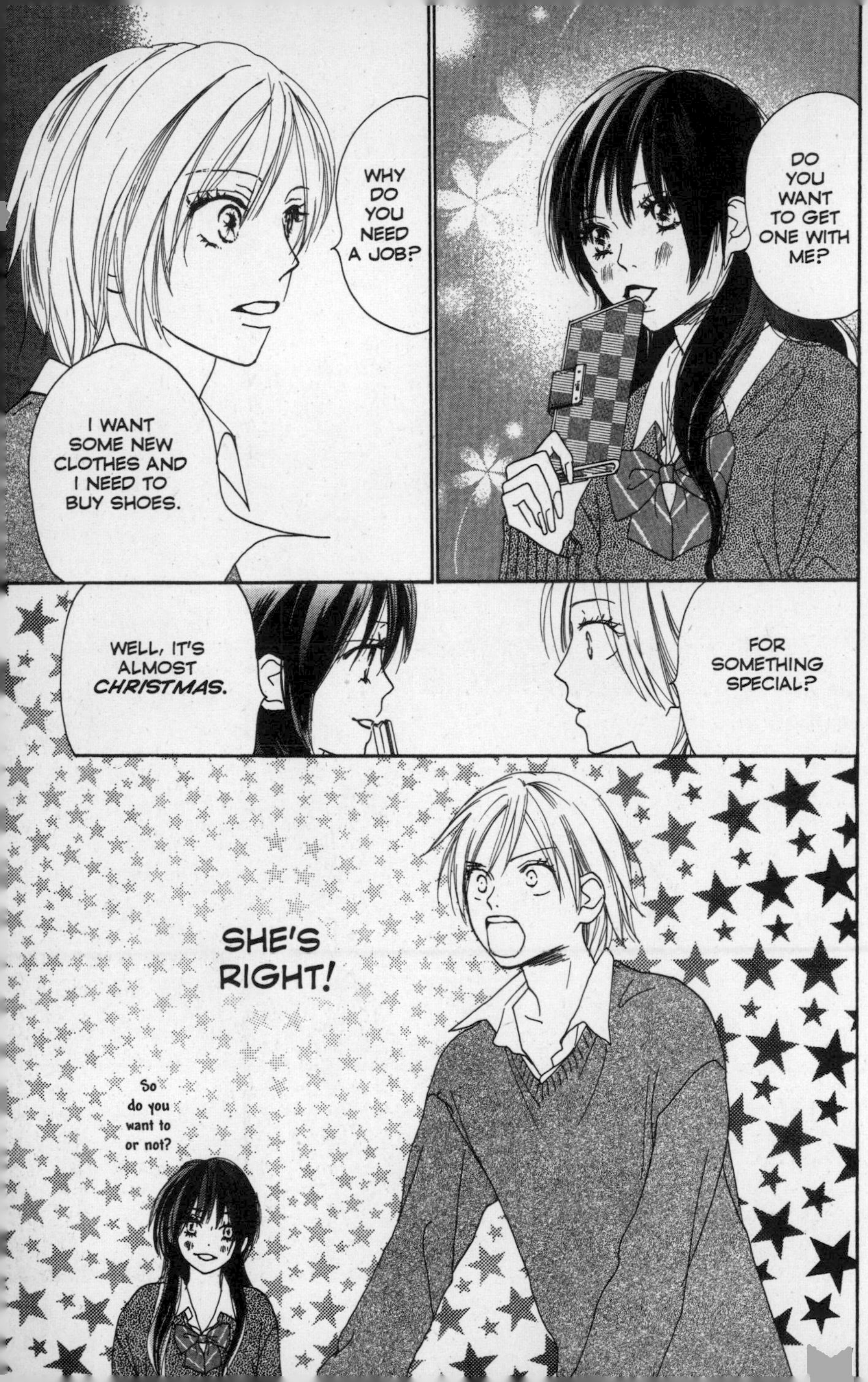
DO YOU WANT TO GET ONE WITH ME?
WHY DO YOU NEED A JOB?
I WANT SOME NEW CLOTHES AND I NEED TO BUY SHOES.
FOR SOMETHING SPECIAL?
WELL, IT'S ALMOST *CHRISTMAS*.
SHE'S RIGHT!
So do you want to or not?

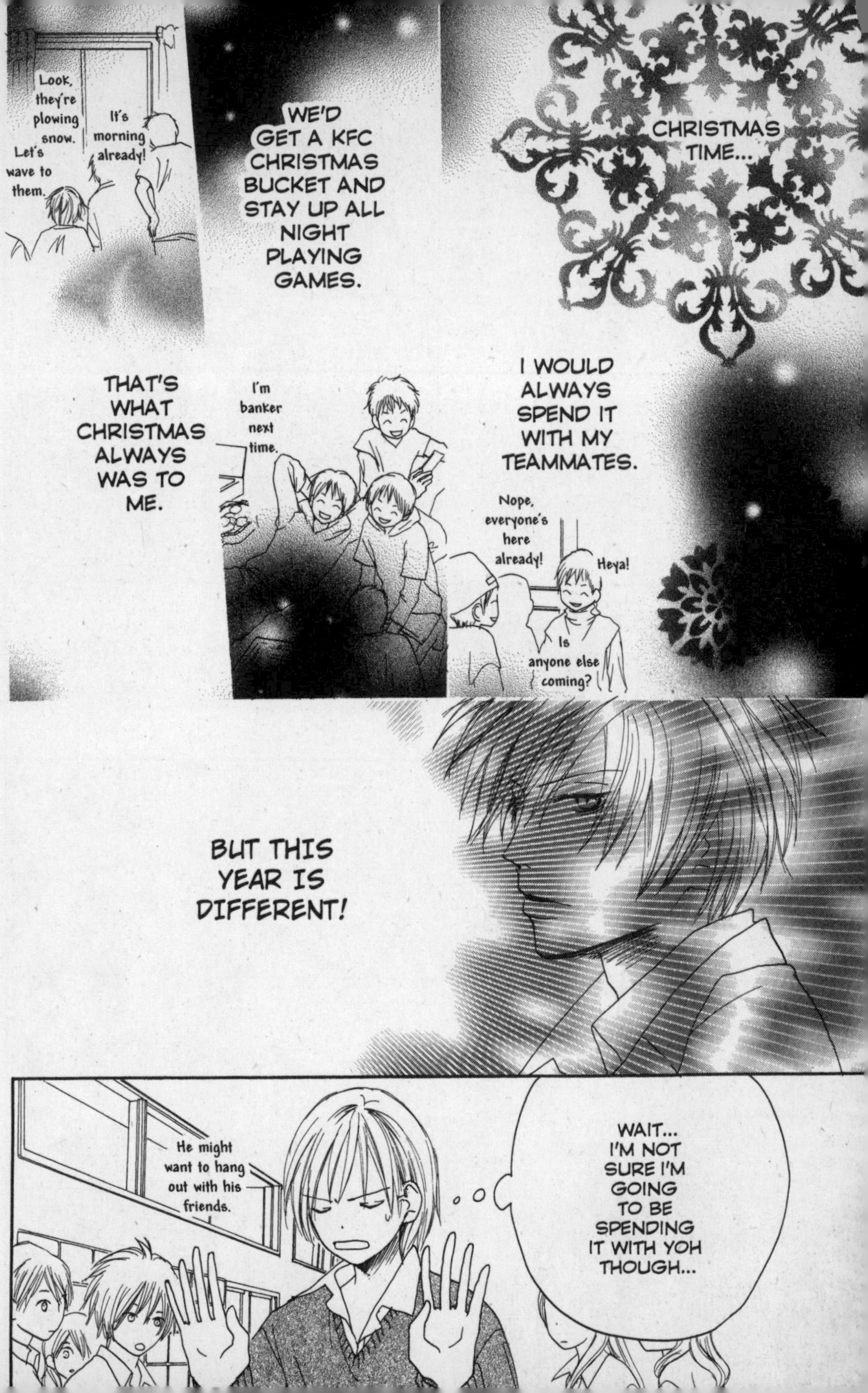
CHRISTMAS TIME...
I WOULD ALWAYS SPEND IT WITH MY TEAMMATES.
Heya!
Is anyone else coming?
Nope, everyone's here already!
WE'D GET A KFC CHRISTMAS BUCKET AND STAY UP ALL NIGHT PLAYING GAMES.
It's morning already!
Look, they're plowing snow.
Let's wave to them.
I'm banker next time.
THAT'S WHAT CHRISTMAS ALWAYS WAS TO ME.
BUT THIS YEAR IS DIFFERENT!
WAIT... I'M NOT SURE I'M GOING TO BE SPENDING IT WITH YOH THOUGH...
He might want to hang out with his friends.

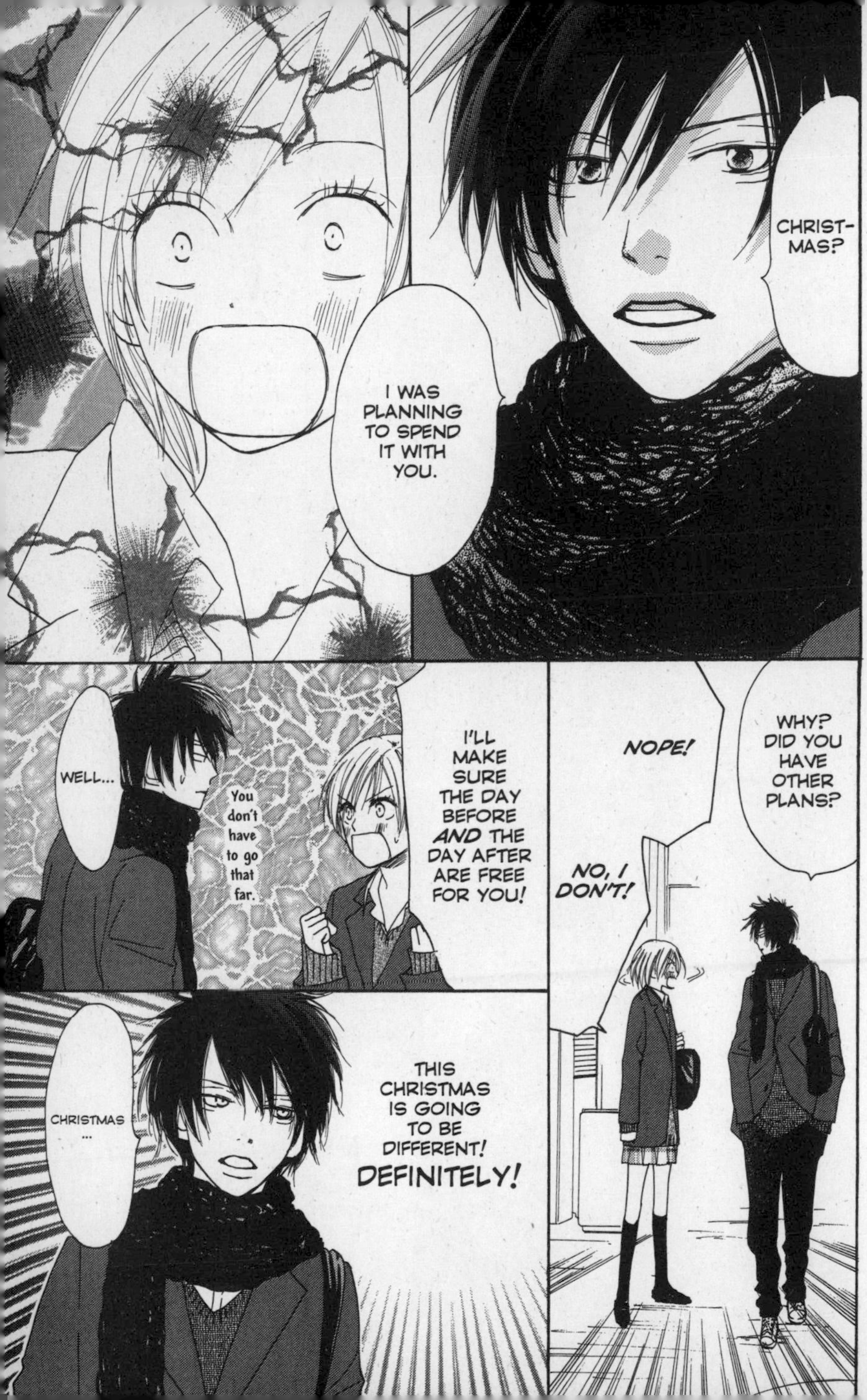
CHRIST-MAS?
I WAS PLANNING TO SPEND IT WITH YOU.
WHY? DID YOU HAVE OTHER PLANS?
NOPE!
NO, I DON'T!
I'LL MAKE SURE THE DAY BEFORE *AND* THE DAY AFTER ARE FREE FOR YOU!
You don't have to go that far.
WELL...
THIS CHRISTMAS IS GOING TO BE DIFFERENT! DEFINITELY!
CHRISTMAS ...

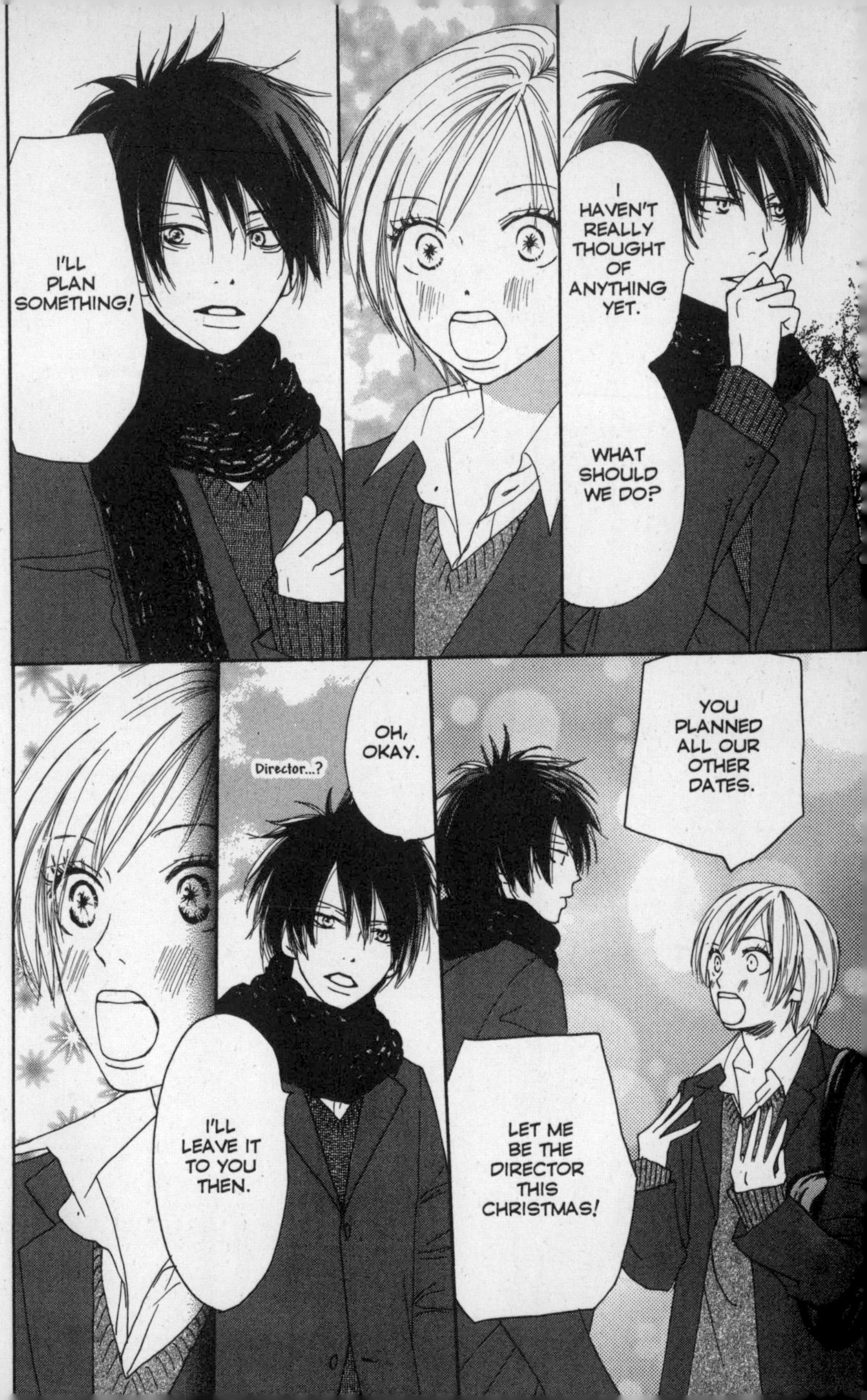
I HAVEN'T REALLY THOUGHT OF ANYTHING YET.
WHAT SHOULD WE DO?
I'LL PLAN SOMETHING!
YOU PLANNED ALL OUR OTHER DATES.
LET ME BE THE DIRECTOR THIS CHRISTMAS!
OH, OKAY.
Director...?
I'LL LEAVE IT TO YOU THEN.

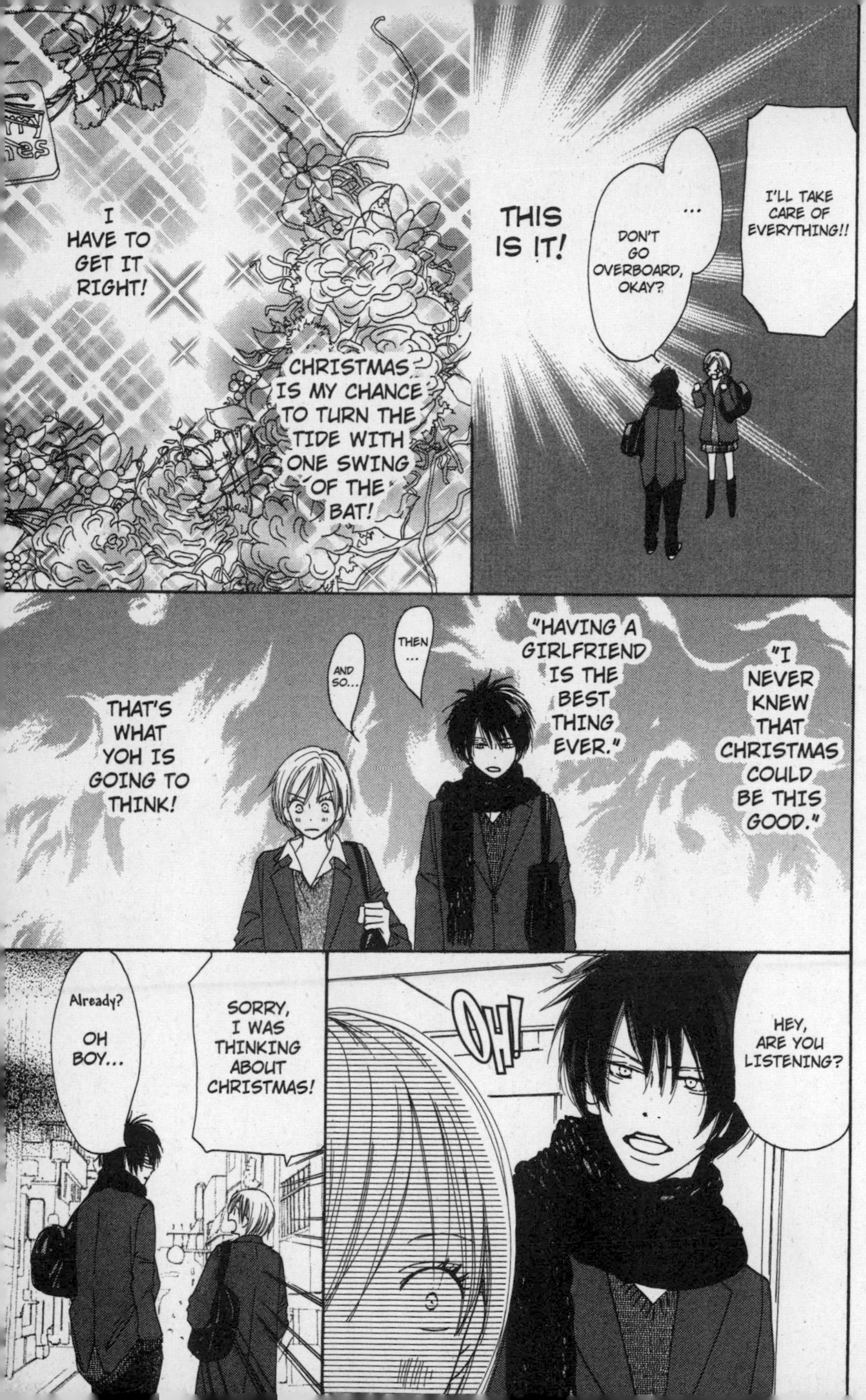
I'LL TAKE CARE OF EVERYTHING!!
...
DON'T GO OVERBOARD, OKAY?
THIS IS IT!
CHRISTMAS IS MY CHANCE TO TURN THE TIDE WITH ONE SWING OF THE BAT!
I HAVE TO GET IT RIGHT!
"I NEVER KNEW THAT CHRISTMAS COULD BE THIS GOOD."
"HAVING A GIRLFRIEND IS THE BEST THING EVER."
THEN ...
AND SO...
THAT'S WHAT YOH IS GOING TO THINK!
HEY, ARE YOU LISTENING?
OH!
SORRY, I WAS THINKING ABOUT CHRISTMAS!
Already?
OH BOY...

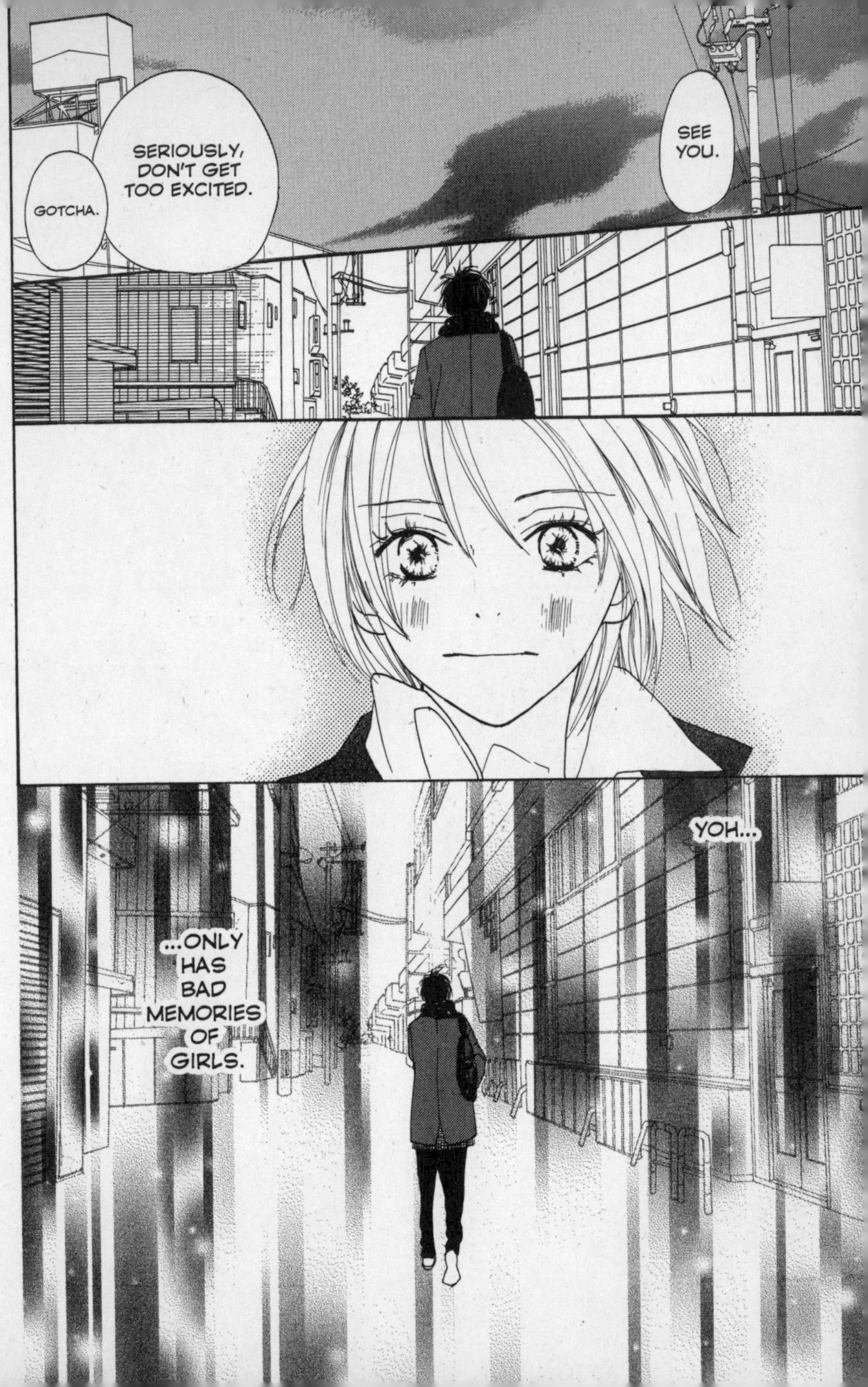
SEE YOU.
SERIOUSLY, DON'T GET TOO EXCITED.
GOTCHA.
YOH...
...ONLY HAS BAD MEMORIES OF GIRLS.

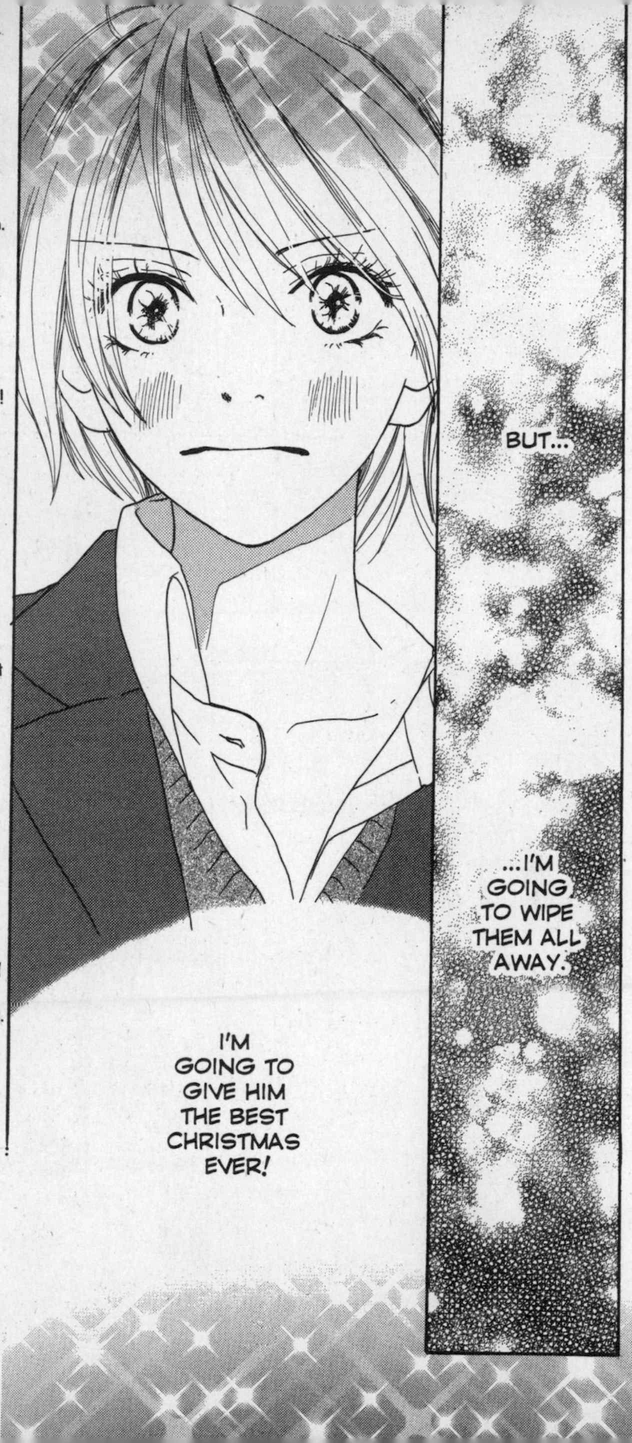
BUT...
...I'M GOING TO WIPE THEM ALL AWAY.
I'M GOING TO GIVE HIM THE BEST CHRISTMAS EVER!

1

Hello. This is Kawahara. Thank you for reading this bit.

I'm always saying silly things here. Sorry, but I'm going to do it again. So let the silly talk begin!

↓

The clocks in my house are all wrong. The main clock is set fast. I did that on purpose. I always rush out at the last minute so having it set a little early is better. Means I'm never late. To catch the 5:00 train, I leave the house when that clock says 5:01. If I rush, I reach the station at 4:55. I don't know how many minutes ahead that clock is, so I did the same thing today.

There's a clock that I don't use much-it's slow. I looked at it closely the other day and discovered that the second hand only moved ten seconds when it should have moved fifty. That's slow...
The cuckoo clock at my sister's house doesn't chime the same number of times as when the cuckoo comes out. →

Continued in part 2

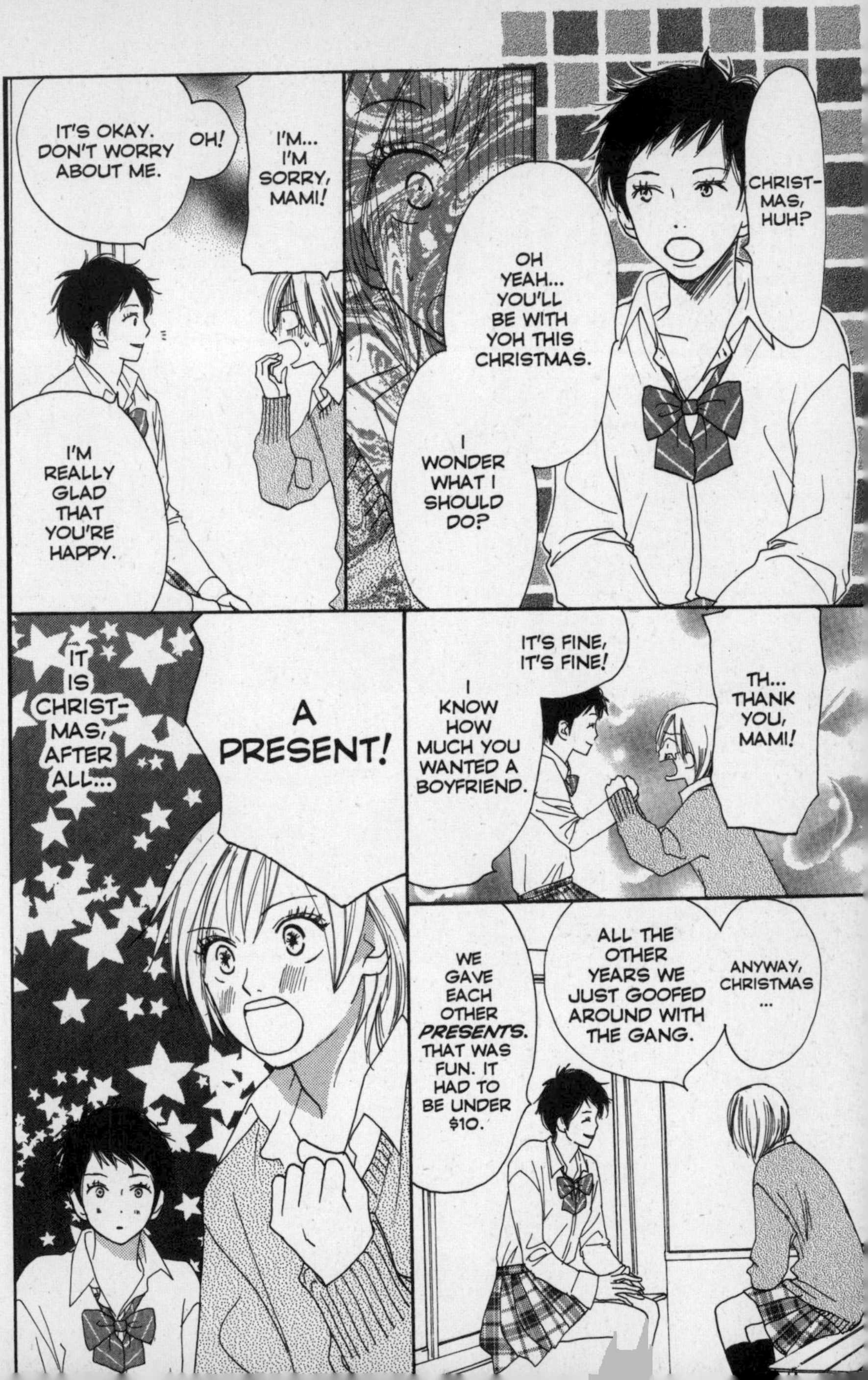
CHRISTMAS, HUH?
OH YEAH... YOU'LL BE WITH YOH THIS CHRISTMAS.
I WONDER WHAT I SHOULD DO?
I'M... I'M SORRY, MAMI!
OH!
IT'S OKAY. DON'T WORRY ABOUT ME.
I'M REALLY GLAD THAT YOU'RE HAPPY.
TH... THANK YOU, MAMI!
IT'S FINE, IT'S FINE!
I KNOW HOW MUCH YOU WANTED A BOYFRIEND.
ANYWAY, CHRISTMAS ...
ALL THE OTHER YEARS WE JUST GOOFED AROUND WITH THE GANG.
WE GAVE EACH OTHER *PRESENTS*. THAT WAS FUN. IT HAD TO BE UNDER $10.
A PRESENT!
IT IS CHRISTMAS, AFTER ALL...

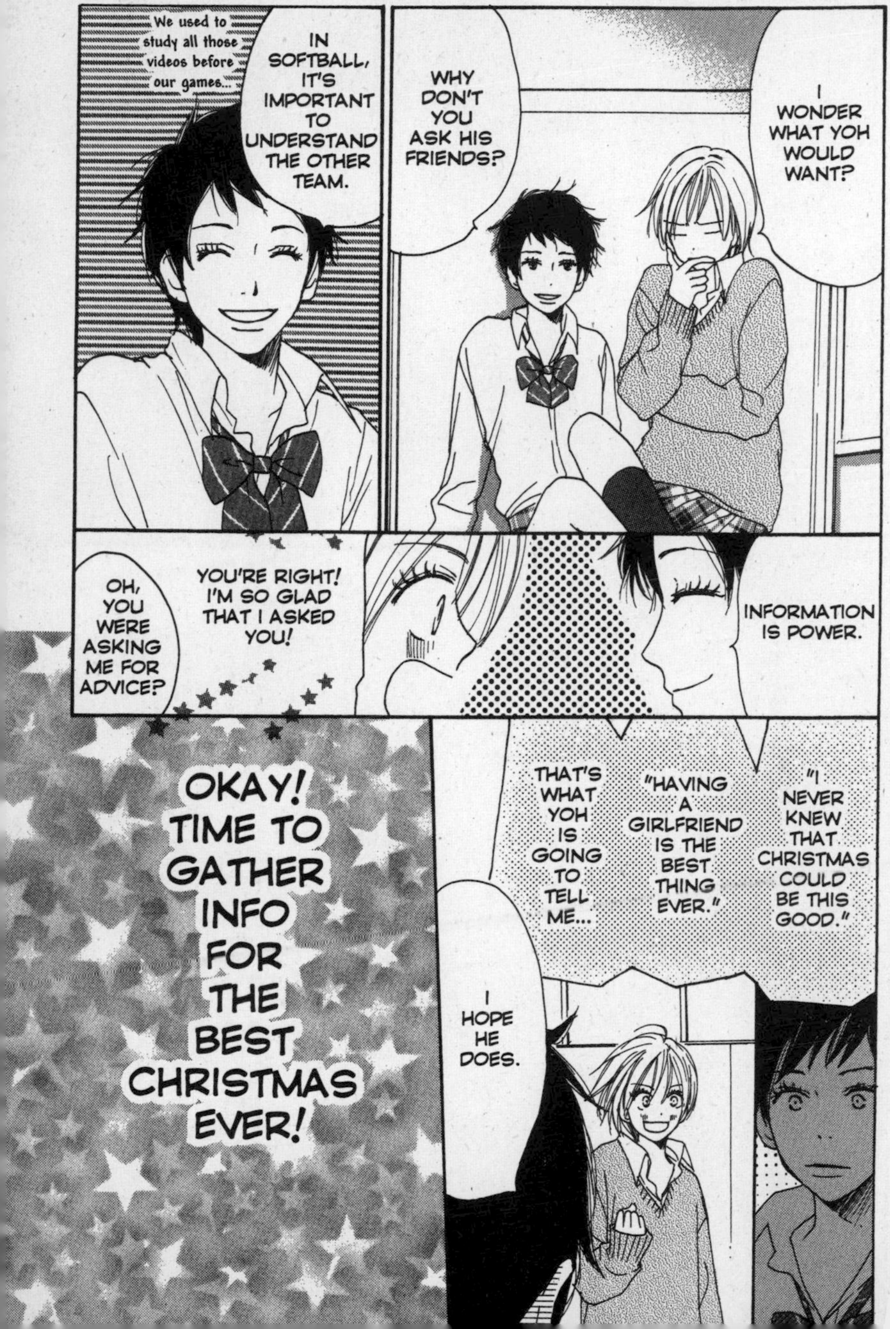
I WONDER WHAT YOH WOULD WANT?
WHY DON'T YOU ASK HIS FRIENDS?
IN SOFTBALL, IT'S IMPORTANT TO UNDERSTAND THE OTHER TEAM.
We used to study all those videos before our games...
INFORMATION IS POWER.
YOU'RE RIGHT! I'M SO GLAD THAT I ASKED YOU!
OH, YOU WERE ASKING ME FOR ADVICE?
"I NEVER KNEW THAT CHRISTMAS COULD BE THIS GOOD."
"HAVING A GIRLFRIEND IS THE BEST THING EVER."
THAT'S WHAT YOH IS GOING TO TELL ME...
I HOPE HE DOES.
OKAY! TIME TO GATHER INFO FOR THE BEST CHRISTMAS EVER!

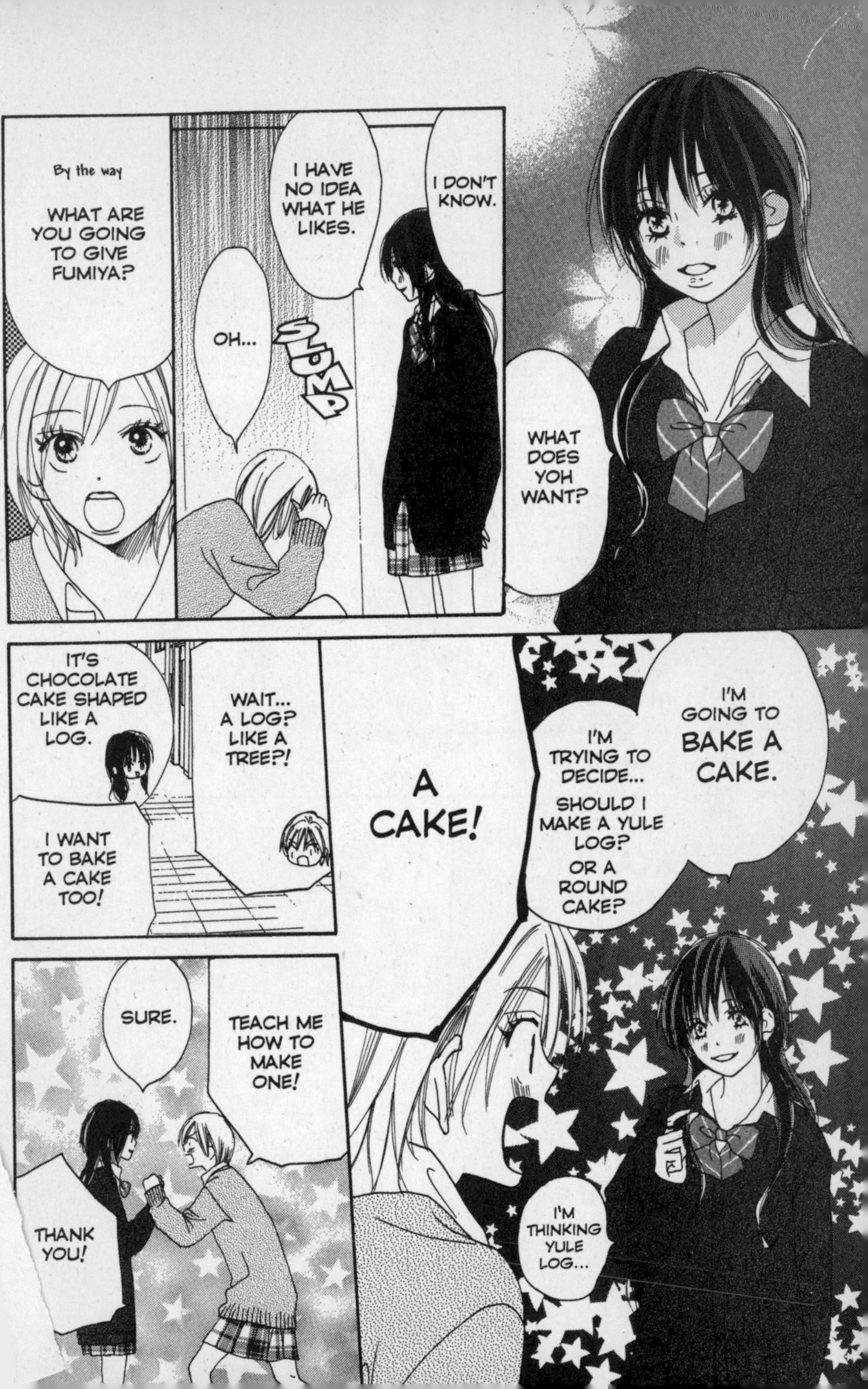
WHAT DOES YOH WANT?
I DON'T KNOW.
I HAVE NO IDEA WHAT HE LIKES.
OH...
SLUMP
By the way
WHAT ARE YOU GOING TO GIVE FUMIYA?
I'M GOING TO BAKE A CAKE.
I'M TRYING TO DECIDE...
SHOULD I MAKE A YULE LOG?
OR A ROUND CAKE?
A CAKE!
WAIT... A LOG? LIKE A TREE?!
IT'S CHOCOLATE CAKE SHAPED LIKE A LOG.
I WANT TO BAKE A CAKE TOO!
I'M THINKING YULE LOG...
TEACH ME HOW TO MAKE ONE!
SURE.
THANK YOU!

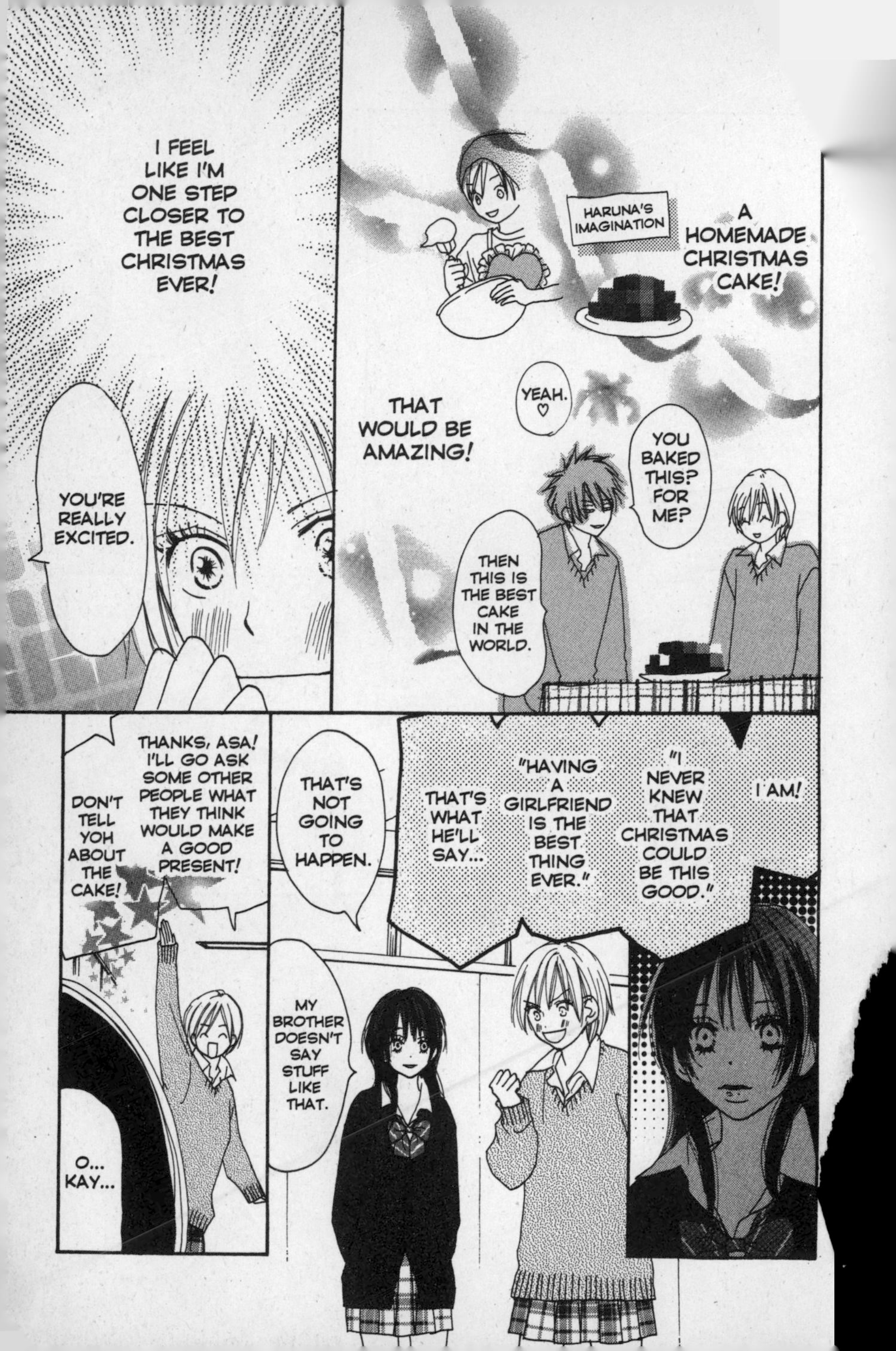
HARUNA'S IMAGINATION
A HOMEMADE CHRISTMAS CAKE!
YOU BAKED THIS? FOR ME?
YEAH. ♡
THEN THIS IS THE BEST CAKE IN THE WORLD.
THAT WOULD BE AMAZING!
I FEEL LIKE I'M ONE STEP CLOSER TO THE BEST CHRISTMAS EVER!
YOU'RE REALLY EXCITED.
I AM!
"I NEVER KNEW THAT CHRISTMAS COULD BE THIS GOOD."
"HAVING A GIRLFRIEND IS THE BEST THING EVER."
THAT'S WHAT HE'LL SAY...
THAT'S NOT GOING TO HAPPEN.
MY BROTHER DOESN'T SAY STUFF LIKE THAT.
THANKS, ASA! I'LL GO ASK SOME OTHER PEOPLE WHAT THEY THINK WOULD MAKE A GOOD PRESENT!
DON'T TELL YOH ABOUT THE CAKE!
O... KAY...

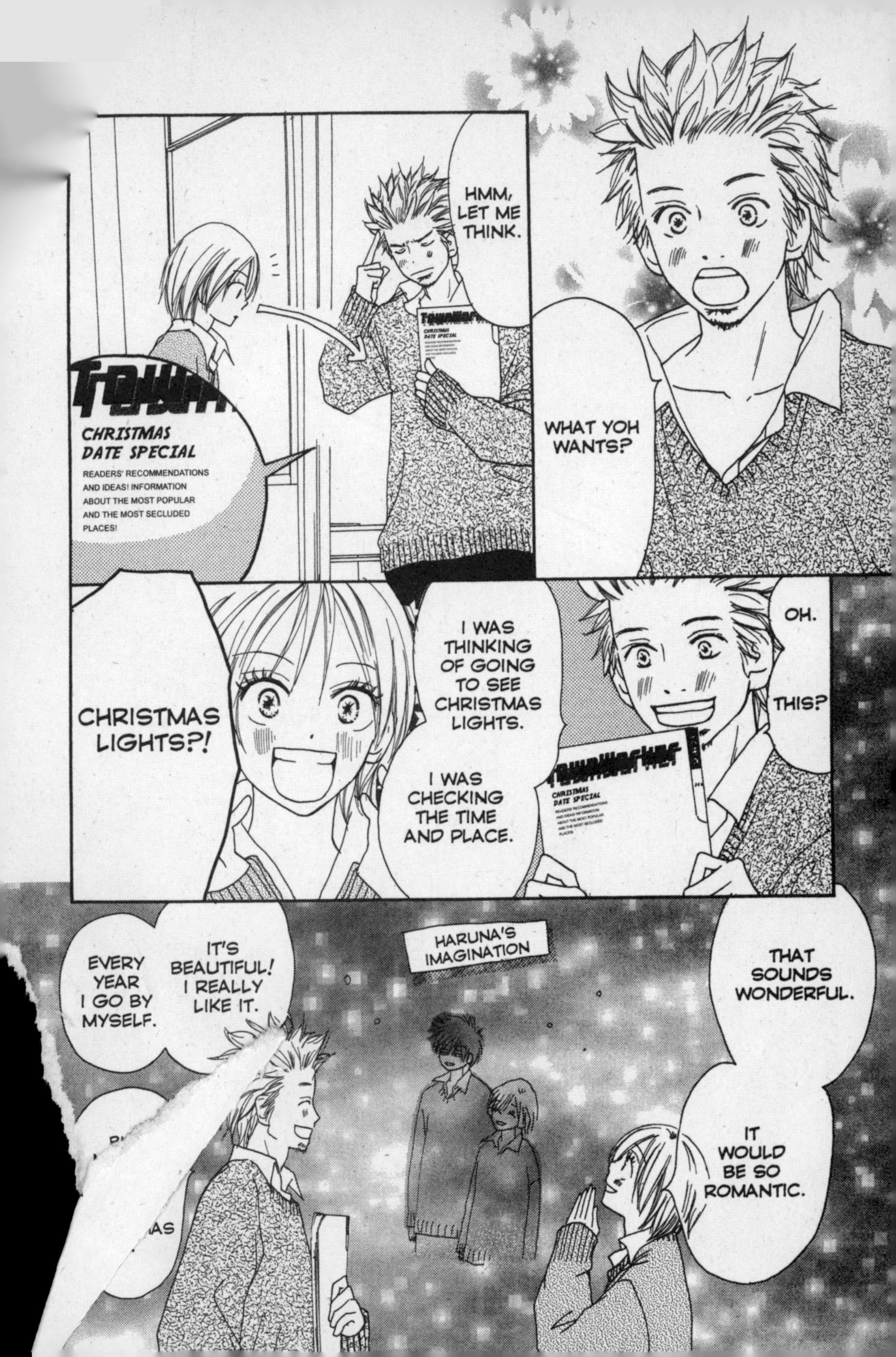
WHAT YOH WANTS?
HMM, LET ME THINK.
CHRISTMAS DATE SPECIAL
READERS' RECOMMENDATIONS AND IDEAS! INFORMATION ABOUT THE MOST POPULAR AND THE MOST SECLUDED PLACES!
OH.
THIS?
I WAS THINKING OF GOING TO SEE CHRISTMAS LIGHTS.
I WAS CHECKING THE TIME AND PLACE.
CHRISTMAS LIGHTS?!
HARUNA'S IMAGINATION
THAT SOUNDS WONDERFUL.
IT WOULD BE SO ROMANTIC.
IT'S BEAUTIFUL! I REALLY LIKE IT.
EVERY YEAR I GO BY MYSELF.

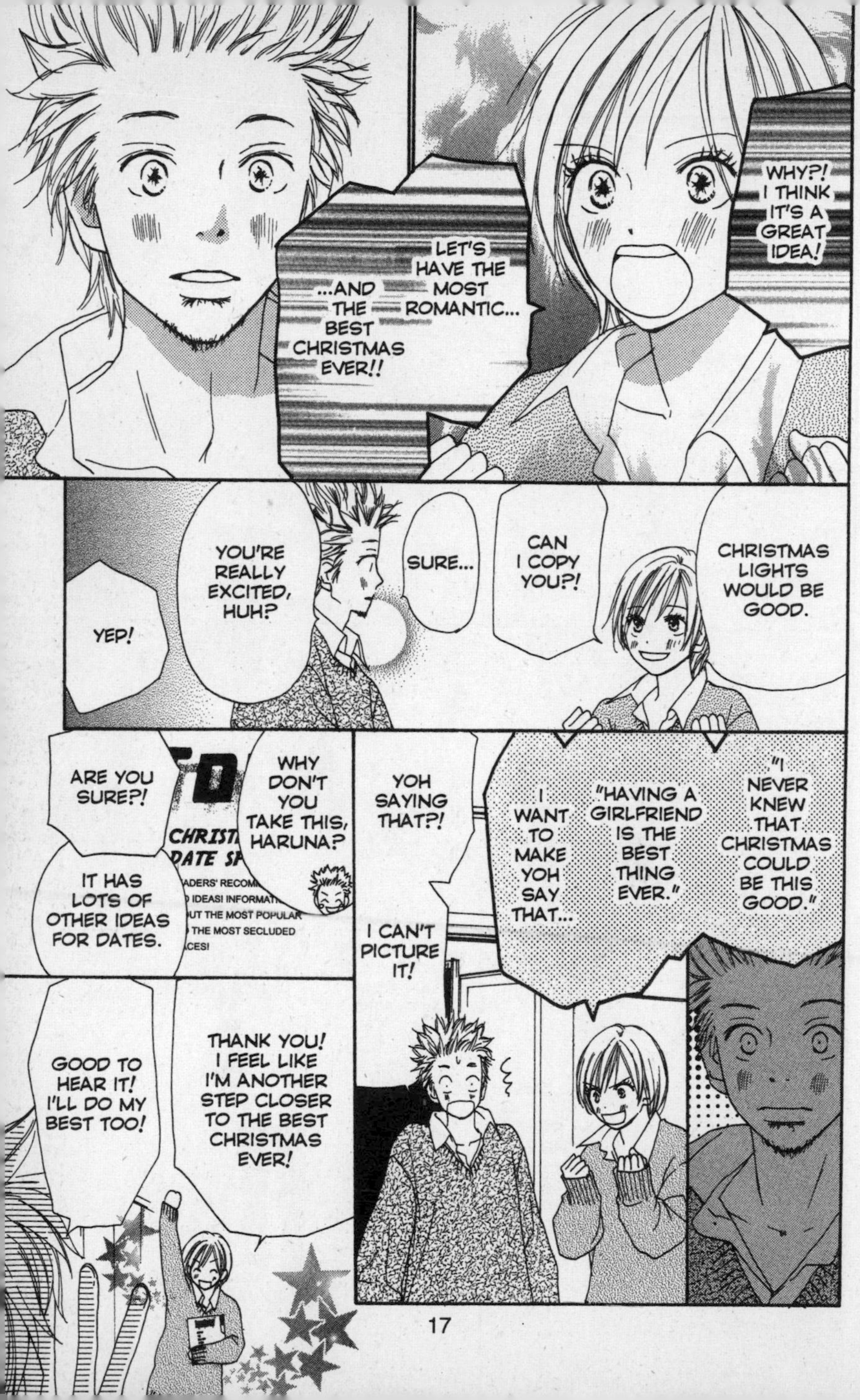
WHY?! I THINK IT'S A GREAT IDEA!
LET'S HAVE THE MOST ROMANTIC...
...AND THE BEST CHRISTMAS EVER!!
CHRISTMAS LIGHTS WOULD BE GOOD.
CAN I COPY YOU?!
SURE...
YOU'RE REALLY EXCITED, HUH?
YEP!
"I NEVER KNEW THAT CHRISTMAS COULD BE THIS GOOD."
"HAVING A GIRLFRIEND IS THE BEST THING EVER."
I WANT TO MAKE YOH SAY THAT...
YOH SAYING THAT?!
I CAN'T PICTURE IT!
WHY DON'T YOU TAKE THIS, HARUNA?
ARE YOU SURE?!
IT HAS LOTS OF OTHER IDEAS FOR DATES.
THANK YOU! I FEEL LIKE I'M ANOTHER STEP CLOSER TO THE BEST CHRISTMAS EVER!
GOOD TO HEAR IT! I'LL DO MY BEST TOO!

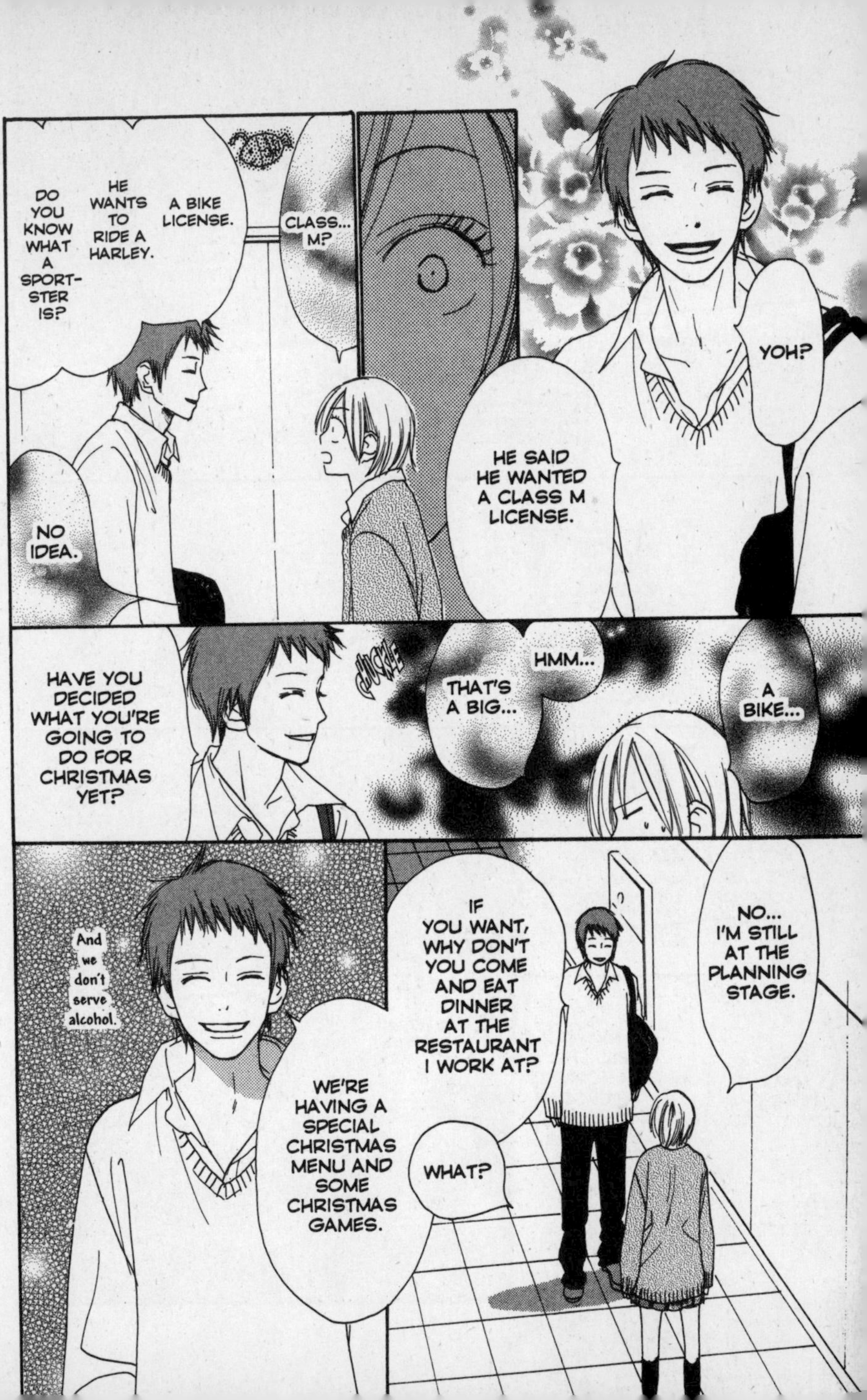
YOH?
HE SAID HE WANTED A CLASS M LICENSE.
CLASS... M?
A BIKE LICENSE.
HE WANTS TO RIDE A HARLEY.
DO YOU KNOW WHAT A SPORT-STER IS?
NO IDEA.
A BIKE...
HMM...
THAT'S A BIG...
HAVE YOU DECIDED WHAT YOU'RE GOING TO DO FOR CHRISTMAS YET?
NO... I'M STILL AT THE PLANNING STAGE.
IF YOU WANT, WHY DON'T YOU COME AND EAT DINNER AT THE RESTAURANT I WORK AT?
WHAT?
WE'RE HAVING A SPECIAL CHRISTMAS MENU AND SOME CHRISTMAS GAMES.
And we don't serve alcohol.

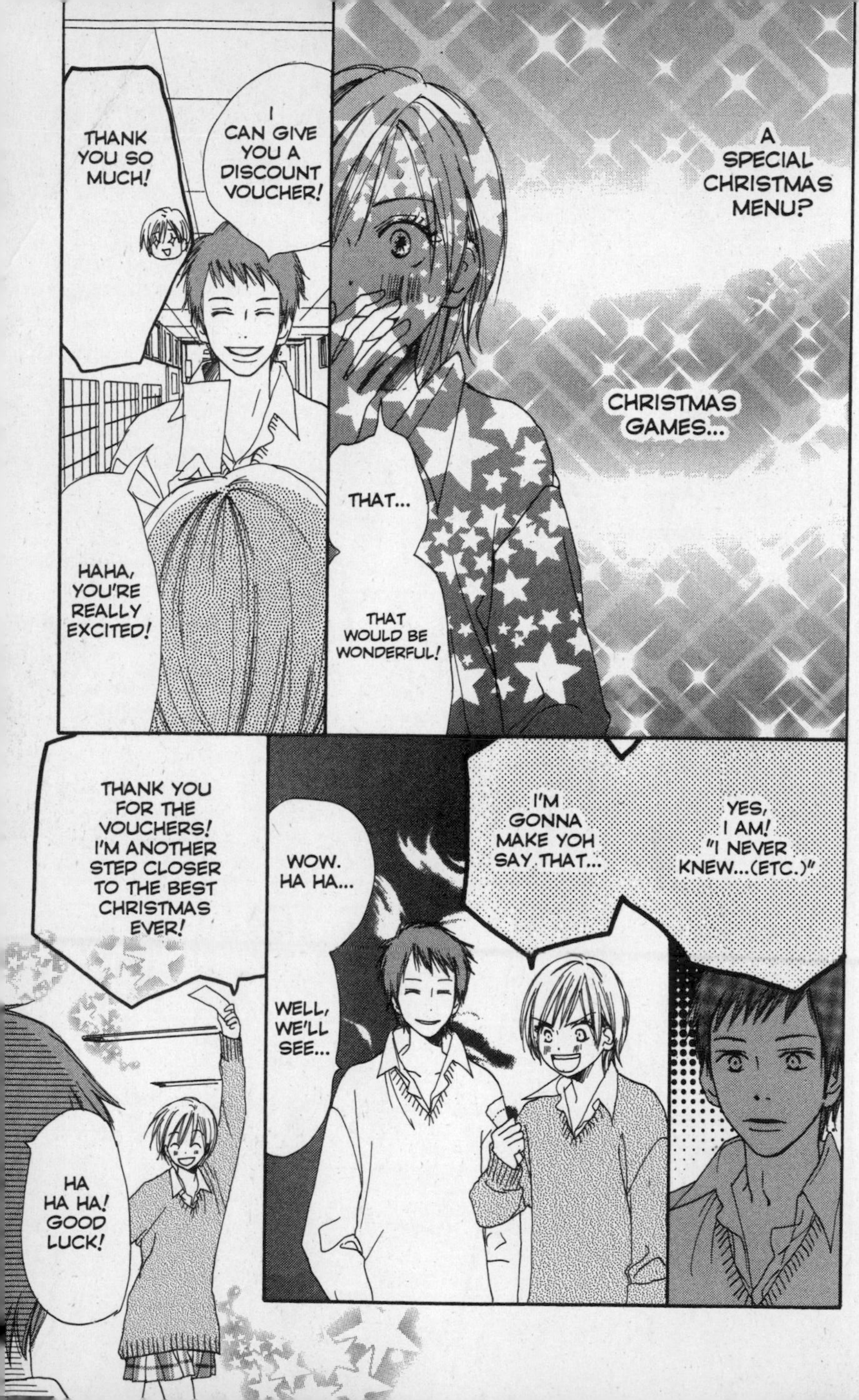
A SPECIAL CHRISTMAS MENU?
CHRISTMAS GAMES...
THAT...
THAT WOULD BE WONDERFUL!
I CAN GIVE YOU A DISCOUNT VOUCHER!
THANK YOU SO MUCH!
HAHA, YOU'RE REALLY EXCITED!
YES, I AM! "I NEVER KNEW...(ETC.)"
I'M GONNA MAKE YOH SAY THAT...
WOW. HA HA...
WELL, WE'LL SEE...
THANK YOU FOR THE VOUCHERS! I'M ANOTHER STEP CLOSER TO THE BEST CHRISTMAS EVER!
HA HA HA! GOOD LUCK!

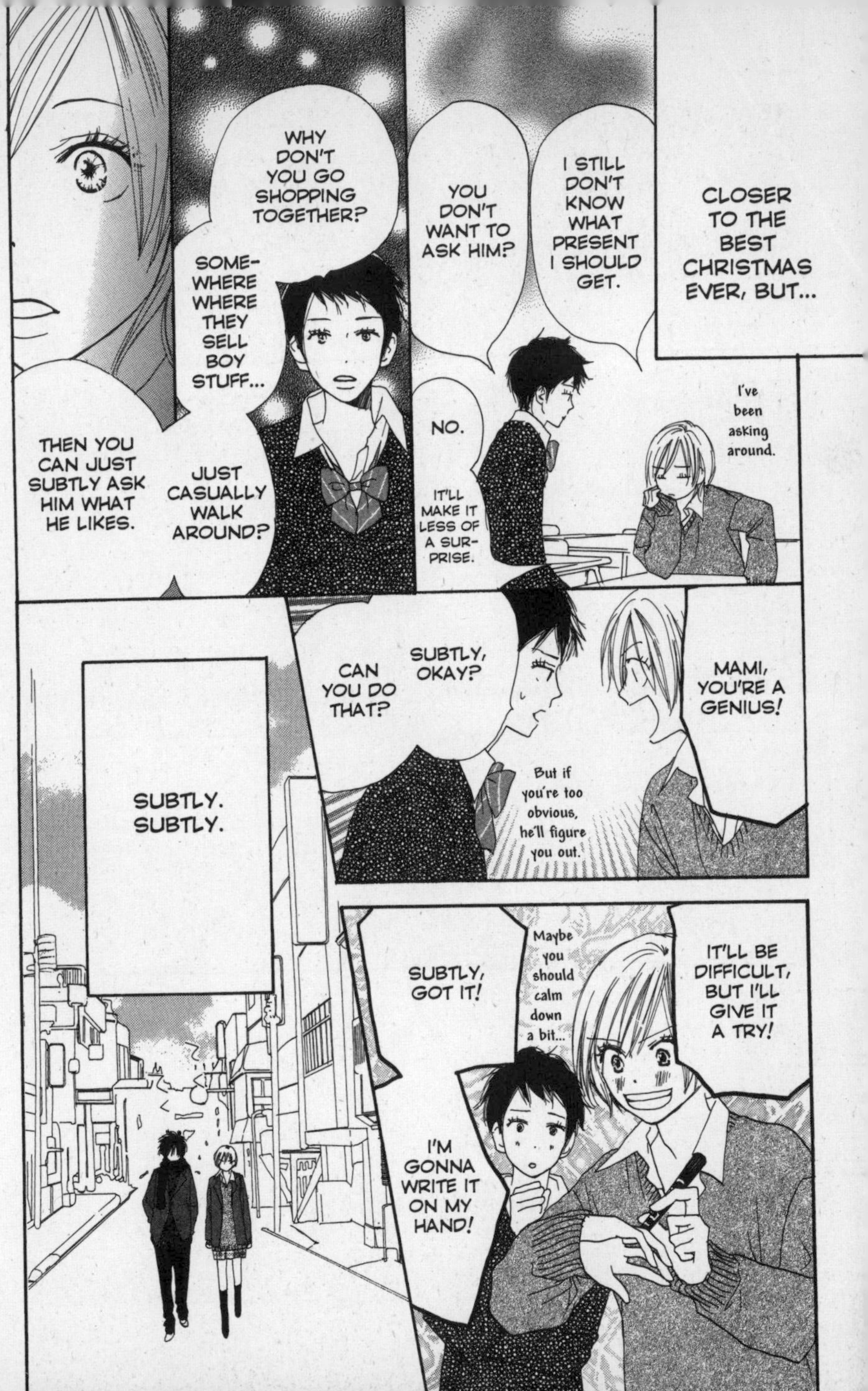
CLOSER TO THE BEST CHRISTMAS EVER, BUT...
I've been asking around.
I STILL DON'T KNOW WHAT PRESENT I SHOULD GET.
YOU DON'T WANT TO ASK HIM?
NO.
IT'LL MAKE IT LESS OF A SUR-PRISE.
WHY DON'T YOU GO SHOPPING TOGETHER?
SOME-WHERE WHERE THEY SELL BOY STUFF...
JUST CASUALLY WALK AROUND?
THEN YOU CAN JUST SUBTLY ASK HIM WHAT HE LIKES.
MAMI, YOU'RE A GENIUS!
SUBTLY, OKAY?
CAN YOU DO THAT?
But if you're too obvious, he'll figure you out.
IT'LL BE DIFFICULT, BUT I'LL GIVE IT A TRY!
Maybe you should calm down a bit...
SUBTLY, GOT IT!
I'M GONNA WRITE IT ON MY HAND!
SUBTLY. SUBTLY.

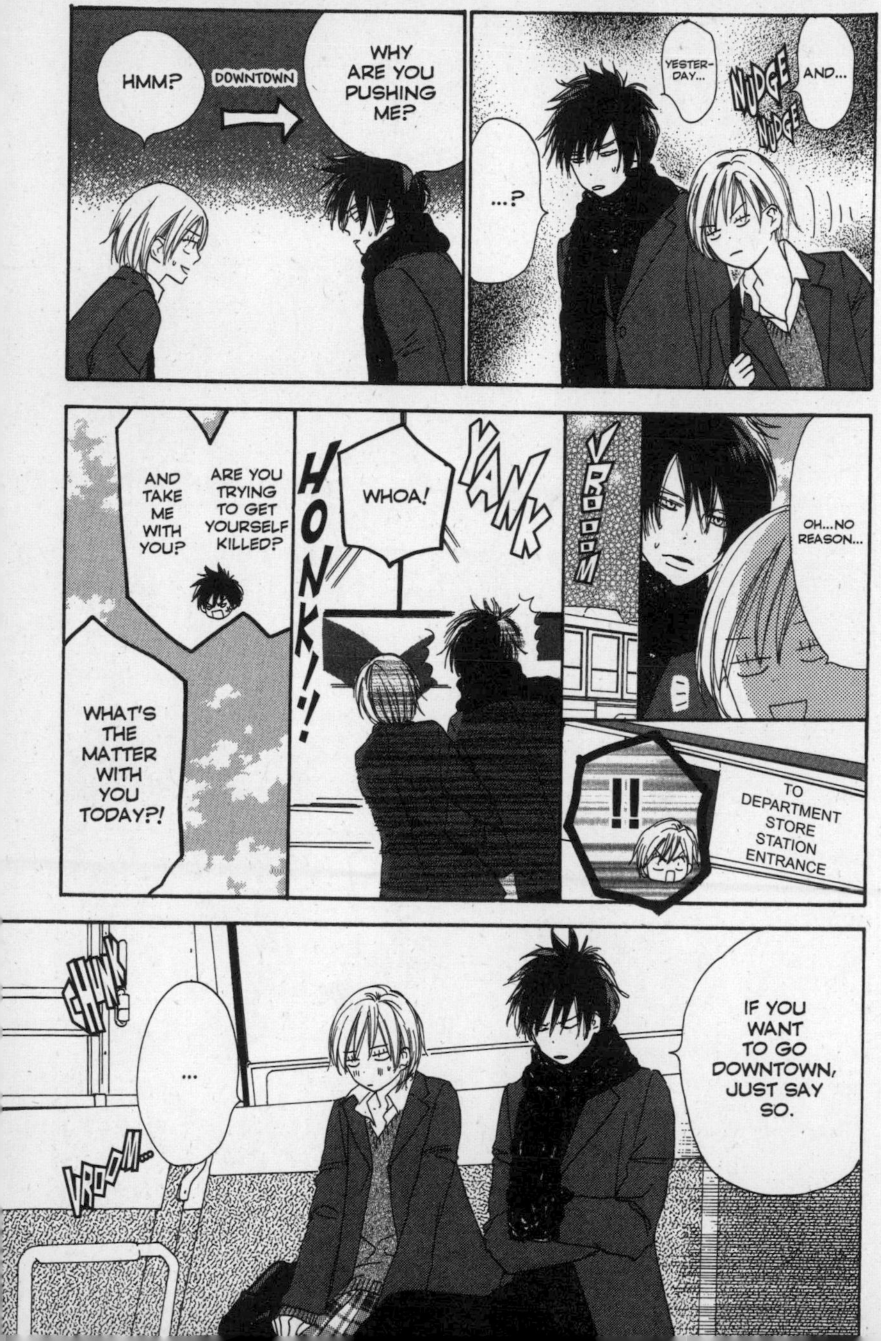
AND...
YESTER-DAY...
NUDGE NUDGE
...?
WHY ARE YOU PUSHING ME?
DOWNTOWN
HMM?
VROOOM
OH...NO REASON...
!!
TO DEPARTMENT STORE STATION ENTRANCE
YANK
WHOA!
HONK!!
ARE YOU TRYING TO GET YOURSELF KILLED?
AND TAKE ME WITH YOU?
WHAT'S THE MATTER WITH YOU TODAY?!
IF YOU WANT TO GO DOWNTOWN, JUST SAY SO.
...
CHUNK
VROOM...

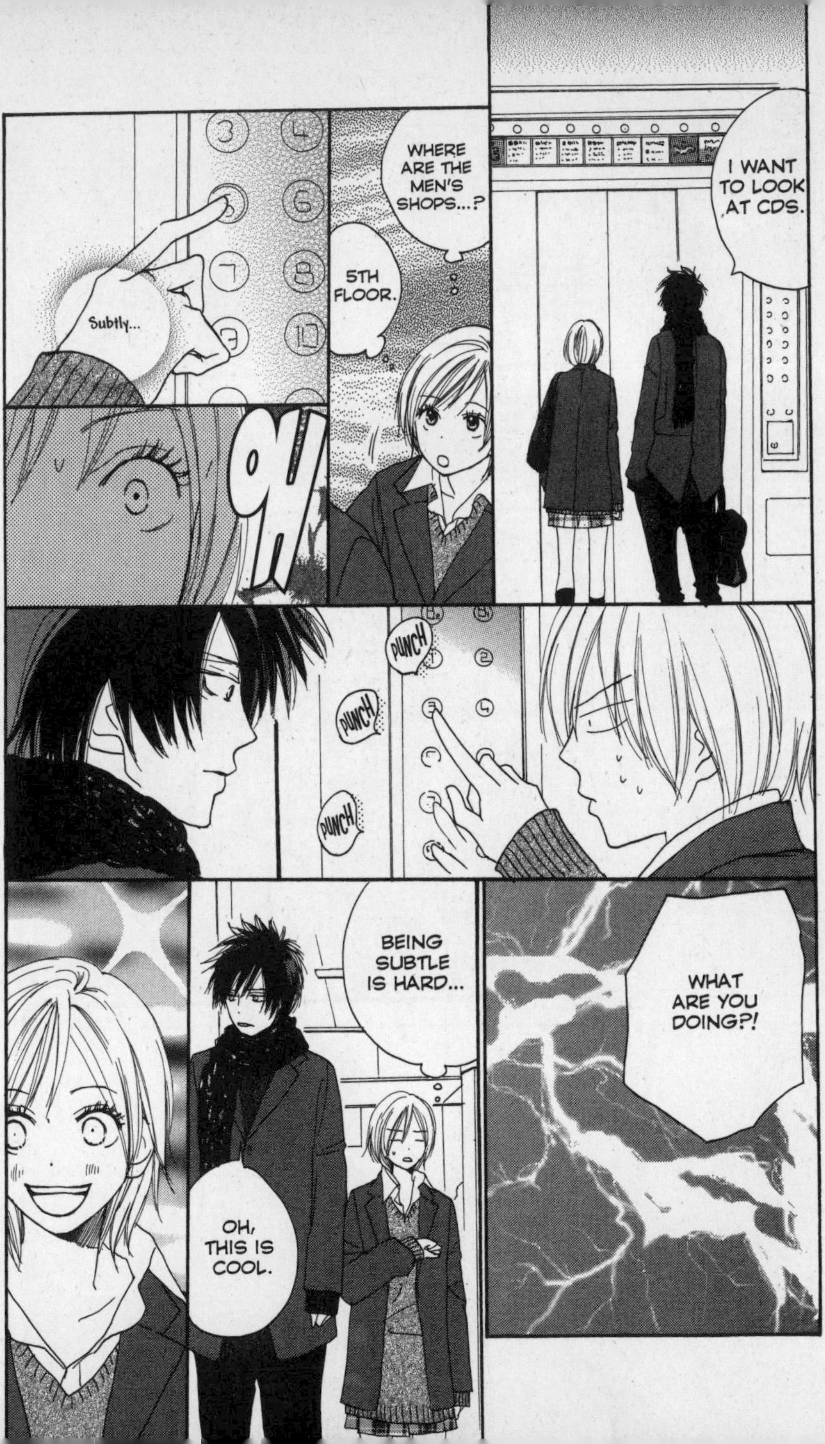
I WANT TO LOOK AT CDS.
WHERE ARE THE MEN'S SHOPS...?
5TH FLOOR.
Subtly...
OH
PUNCH
PUNCH
PUNCH
WHAT ARE YOU DOING?!
BEING SUBTLE IS HARD...
OH, THIS IS COOL.

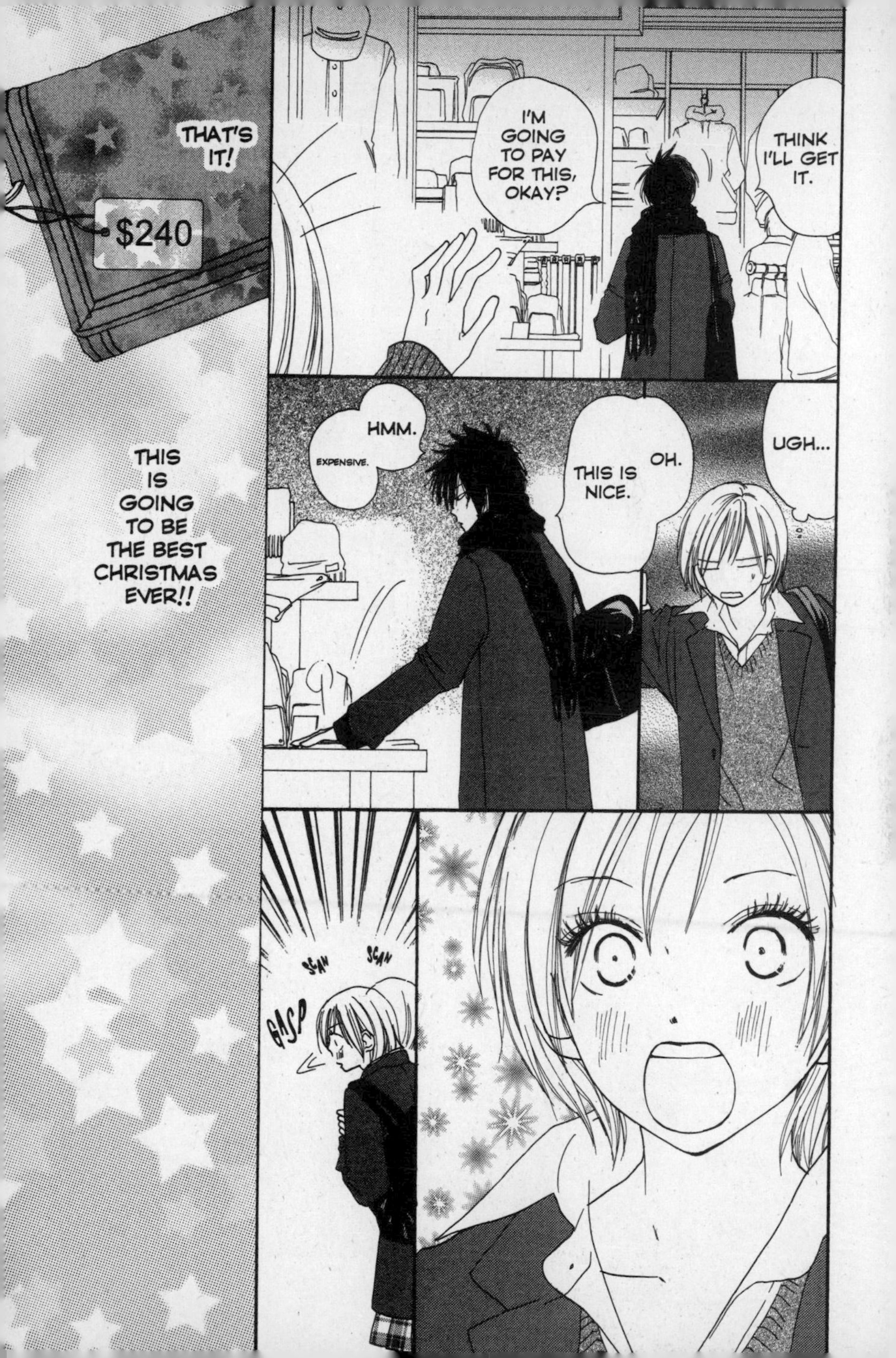
THINK I'LL GET IT.
I'M GOING TO PAY FOR THIS, OKAY?
UGH...
OH. THIS IS NICE.
HMM.
EXPENSIVE.
SCAN SCAN
GASP
THAT'S IT!
$240
THIS IS GOING TO BE THE BEST CHRISTMAS EVER!!

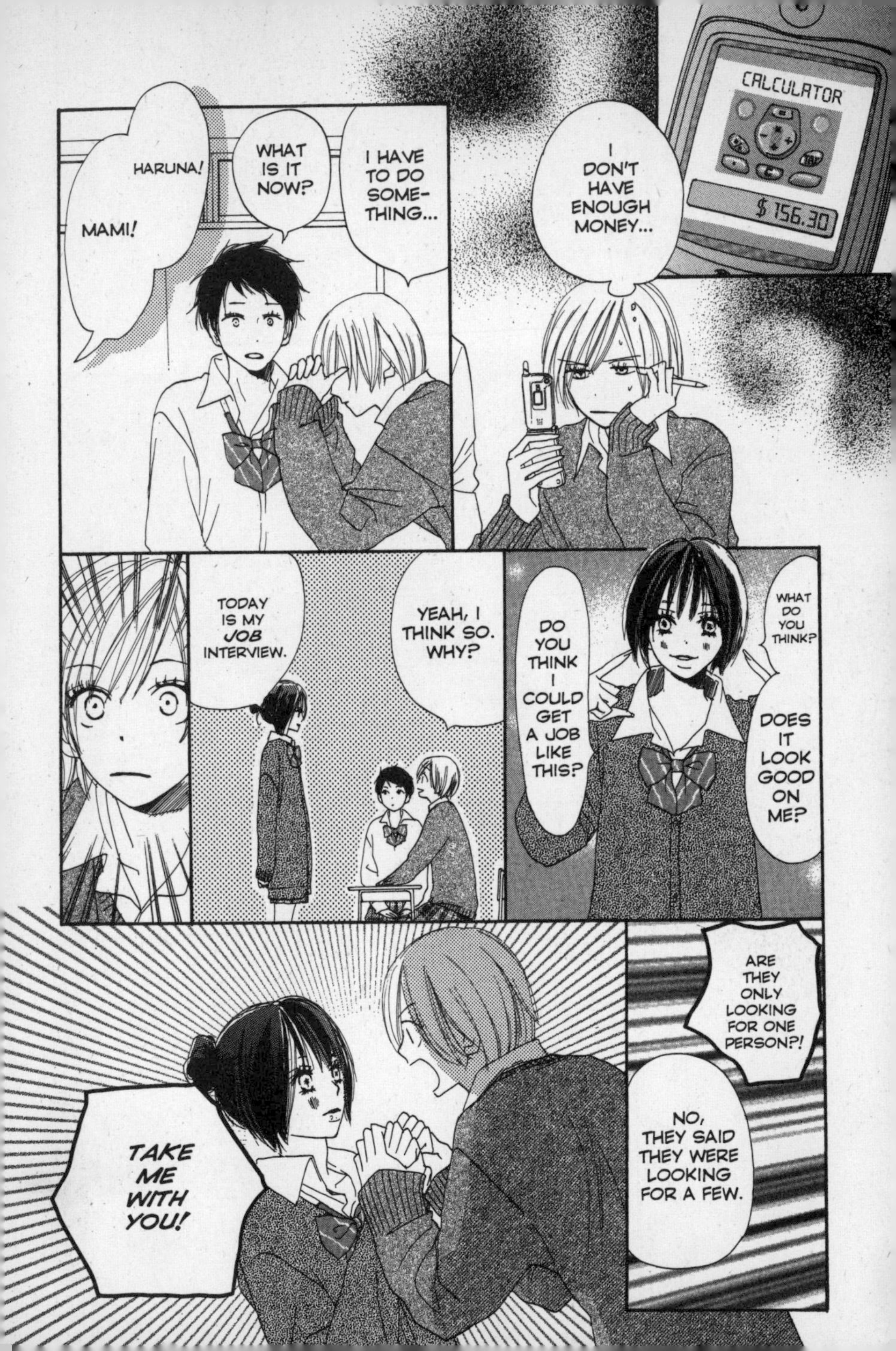
CALCULATOR
$ 156.30
I DON'T HAVE ENOUGH MONEY...
I HAVE TO DO SOMETHING...
WHAT IS IT NOW?
HARUNA!
MAMI!
WHAT DO YOU THINK?
DOES IT LOOK GOOD ON ME?
DO YOU THINK I COULD GET A JOB LIKE THIS?
YEAH, I THINK SO. WHY?
TODAY IS MY *JOB* INTERVIEW.
ARE THEY ONLY LOOKING FOR ONE PERSON?!
NO, THEY SAID THEY WERE LOOKING FOR A FEW.
TAKE ME WITH YOU!

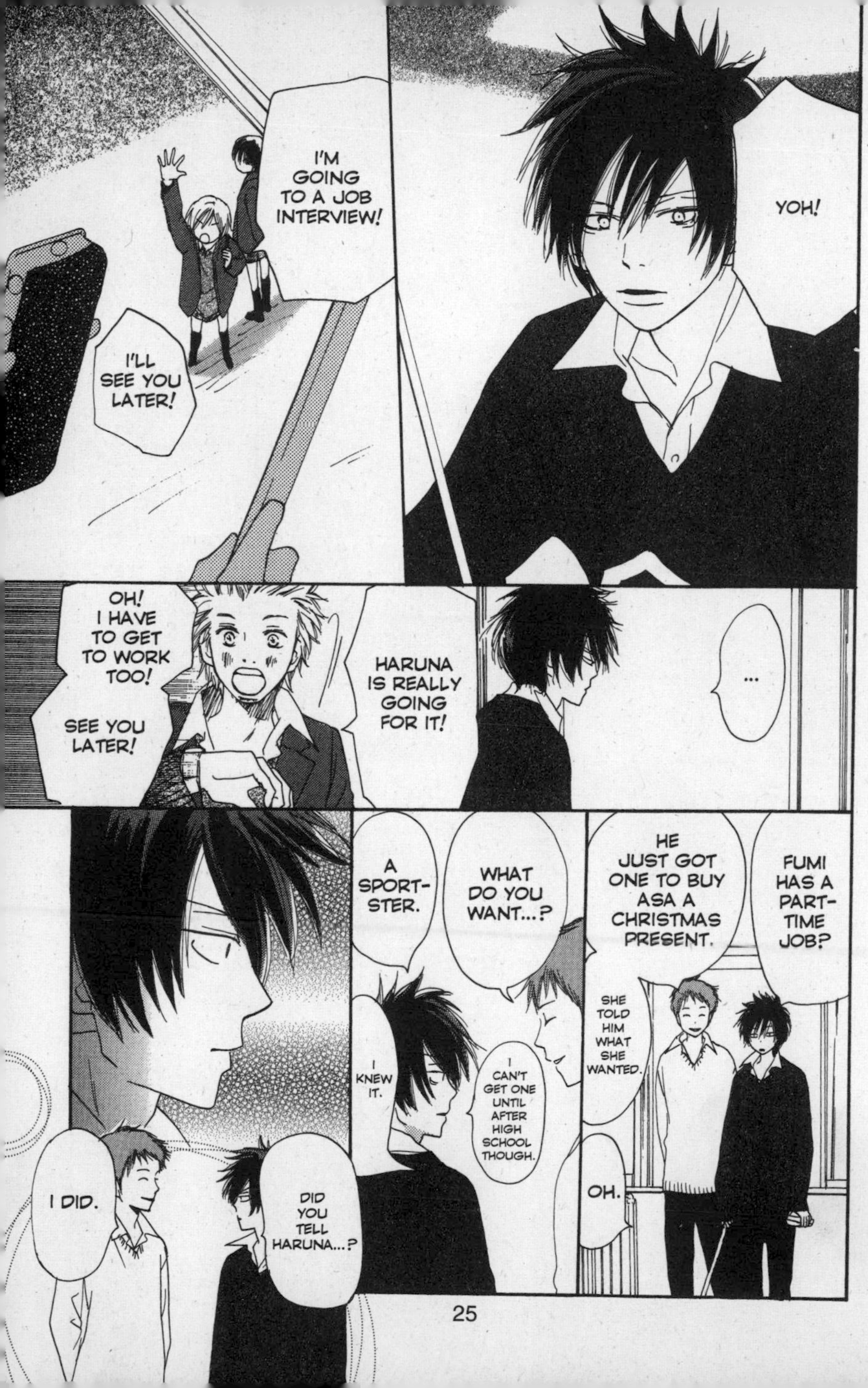
YOH!
I'M GOING TO A JOB INTERVIEW!
I'LL SEE YOU LATER!
...
HARUNA IS REALLY GOING FOR IT!
OH! I HAVE TO GET TO WORK TOO!
SEE YOU LATER!
FUMI HAS A PART-TIME JOB?
HE JUST GOT ONE TO BUY ASA A CHRISTMAS PRESENT.
SHE TOLD HIM WHAT SHE WANTED.
OH.
WHAT DO YOU WANT...?
A SPORT-STER.
I CAN'T GET ONE UNTIL AFTER HIGH SCHOOL THOUGH.
I KNEW IT.
DID YOU TELL HARUNA...?
I DID.

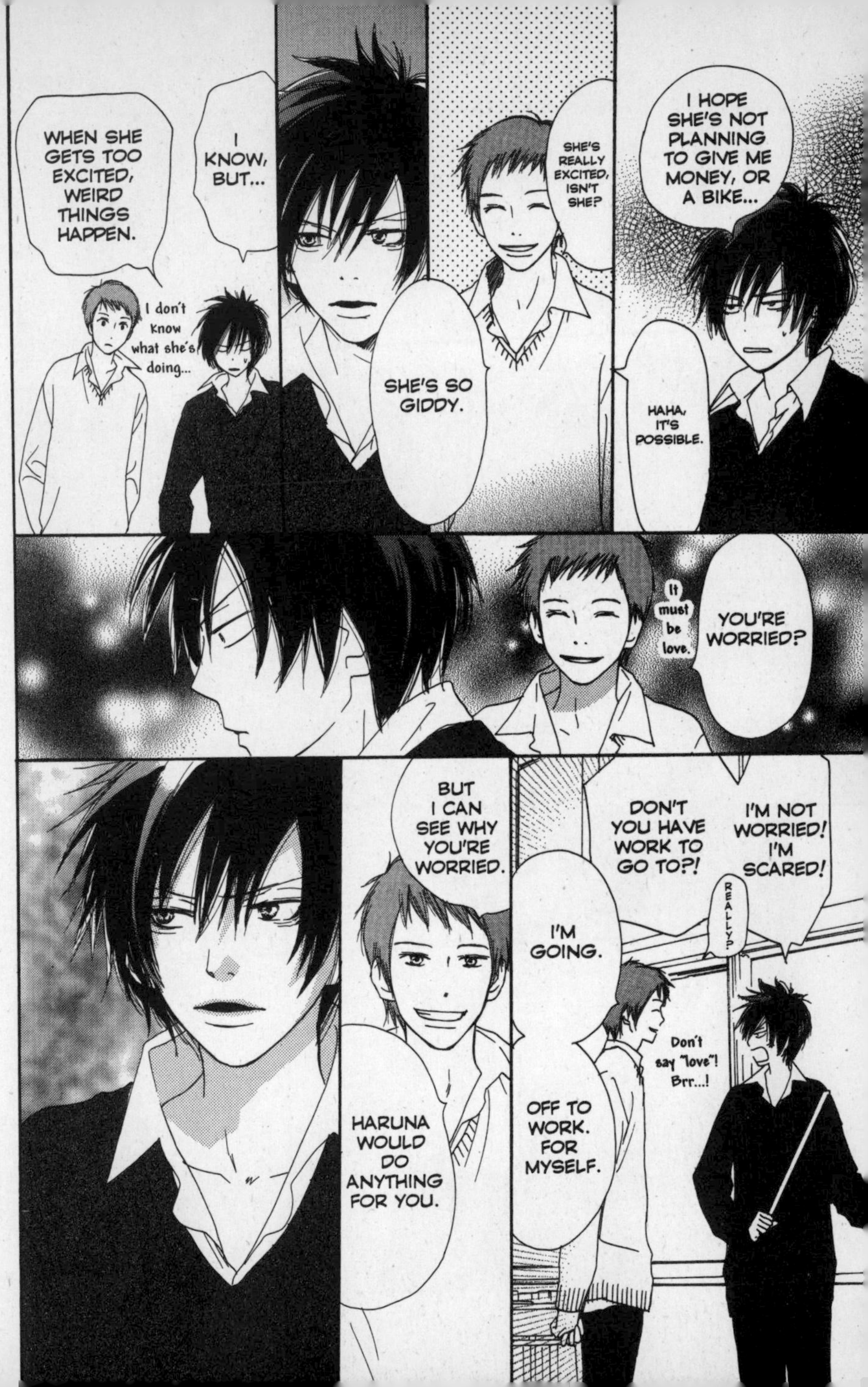
I HOPE SHE'S NOT PLANNING TO GIVE ME MONEY, OR A BIKE...
HAHA, IT'S POSSIBLE.
SHE'S REALLY EXCITED, ISN'T SHE?
SHE'S SO GIDDY.
I KNOW, BUT...
WHEN SHE GETS TOO EXCITED, WEIRD THINGS HAPPEN.
I don't know what she's doing...
YOU'RE WORRIED?
It must be love.
I'M NOT WORRIED! I'M SCARED!
REALLY?
DON'T YOU HAVE WORK TO GO TO?!
I'M GOING.
OFF TO WORK. FOR MYSELF.
Don't say "love"! Brr...!
BUT I CAN SEE WHY YOU'RE WORRIED.
HARUNA WOULD DO ANYTHING FOR YOU.

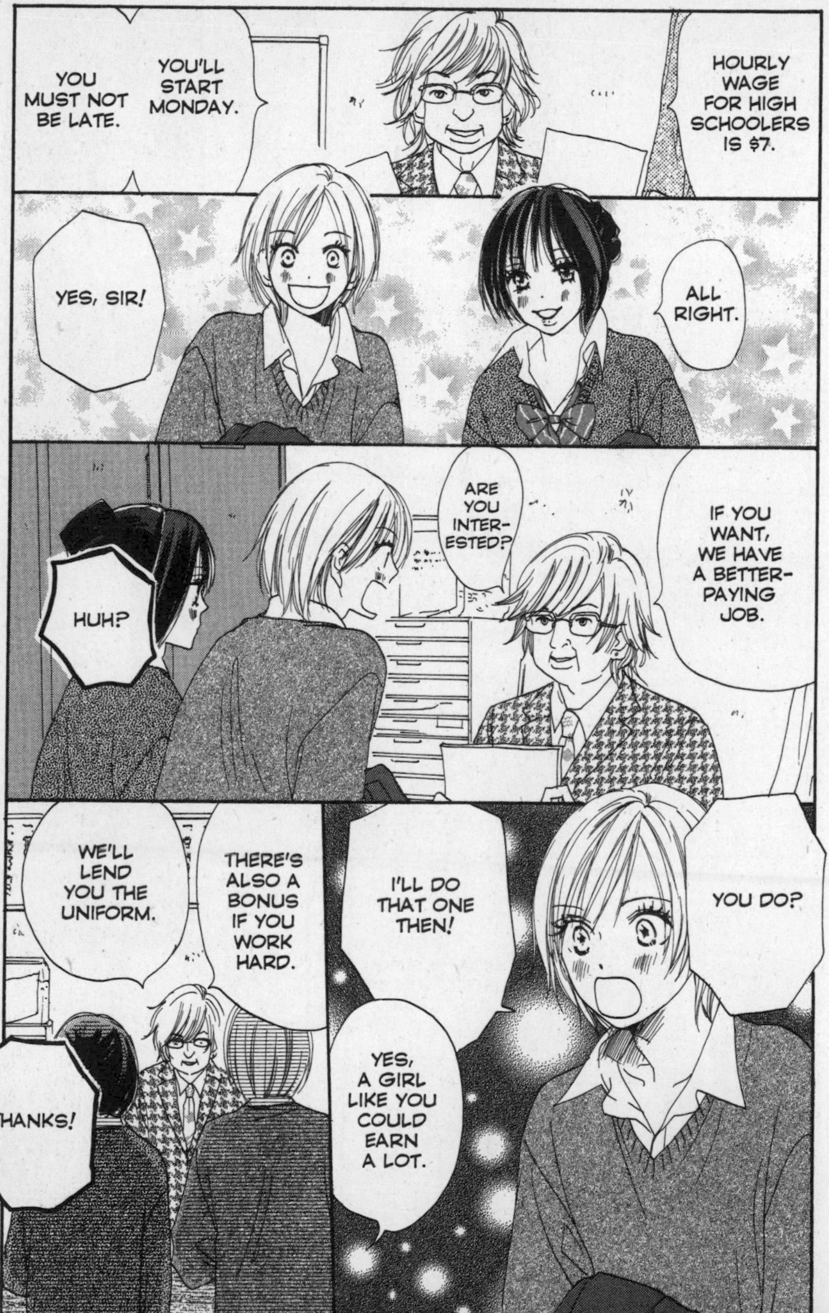
HOURLY WAGE FOR HIGH SCHOOLERS IS $7.
YOU'LL START MONDAY.
YOU MUST NOT BE LATE.
ALL RIGHT.
YES, SIR!
IF YOU WANT, WE HAVE A BETTER-PAYING JOB.
ARE YOU INTERESTED?
HUH?
YOU DO?
I'LL DO THAT ONE THEN!
YES, A GIRL LIKE YOU COULD EARN A LOT.
THERE'S ALSO A BONUS IF YOU WORK HARD.
WE'LL LEND YOU THE UNIFORM.
THANKS!

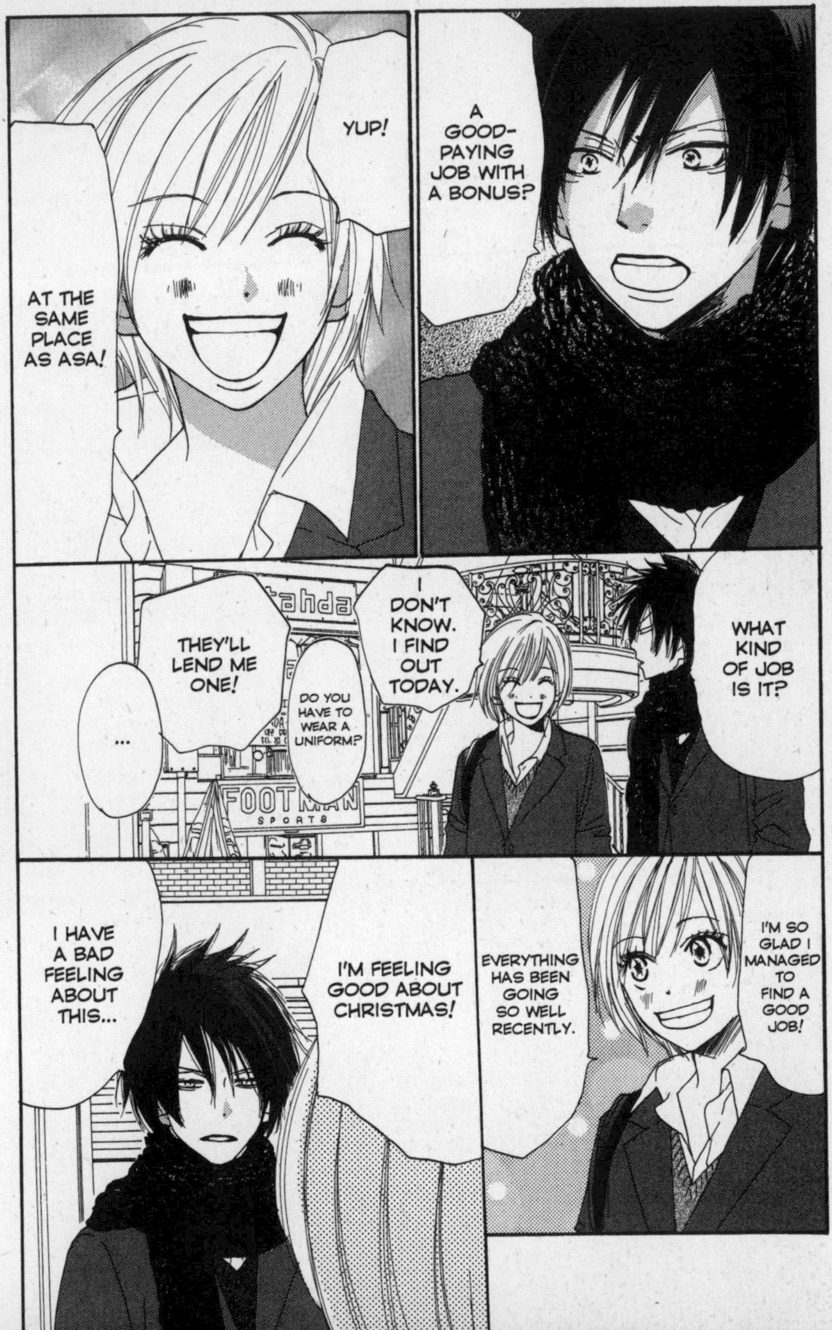
A GOOD-PAYING JOB WITH A BONUS?
YUP!
AT THE SAME PLACE AS ASA!
WHAT KIND OF JOB IS IT?
I DON'T KNOW. I FIND OUT TODAY.
DO YOU HAVE TO WEAR A UNIFORM?
THEY'LL LEND ME ONE!
...
FOOTMAN
SPORTS
I'M SO GLAD I MANAGED TO FIND A GOOD JOB!
EVERYTHING HAS BEEN GOING SO WELL RECENTLY.
I'M FEELING GOOD ABOUT CHRISTMAS!
I HAVE A BAD FEELING ABOUT THIS...

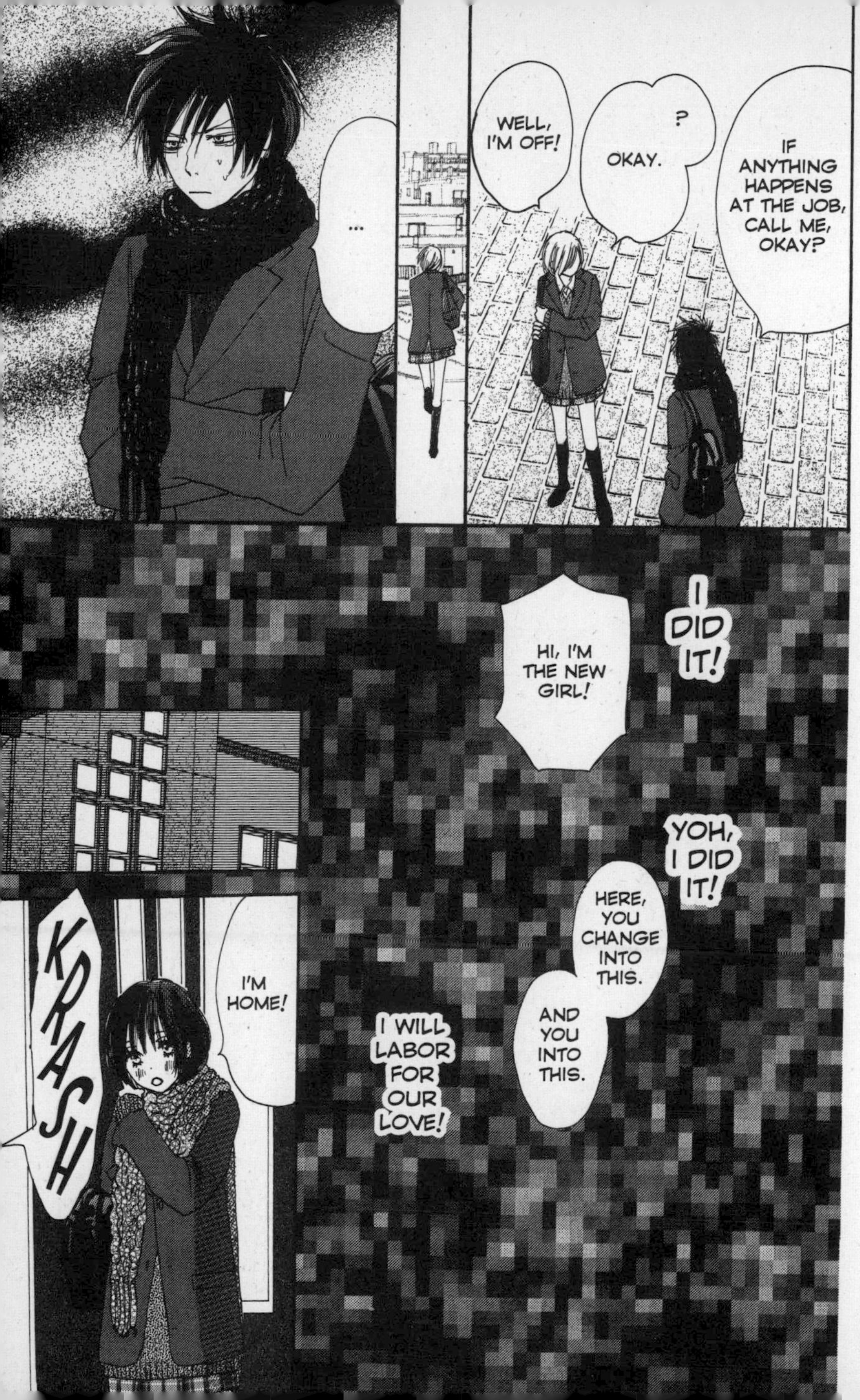
IF ANYTHING HAPPENS AT THE JOB, CALL ME, OKAY?
?
OKAY.
WELL, I'M OFF!
...
I DID IT!
HI, I'M THE NEW GIRL!
YOH, I DID IT!
HERE, YOU CHANGE INTO THIS.
AND YOU INTO THIS.
I WILL LABOR FOR OUR LOVE!
I'M HOME!
KRASH

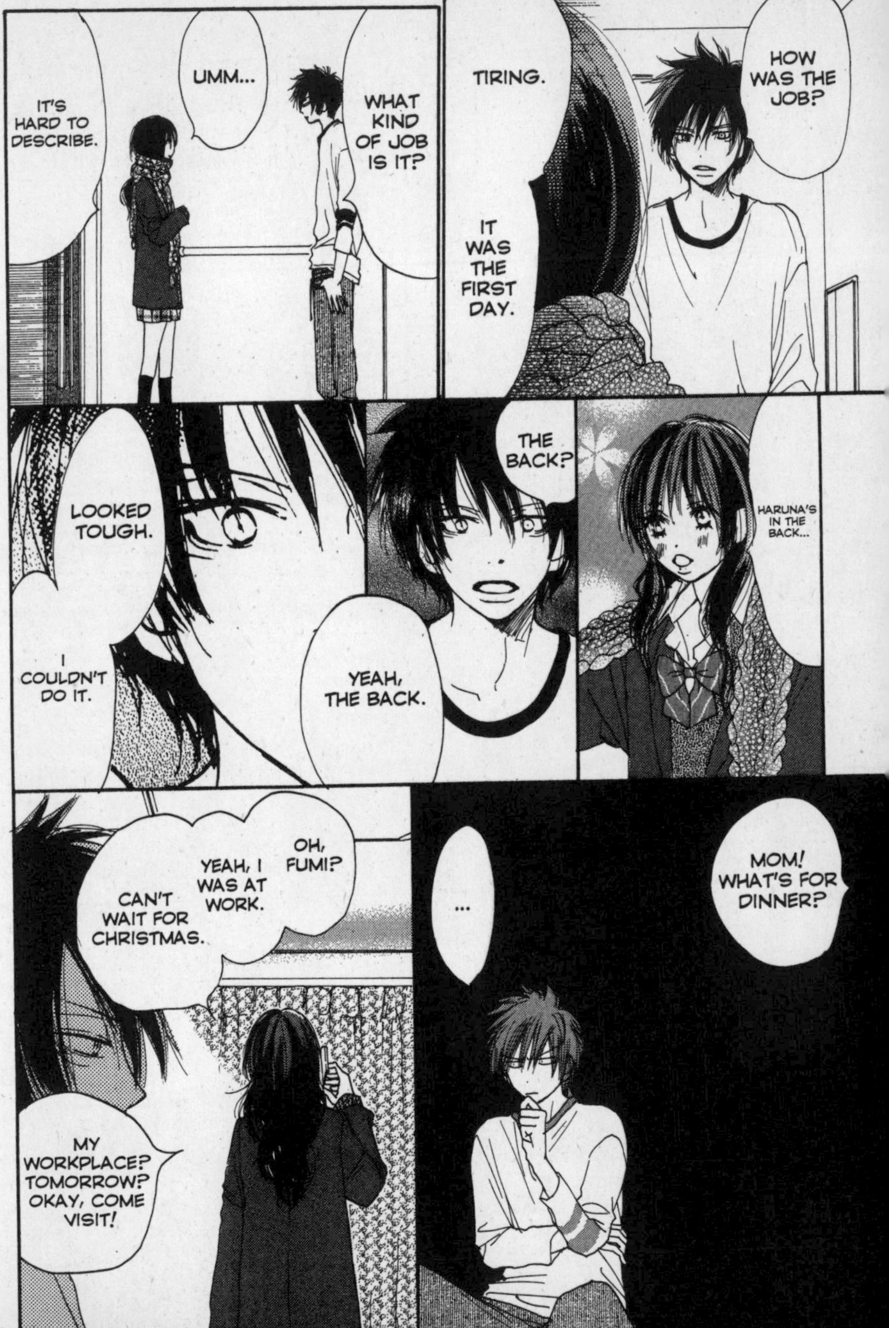
HOW WAS THE JOB?
TIRING.
IT WAS THE FIRST DAY.
WHAT KIND OF JOB IS IT?
UMM...
IT'S HARD TO DESCRIBE.
HARUNA'S IN THE BACK...
THE BACK?
YEAH, THE BACK.
LOOKED TOUGH.
I COULDN'T DO IT.
MOM! WHAT'S FOR DINNER?
...
OH, FUMI?
YEAH, I WAS AT WORK.
CAN'T WAIT FOR CHRISTMAS.
MY WORKPLACE? TOMORROW? OKAY, COME VISIT!

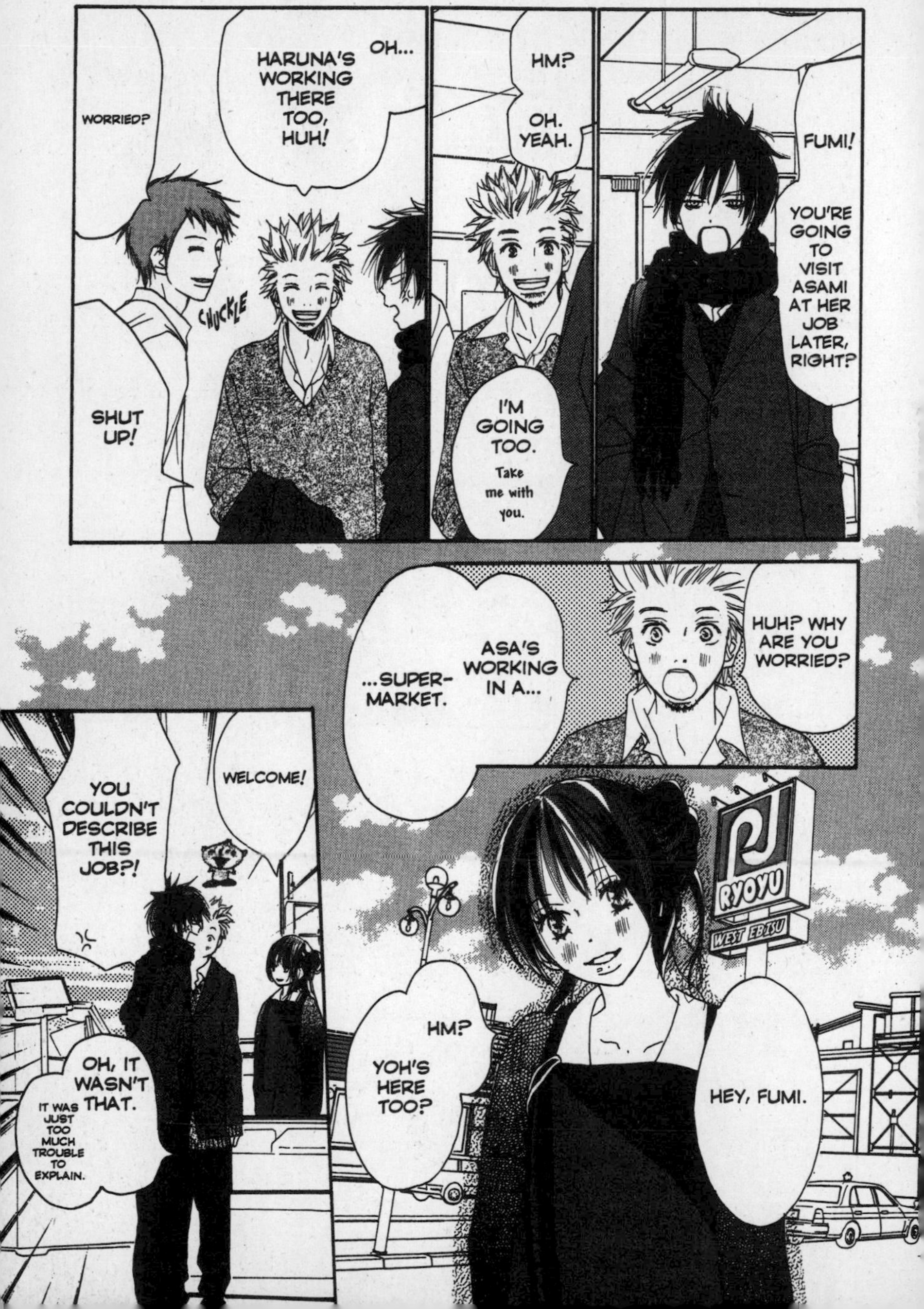
FUMI!
YOU'RE GOING TO VISIT ASAMI AT HER JOB LATER, RIGHT?
HM?
OH. YEAH.
I'M GOING TOO.
Take me with you.
OH...
HARUNA'S WORKING THERE TOO, HUH!
WORRIED?
CHUCKLE
SHUT UP!
HUH? WHY ARE YOU WORRIED?
ASA'S WORKING IN A...
...SUPER-MARKET.
HEY, FUMI.
HM?
YOH'S HERE TOO?
RYOYU
WEST EBISU
WELCOME!
YOU COULDN'T DESCRIBE THIS JOB?!
OH, IT WASN'T THAT.
IT WAS JUST TOO MUCH TROUBLE TO EXPLAIN.

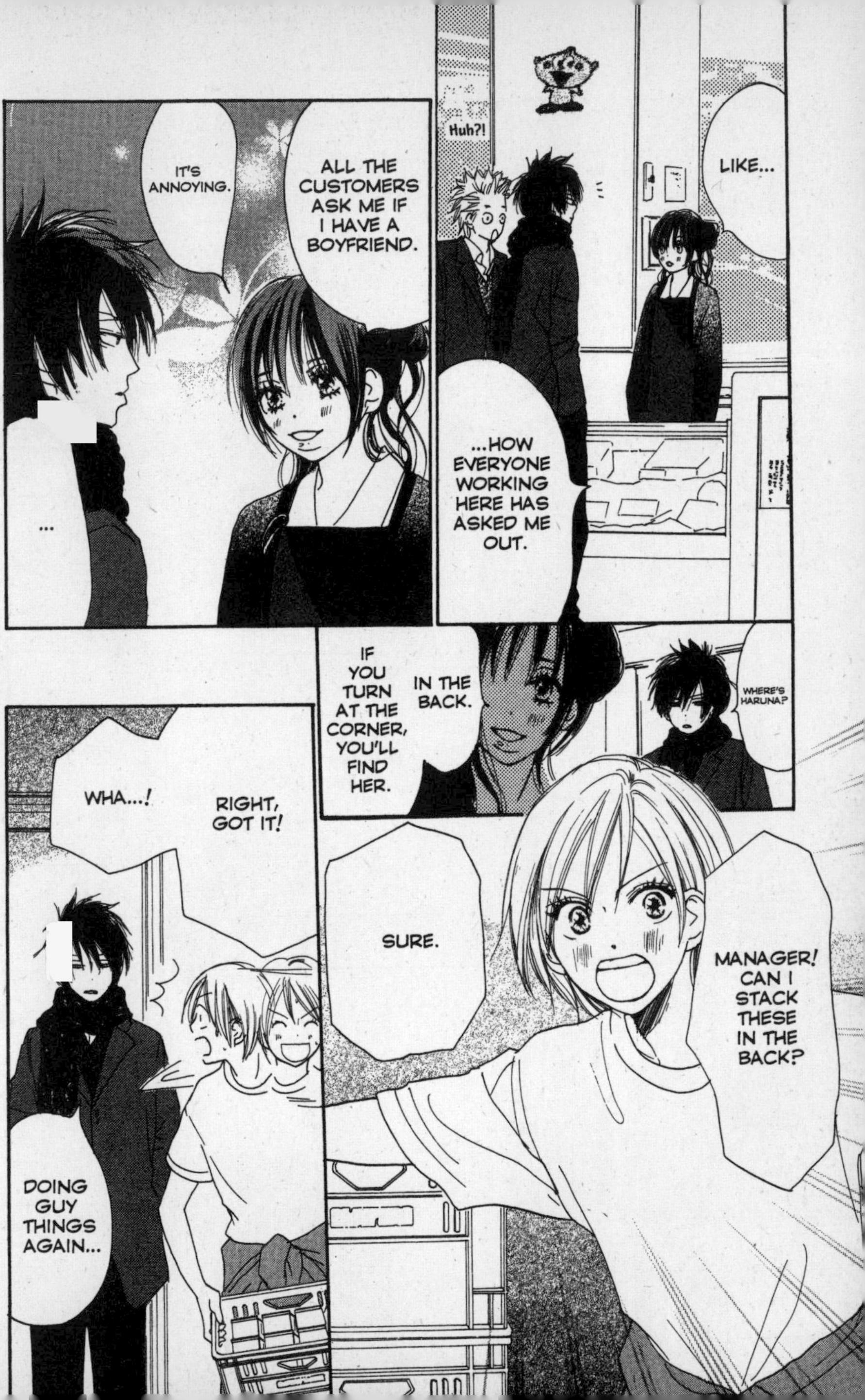
Huh?!
LIKE...
...HOW EVERYONE WORKING HERE HAS ASKED ME OUT.
ALL THE CUSTOMERS ASK ME IF I HAVE A BOYFRIEND.
IT'S ANNOYING.
...
WHERE'S HARUNA?
IN THE BACK.
IF YOU TURN AT THE CORNER, YOU'LL FIND HER.
MANAGER! CAN I STACK THESE IN THE BACK?
SURE.
RIGHT, GOT IT!
WHA...!
DOING GUY THINGS AGAIN...

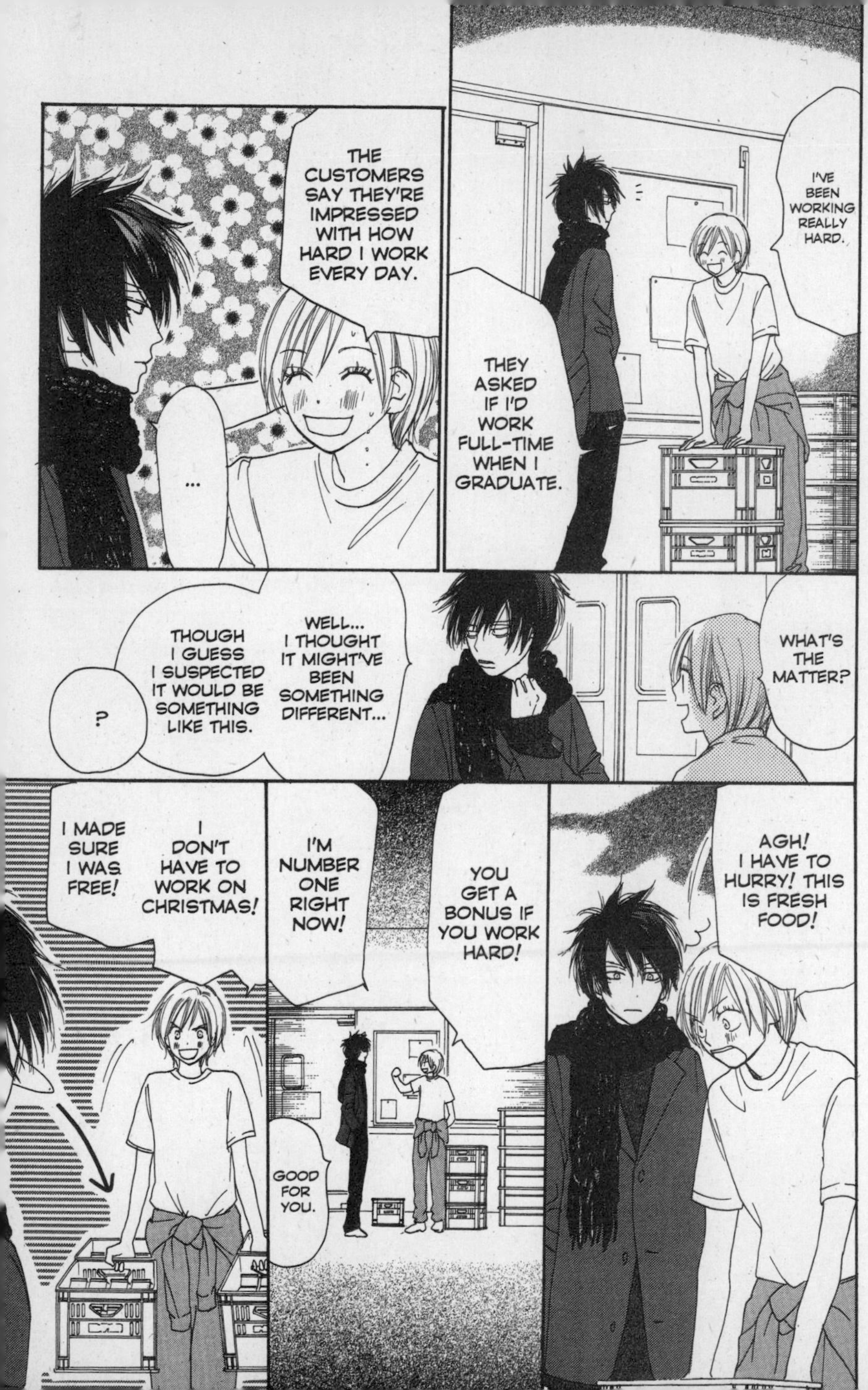
I'VE BEEN WORKING REALLY HARD.
THEY ASKED IF I'D WORK FULL-TIME WHEN I GRADUATE.
THE CUSTOMERS SAY THEY'RE IMPRESSED WITH HOW HARD I WORK EVERY DAY.
...
WHAT'S THE MATTER?
WELL... I THOUGHT IT MIGHT'VE BEEN SOMETHING DIFFERENT...
THOUGH I GUESS I SUSPECTED IT WOULD BE SOMETHING LIKE THIS.
?
AGH! I HAVE TO HURRY! THIS IS FRESH FOOD!
YOU GET A BONUS IF YOU WORK HARD!
I'M NUMBER ONE RIGHT NOW!
GOOD FOR YOU.
I DON'T HAVE TO WORK ON CHRISTMAS!
I MADE SURE I WAS FREE!

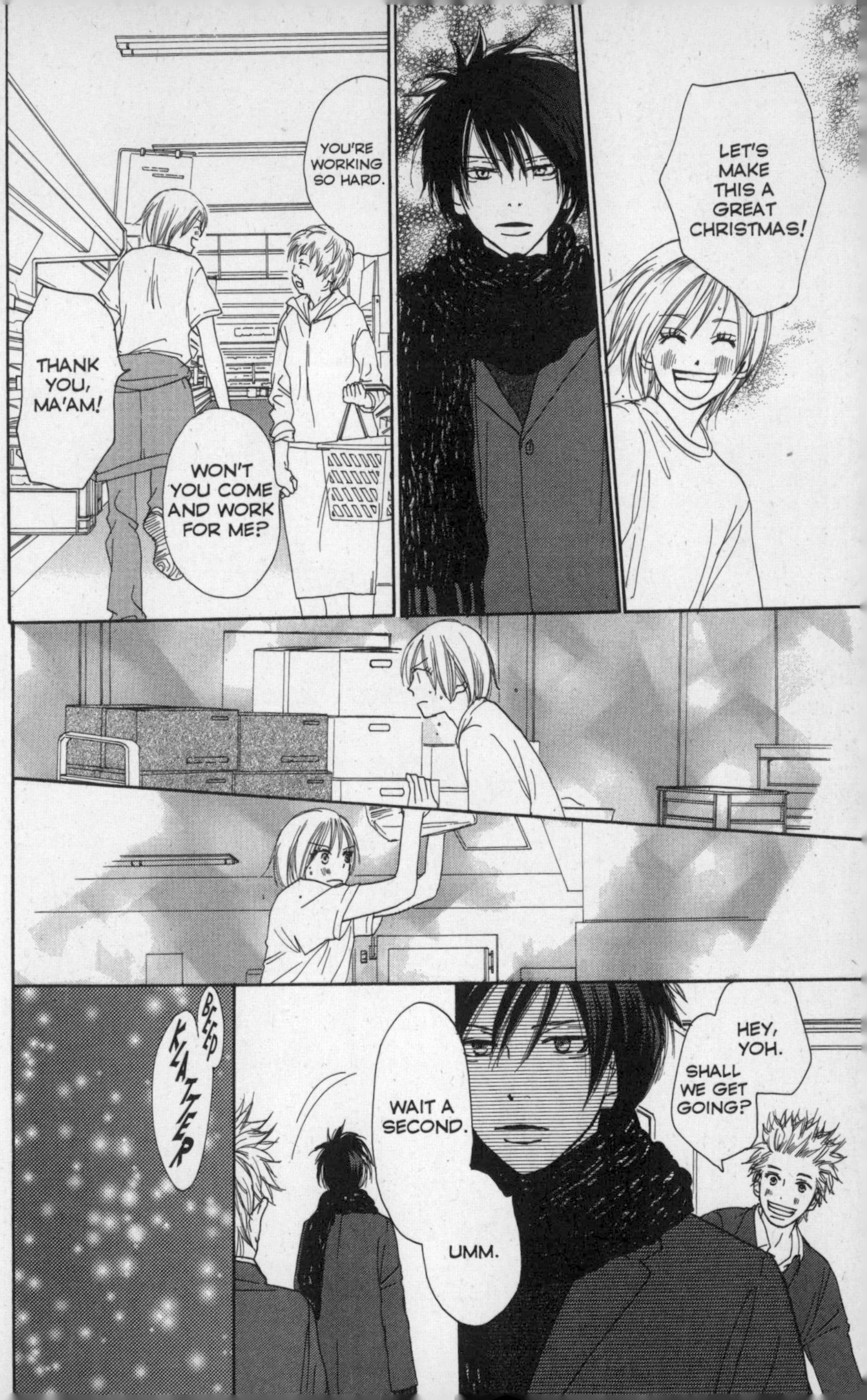
LET'S MAKE THIS A GREAT CHRISTMAS!
YOU'RE WORKING SO HARD.
THANK YOU, MA'AM!
WON'T YOU COME AND WORK FOR ME?
HEY, YOH.
SHALL WE GET GOING?
WAIT A SECOND.
UMM.
BEEP
KLATTER

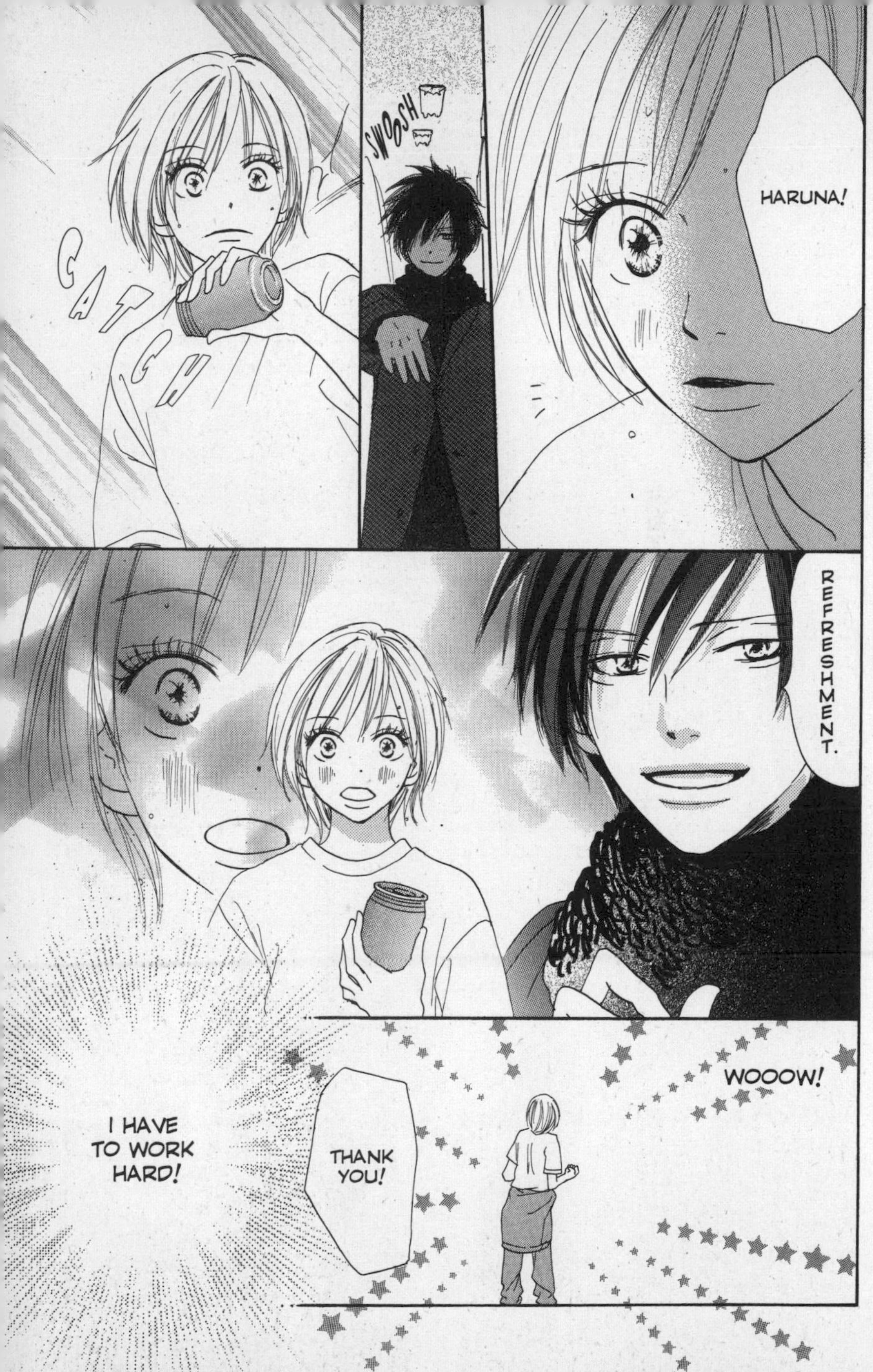
HARUNA!
SWOOSH
CATCH
REFRESHMENT.
WOOOW!
THANK YOU!
I HAVE TO WORK HARD!

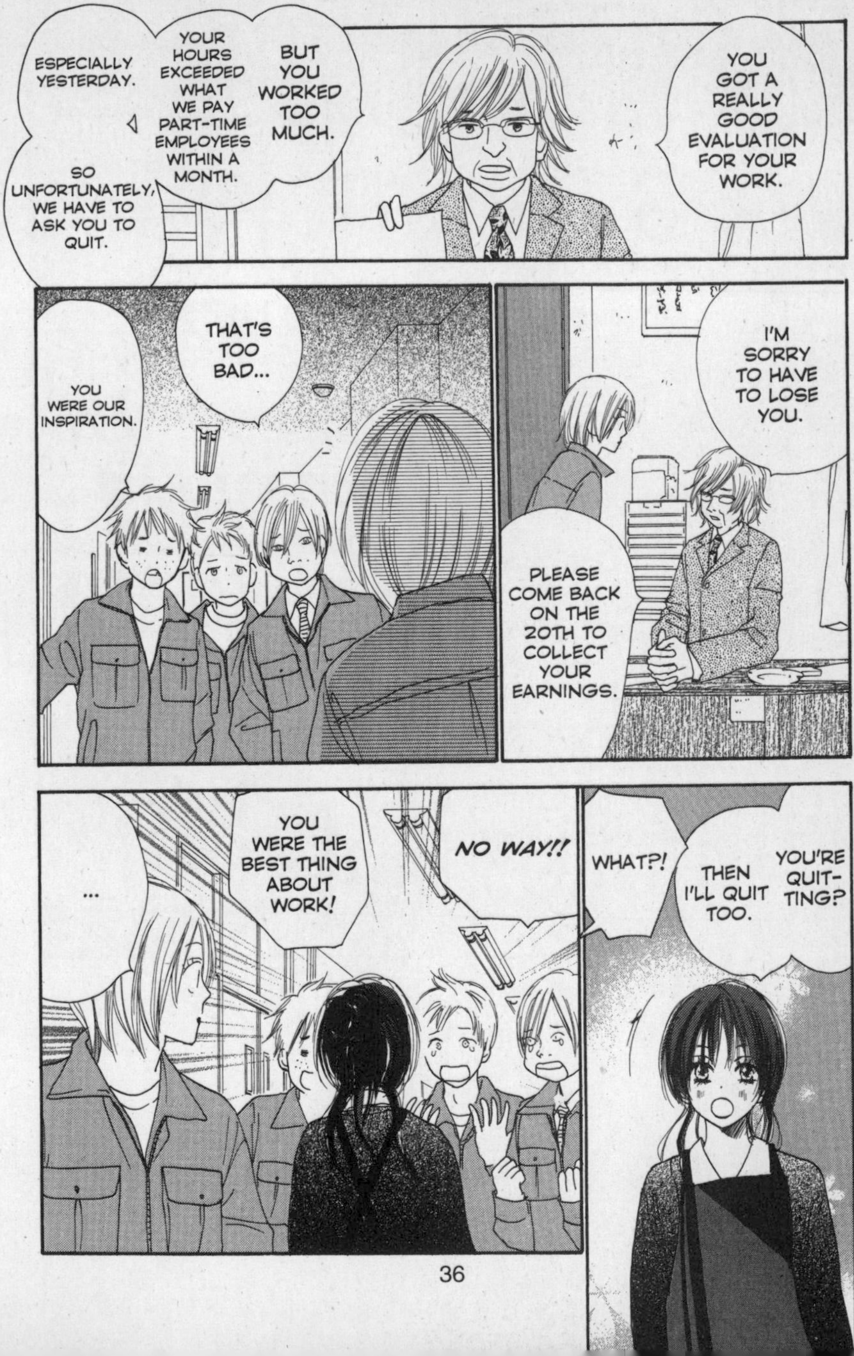
YOU GOT A REALLY GOOD EVALUATION FOR YOUR WORK.
BUT YOU WORKED TOO MUCH.
YOUR HOURS EXCEEDED WHAT WE PAY PART-TIME EMPLOYEES WITHIN A MONTH.
ESPECIALLY YESTERDAY.
SO UNFORTUNATELY, WE HAVE TO ASK YOU TO QUIT.
I'M SORRY TO HAVE TO LOSE YOU.
PLEASE COME BACK ON THE 20TH TO COLLECT YOUR EARNINGS.
THAT'S TOO BAD...
YOU WERE OUR INSPIRATION.
YOU'RE QUIT-TING?
THEN I'LL QUIT TOO.
WHAT?!
NO WAY!!
YOU WERE THE BEST THING ABOUT WORK!
...

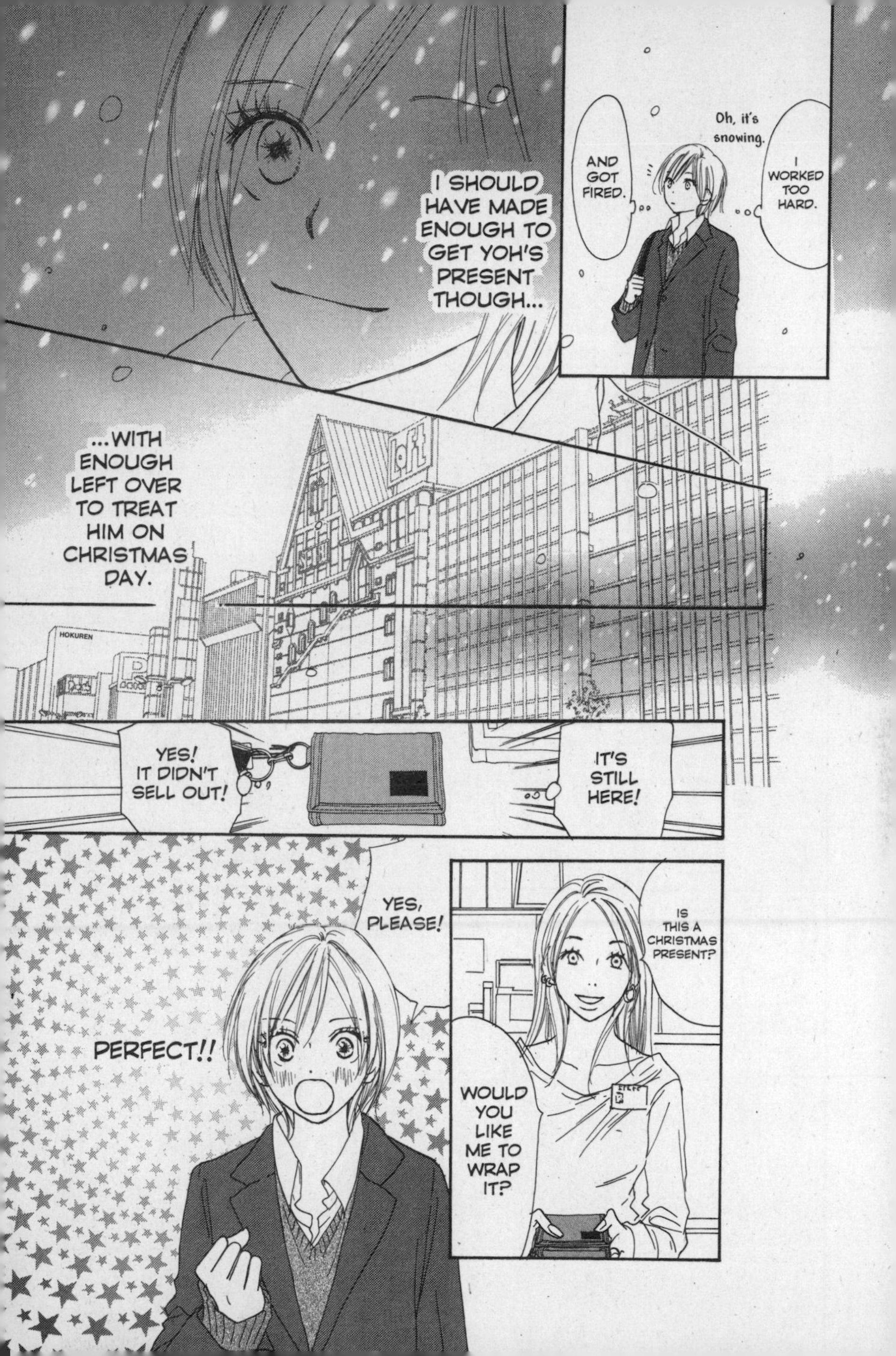
Oh, it's snowing.
I WORKED TOO HARD.
AND GOT FIRED.
I SHOULD HAVE MADE ENOUGH TO GET YOH'S PRESENT THOUGH...
...WITH ENOUGH LEFT OVER TO TREAT HIM ON CHRISTMAS DAY.
loft
HOKUREN
IT'S STILL HERE!
YES! IT DIDN'T SELL OUT!
IS THIS A CHRISTMAS PRESENT?
WOULD YOU LIKE ME TO WRAP IT?
YES, PLEASE!
PERFECT!!

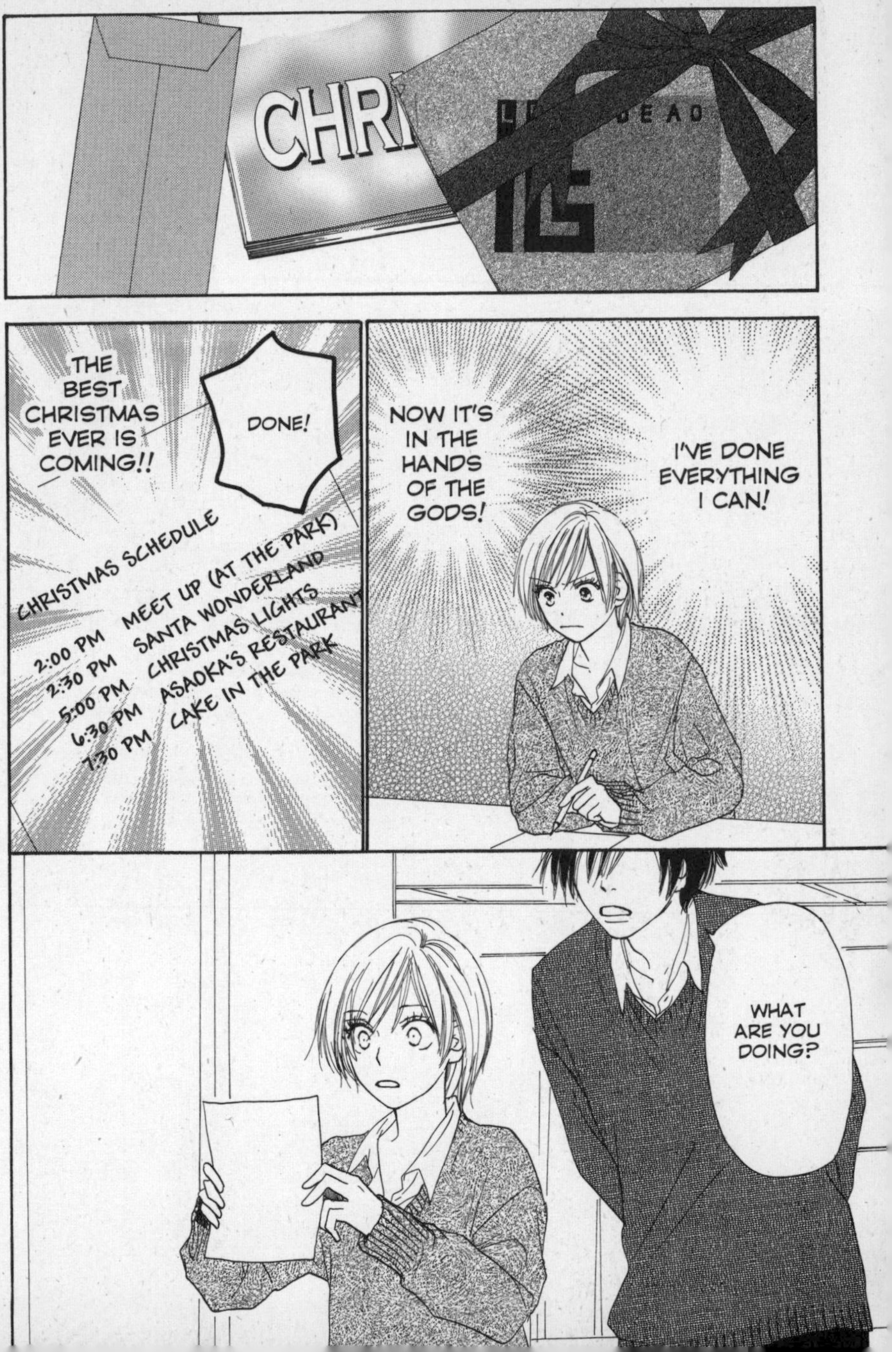
CHRI
I'VE DONE EVERYTHING I CAN!
NOW IT'S IN THE HANDS OF THE GODS!
DONE!
THE BEST CHRISTMAS EVER IS COMING!!
CHRISTMAS SCHEDULE
2:00 PM MEET UP (AT THE PARK)
2:30 PM SANTA WONDERLAND
5:00 PM CHRISTMAS LIGHTS
6:30 PM ASAOKA'S RESTAURANT
7:30 PM CAKE IN THE PARK
WHAT ARE YOU DOING?

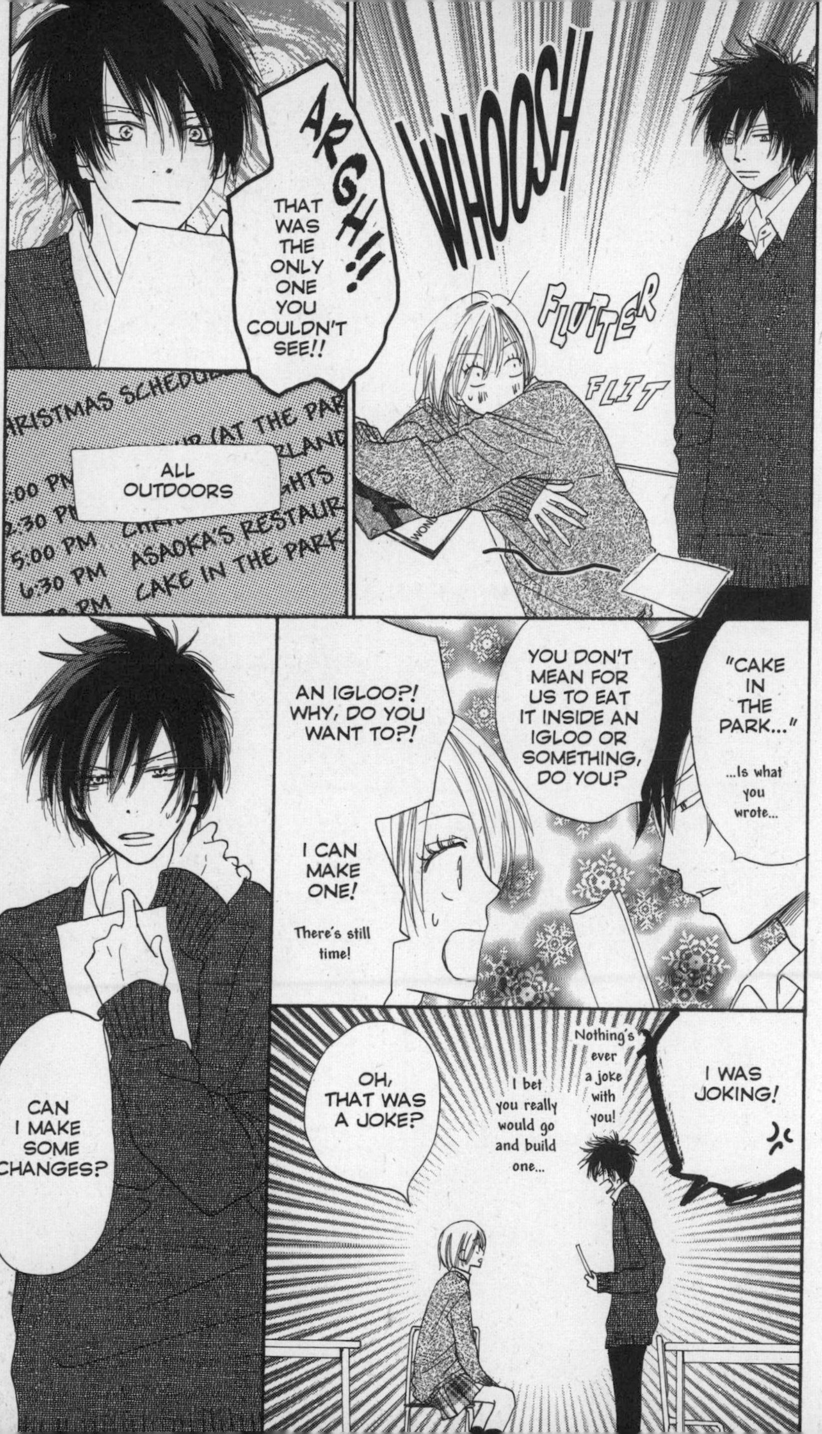
WHOOSH
FLUTTER
FLIT
ARGH!!
THAT WAS THE ONLY ONE YOU COULDN'T SEE!!
ALL OUTDOORS
ASAOKA'S RESTAUR
5:00 PM
6:30 PM CAKE IN THE PARK
"CAKE IN THE PARK..."
...Is what you wrote...
YOU DON'T MEAN FOR US TO EAT IT INSIDE AN IGLOO OR SOMETHING, DO YOU?
AN IGLOO?! WHY, DO YOU WANT TO?!
I CAN MAKE ONE!
There's still time!
I WAS JOKING!
Nothing's ever a joke with you!
I bet you really would go and build one...
OH, THAT WAS A JOKE?
CAN I MAKE SOME CHANGES?

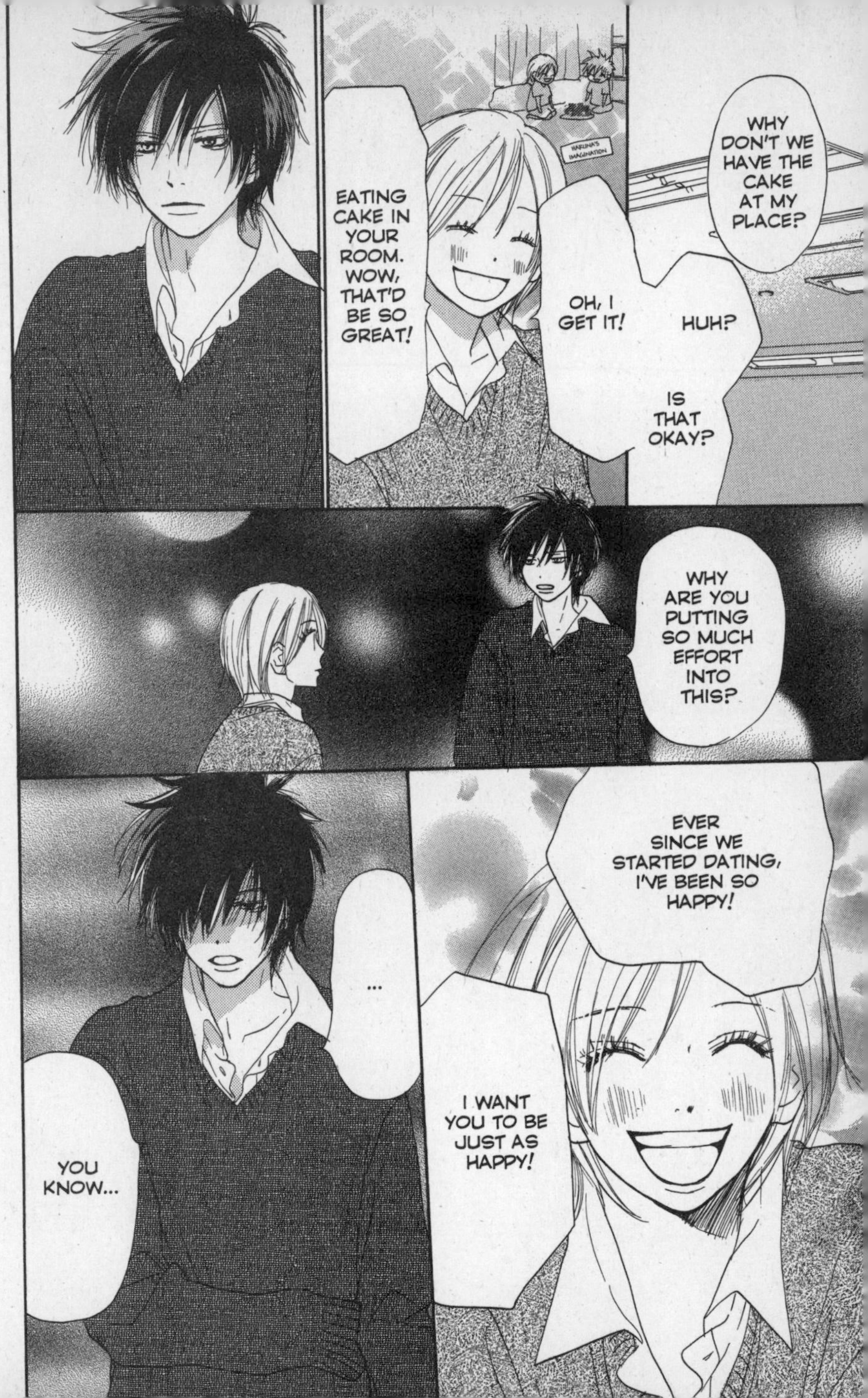
WHY DON'T WE HAVE THE CAKE AT MY PLACE?
HUH?
IS THAT OKAY?
HARUNA'S IMAGINATION
OH, I GET IT!
EATING CAKE IN YOUR ROOM. WOW, THAT'D BE SO GREAT!
WHY ARE YOU PUTTING SO MUCH EFFORT INTO THIS?
EVER SINCE WE STARTED DATING, I'VE BEEN SO HAPPY!
I WANT YOU TO BE JUST AS HAPPY!
...
YOU KNOW...

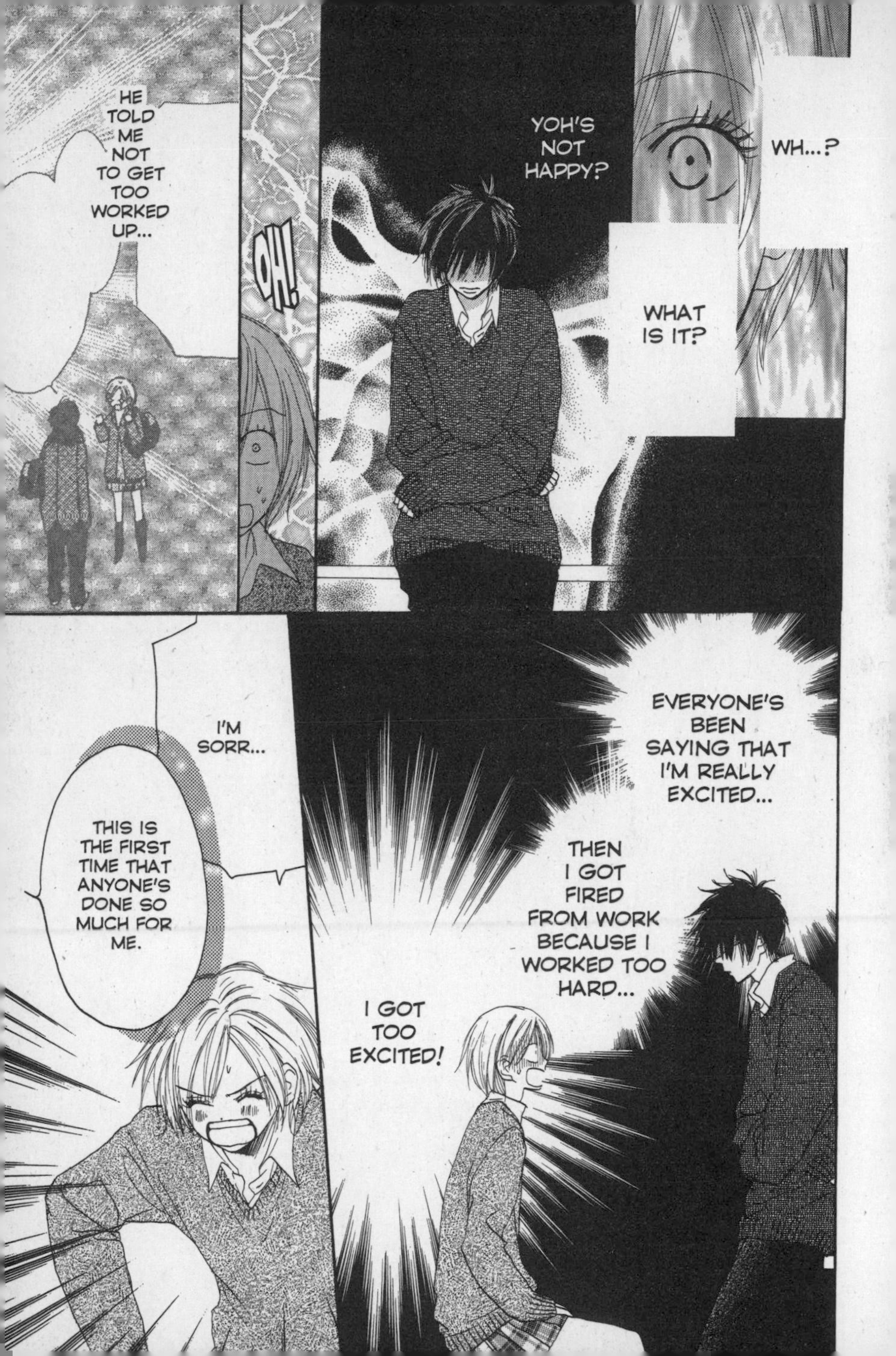
WH...?
WHAT IS IT?
YOH'S NOT HAPPY?
OH!
HE TOLD ME NOT TO GET TOO WORKED UP...
EVERYONE'S BEEN SAYING THAT I'M REALLY EXCITED...
THEN I GOT FIRED FROM WORK BECAUSE I WORKED TOO HARD...
I GOT TOO EXCITED!
I'M SORR...
THIS IS THE FIRST TIME THAT ANYONE'S DONE SO MUCH FOR ME.

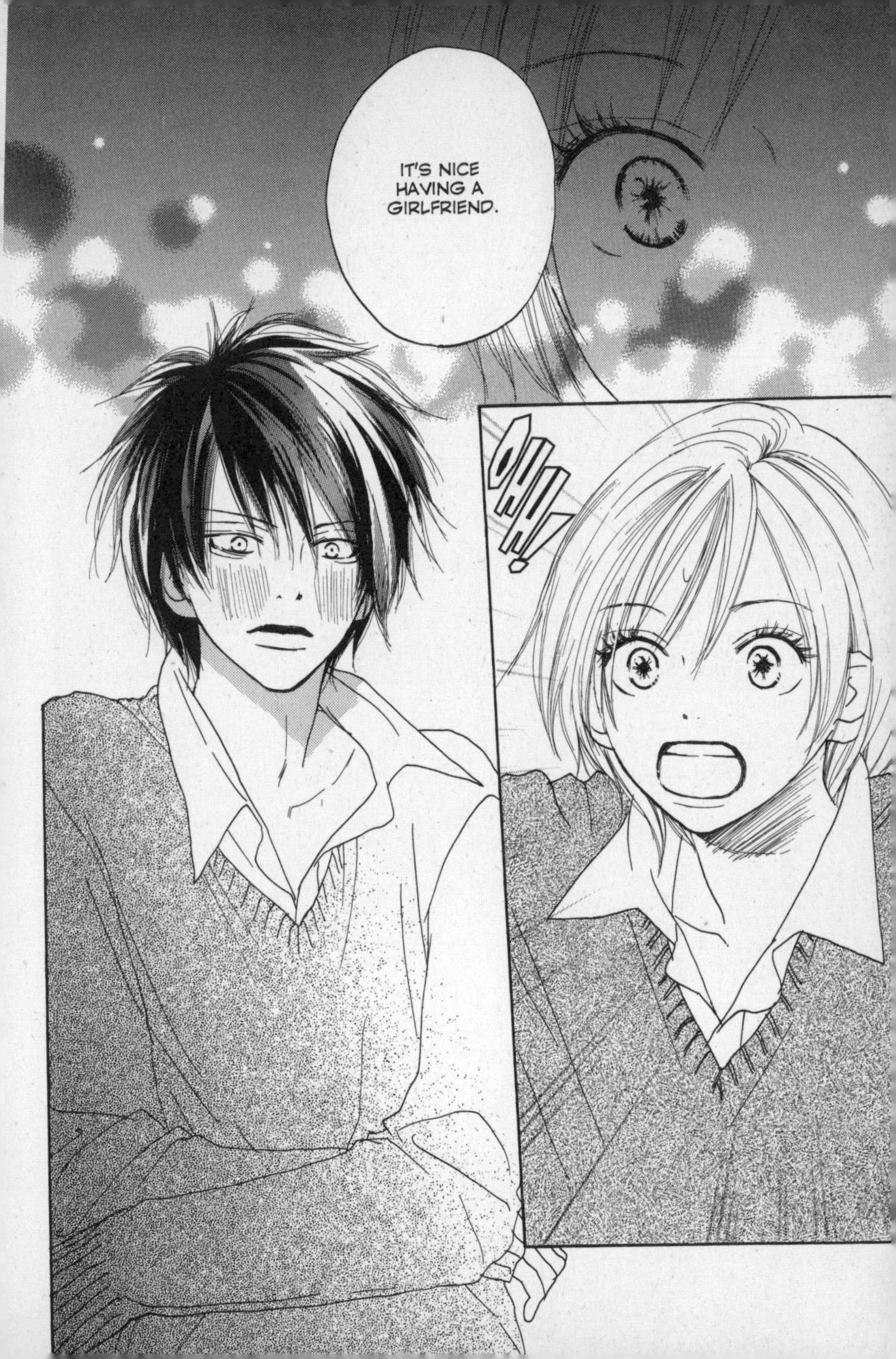
IT'S NICE HAVING A GIRLFRIEND.
OH!!

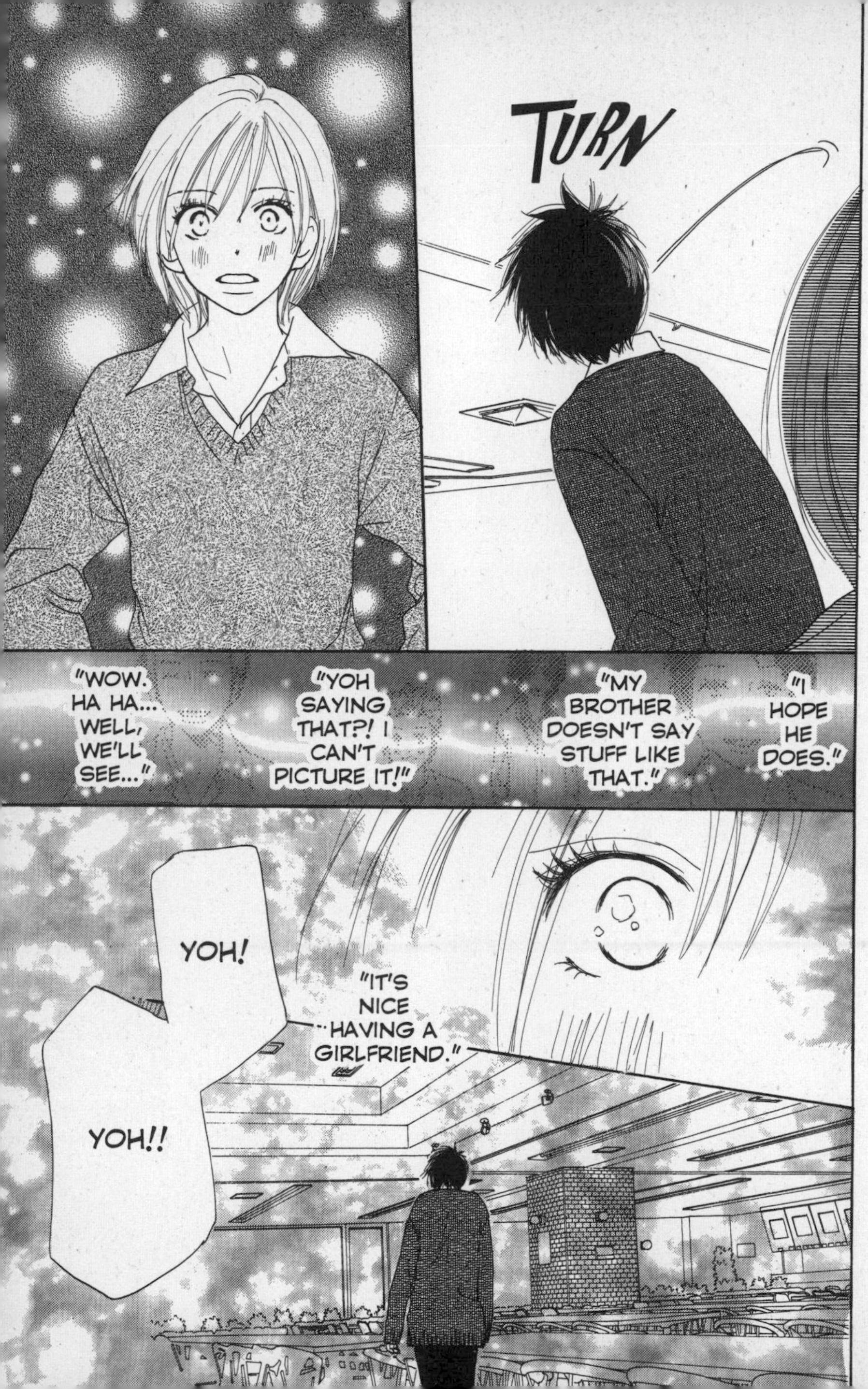
TURN
"I HOPE HE DOES."
"MY BROTHER DOESN'T SAY STUFF LIKE THAT."
"YOH SAYING THAT?! I CAN'T PICTURE IT!"
"WOW. HA HA... WELL, WE'LL SEE..."
"IT'S NICE HAVING A GIRLFRIEND."
YOH!
YOH!!

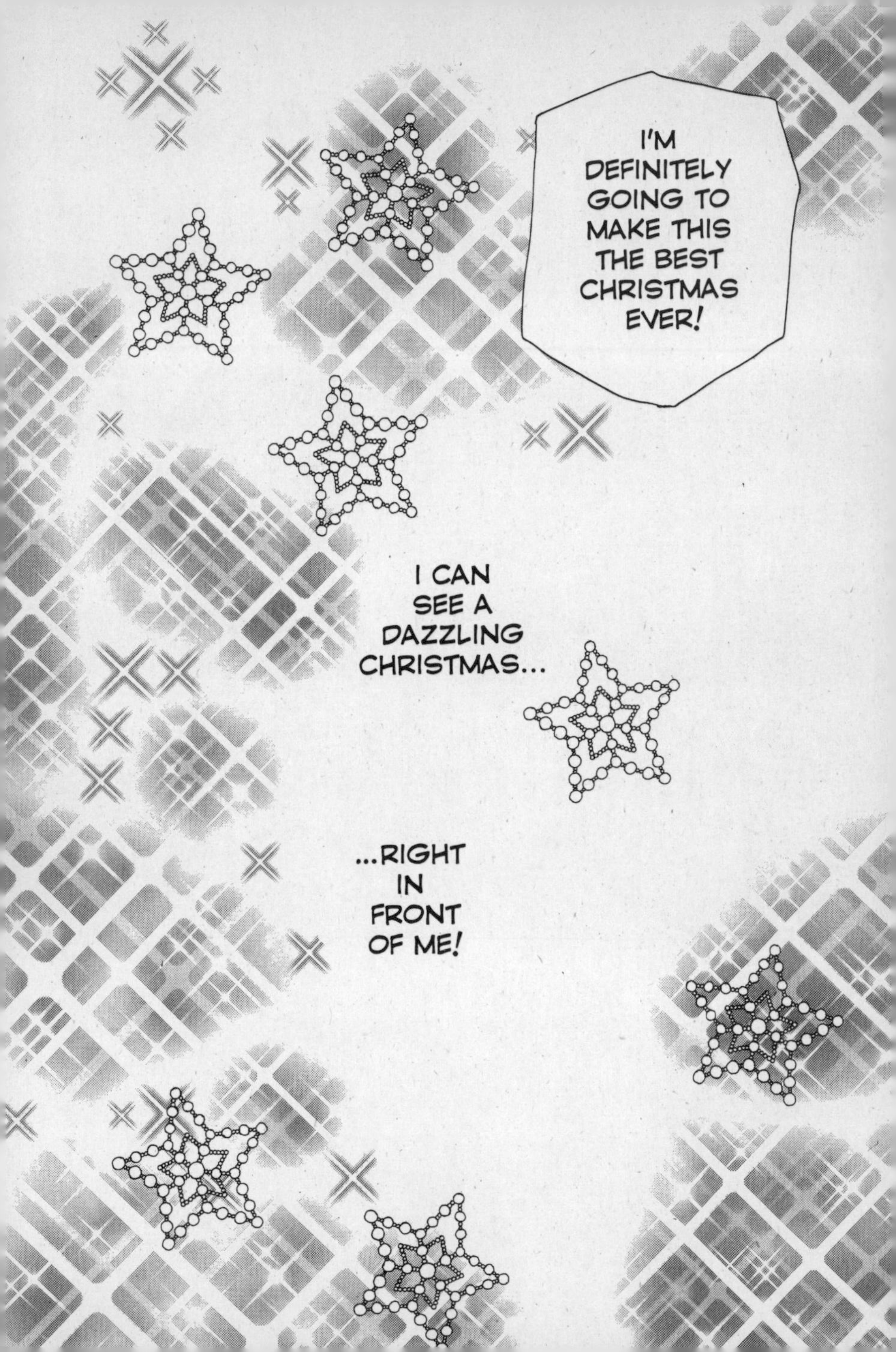
I'M DEFINITELY GOING TO MAKE THIS THE BEST CHRISTMAS EVER!
I CAN SEE A DAZZLING CHRISTMAS...
...RIGHT IN FRONT OF ME!

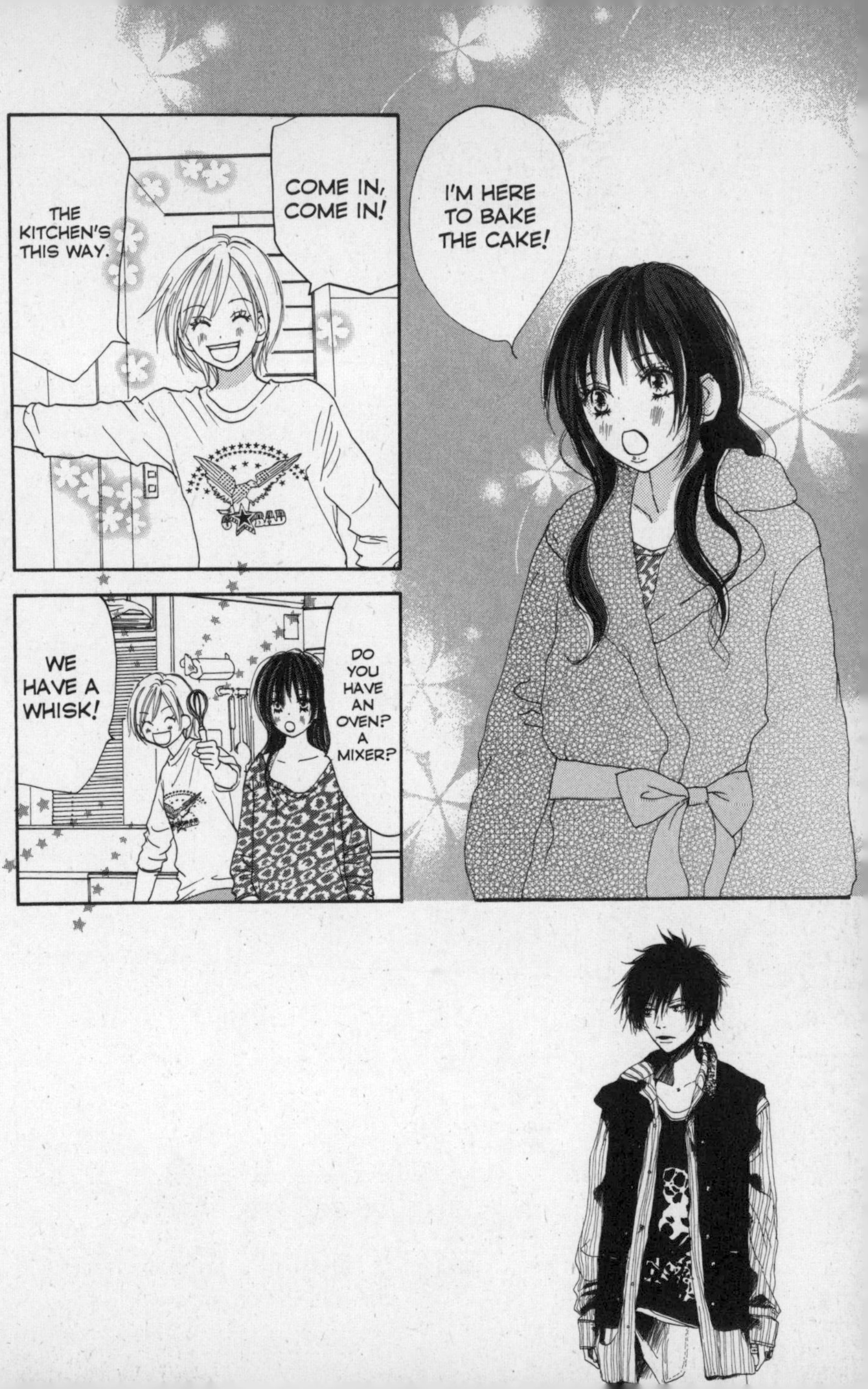
I'M HERE TO BAKE THE CAKE!
COME IN, COME IN!
THE KITCHEN'S THIS WAY.
DO YOU HAVE AN OVEN? A MIXER?
WE HAVE A WHISK!

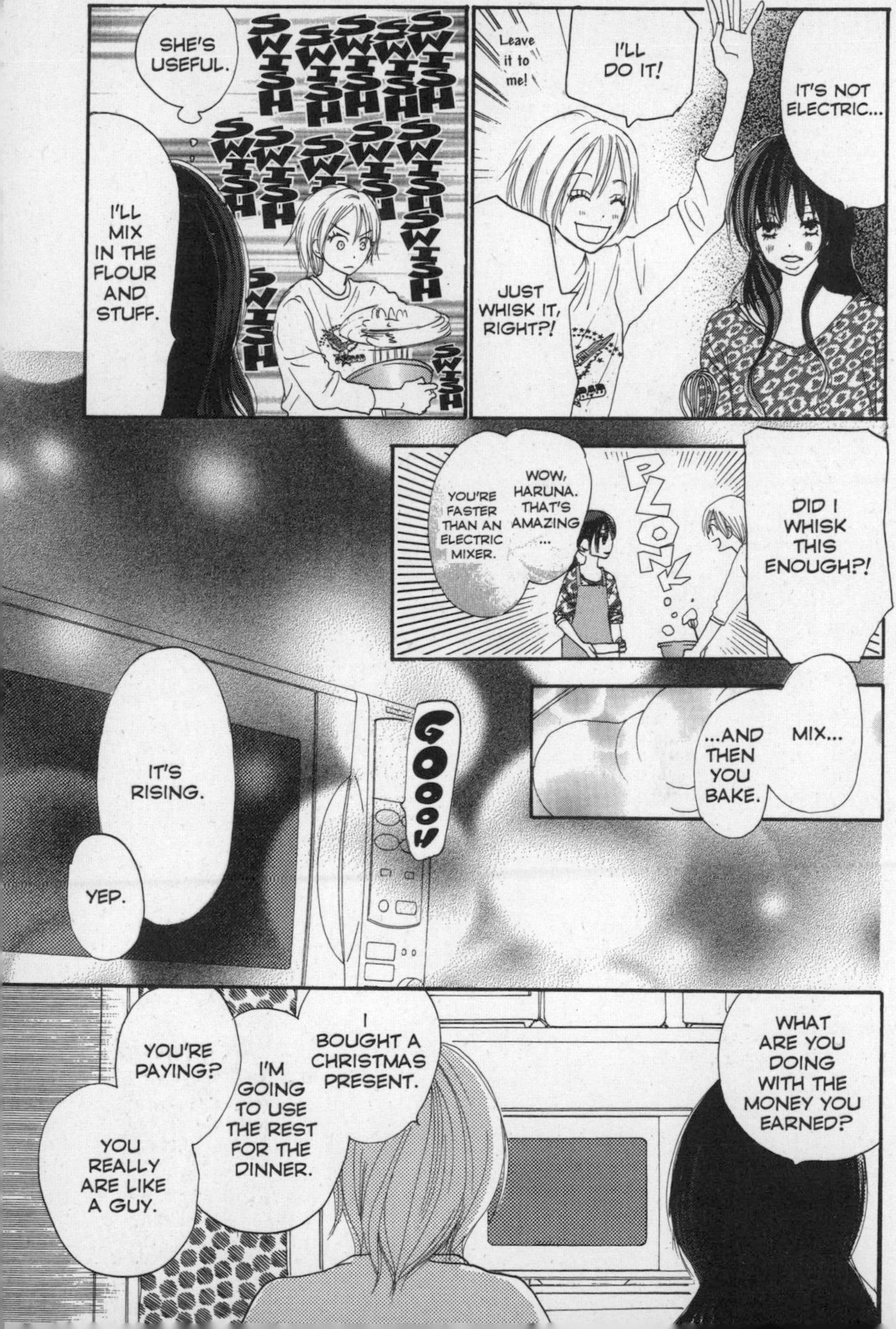
IT'S NOT ELECTRIC...
I'LL DO IT!
Leave it to me!
JUST WHISK IT, RIGHT?!
SWISH SWISH SWISH SWISH SWISH
SHE'S USEFUL.
SWISH SWISH SWISH SWISH SWISH SWISH SWISH
I'LL MIX IN THE FLOUR AND STUFF.
DID I WHISK THIS ENOUGH?!
PLONK
WOW, HARUNA. THAT'S AMAZING...
YOU'RE FASTER THAN AN ELECTRIC MIXER.
MIX...
...AND THEN YOU BAKE.
GOOOOH
IT'S RISING.
YEP.
WHAT ARE YOU DOING WITH THE MONEY YOU EARNED?
I BOUGHT A CHRISTMAS PRESENT.
I'M GOING TO USE THE REST FOR THE DINNER.
YOU'RE PAYING?
YOU REALLY ARE LIKE A GUY.

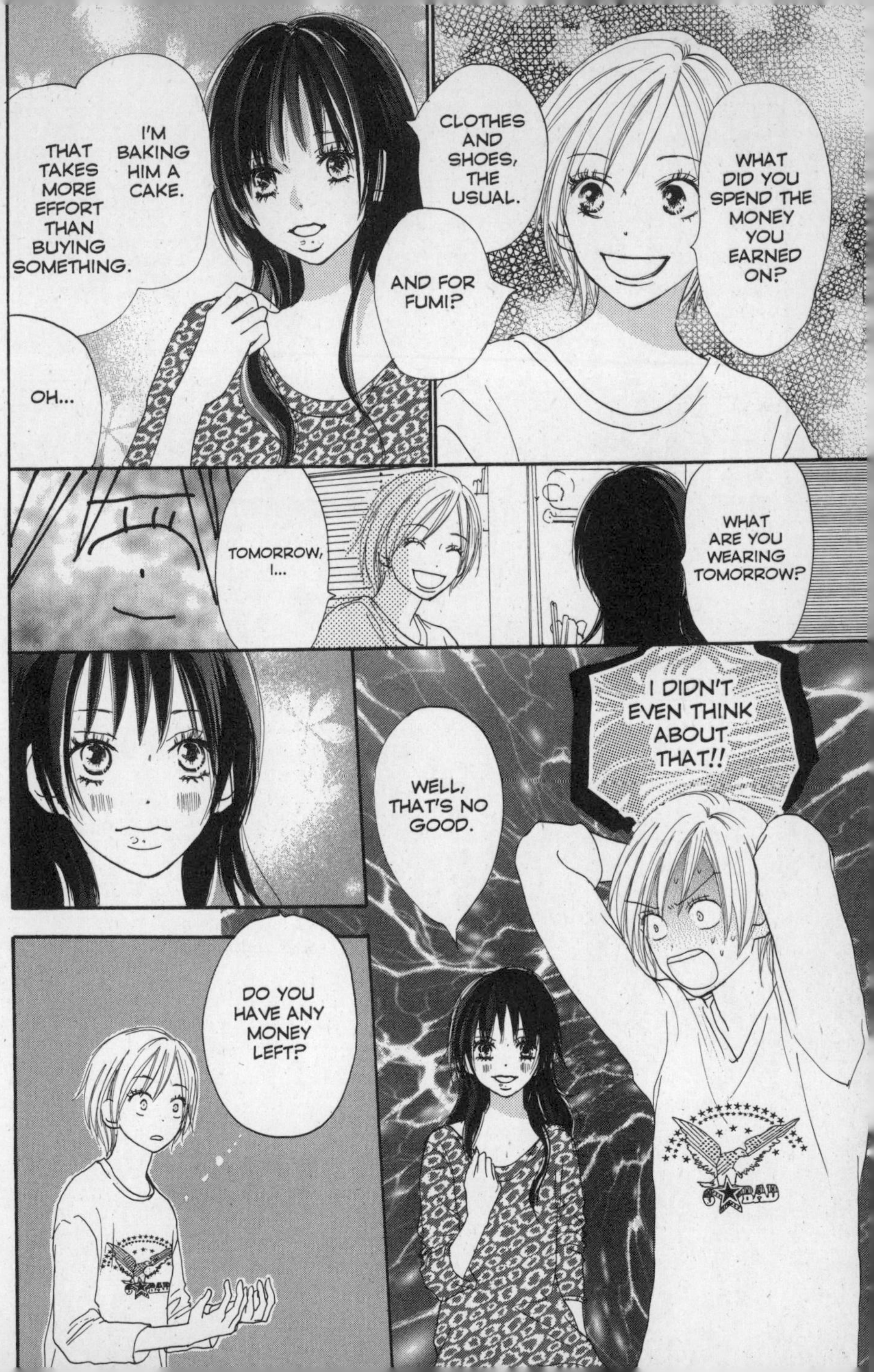
WHAT DID YOU SPEND THE MONEY YOU EARNED ON?
CLOTHES AND SHOES, THE USUAL.
AND FOR FUMI?
I'M BAKING HIM A CAKE.
THAT TAKES MORE EFFORT THAN BUYING SOMETHING.
OH...
WHAT ARE YOU WEARING TOMORROW?
TOMORROW, I...
I DIDN'T EVEN THINK ABOUT THAT!!
WELL, THAT'S NO GOOD.
DO YOU HAVE ANY MONEY LEFT?

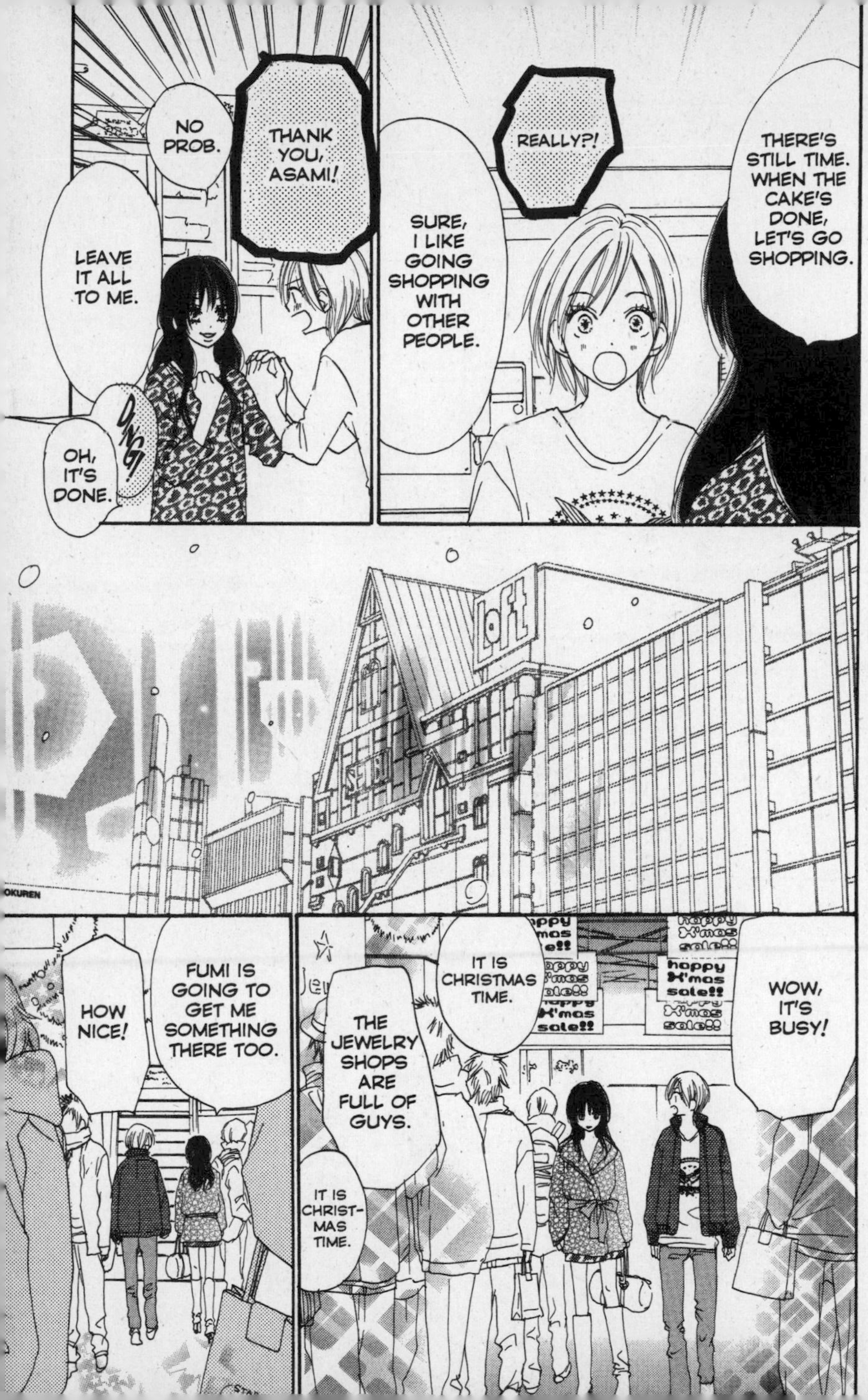
THERE'S STILL TIME. WHEN THE CAKE'S DONE, LET'S GO SHOPPING.
REALLY?!
SURE, I LIKE GOING SHOPPING WITH OTHER PEOPLE.
THANK YOU, ASAMI!
NO PROB.
LEAVE IT ALL TO ME.
DING!
OH, IT'S DONE.
LOFT
WOW, IT'S BUSY!
happy X'mas sale!!
IT IS CHRISTMAS TIME.
THE JEWELRY SHOPS ARE FULL OF GUYS.
IT IS CHRIST-MAS TIME.
FUMI IS GOING TO GET ME SOMETHING THERE TOO.
HOW NICE!

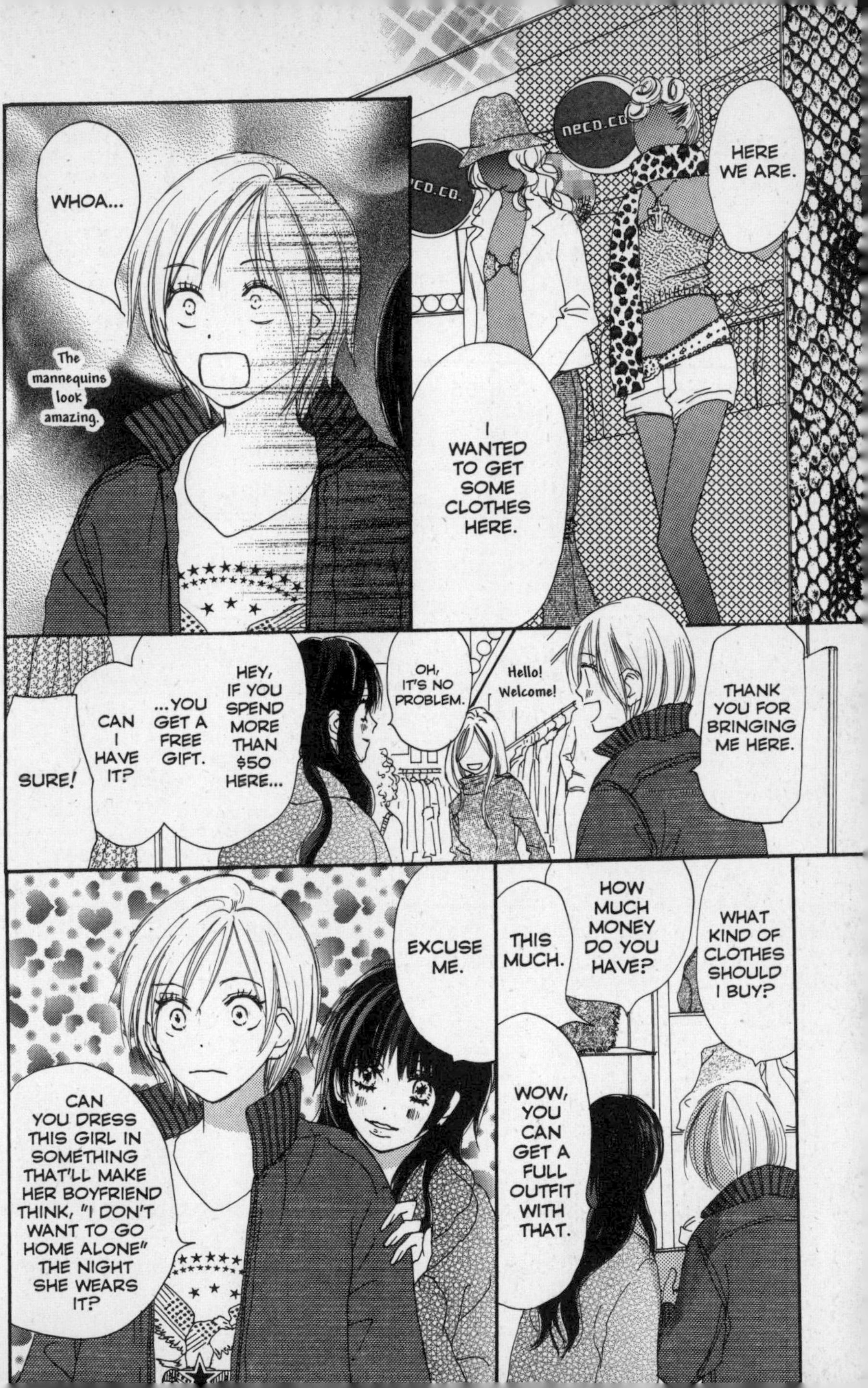
HERE WE ARE.
I WANTED TO GET SOME CLOTHES HERE.
WHOA...
The mannequins look amazing.
THANK YOU FOR BRINGING ME HERE.
Hello! Welcome!
OH, IT'S NO PROBLEM.
HEY, IF YOU SPEND MORE THAN $50 HERE...
...YOU GET A FREE GIFT.
CAN I HAVE IT?
SURE!
WHAT KIND OF CLOTHES SHOULD I BUY?
HOW MUCH MONEY DO YOU HAVE?
THIS MUCH.
WOW, YOU CAN GET A FULL OUTFIT WITH THAT.
EXCUSE ME.
CAN YOU DRESS THIS GIRL IN SOMETHING THAT'LL MAKE HER BOYFRIEND THINK, "I DON'T WANT TO GO HOME ALONE" THE NIGHT SHE WEARS IT?

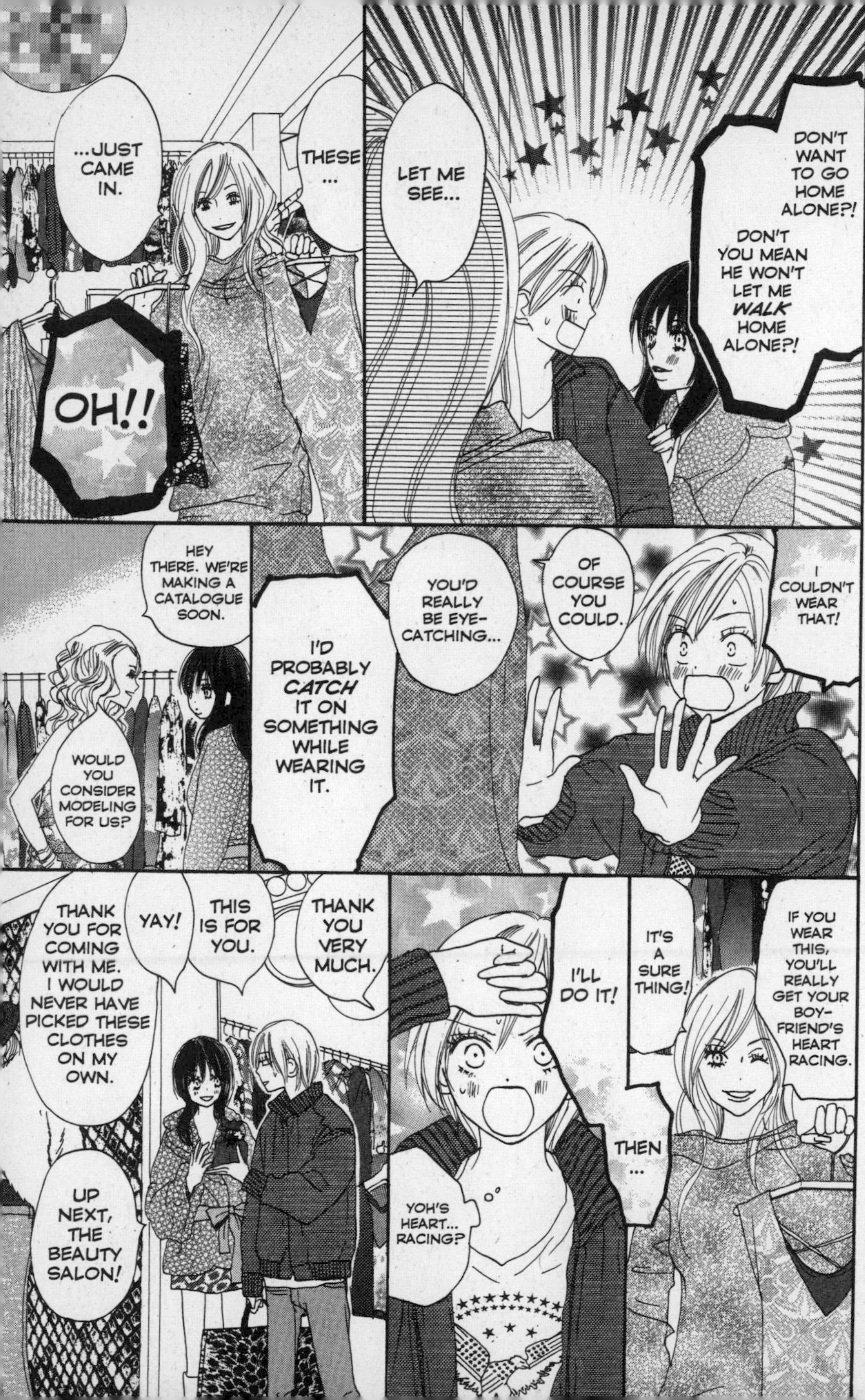
DON'T WANT TO GO HOME ALONE?!
DON'T YOU MEAN HE WON'T LET ME *WALK* HOME ALONE?!
LET ME SEE...
THESE ...
...JUST CAME IN.
OH!!
I COULDN'T WEAR THAT!
OF COURSE YOU COULD.
YOU'D REALLY BE EYE-CATCHING...
I'D PROBABLY *CATCH* IT ON SOMETHING WHILE WEARING IT.
HEY THERE. WE'RE MAKING A CATALOGUE SOON.
WOULD YOU CONSIDER MODELING FOR US?
IF YOU WEAR THIS, YOU'LL REALLY GET YOUR BOY-FRIEND'S HEART RACING.
IT'S A SURE THING!
I'LL DO IT!
THEN ...
YOH'S HEART... RACING?
THANK YOU VERY MUCH.
THIS IS FOR YOU.
YAY!
THANK YOU FOR COMING WITH ME. I WOULD NEVER HAVE PICKED THESE CLOTHES ON MY OWN.
UP NEXT, THE BEAUTY SALON!

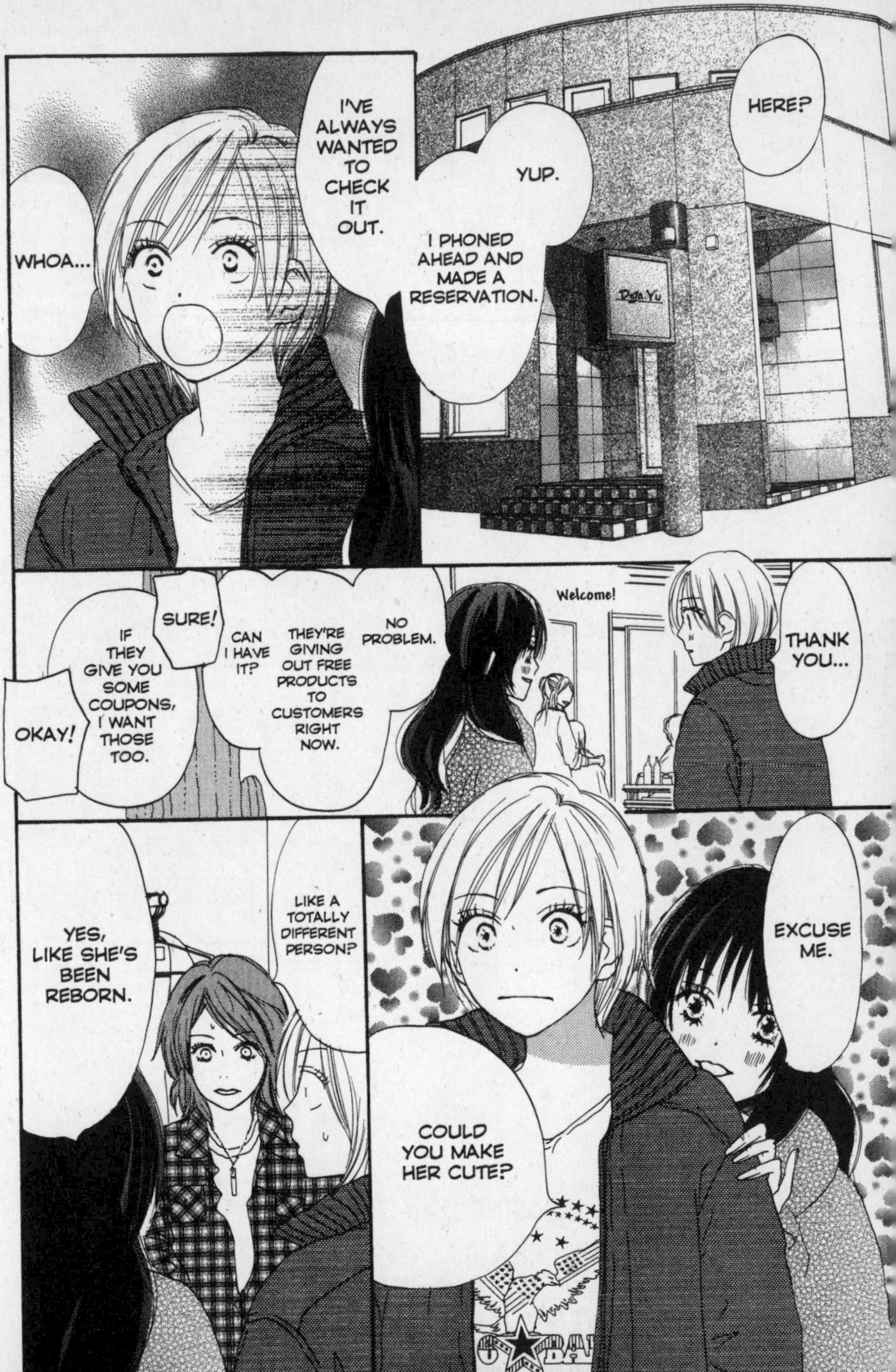
HERE?
YUP.
I PHONED AHEAD AND MADE A RESERVATION.
I'VE ALWAYS WANTED TO CHECK IT OUT.
WHOA...
Welcome!
THANK YOU...
NO PROBLEM.
THEY'RE GIVING OUT FREE PRODUCTS TO CUSTOMERS RIGHT NOW.
CAN I HAVE IT?
SURE!
IF THEY GIVE YOU SOME COUPONS, I WANT THOSE TOO.
OKAY!
EXCUSE ME.
COULD YOU MAKE HER CUTE?
LIKE A TOTALLY DIFFERENT PERSON?
YES, LIKE SHE'S BEEN REBORN.

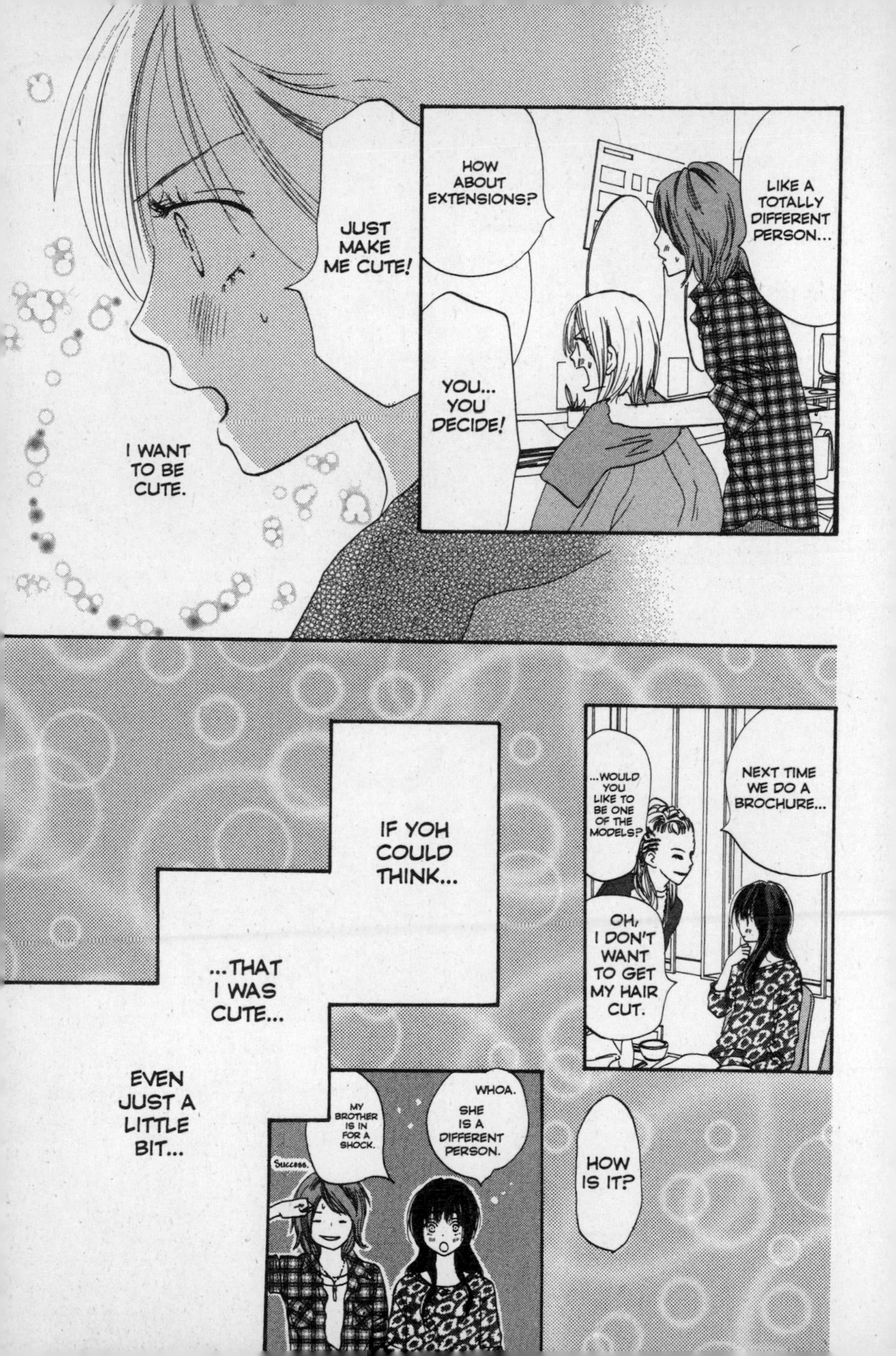
LIKE A TOTALLY DIFFERENT PERSON...
HOW ABOUT EXTENSIONS?
YOU... YOU DECIDE!
JUST MAKE ME CUTE!
I WANT TO BE CUTE.
NEXT TIME WE DO A BROCHURE...
...WOULD YOU LIKE TO BE ONE OF THE MODELS?
OH, I DON'T WANT TO GET MY HAIR CUT.
IF YOH COULD THINK...
...THAT I WAS CUTE...
HOW IS IT?
WHOA. SHE IS A DIFFERENT PERSON.
MY BROTHER IS IN FOR A SHOCK.
Success.
EVEN JUST A LITTLE BIT...

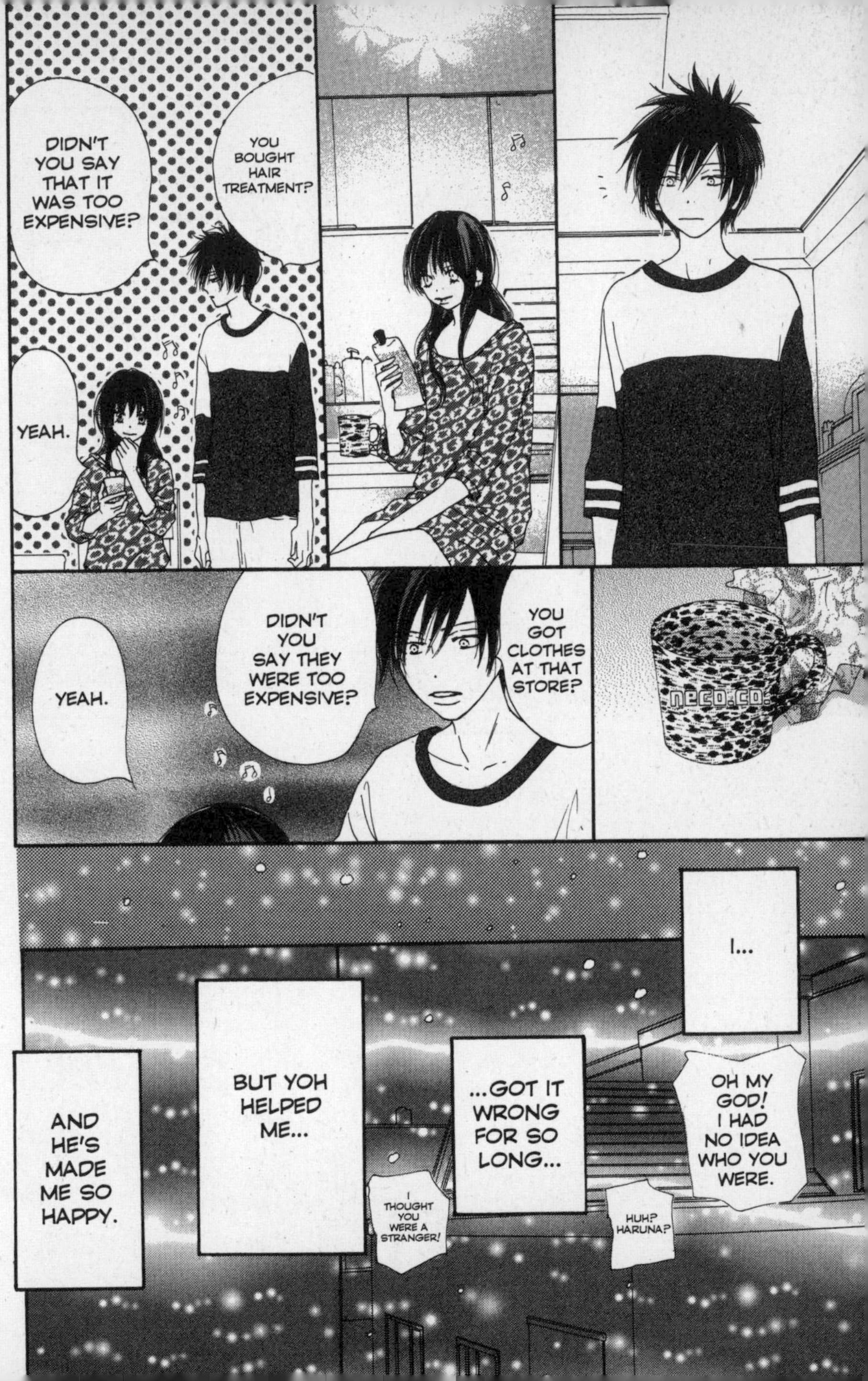
YOU BOUGHT HAIR TREATMENT?
DIDN'T YOU SAY THAT IT WAS TOO EXPENSIVE?
YEAH.
neco.co.
YOU GOT CLOTHES AT THAT STORE?
DIDN'T YOU SAY THEY WERE TOO EXPENSIVE?
YEAH.
I...
OH MY GOD! I HAD NO IDEA WHO YOU WERE.
HUH? HARUNA?
...GOT IT WRONG FOR SO LONG...
I THOUGHT YOU WERE A STRANGER!
BUT YOH HELPED ME...
AND HE'S MADE ME SO HAPPY.

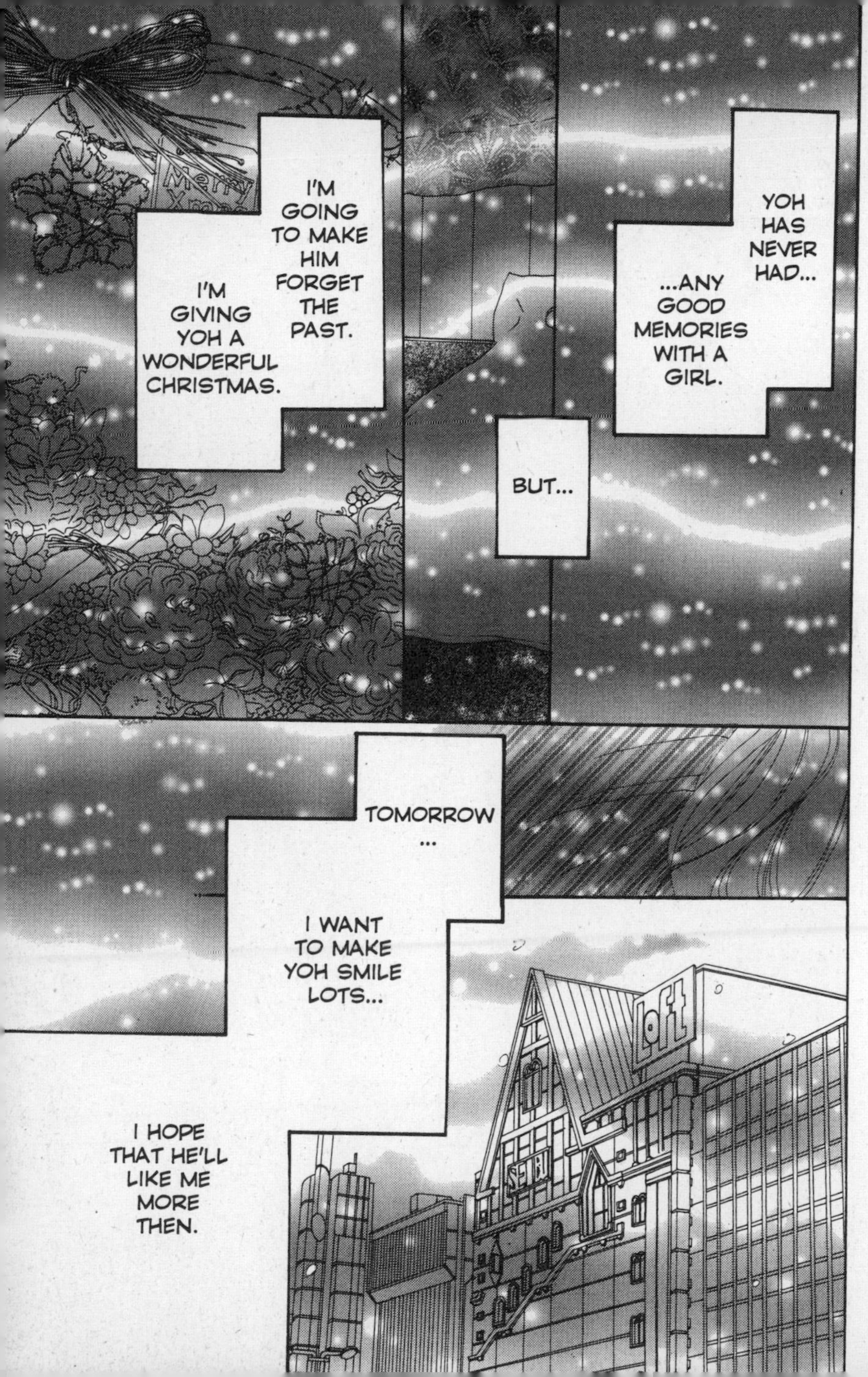
YOH HAS NEVER HAD...
...ANY GOOD MEMORIES WITH A GIRL.
BUT...
I'M GOING TO MAKE HIM FORGET THE PAST.
I'M GIVING YOH A WONDERFUL CHRISTMAS.
TOMORROW...
I WANT TO MAKE YOH SMILE LOTS...
I HOPE THAT HE'LL LIKE ME MORE THEN.
Loft

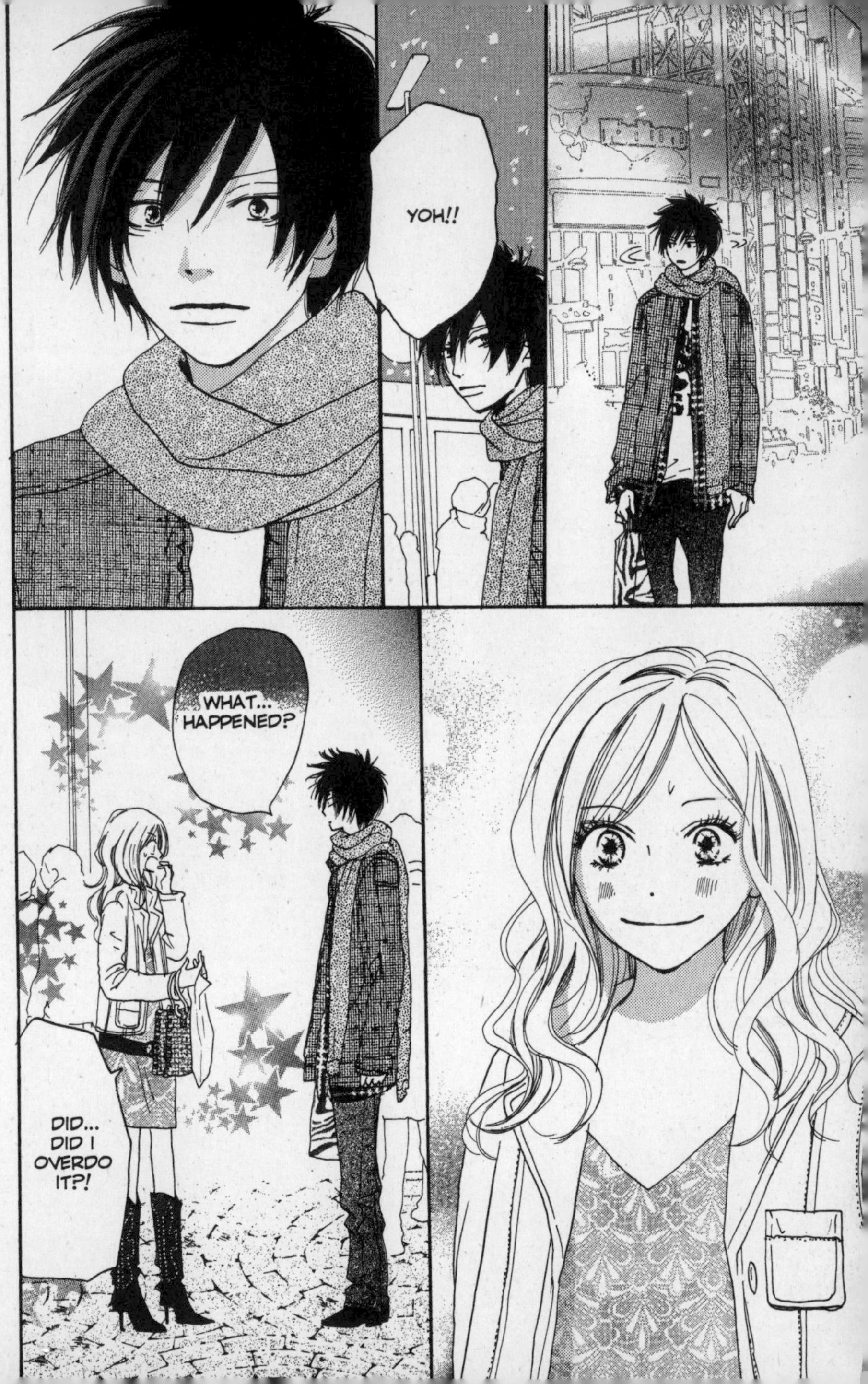
YOH!!
WHAT... HAPPENED?
DID... DID I OVERDO IT?!

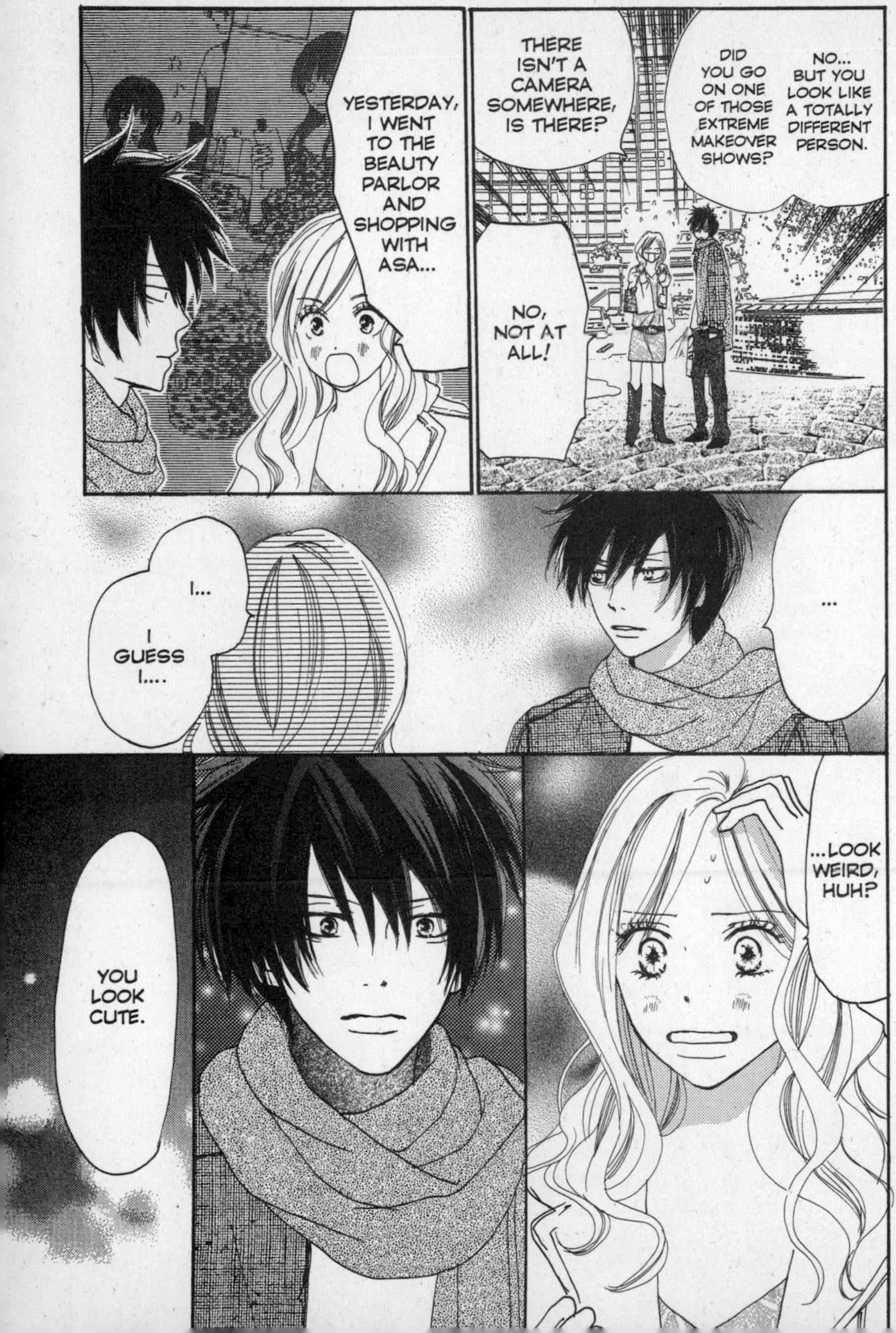
NO... BUT YOU LOOK LIKE A TOTALLY DIFFERENT PERSON.
DID YOU GO ON ONE OF THOSE EXTREME MAKEOVER SHOWS?
THERE ISN'T A CAMERA SOMEWHERE, IS THERE?
NO, NOT AT ALL!
YESTERDAY, I WENT TO THE BEAUTY PARLOR AND SHOPPING WITH ASA...
...
I... I GUESS I....
...LOOK WEIRD, HUH?
YOU LOOK CUTE.

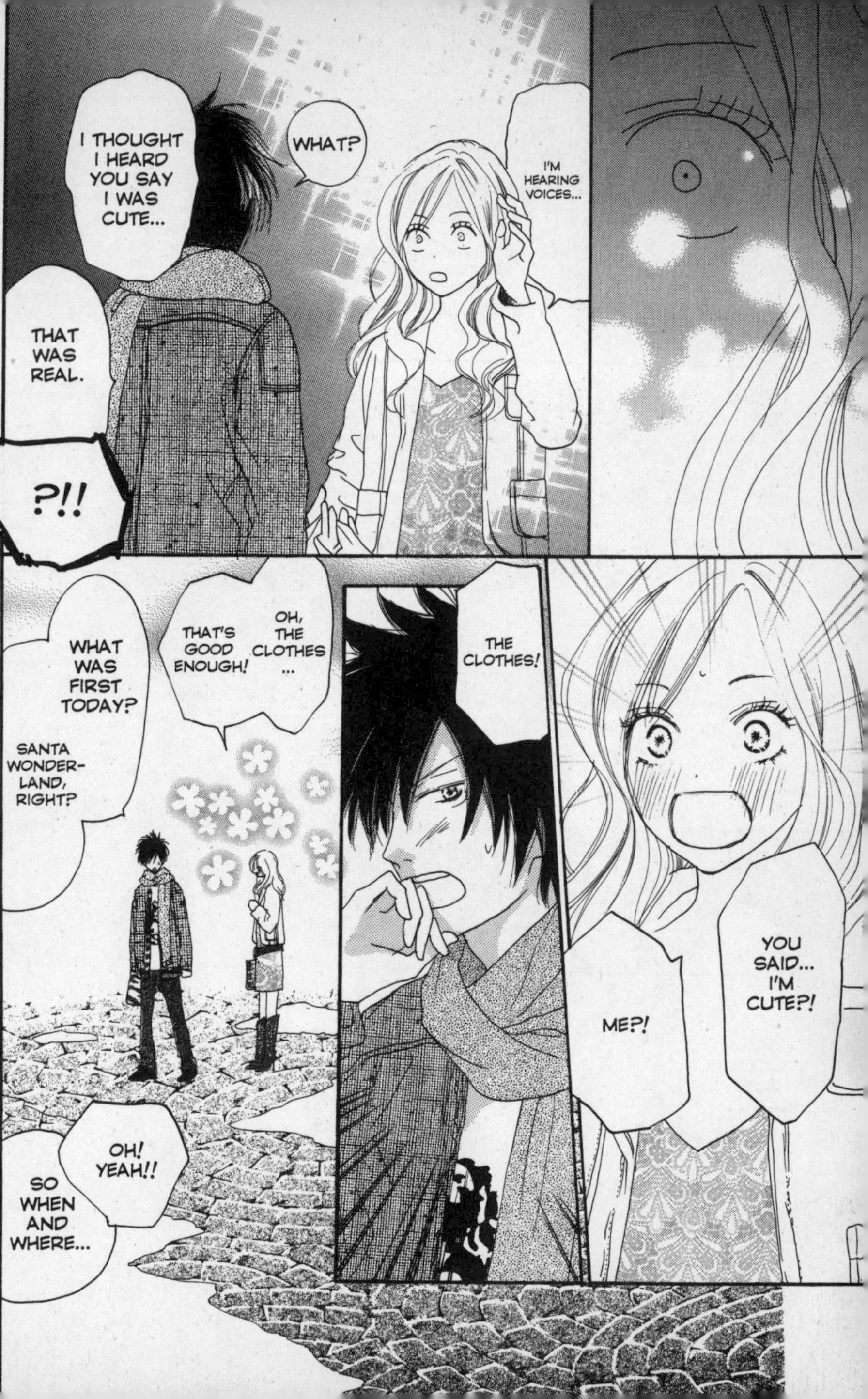
I'M HEARING VOICES...
WHAT?
I THOUGHT I HEARD YOU SAY I WAS CUTE...
THAT WAS REAL.
?!!
YOU SAID... I'M CUTE?!
ME?!
THE CLOTHES!
OH, THE CLOTHES...
THAT'S GOOD ENOUGH!
WHAT WAS FIRST TODAY?
SANTA WONDER-LAND, RIGHT?
OH! YEAH!!
SO WHEN AND WHERE...

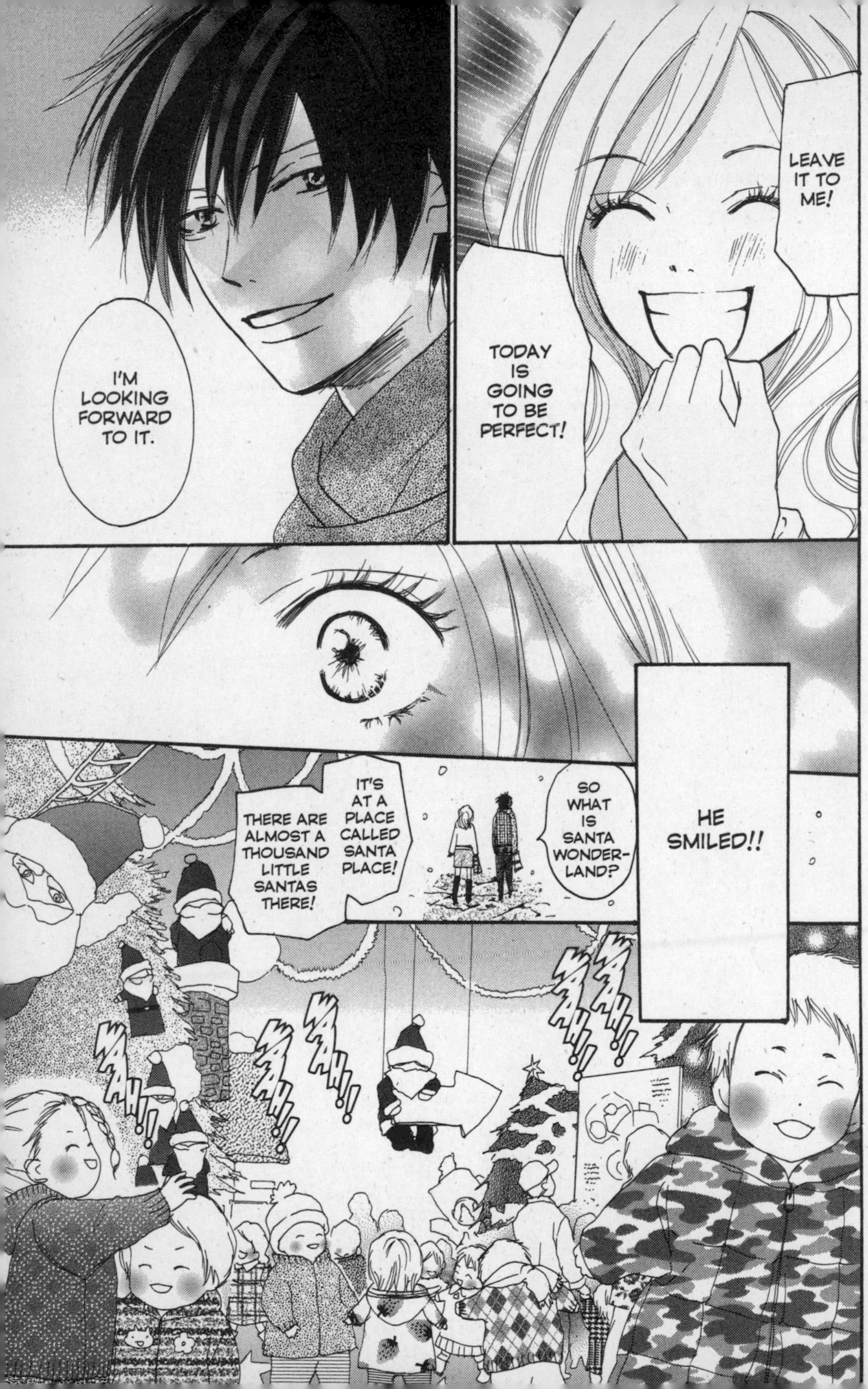
LEAVE IT TO ME!
TODAY IS GOING TO BE PERFECT!
I'M LOOKING FORWARD TO IT.
HE SMILED!!
SO WHAT IS SANTA WONDER-LAND?
IT'S AT A PLACE CALLED SANTA PLACE!
THERE ARE ALMOST A THOUSAND LITTLE SANTAS THERE!

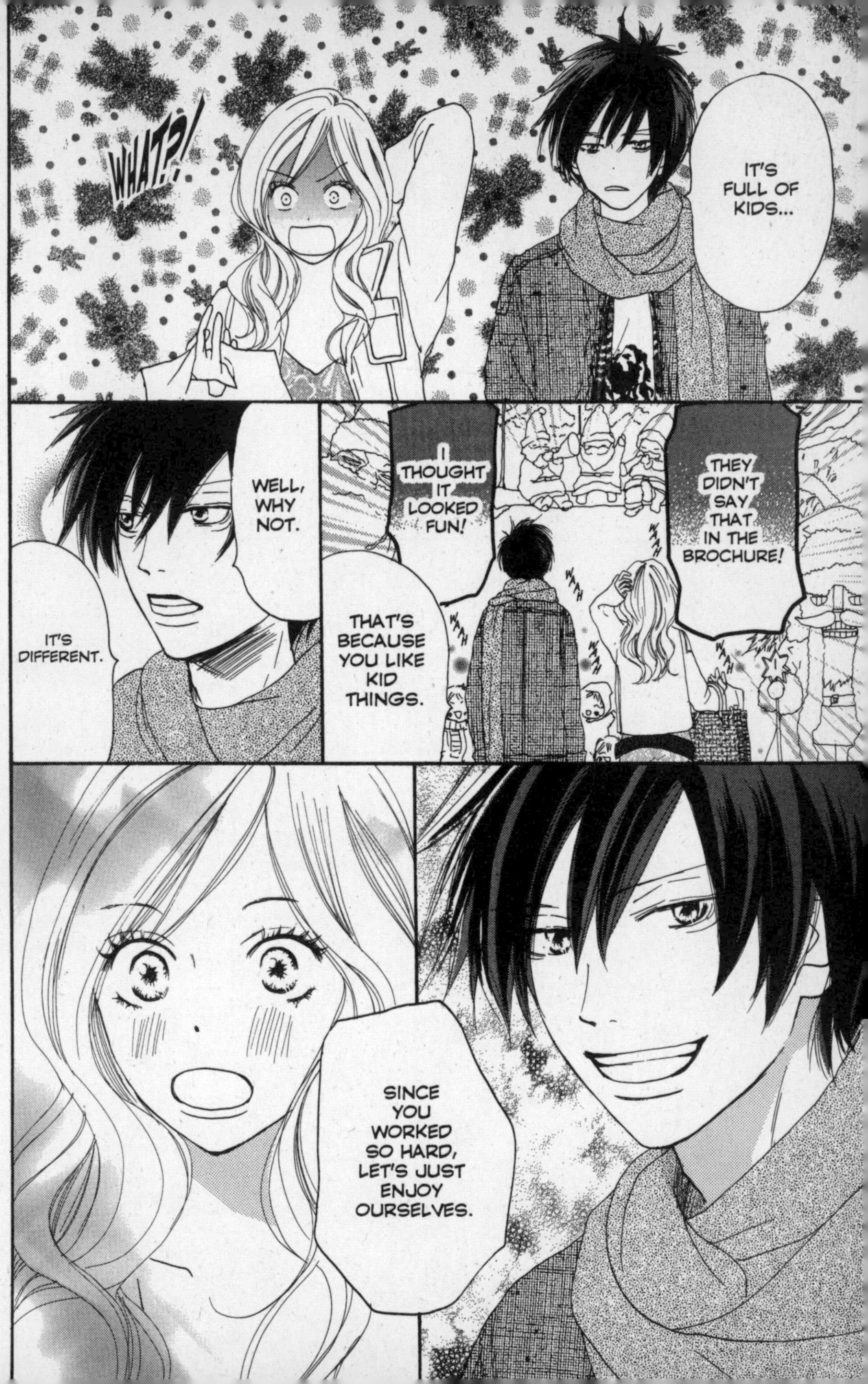
IT'S FULL OF KIDS...
WHAT?!
THEY DIDN'T SAY THAT IN THE BROCHURE!
I THOUGHT IT LOOKED FUN!
THAT'S BECAUSE YOU LIKE KID THINGS.
WELL, WHY NOT.
IT'S DIFFERENT.
SINCE YOU WORKED SO HARD, LET'S JUST ENJOY OURSELVES.

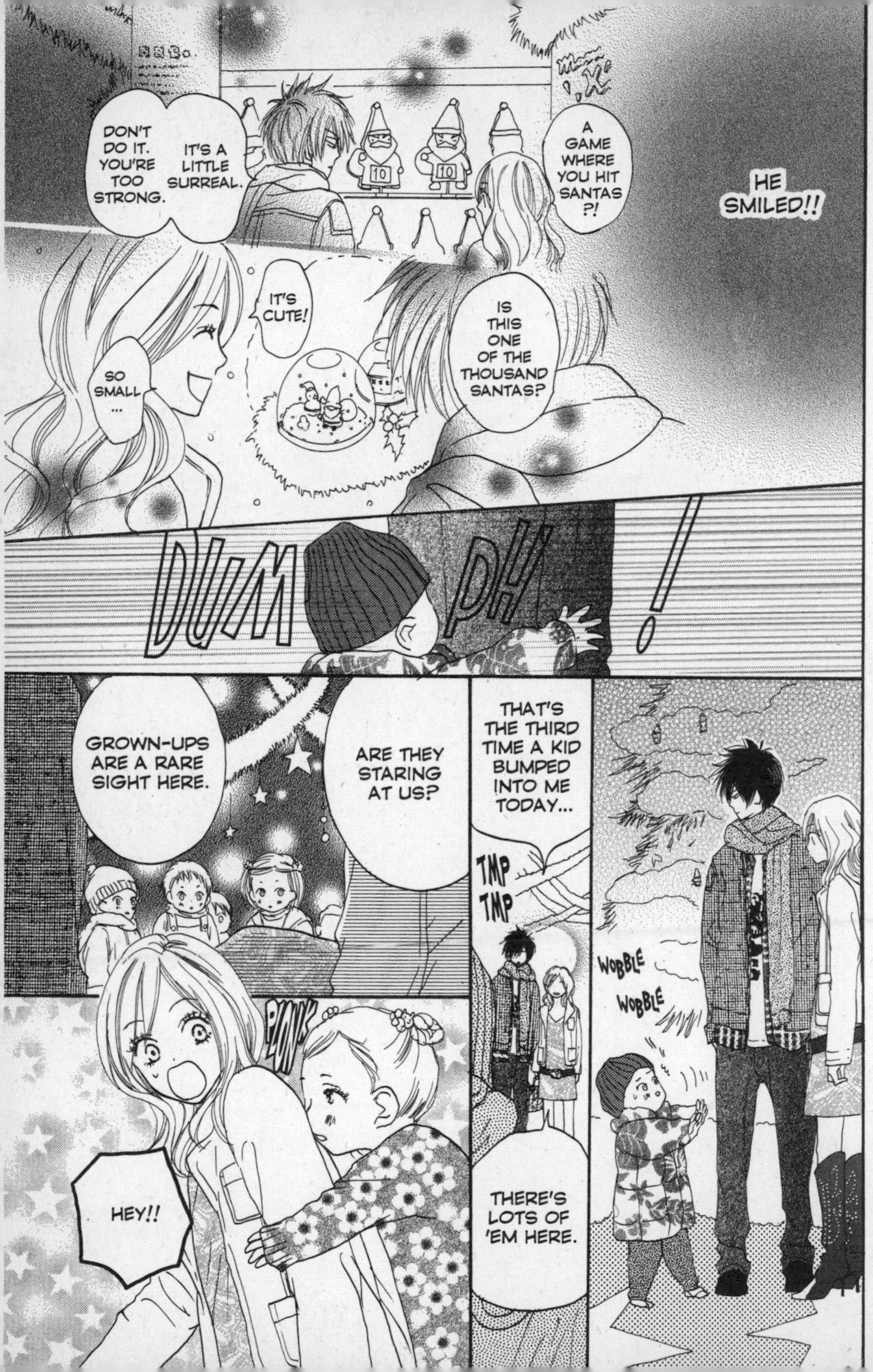

HE SMILED!!
A GAME WHERE YOU HIT SANTAS?!
IT'S A LITTLE SURREAL.
DON'T DO IT. YOU'RE TOO STRONG.
IS THIS ONE OF THE THOUSAND SANTAS?
IT'S CUTE!
SO SMALL...
DUMPH
!
THAT'S THE THIRD TIME A KID BUMPED INTO ME TODAY...
TMP TMP
WOBBLE WOBBLE
THERE'S LOTS OF 'EM HERE.
ARE THEY STARING AT US?
GROWN-UPS ARE A RARE SIGHT HERE.
PLINK
HEY!!

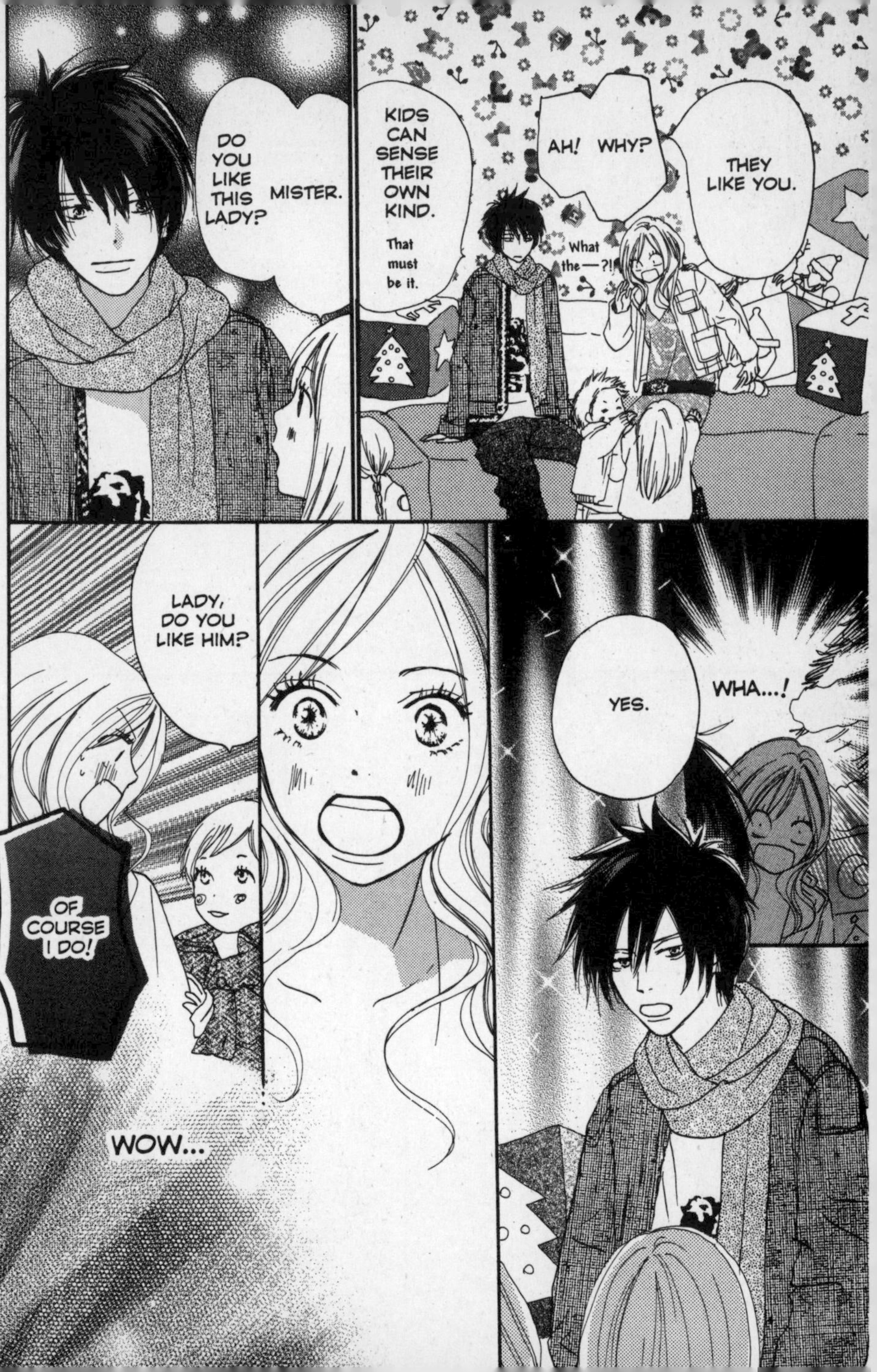
THEY LIKE YOU.
AH! WHY?
What the—?!
KIDS CAN SENSE THEIR OWN KIND.
That must be it.
DO YOU LIKE THIS LADY? MISTER.
WHA...!
YES.
LADY, DO YOU LIKE HIM?
OF COURSE I DO!
WOW...

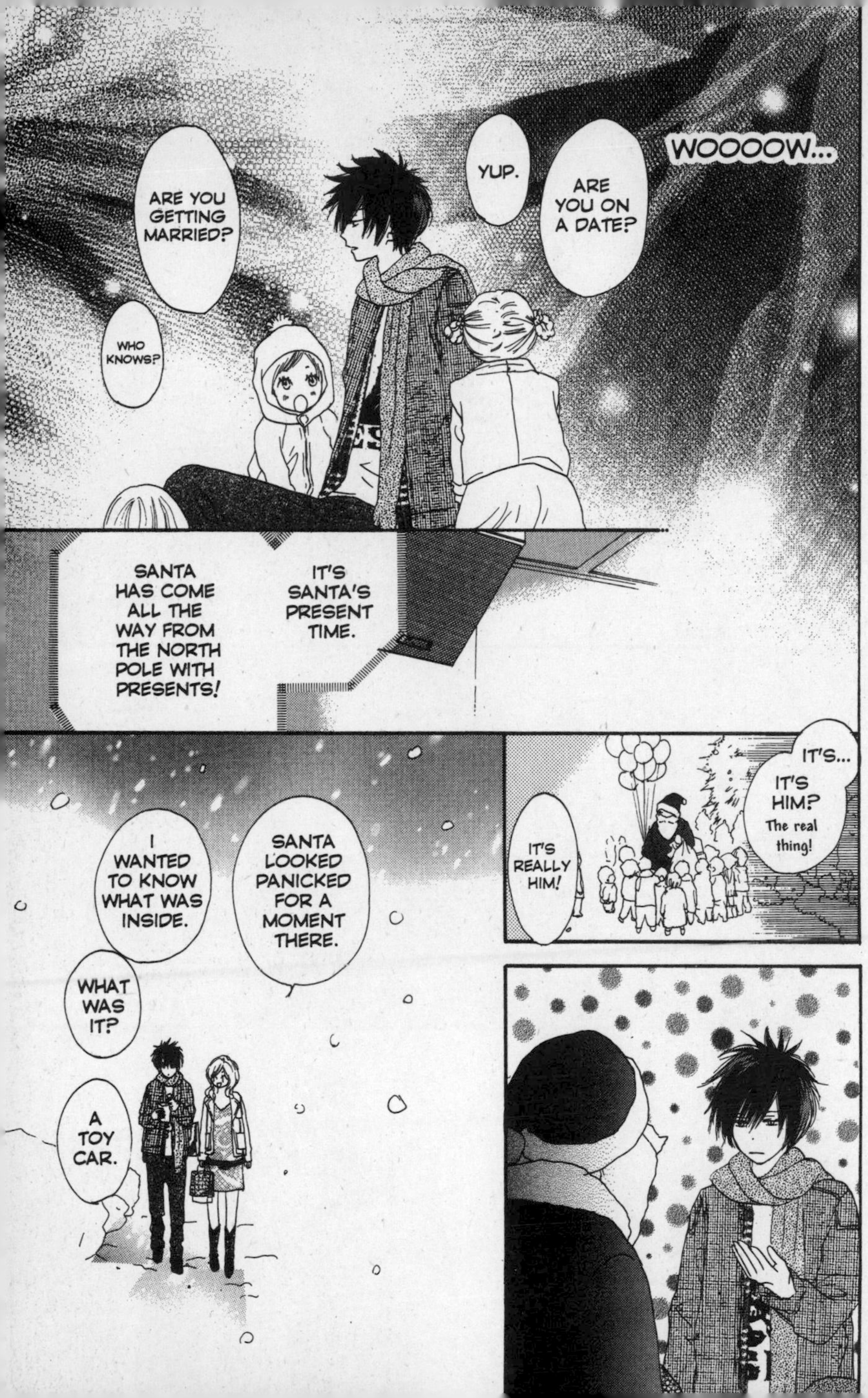
WOOOOW...
ARE YOU ON A DATE?
YUP.
ARE YOU GETTING MARRIED?
WHO KNOWS?
IT'S SANTA'S PRESENT TIME.
SANTA HAS COME ALL THE WAY FROM THE NORTH POLE WITH PRESENTS!
IT'S... IT'S HIM? The real thing!
IT'S REALLY HIM!
SANTA LOOKED PANICKED FOR A MOMENT THERE.
I WANTED TO KNOW WHAT WAS INSIDE.
WHAT WAS IT?
A TOY CAR.

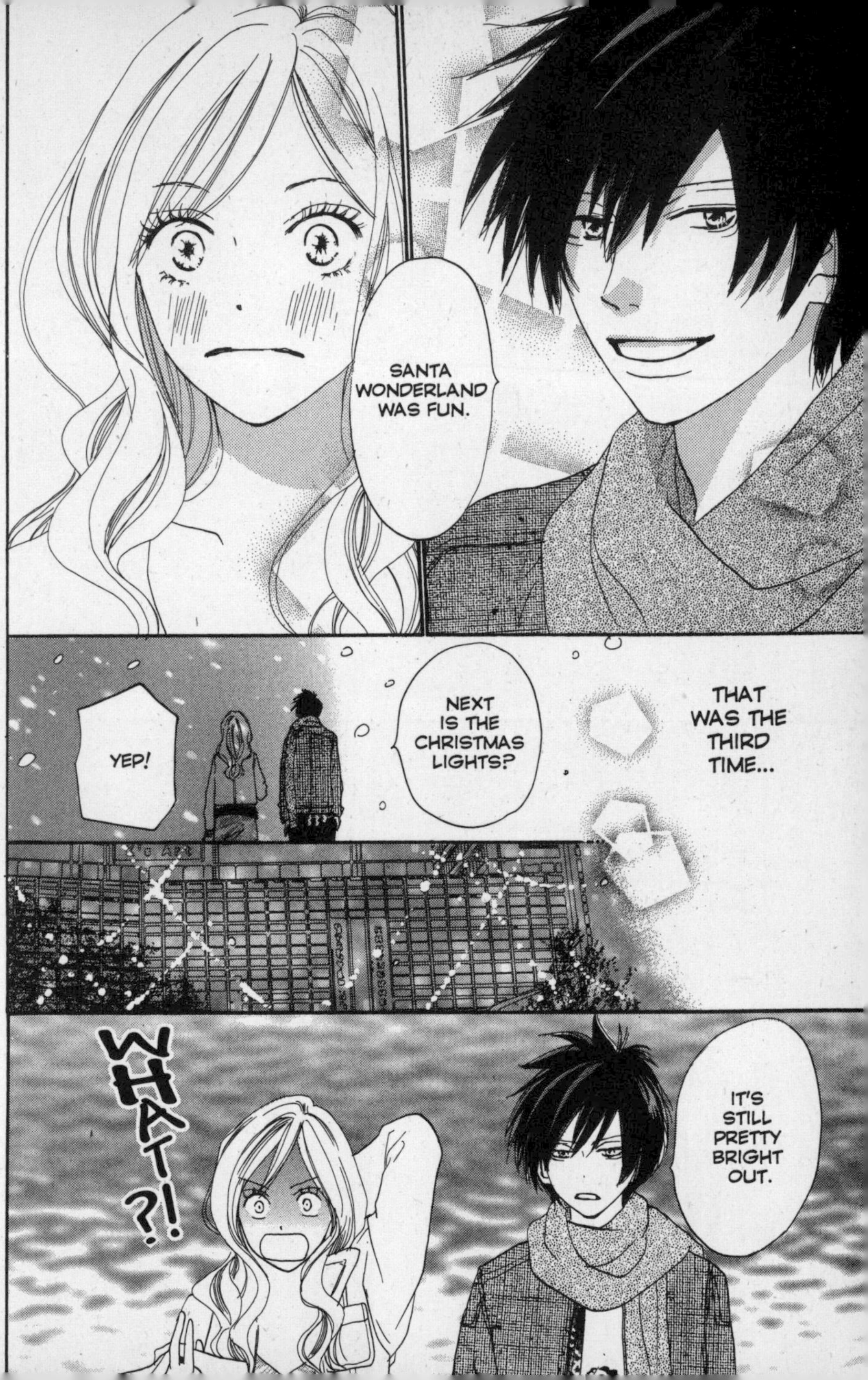
SANTA WONDERLAND WAS FUN.
THAT WAS THE THIRD TIME...
NEXT IS THE CHRISTMAS LIGHTS?
YEP!
IT'S STILL PRETTY BRIGHT OUT.
WHAT?!

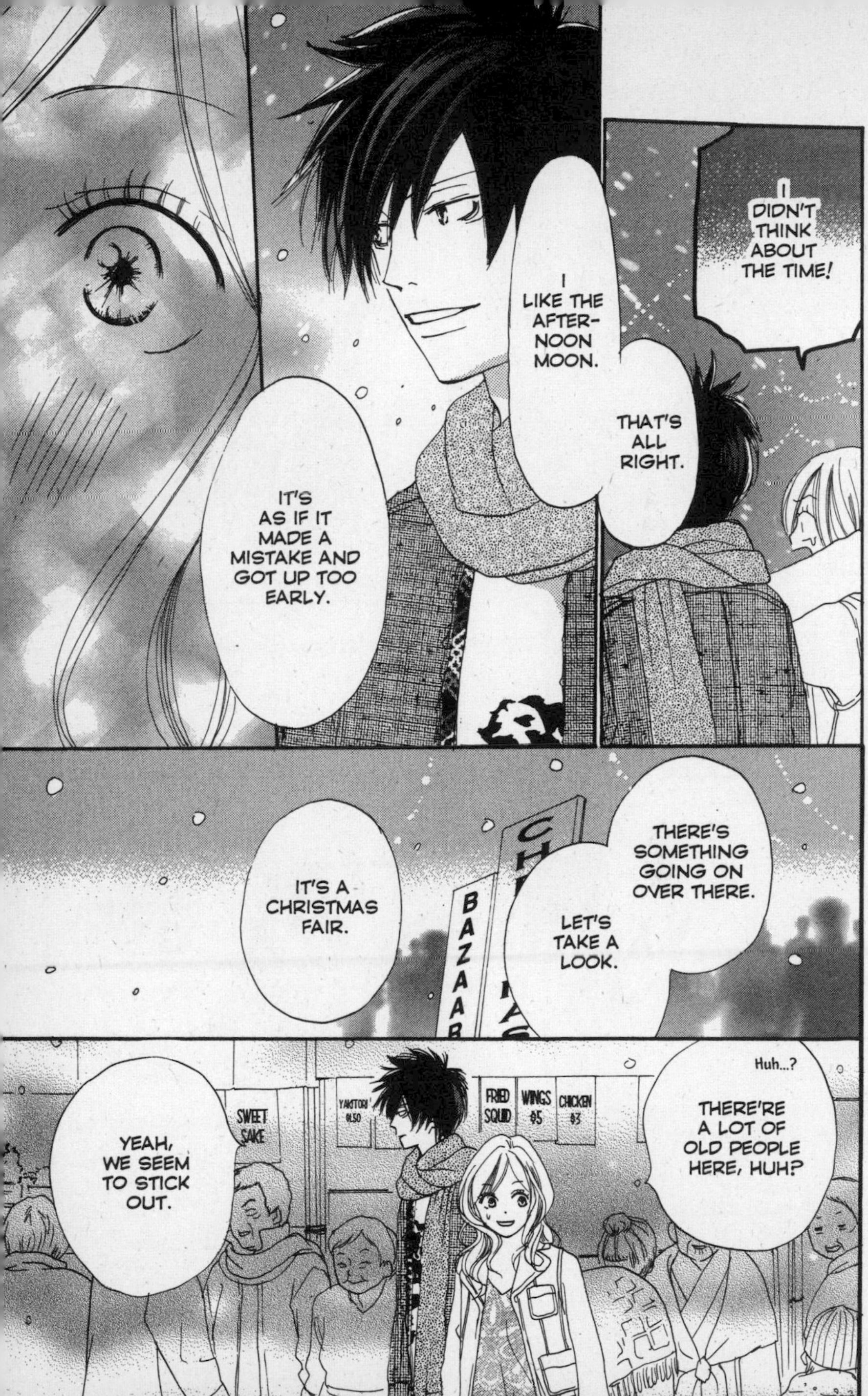
I DIDN'T THINK ABOUT THE TIME!
THAT'S ALL RIGHT.
I LIKE THE AFTER-NOON MOON.
IT'S AS IF IT MADE A MISTAKE AND GOT UP TOO EARLY.
THERE'S SOMETHING GOING ON OVER THERE.
LET'S TAKE A LOOK.
IT'S A CHRISTMAS FAIR.
BAZAAR
Huh...?
THERE'RE A LOT OF OLD PEOPLE HERE, HUH?
CHICKEN $3
WINGS $5
FRIED SQUID
YAKITORI
SWEET SAKE
YEAH, WE SEEM TO STICK OUT.

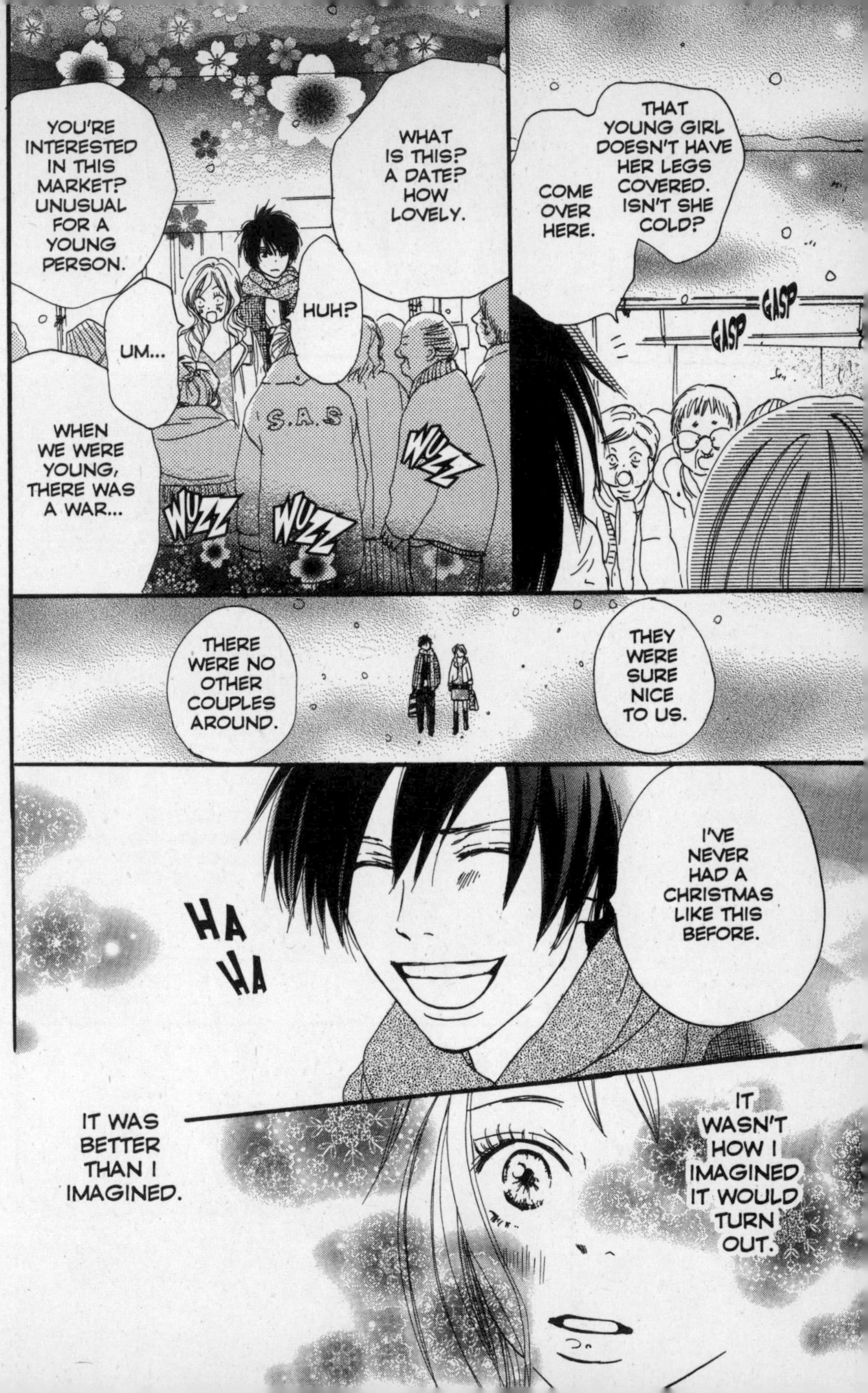
THAT YOUNG GIRL DOESN'T HAVE HER LEGS COVERED. ISN'T SHE COLD?
COME OVER HERE.
GASP
GASP
WHAT IS THIS? A DATE? HOW LOVELY.
YOU'RE INTERESTED IN THIS MARKET? UNUSUAL FOR A YOUNG PERSON.
HUH?
UM...
WUZZ
WUZZ
WUZZ
WHEN WE WERE YOUNG, THERE WAS A WAR...
THEY WERE SURE NICE TO US.
THERE WERE NO OTHER COUPLES AROUND.
I'VE NEVER HAD A CHRISTMAS LIKE THIS BEFORE.
HA HA
IT WASN'T HOW I IMAGINED IT WOULD TURN OUT.
IT WAS BETTER THAN I IMAGINED.

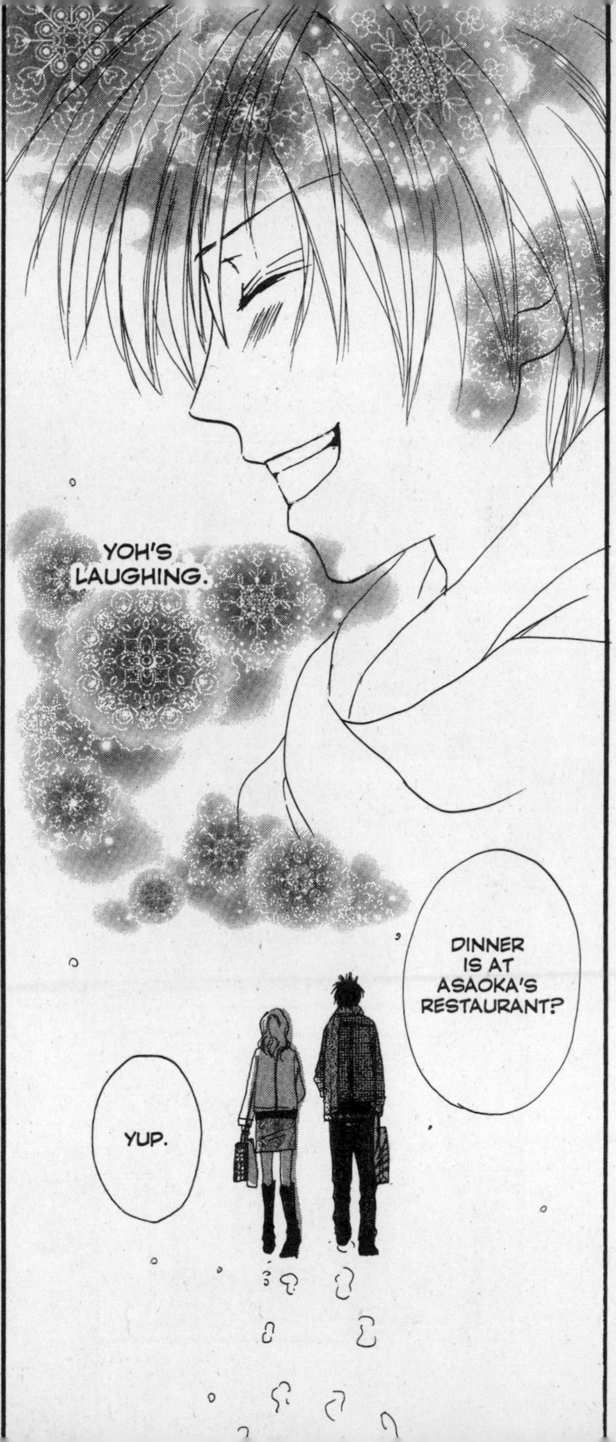
YOH'S LAUGHING.
DINNER IS AT ASAOKA'S RESTAURANT?
YUP.

2

Continued from part 1⇩
She called the manufacturer, and they sent her a replacement. But it was exactly the same, so she called them again and they sent her another one. At one point, she had three cuckoo clocks in her house. My little niece would say to it:

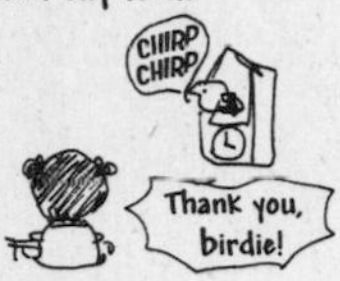
CHIIRP CHIRP
Thank you, birdie!

I could even hear her doing it over the phone. It's a nice memory, but clocks really should be accurate.
The clocks at my parents' place are almost all fast. I wonder why. Whenever I switch to a TV program I want to see, it never starts... If the program I want to watch is on at 7:00 and I turn the TV on at 7:05, it's still the news or the weather report. I should really fix my clocks. I think it would be much more useful. But then maybe I'd always be late.

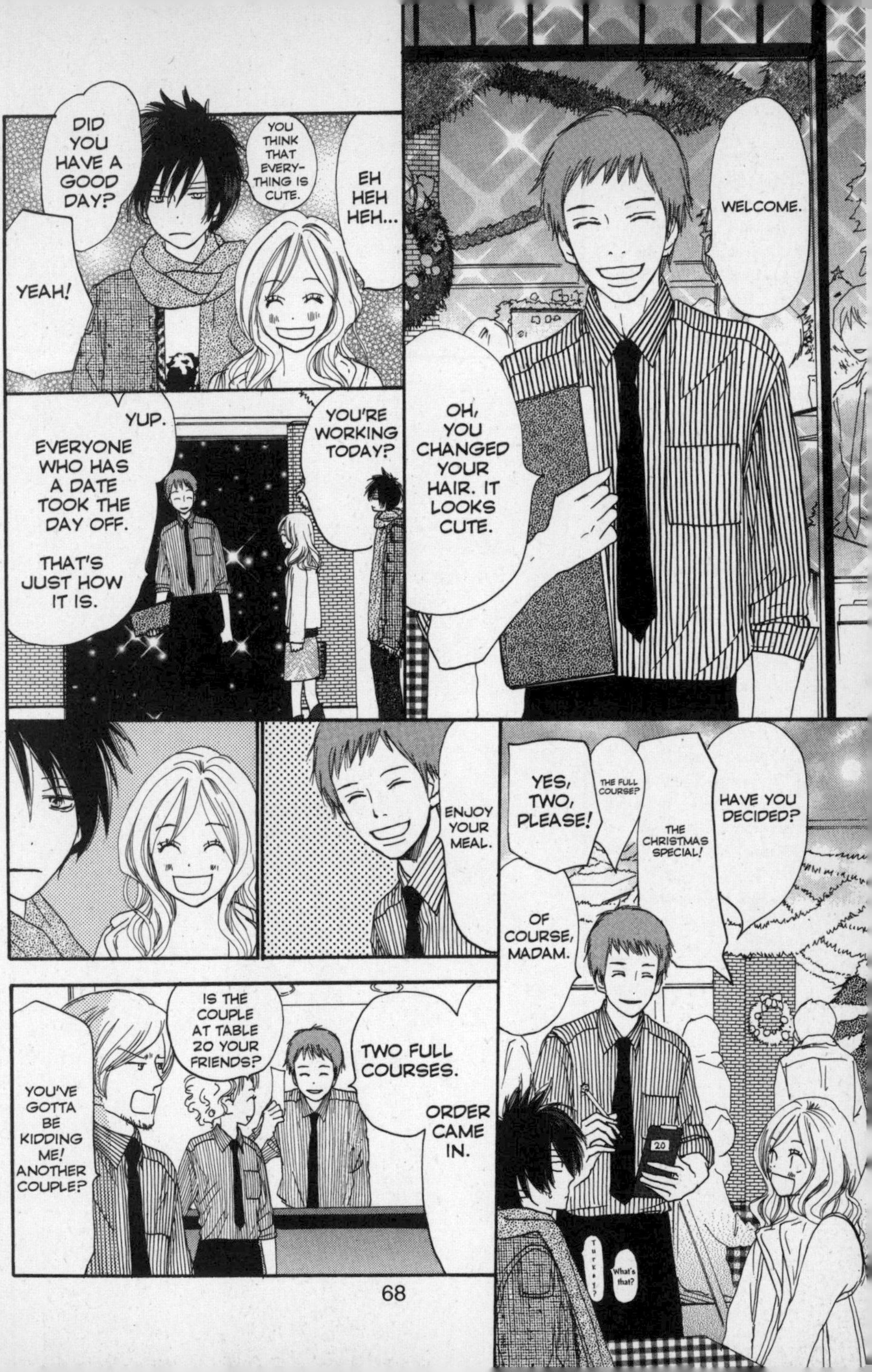
WELCOME.
OH, YOU CHANGED YOUR HAIR. IT LOOKS CUTE.
EH HEH HEH...
YOU THINK THAT EVERY-THING IS CUTE.
DID YOU HAVE A GOOD DAY?
YEAH!
YOU'RE WORKING TODAY?
YUP.
EVERYONE WHO HAS A DATE TOOK THE DAY OFF.
THAT'S JUST HOW IT IS.
HAVE YOU DECIDED?
THE CHRISTMAS SPECIAL!
THE FULL COURSE?
YES, TWO, PLEASE!
OF COURSE, MADAM.
20
What's that?
Turkey?
ENJOY YOUR MEAL.
TWO FULL COURSES.
ORDER CAME IN.
IS THE COUPLE AT TABLE 20 YOUR FRIENDS?
YOU'VE GOTTA BE KIDDING ME! ANOTHER COUPLE?

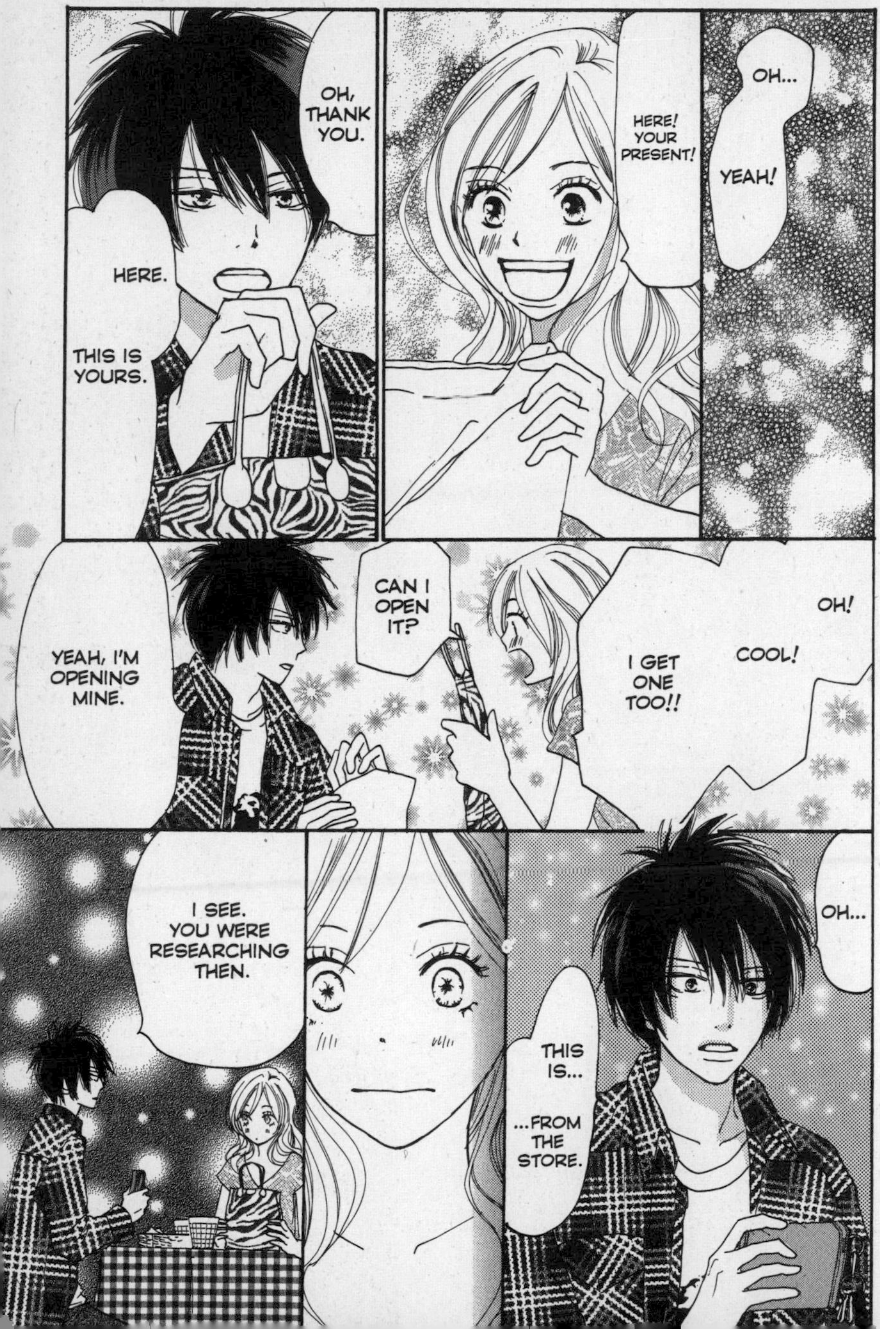
OH... YEAH!
HERE! YOUR PRESENT!
OH, THANK YOU.
HERE.
THIS IS YOURS.
OH!
COOL!
I GET ONE TOO!!
CAN I OPEN IT?
YEAH, I'M OPENING MINE.
OH...
THIS IS...
...FROM THE STORE.
I SEE. YOU WERE RESEARCHING THEN.

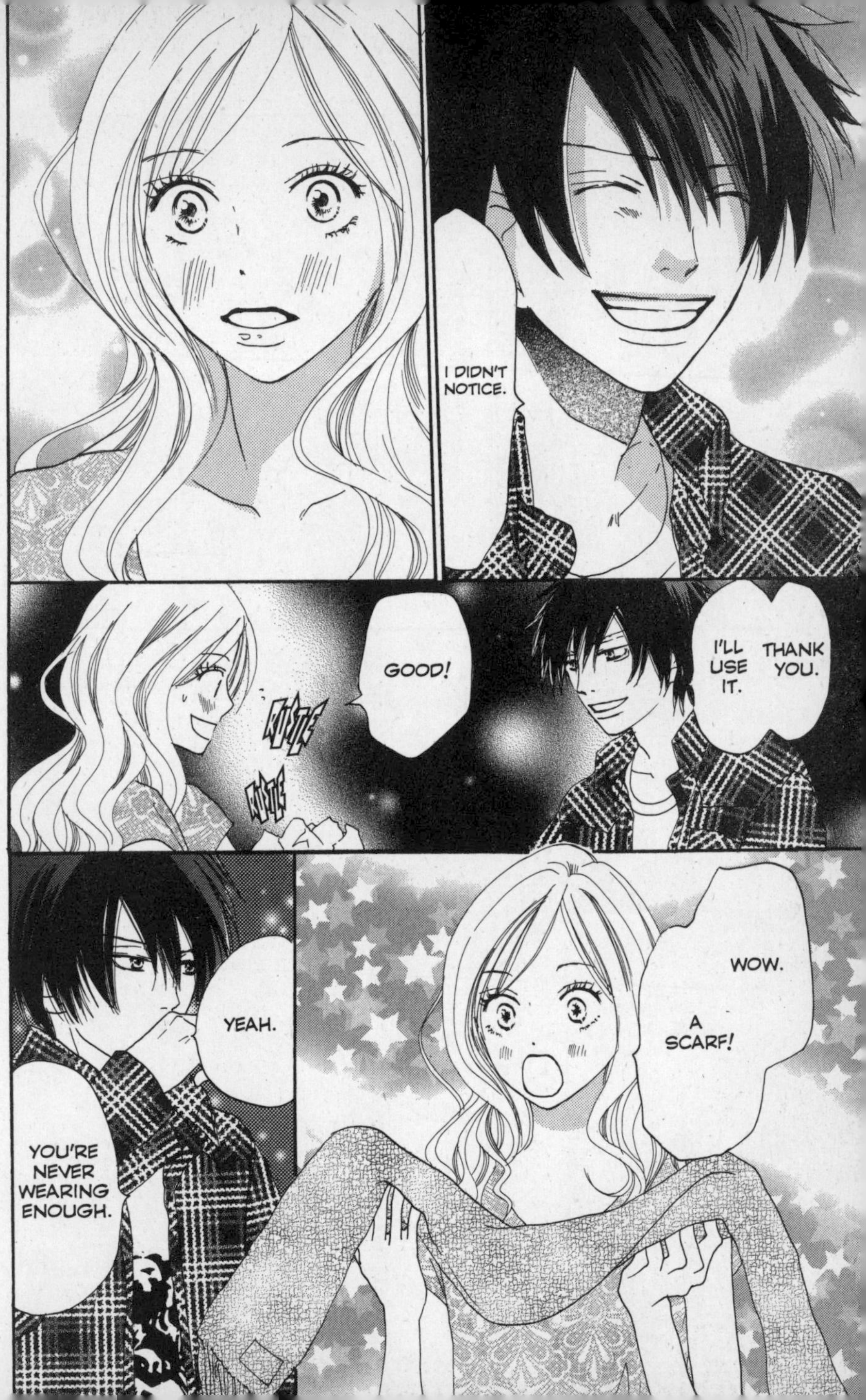
I DIDN'T NOTICE.
THANK YOU.
I'LL USE IT.
GOOD!
RUSTLE
RUSTLE
WOW.
A SCARF!
YEAH.
YOU'RE NEVER WEARING ENOUGH.

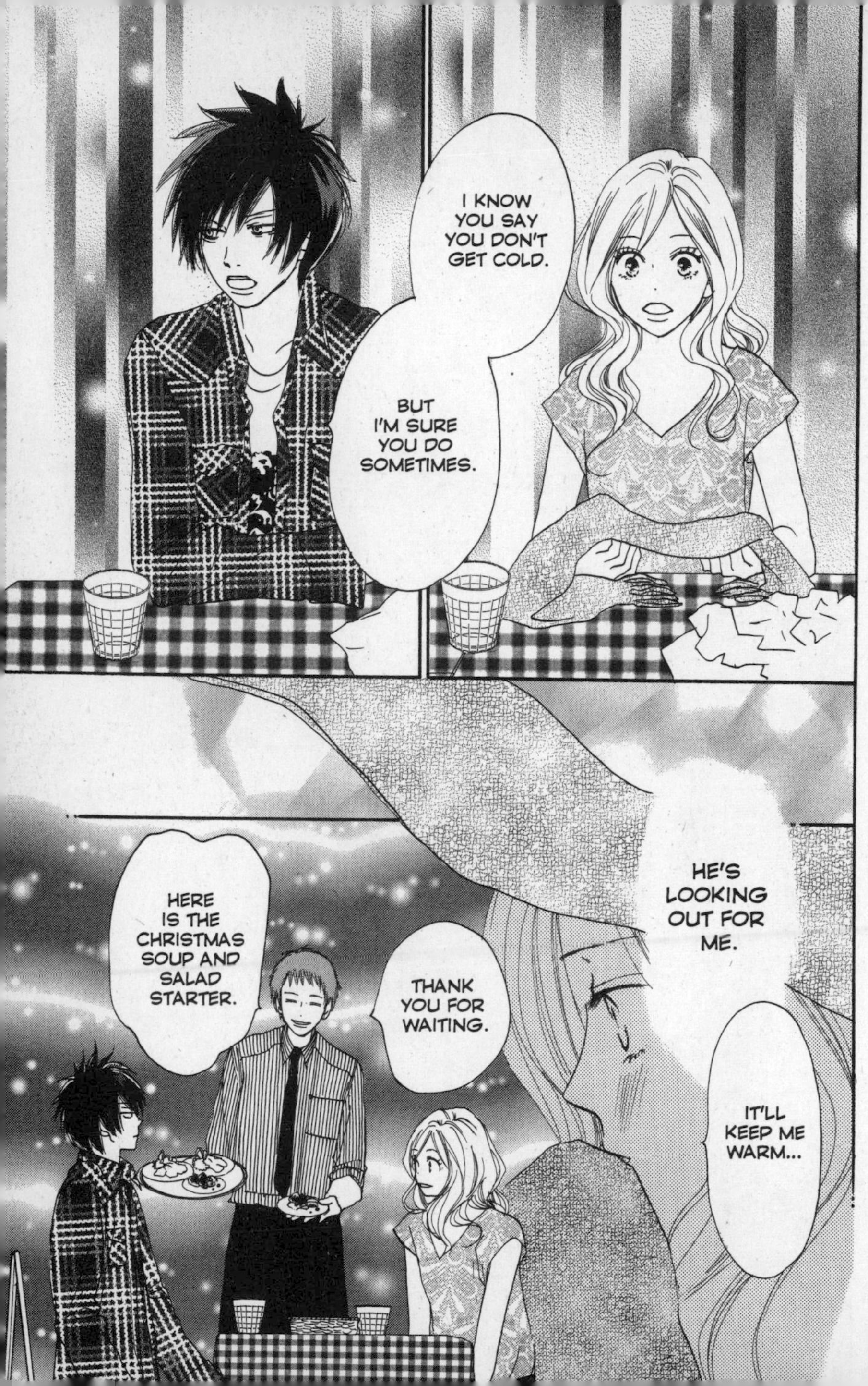
I KNOW YOU SAY YOU DON'T GET COLD.
BUT I'M SURE YOU DO SOMETIMES.
HE'S LOOKING OUT FOR ME.
IT'LL KEEP ME WARM...
THANK YOU FOR WAITING.
HERE IS THE CHRISTMAS SOUP AND SALAD STARTER.

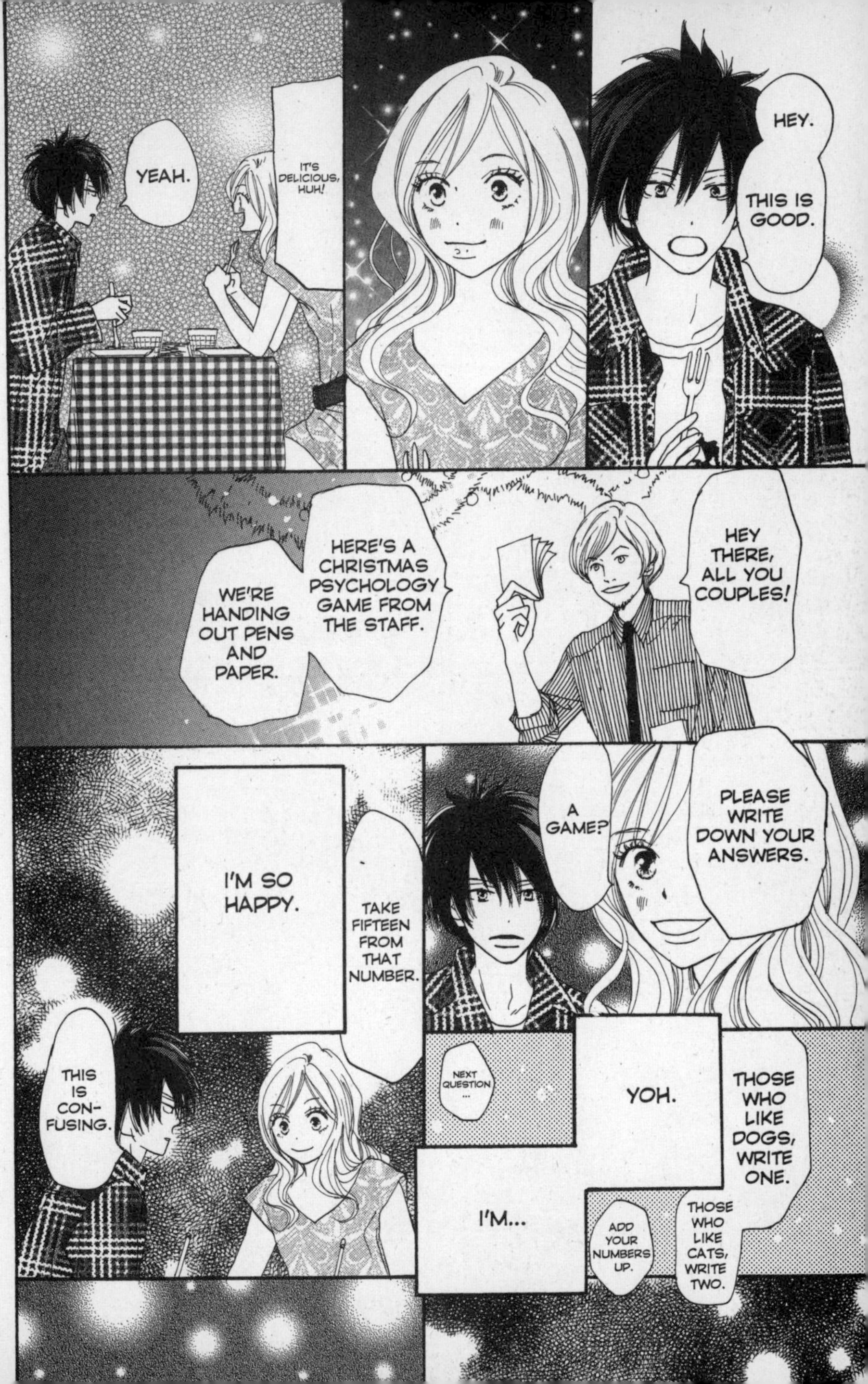
HEY.
THIS IS GOOD.
IT'S DELICIOUS, HUH!
YEAH.
HEY THERE, ALL YOU COUPLES!
HERE'S A CHRISTMAS PSYCHOLOGY GAME FROM THE STAFF.
WE'RE HANDING OUT PENS AND PAPER.
PLEASE WRITE DOWN YOUR ANSWERS.
A GAME?
THOSE WHO LIKE DOGS, WRITE ONE.
THOSE WHO LIKE CATS, WRITE TWO.
ADD YOUR NUMBERS UP.
YOH.
NEXT QUESTION...
I'M...
I'M SO HAPPY.
TAKE FIFTEEN FROM THAT NUMBER.
THIS IS CONFUSING.

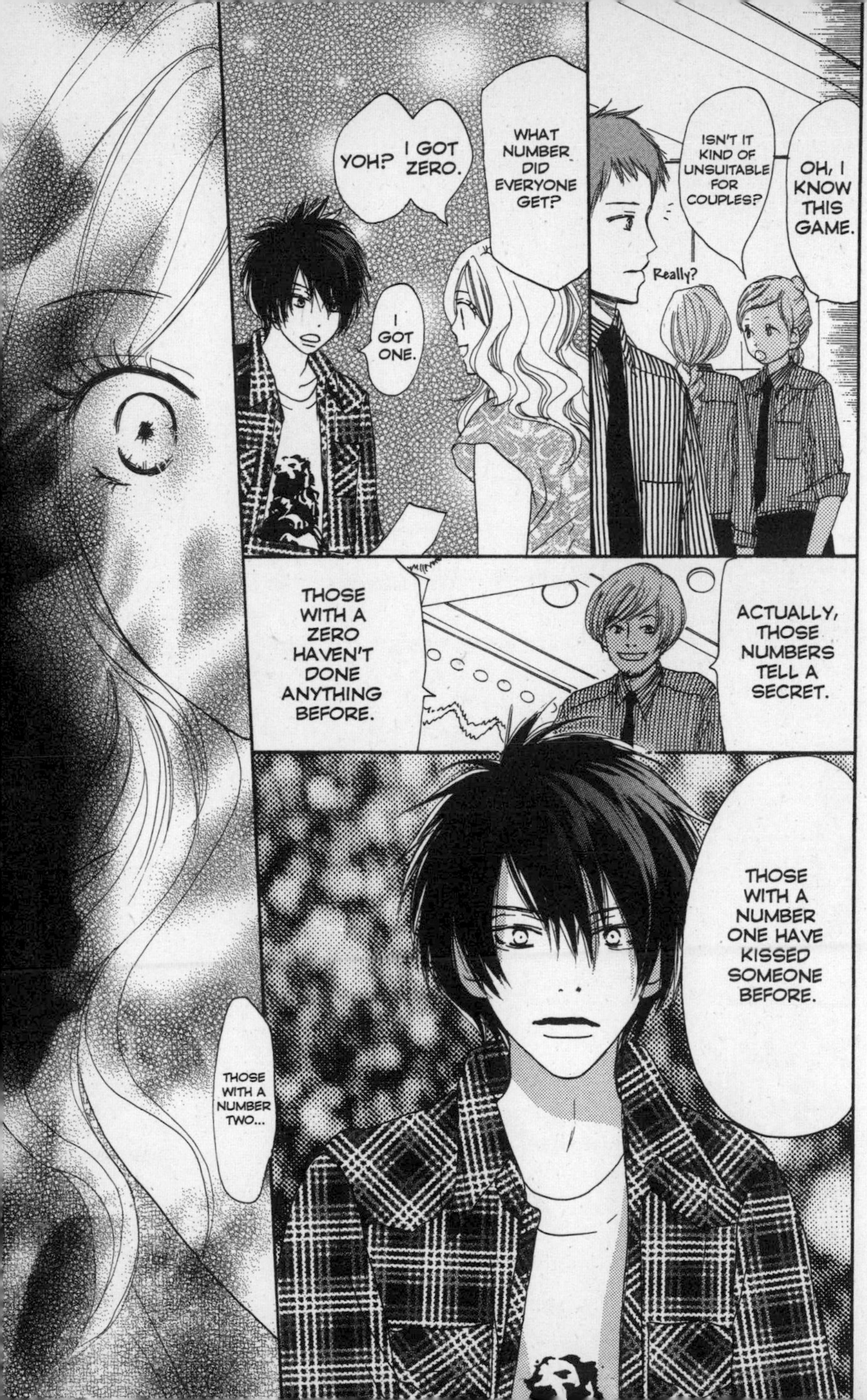

OH, I KNOW THIS GAME.
ISN'T IT KIND OF UNSUITABLE FOR COUPLES?
Really?
WHAT NUMBER DID EVERYONE GET?
YOH? I GOT ZERO.
I GOT ONE.
ACTUALLY, THOSE NUMBERS TELL A SECRET.
THOSE WITH A ZERO HAVEN'T DONE ANYTHING BEFORE.
THOSE WITH A NUMBER ONE HAVE KISSED SOMEONE BEFORE.
THOSE WITH A NUMBER TWO...

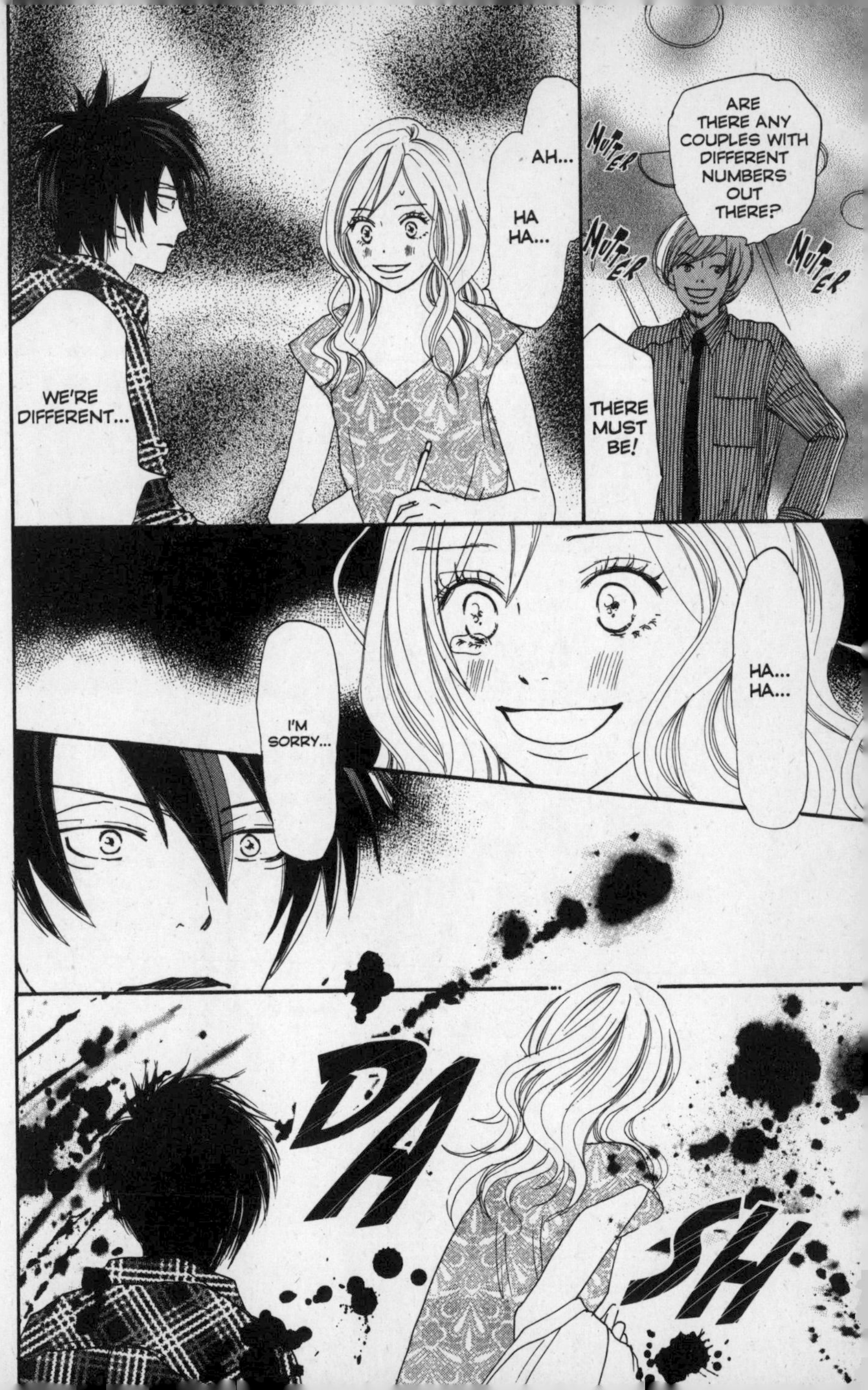
ARE THERE ANY COUPLES WITH DIFFERENT NUMBERS OUT THERE?
MUTTER
MUTTER
MUTTER
THERE MUST BE!
AH...
HA HA...
WE'RE DIFFERENT...
HA... HA...
I'M SORRY...
DASH

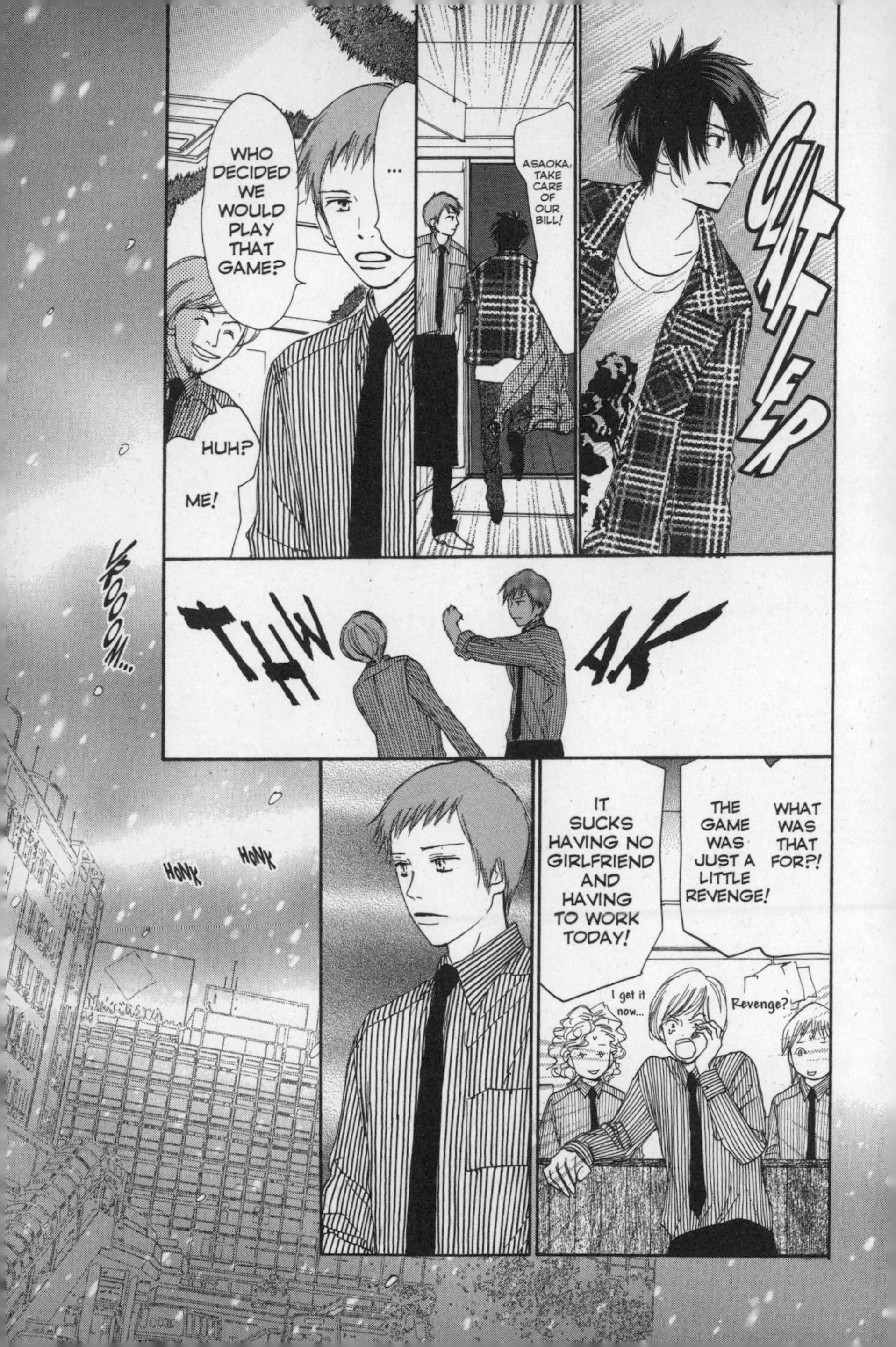
CLATTER
ASAOKA, TAKE CARE OF OUR BILL!
...
WHO DECIDED WE WOULD PLAY THAT GAME?
HUH?
ME!
THWAK
VROOOM...
WHAT WAS THAT FOR?!
THE GAME WAS JUST A LITTLE REVENGE!
IT SUCKS HAVING NO GIRLFRIEND AND HAVING TO WORK TODAY!
Revenge?
I get it now...
HONK
HONK

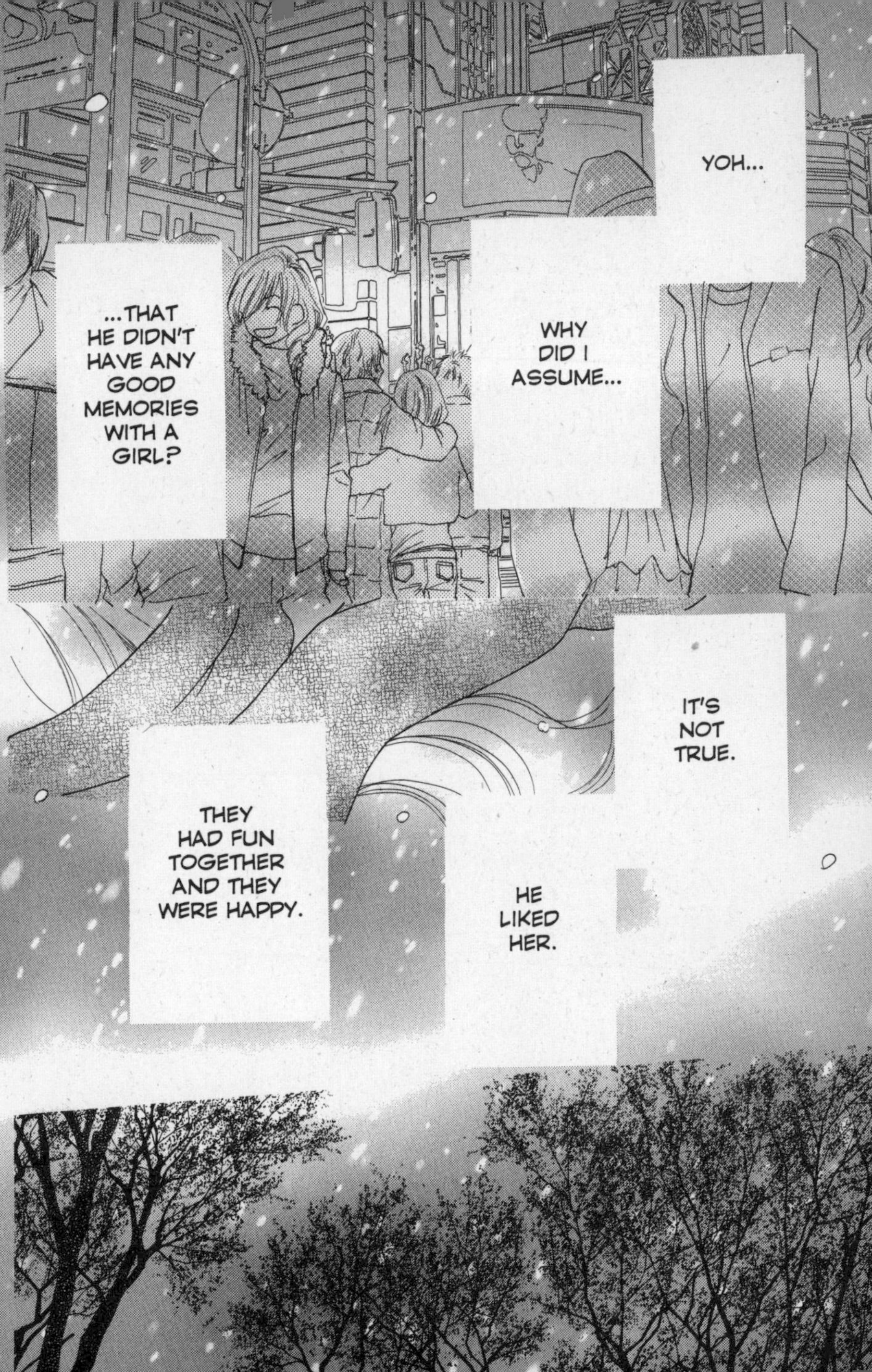
YOH...
WHY DID I ASSUME...
...THAT HE DIDN'T HAVE ANY GOOD MEMORIES WITH A GIRL?
IT'S NOT TRUE.
HE LIKED HER.
THEY HAD FUN TOGETHER AND THEY WERE HAPPY.

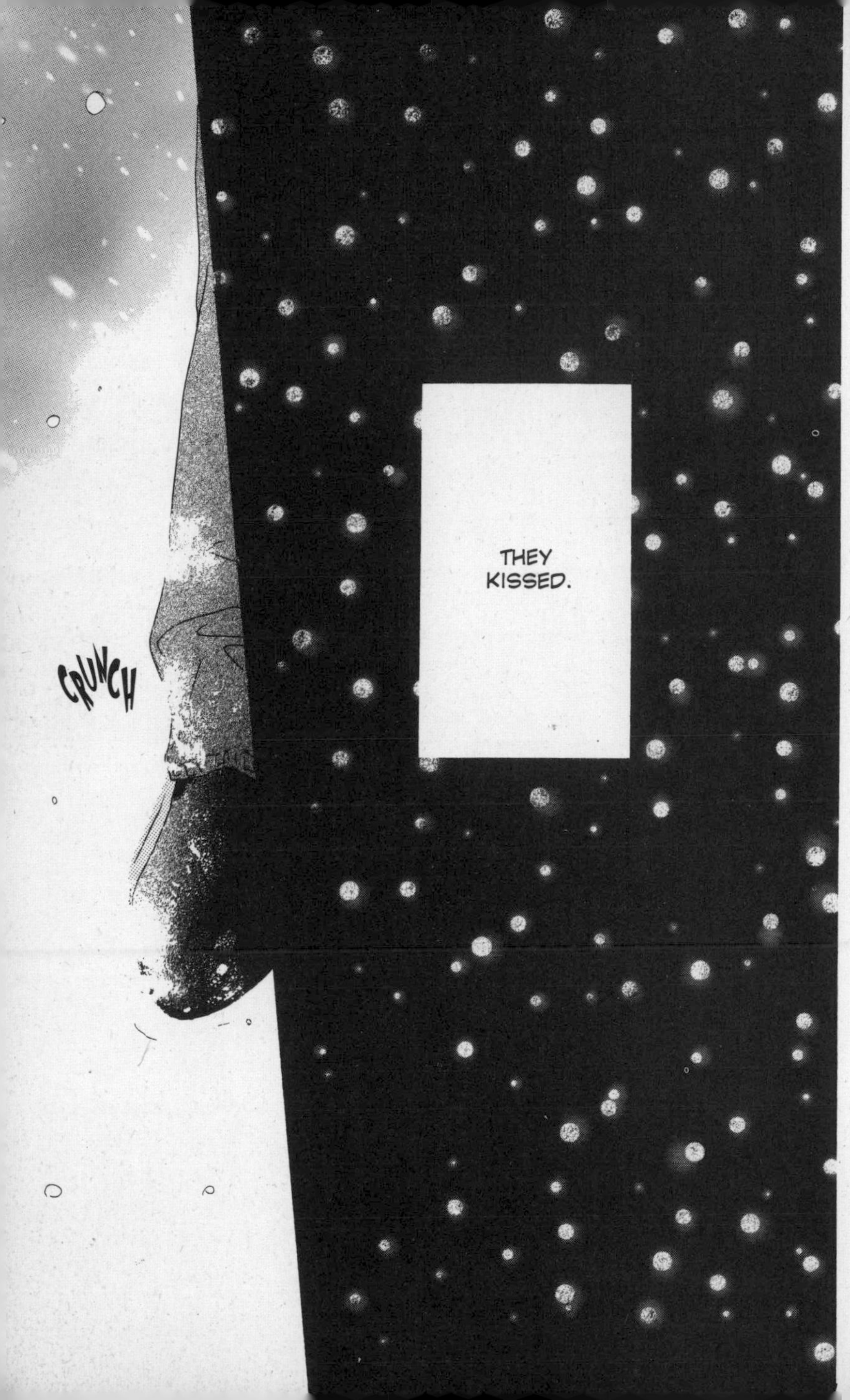
THEY KISSED.
CRUNCH

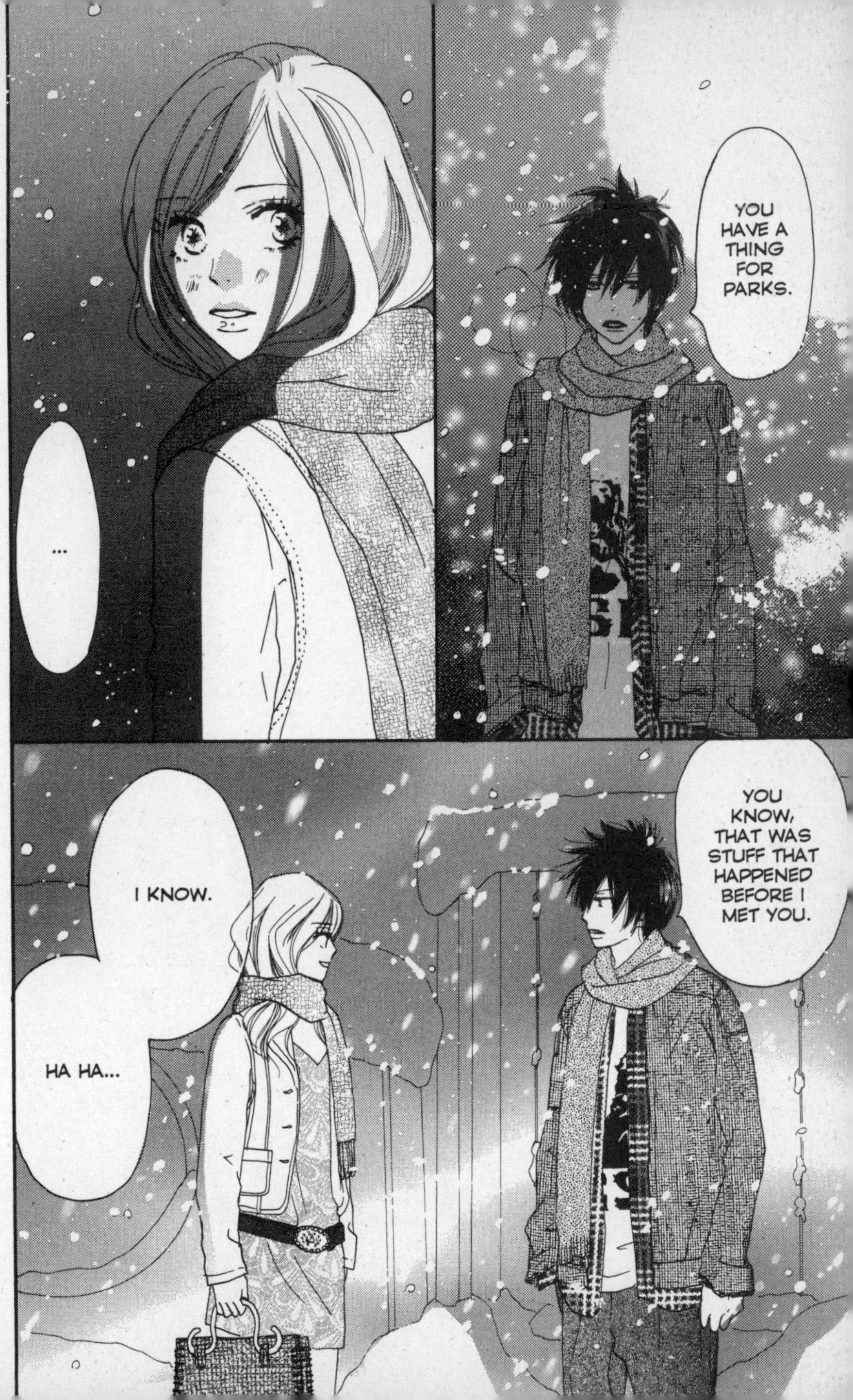
YOU HAVE A THING FOR PARKS.
...
YOU KNOW, THAT WAS STUFF THAT HAPPENED BEFORE I MET YOU.
I KNOW.
HA HA...

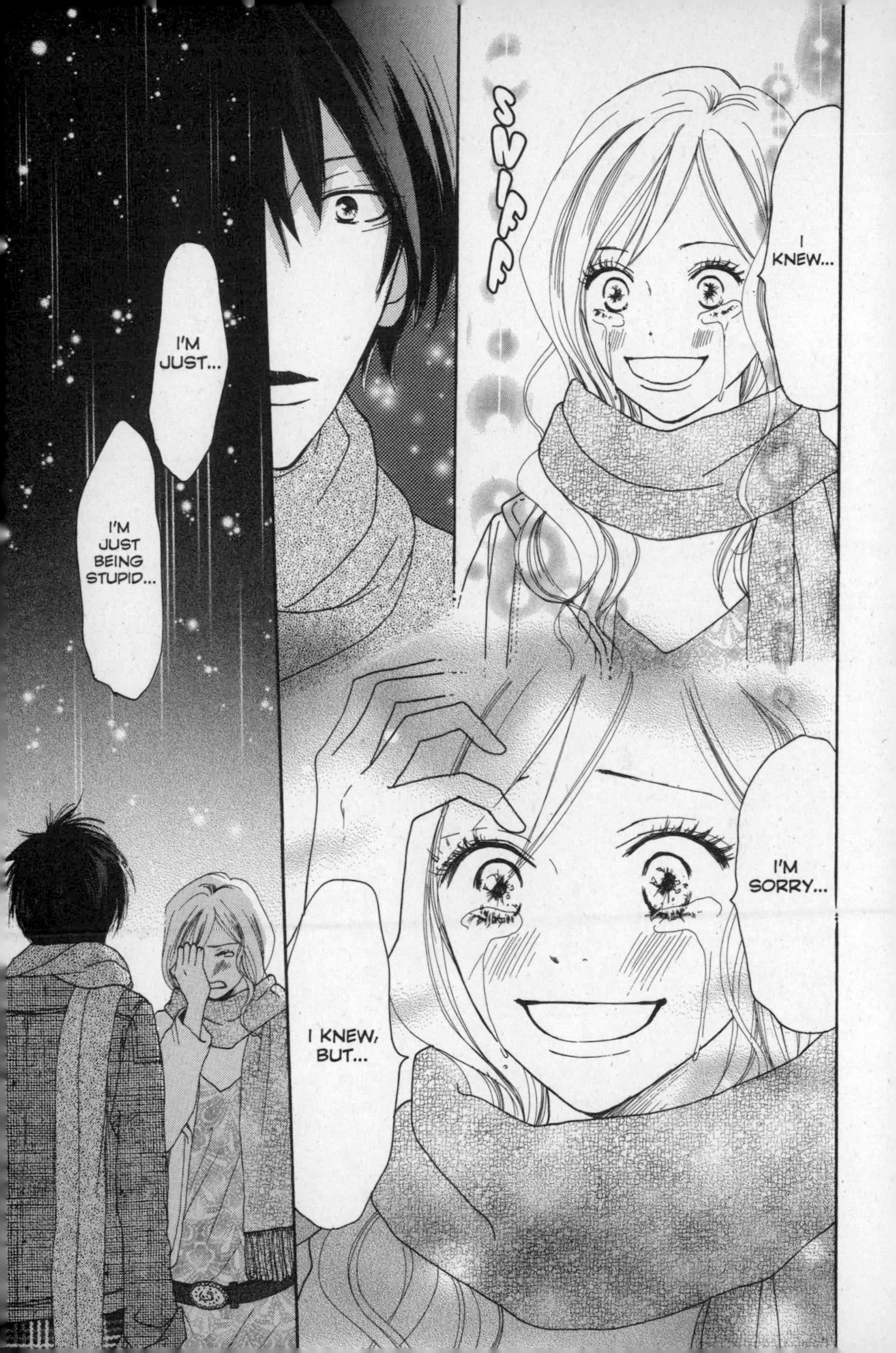
SNIFF
I KNEW...
I'M SORRY...
I KNEW, BUT...
I'M JUST...
I'M JUST BEING STUPID...

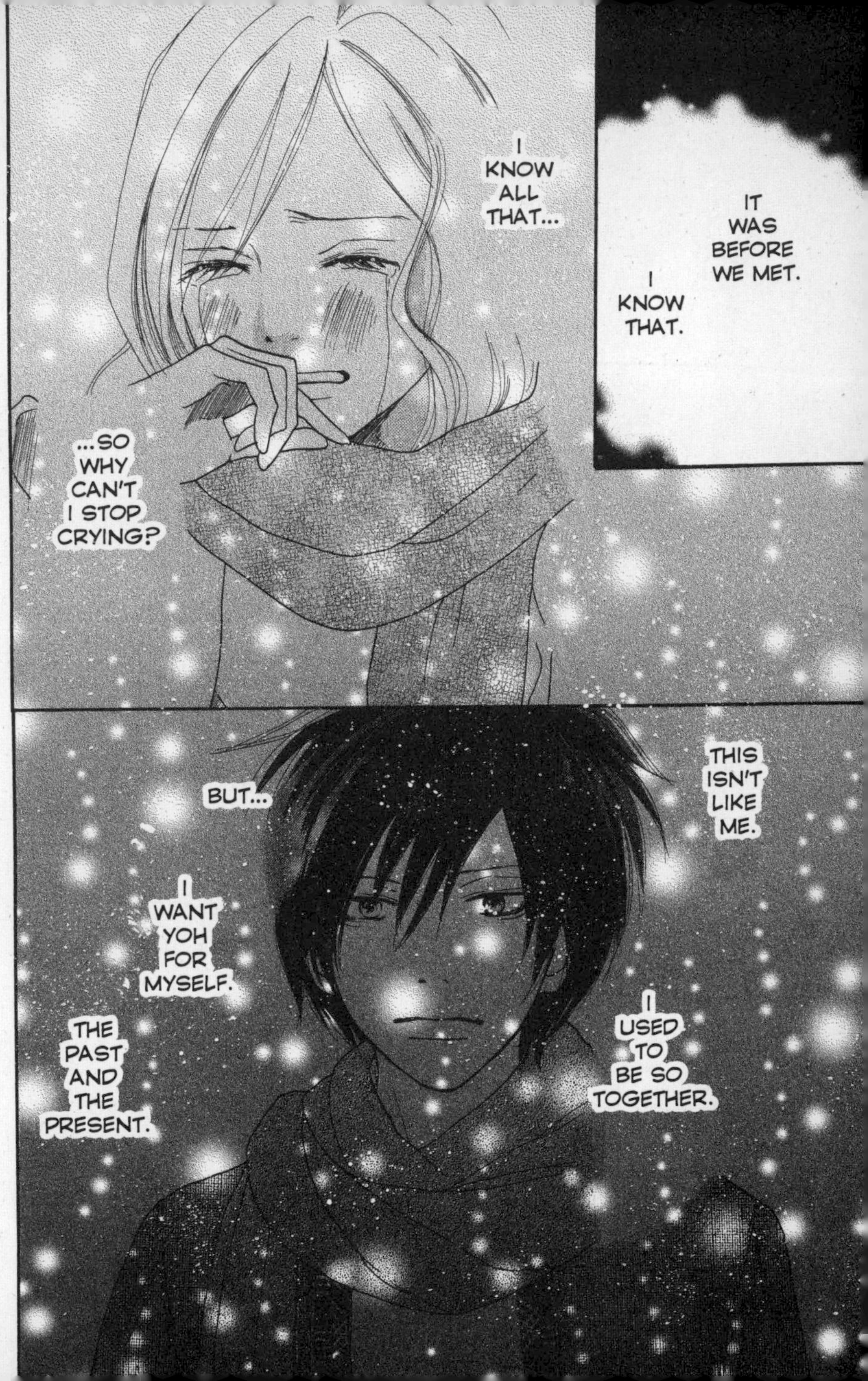
IT WAS BEFORE WE MET.
I KNOW THAT.
I KNOW ALL THAT...
...SO WHY CAN'T I STOP CRYING?
THIS ISN'T LIKE ME.
BUT...
I USED TO BE SO TOGETHER.
I WANT YOH FOR MYSELF.
THE PAST AND THE PRESENT.

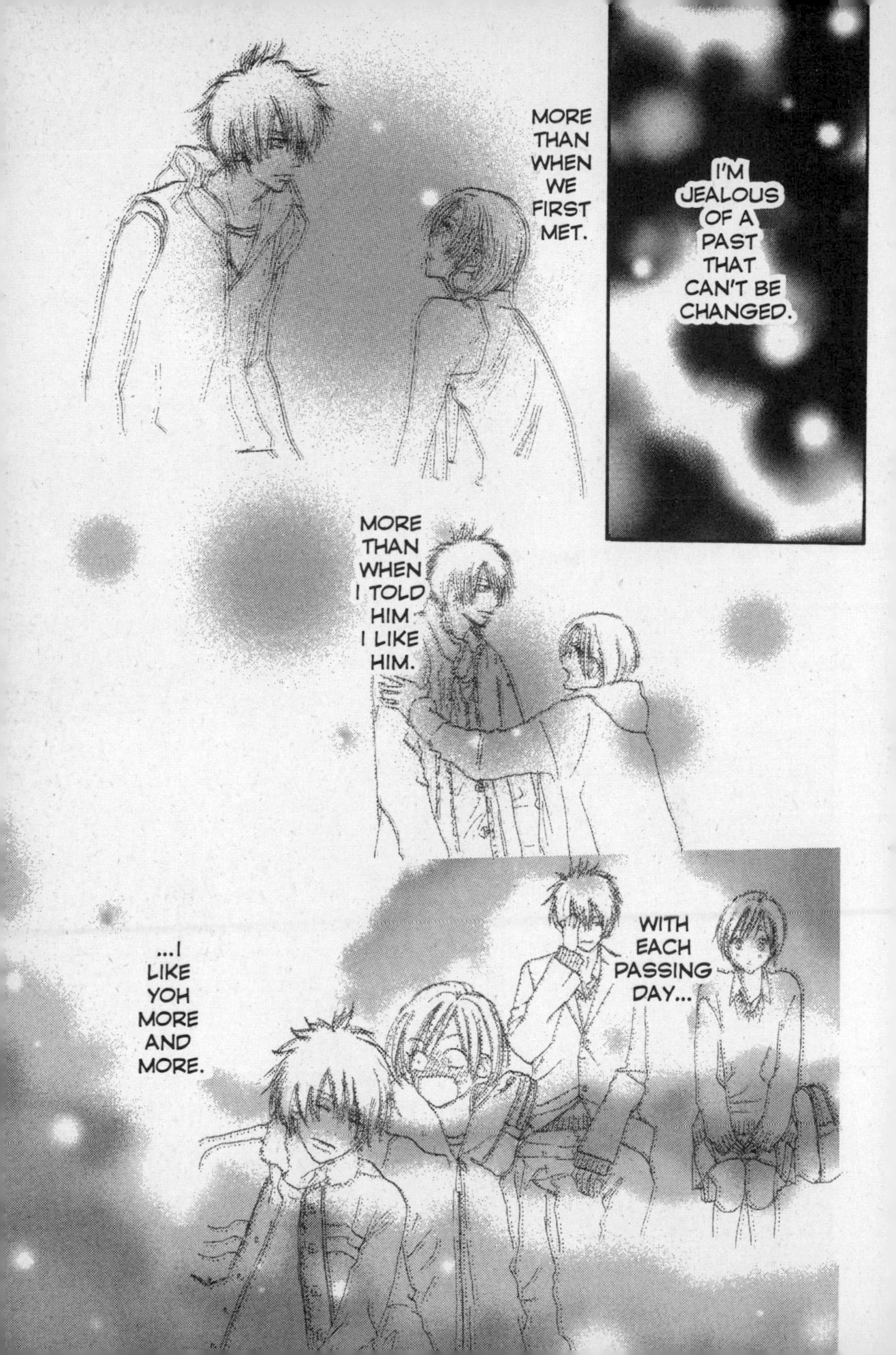
I'M JEALOUS OF A PAST THAT CAN'T BE CHANGED.
MORE THAN WHEN WE FIRST MET.
MORE THAN WHEN I TOLD HIM I LIKE HIM.
WITH EACH PASSING DAY...
...I LIKE YOH MORE AND MORE.

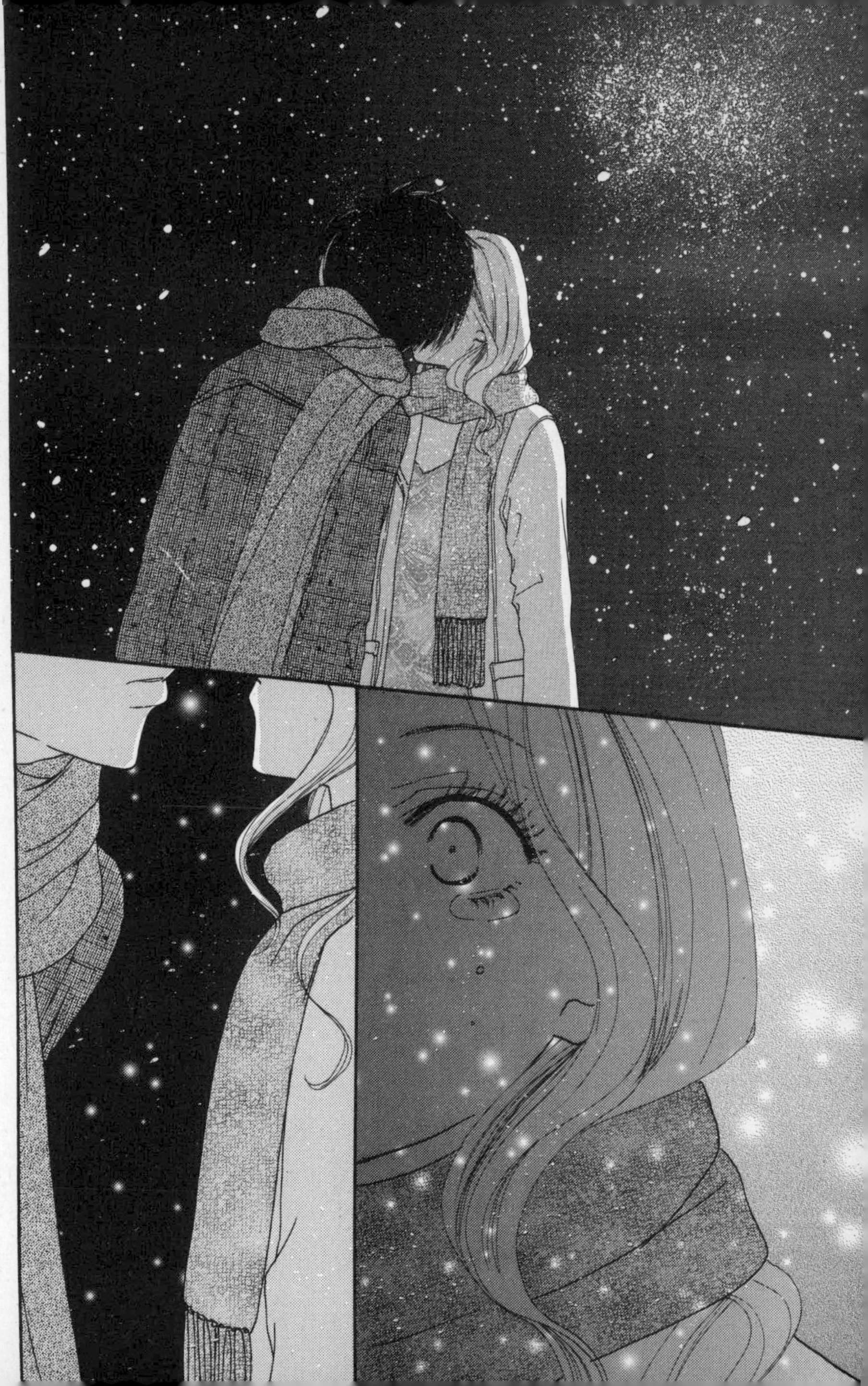

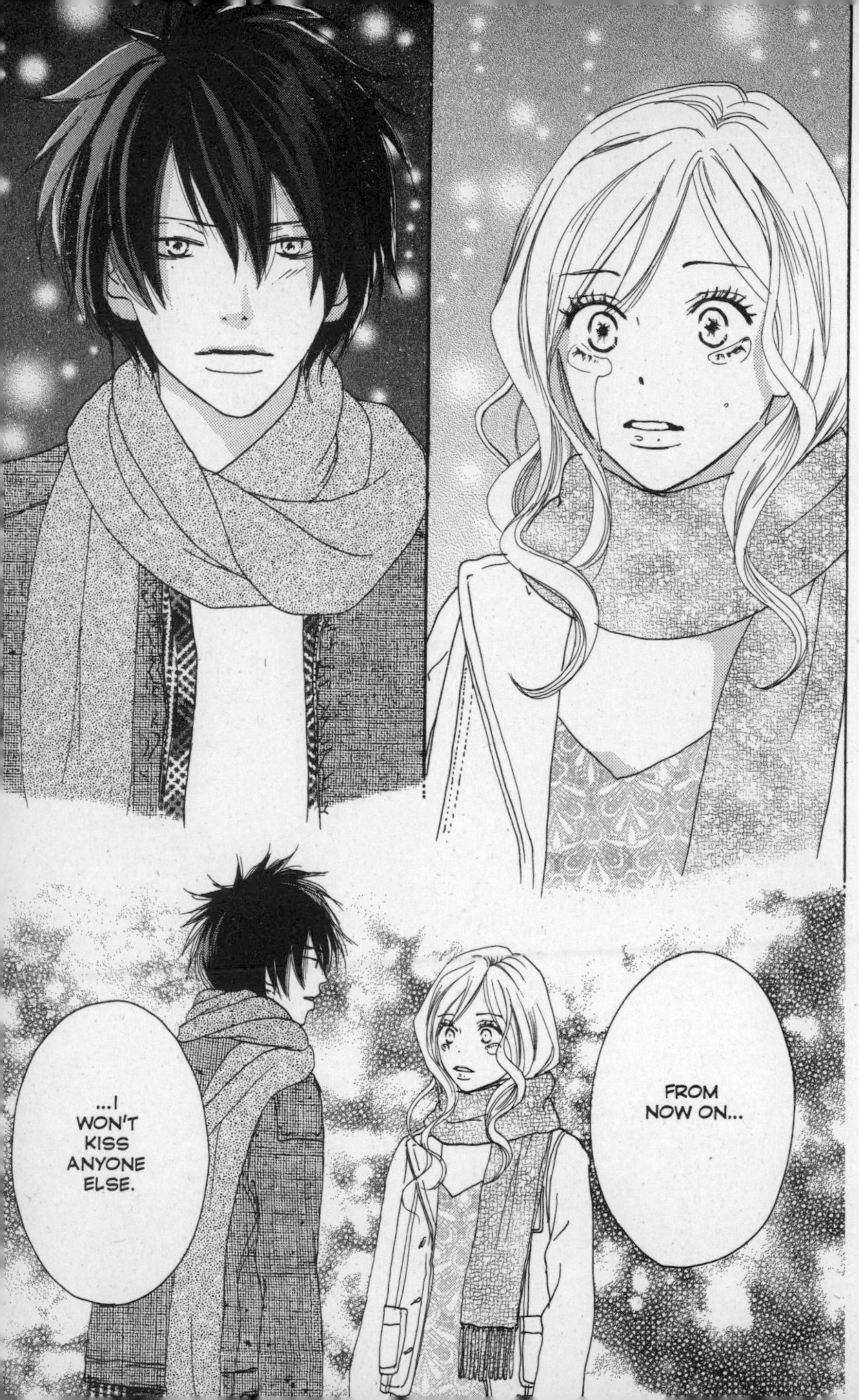
FROM NOW ON...
...I WON'T KISS ANYONE ELSE.

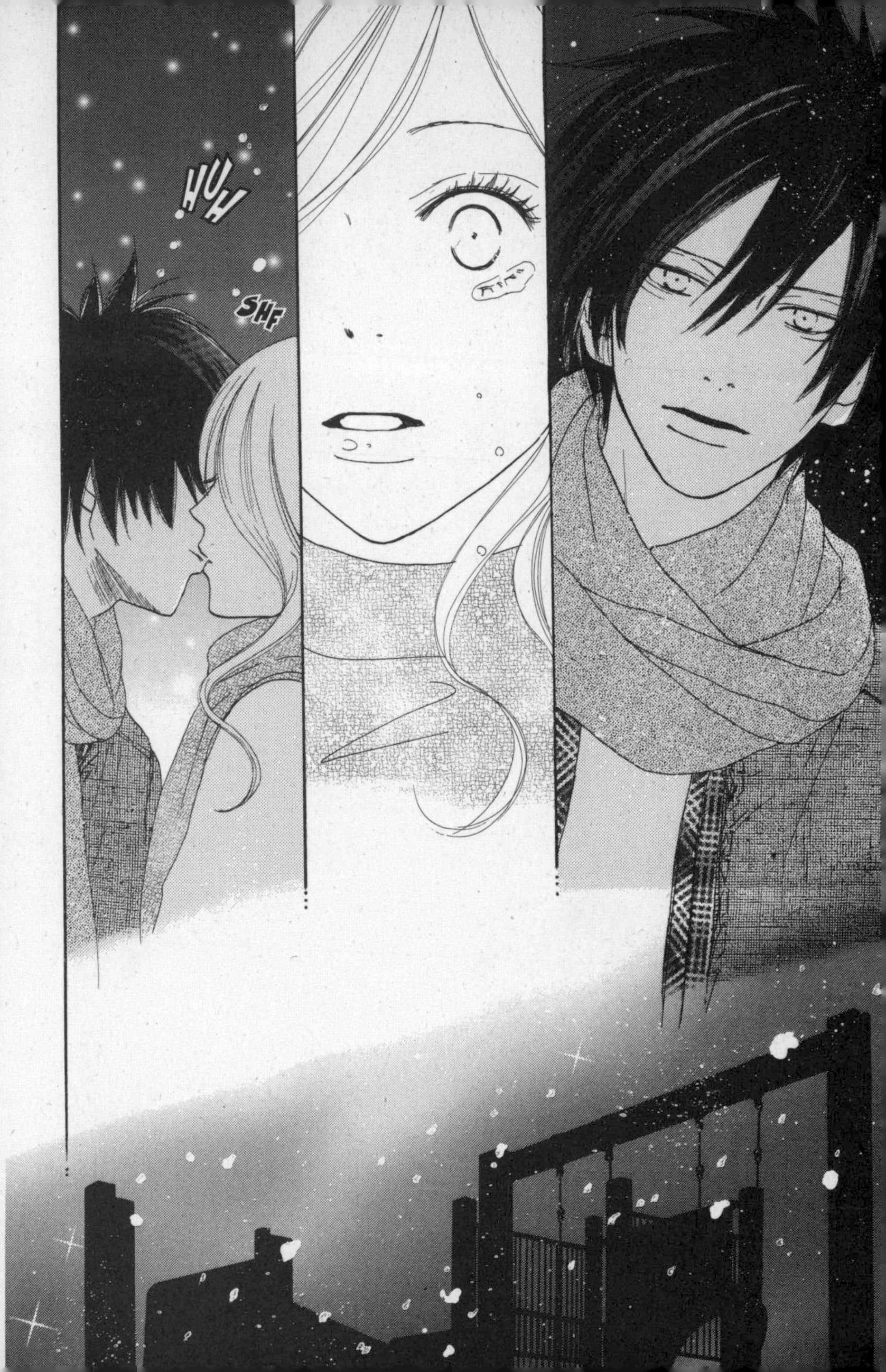
HUH
SHF

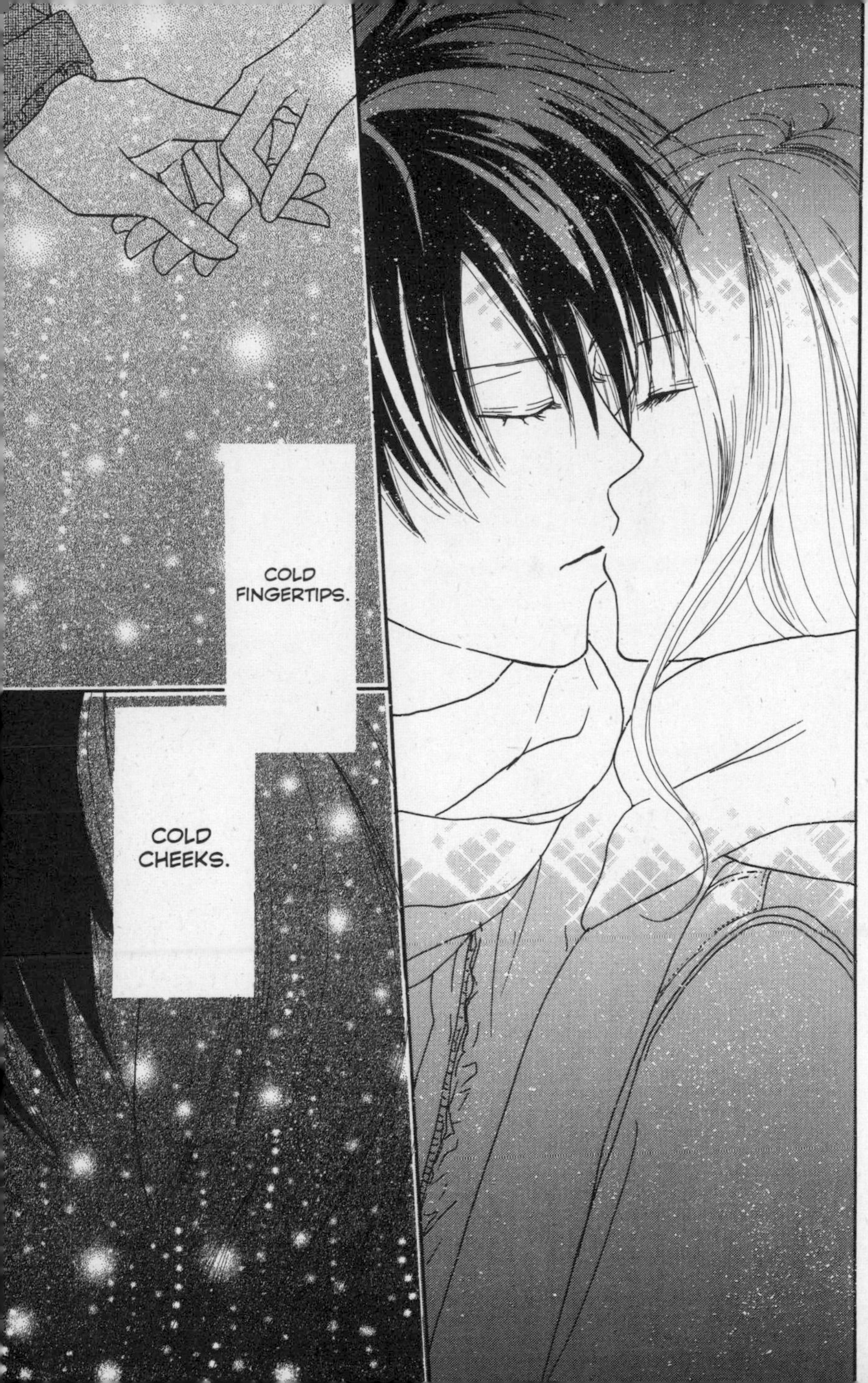
COLD FINGERTIPS.
COLD CHEEKS.

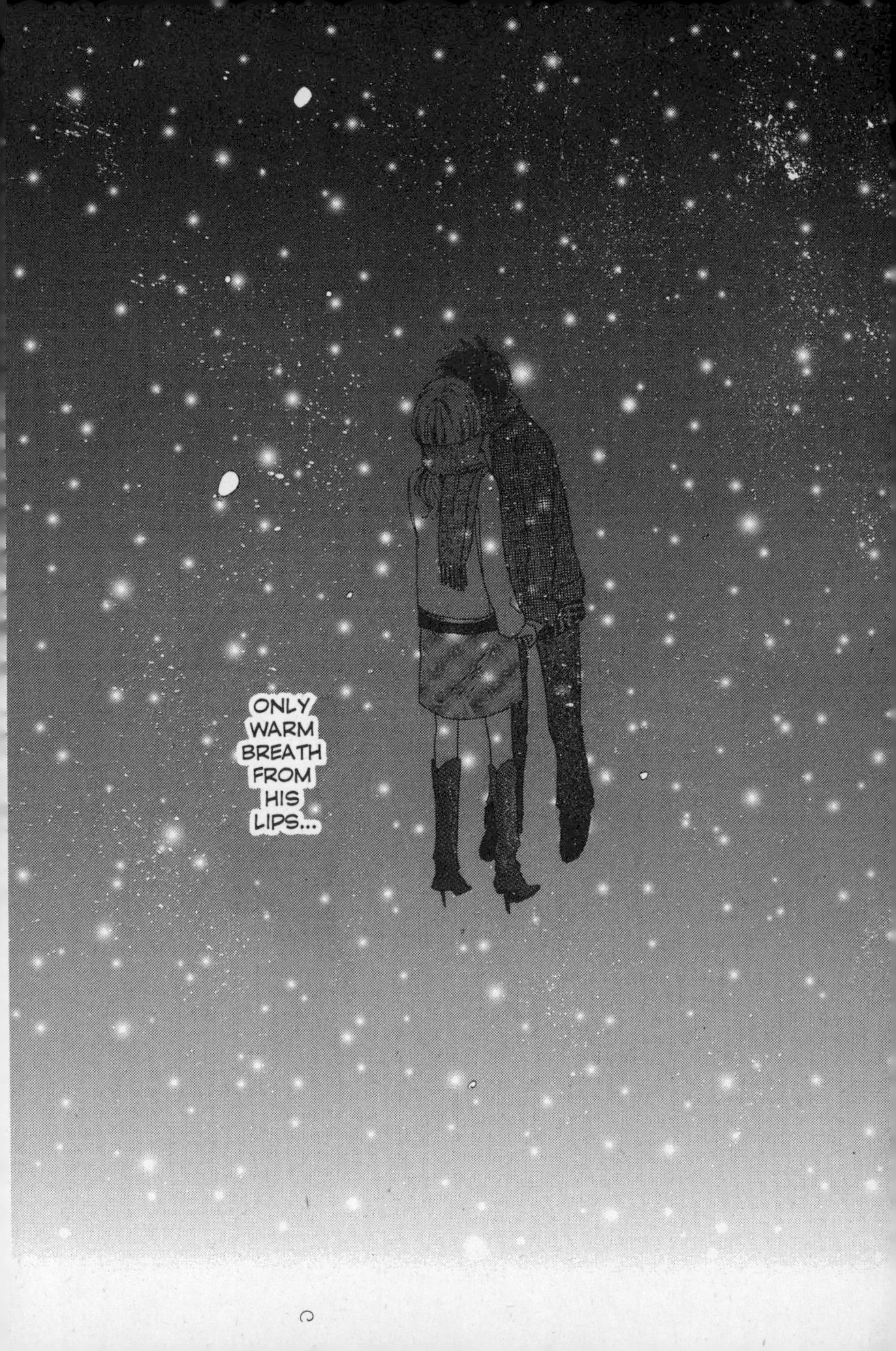
ONLY WARM BREATH FROM HIS LIPS...

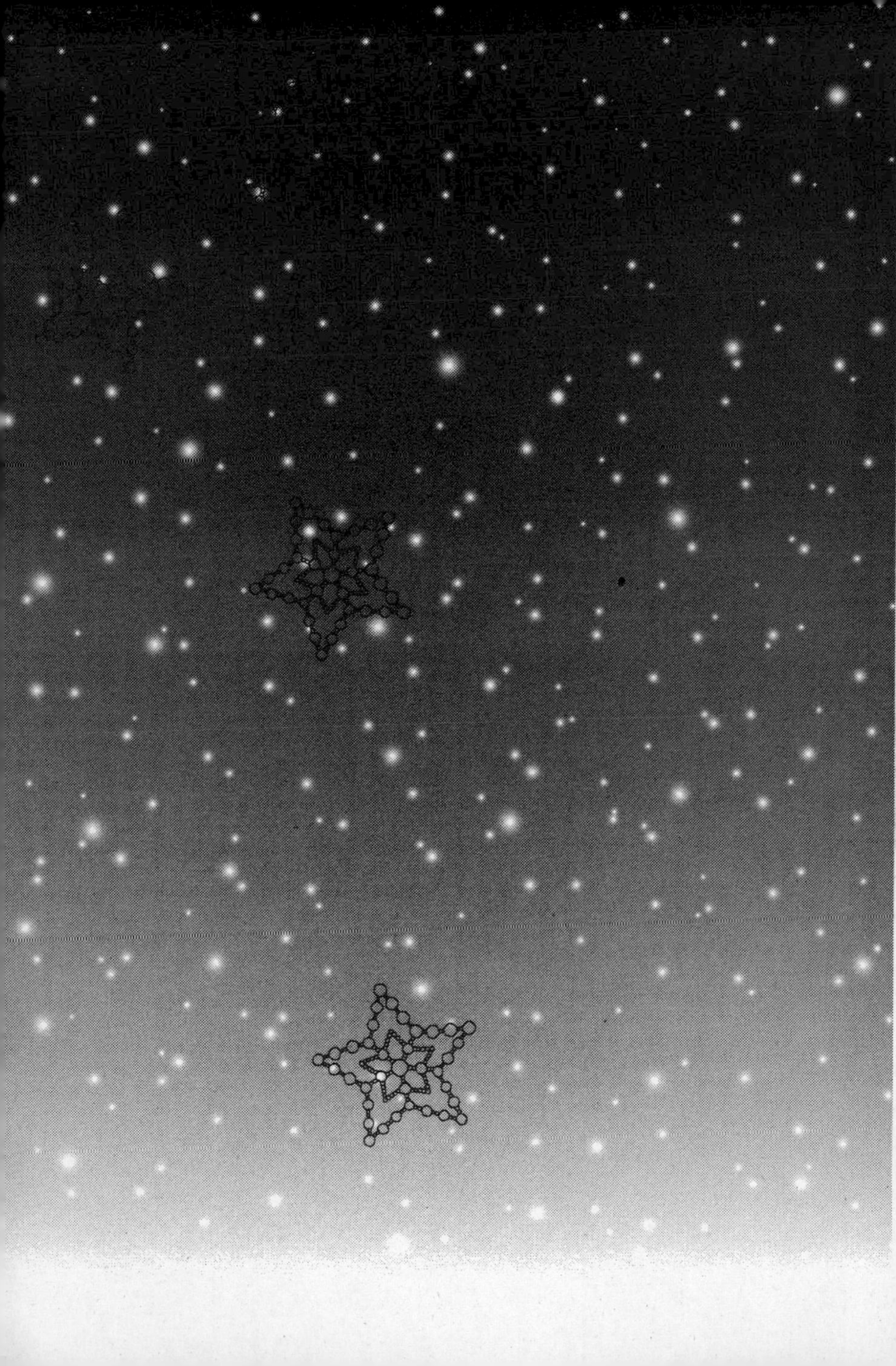

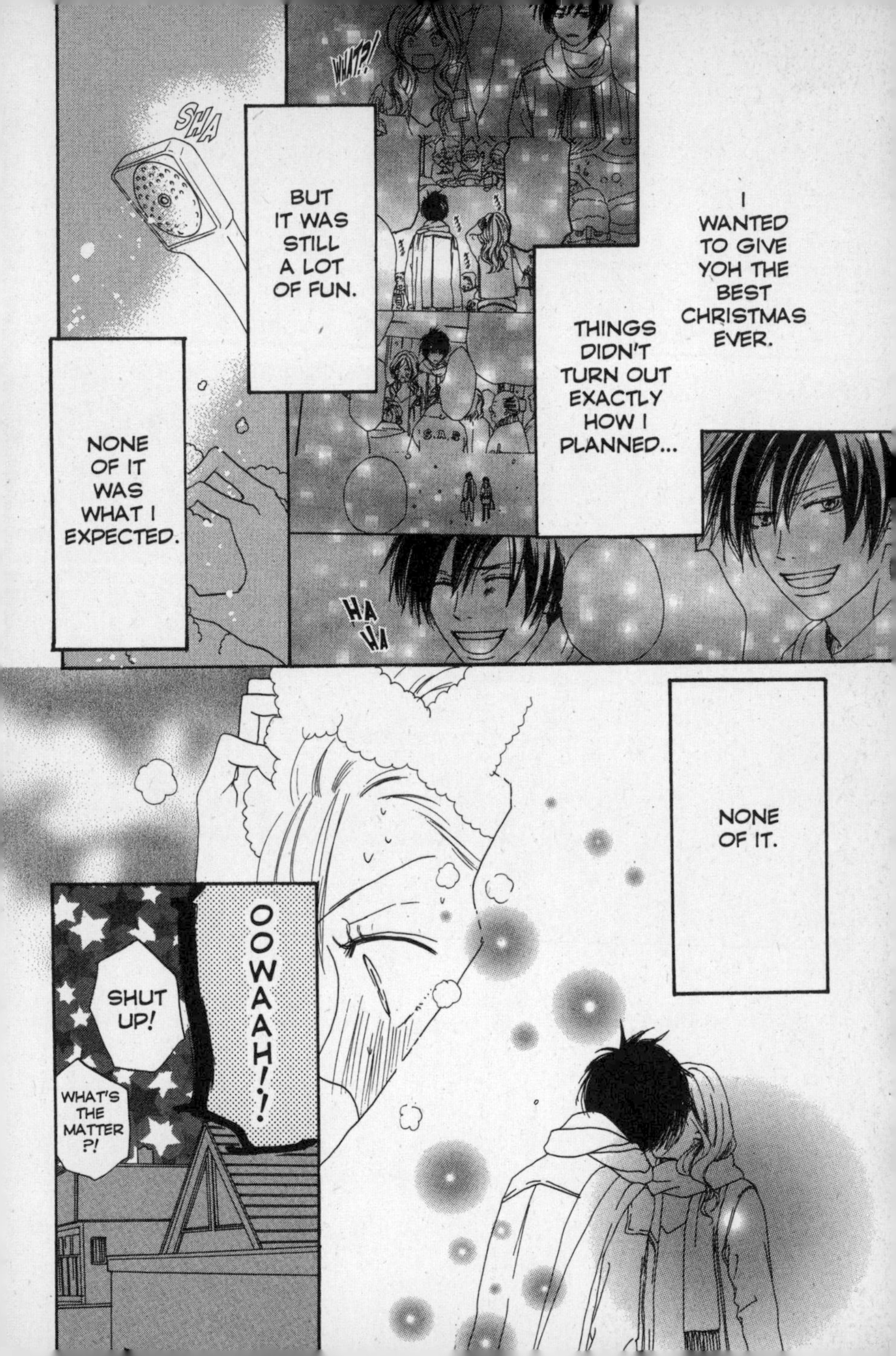
WHAT?!
I WANTED TO GIVE YOH THE BEST CHRISTMAS EVER.
THINGS DIDN'T TURN OUT EXACTLY HOW I PLANNED...
BUT IT WAS STILL A LOT OF FUN.
HA HA
SHA
NONE OF IT WAS WHAT I EXPECTED.
NONE OF IT.
OOWAAAH!!
SHUT UP!
WHAT'S THE MATTER?!

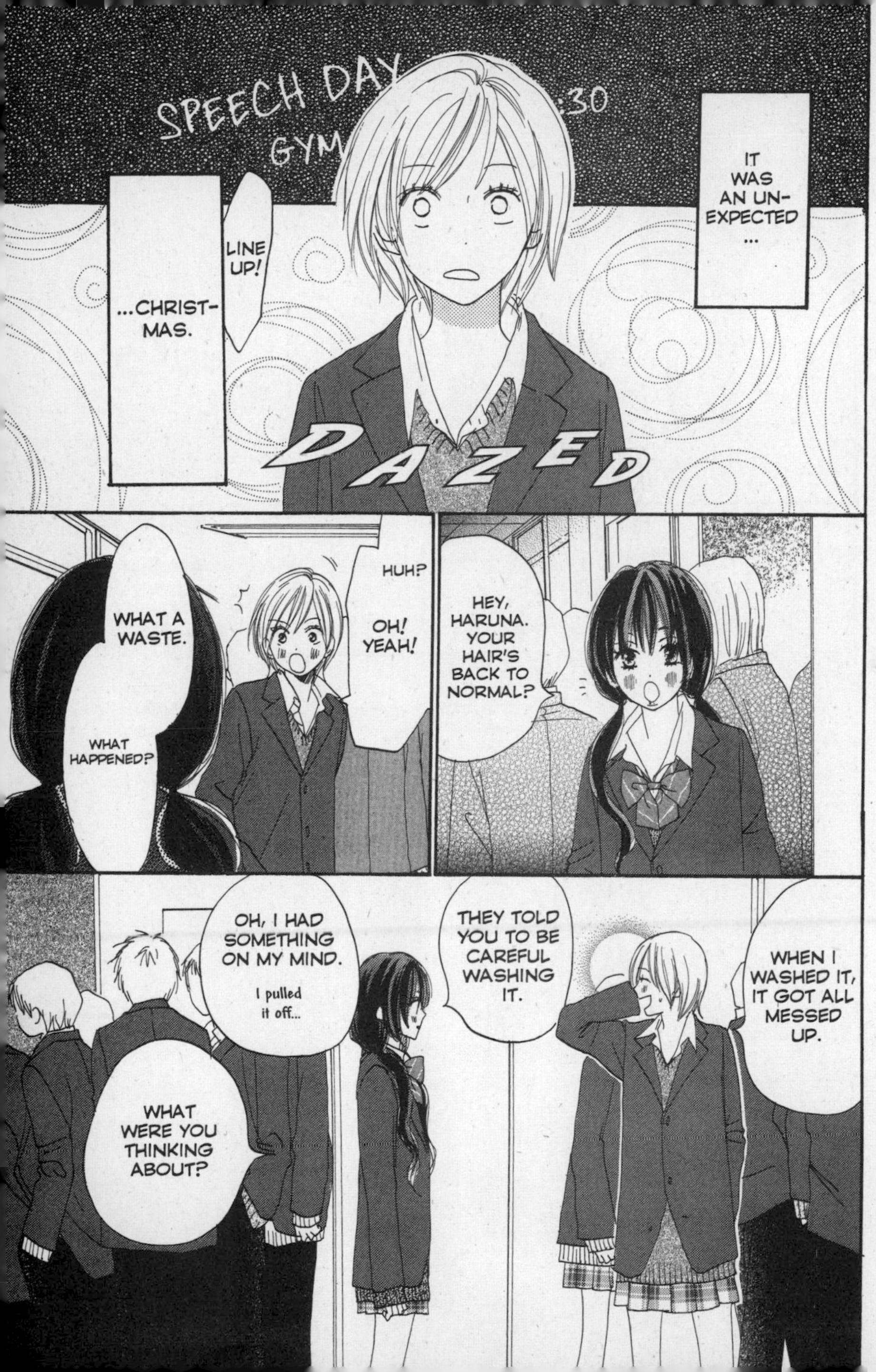
SPEECH DAY
GYM
:30
IT WAS AN UN-EXPECTED ...
LINE UP!
...CHRIST-MAS.
DAZED
HEY, HARUNA. YOUR HAIR'S BACK TO NORMAL?
HUH?
OH! YEAH!
WHAT A WASTE.
WHAT HAPPENED?
WHEN I WASHED IT, IT GOT ALL MESSED UP.
THEY TOLD YOU TO BE CAREFUL WASHING IT.
OH, I HAD SOMETHING ON MY MIND.
I pulled it off...
WHAT WERE YOU THINKING ABOUT?

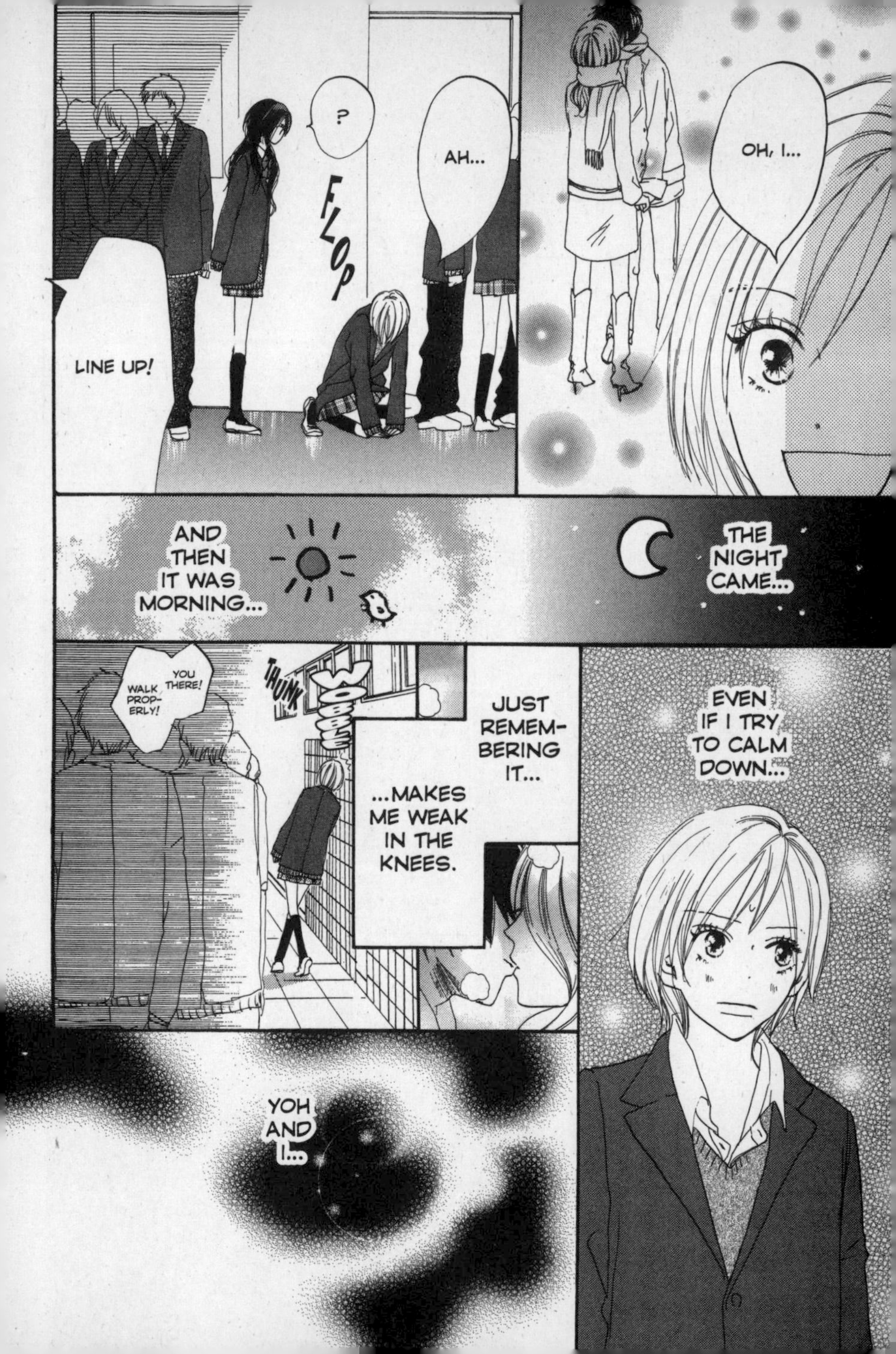
OH, I...
AH...
?
FLOP
LINE UP!
THE NIGHT CAME...
AND THEN IT WAS MORNING...
EVEN IF I TRY TO CALM DOWN...
JUST REMEMBERING IT...
...MAKES ME WEAK IN THE KNEES.
WOBBLE
THUNK
YOU THERE!
WALK PROPERLY!
YOH AND I...

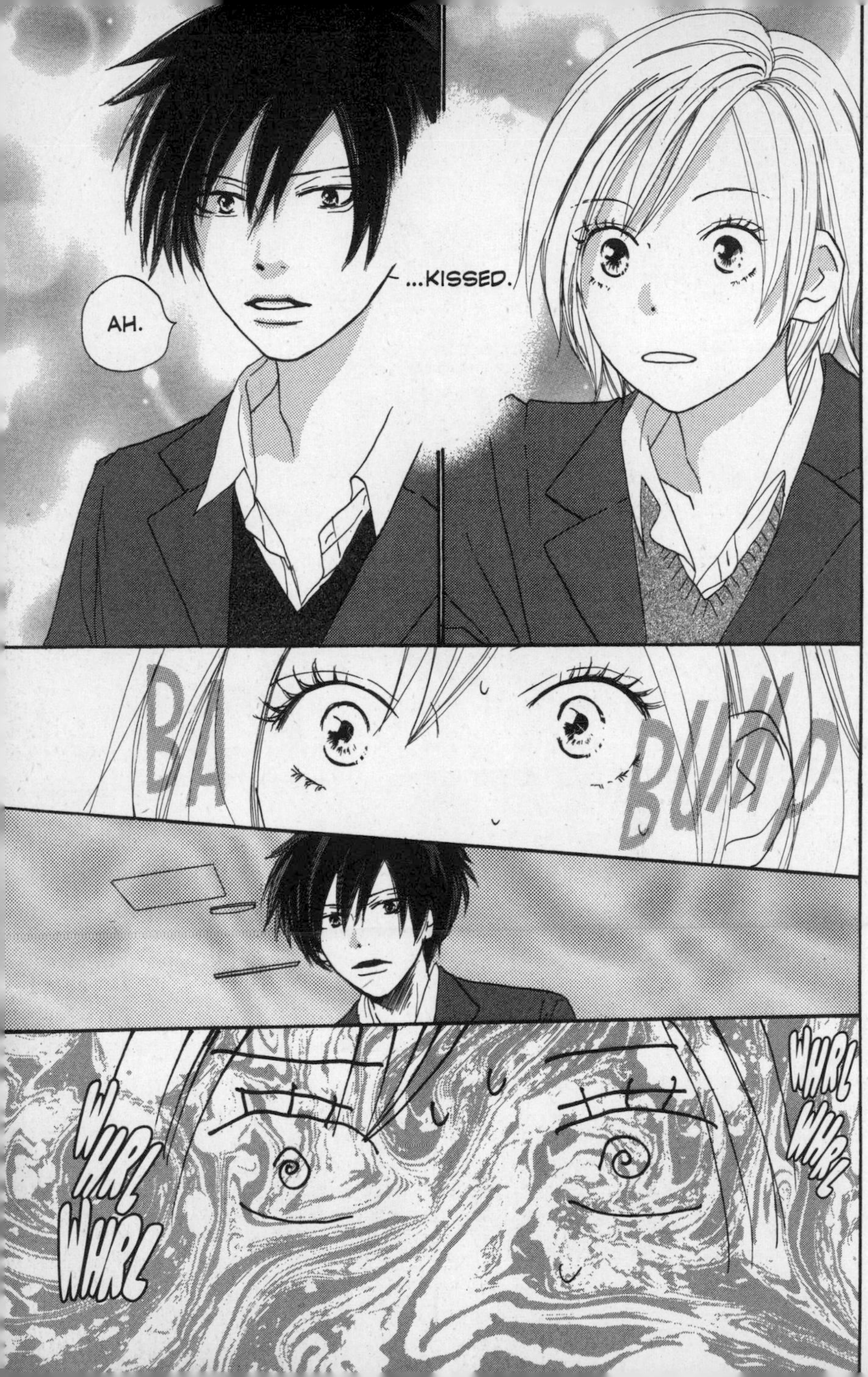
...KISSED.
AH.
BA BUMP
WHIRL WHIRL
WHIRL WHIRL

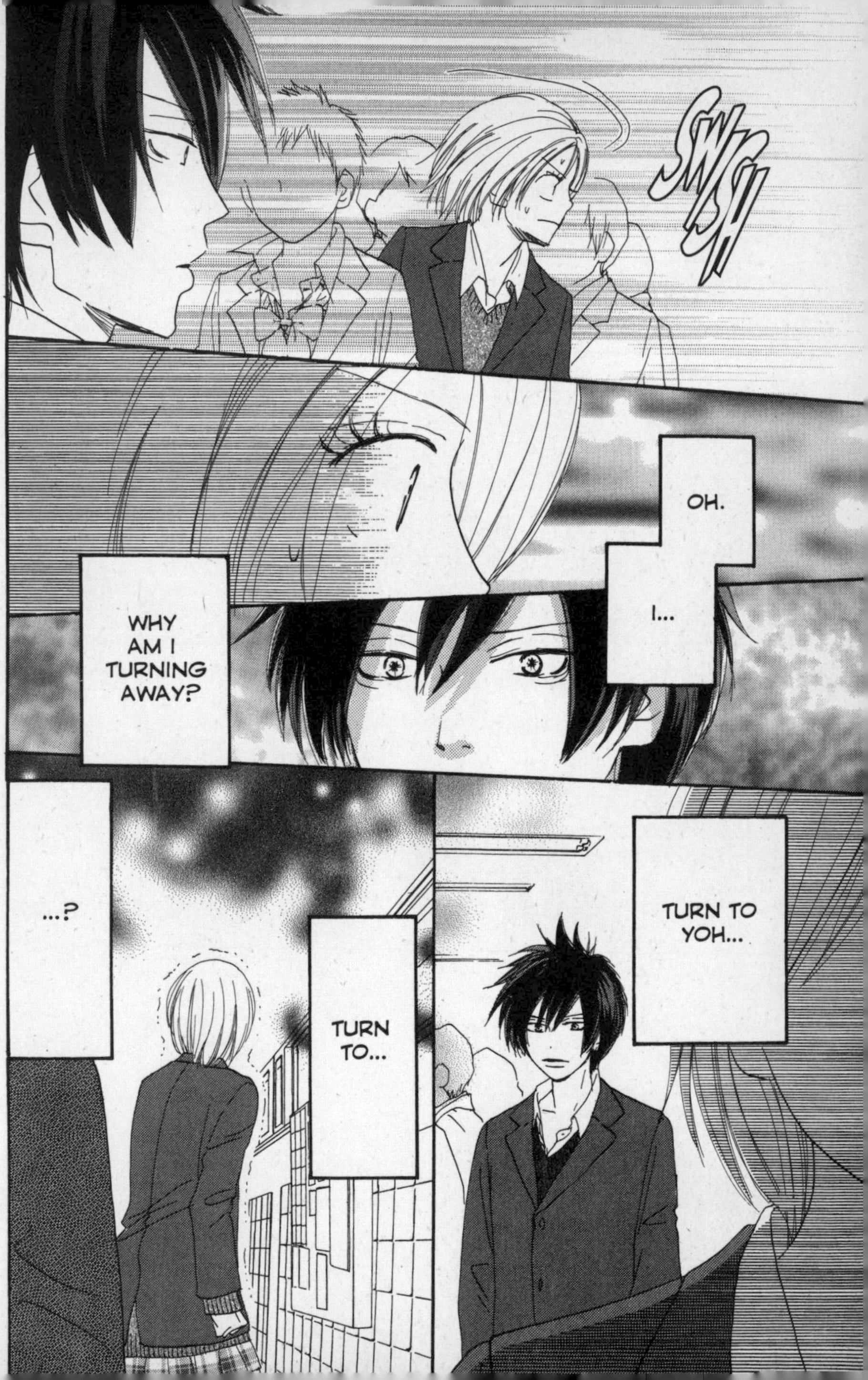
SWISH
OH.
I...
WHY AM I TURNING AWAY?
TURN TO YOH...
TURN TO...
...?

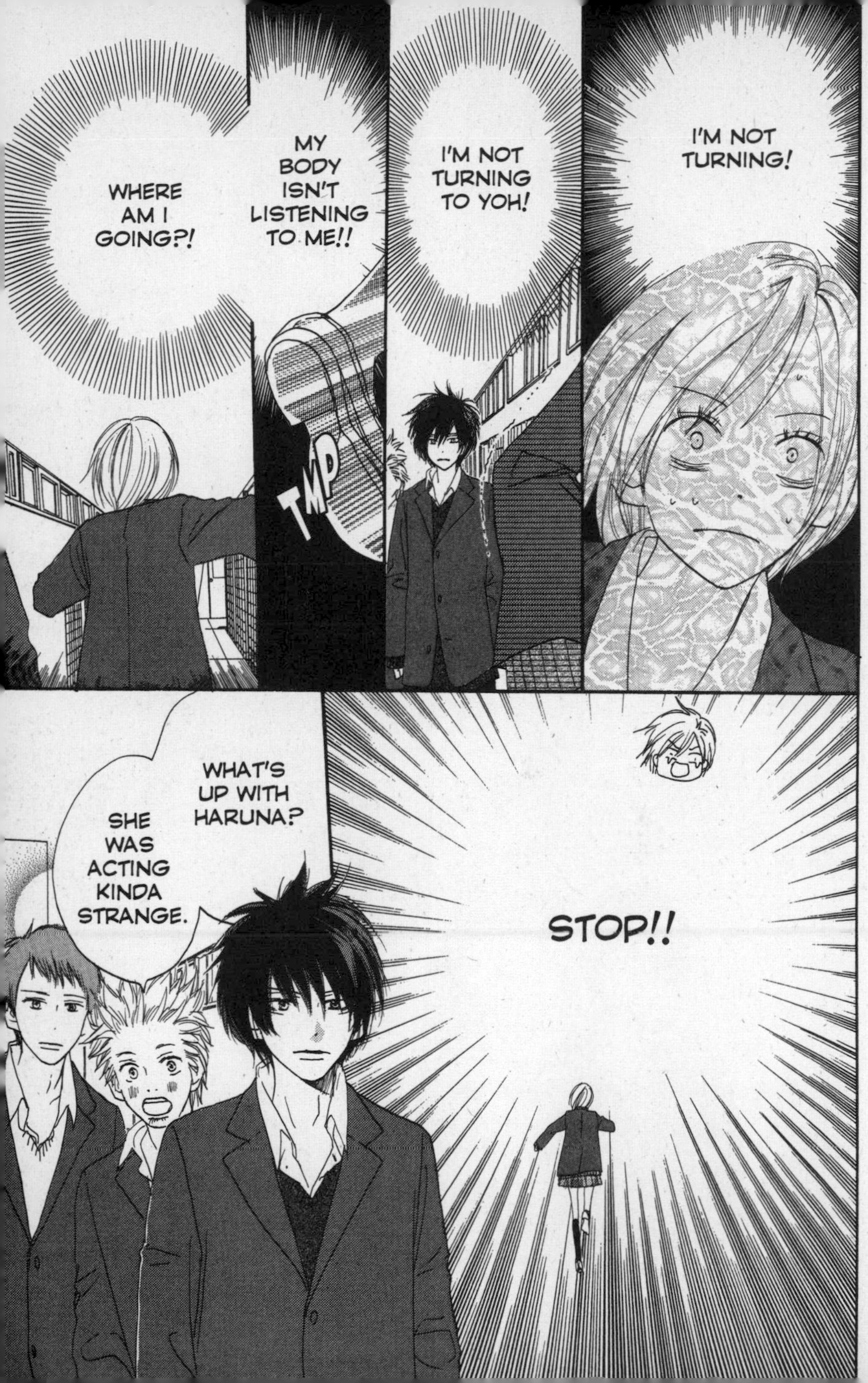
I'M NOT TURNING!
I'M NOT TURNING TO YOH!
MY BODY ISN'T LISTENING TO ME!!
TMP
WHERE AM I GOING?!
STOP!!
WHAT'S UP WITH HARUNA?
SHE WAS ACTING KINDA STRANGE.

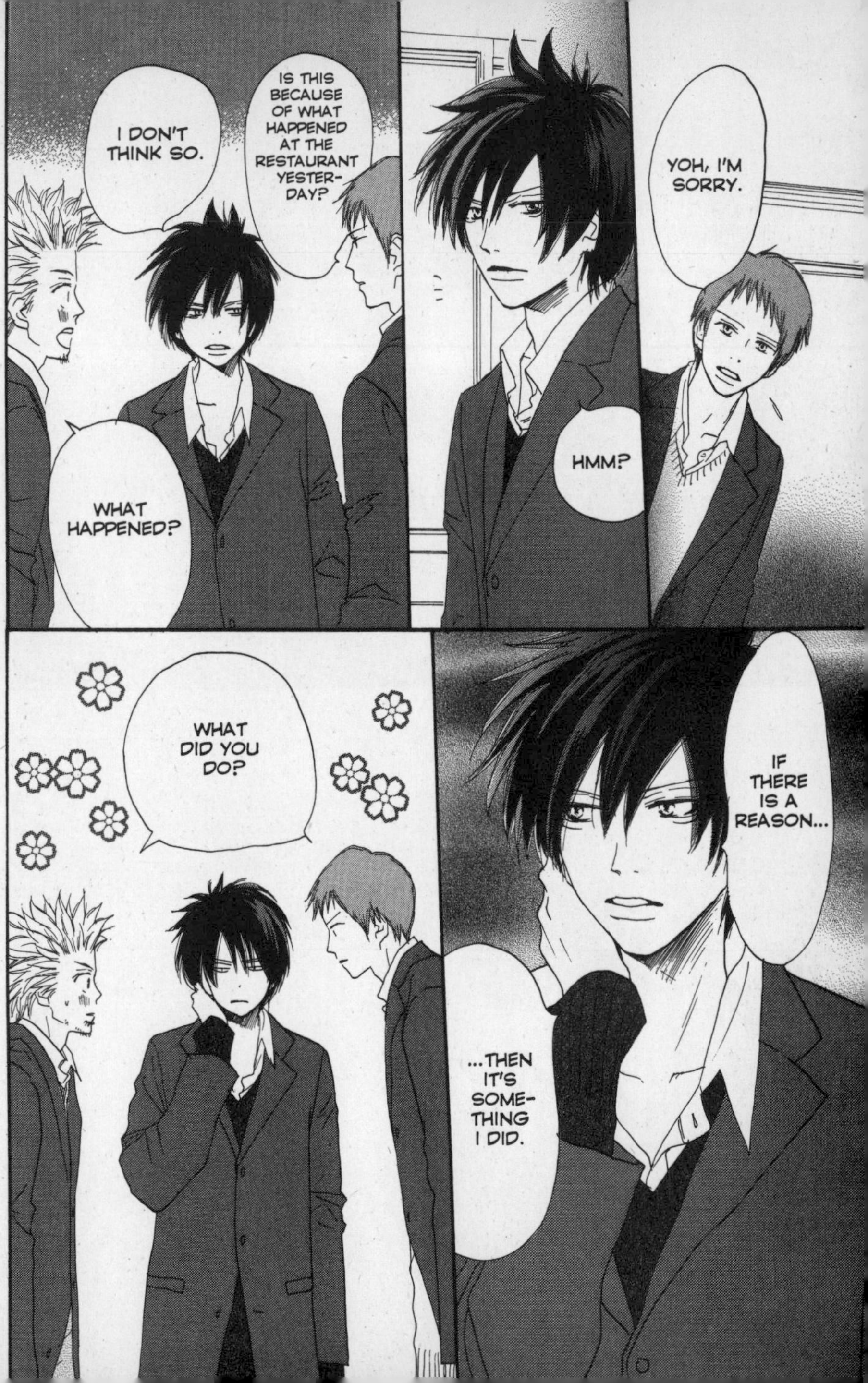
YOH, I'M SORRY.
HMM?
IS THIS BECAUSE OF WHAT HAPPENED AT THE RESTAURANT YESTER-DAY?
I DON'T THINK SO.
WHAT HAPPENED?
IF THERE IS A REASON...
...THEN IT'S SOME-THING I DID.
WHAT DID YOU DO?

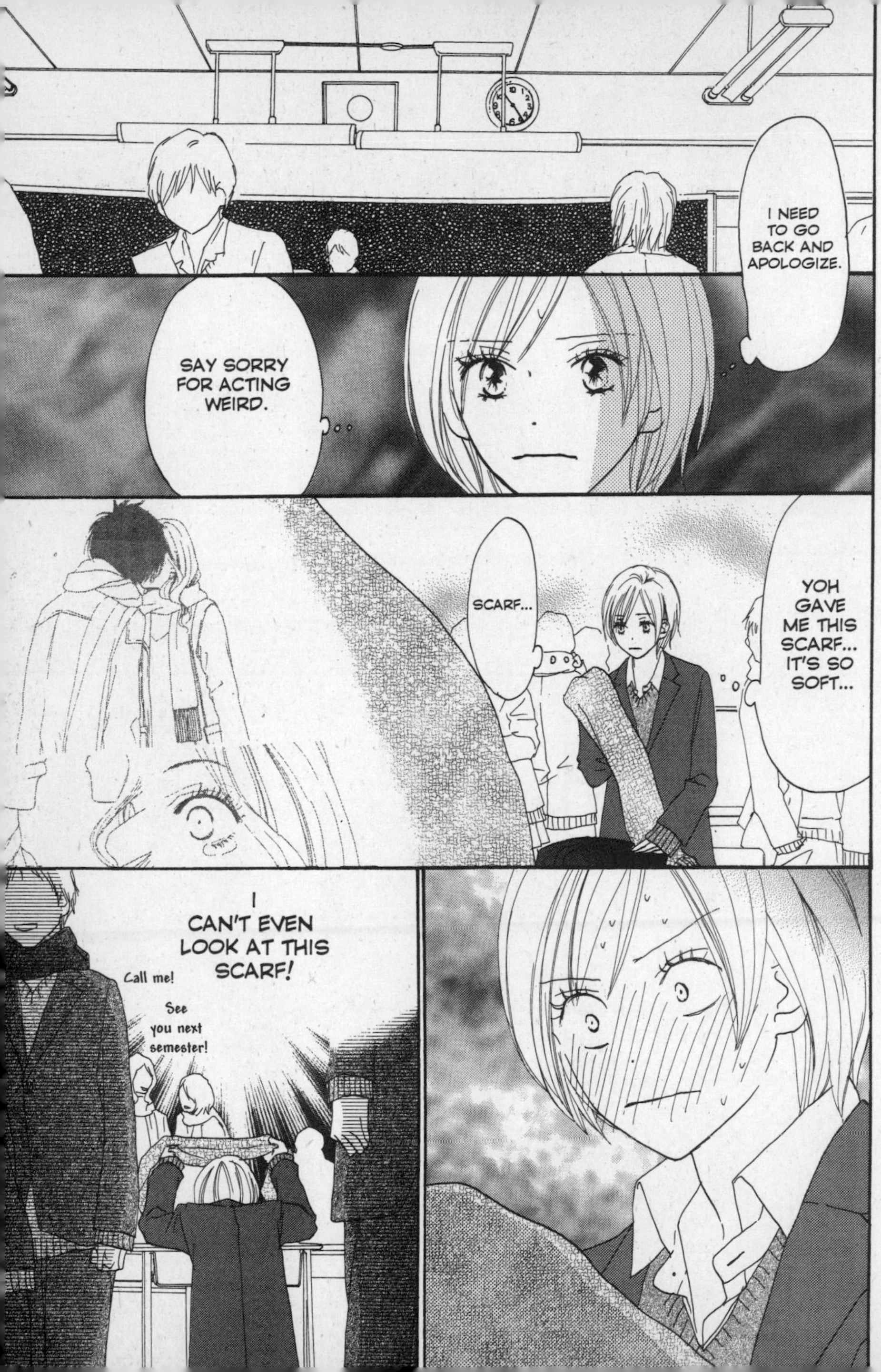
I NEED TO GO BACK AND APOLOGIZE.
SAY SORRY FOR ACTING WEIRD.
YOH GAVE ME THIS SCARF... IT'S SO SOFT...
SCARF...
I CAN'T EVEN LOOK AT THIS SCARF!
Call me!
See you next semester!

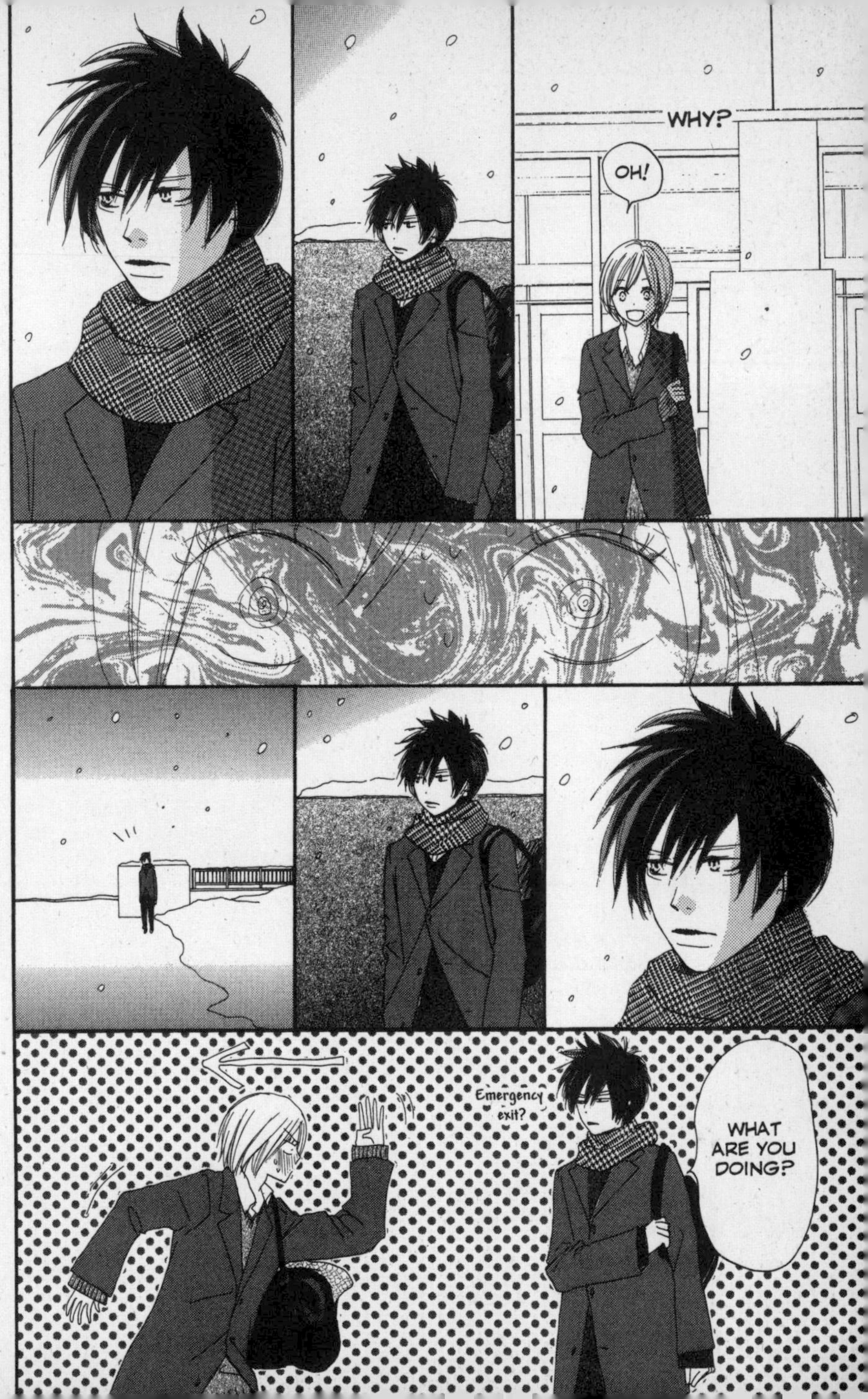
WHY?
OH!
WHAT ARE YOU DOING?
Emergency exit?

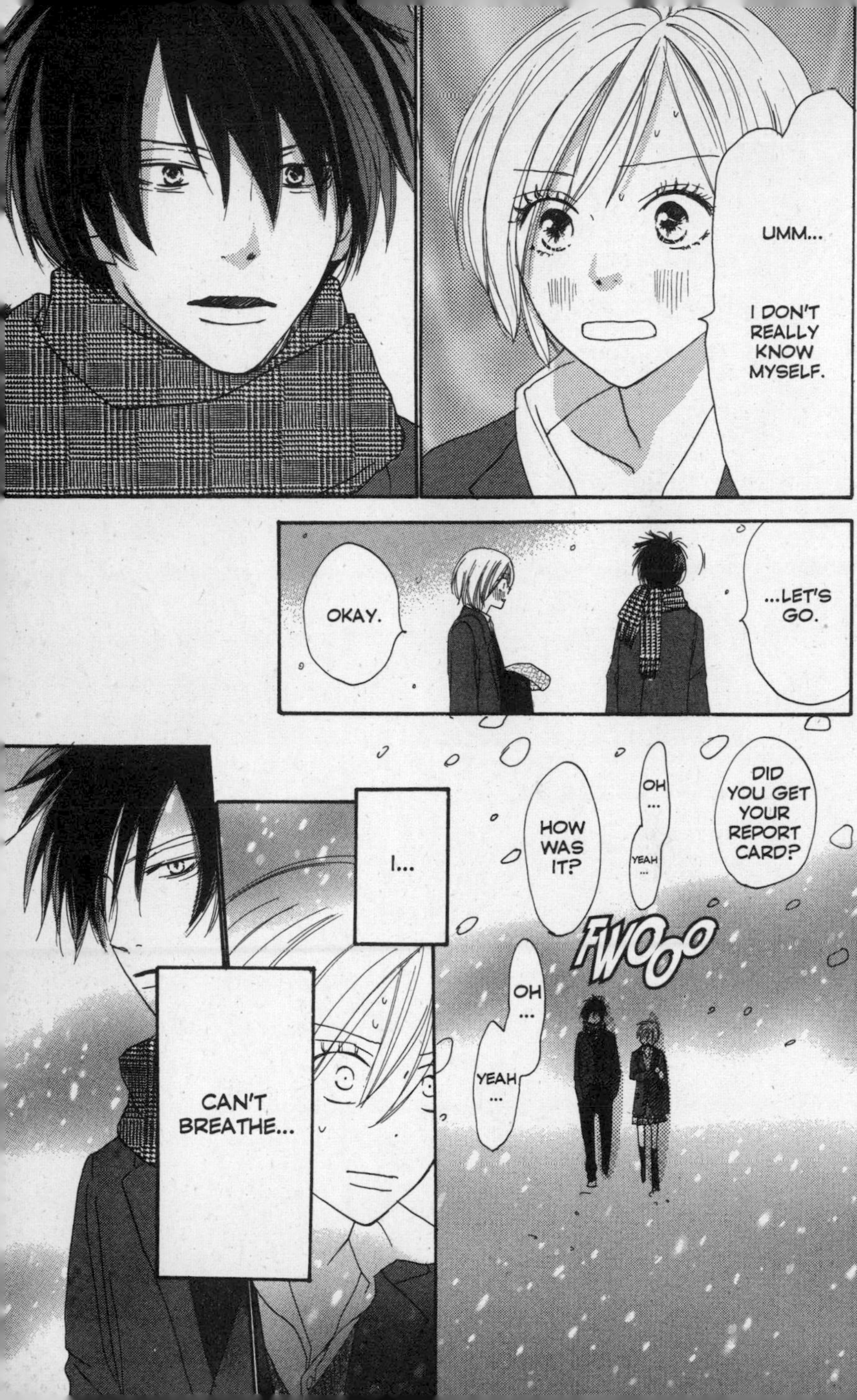
UMM...
I DON'T REALLY KNOW MYSELF.
...LET'S GO.
OKAY.
DID YOU GET YOUR REPORT CARD?
OH ... YEAH ...
HOW WAS IT?
FWOOOO
OH ... YEAH ...
I...
CAN'T BREATHE...

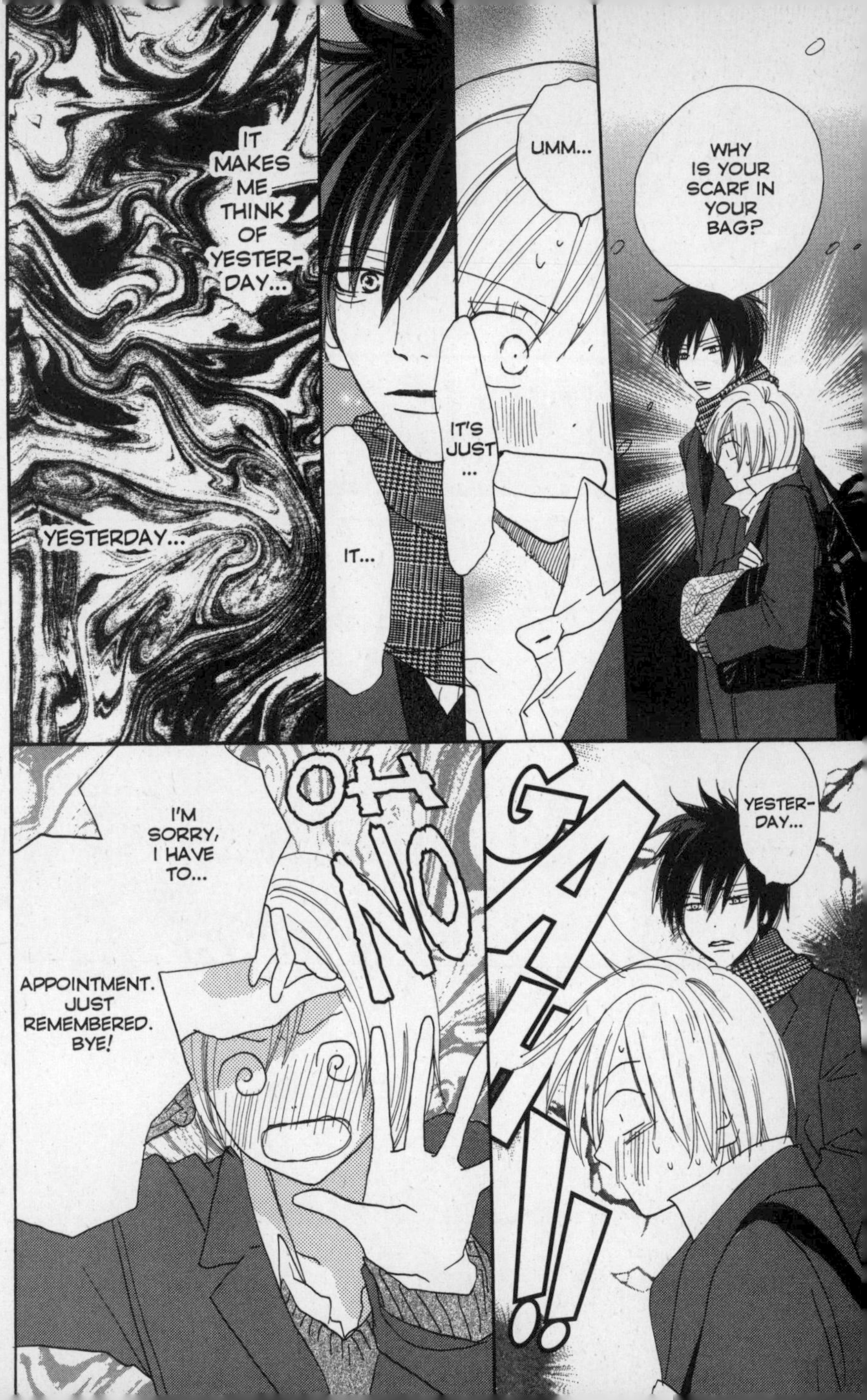
WHY IS YOUR SCARF IN YOUR BAG?
UMM...
IT'S JUST ...
IT...
IT MAKES ME THINK OF YESTER-DAY...
YESTERDAY...
YESTER-DAY...
OH NO
I'M SORRY, I HAVE TO...
APPOINTMENT. JUST REMEMBERED. BYE!

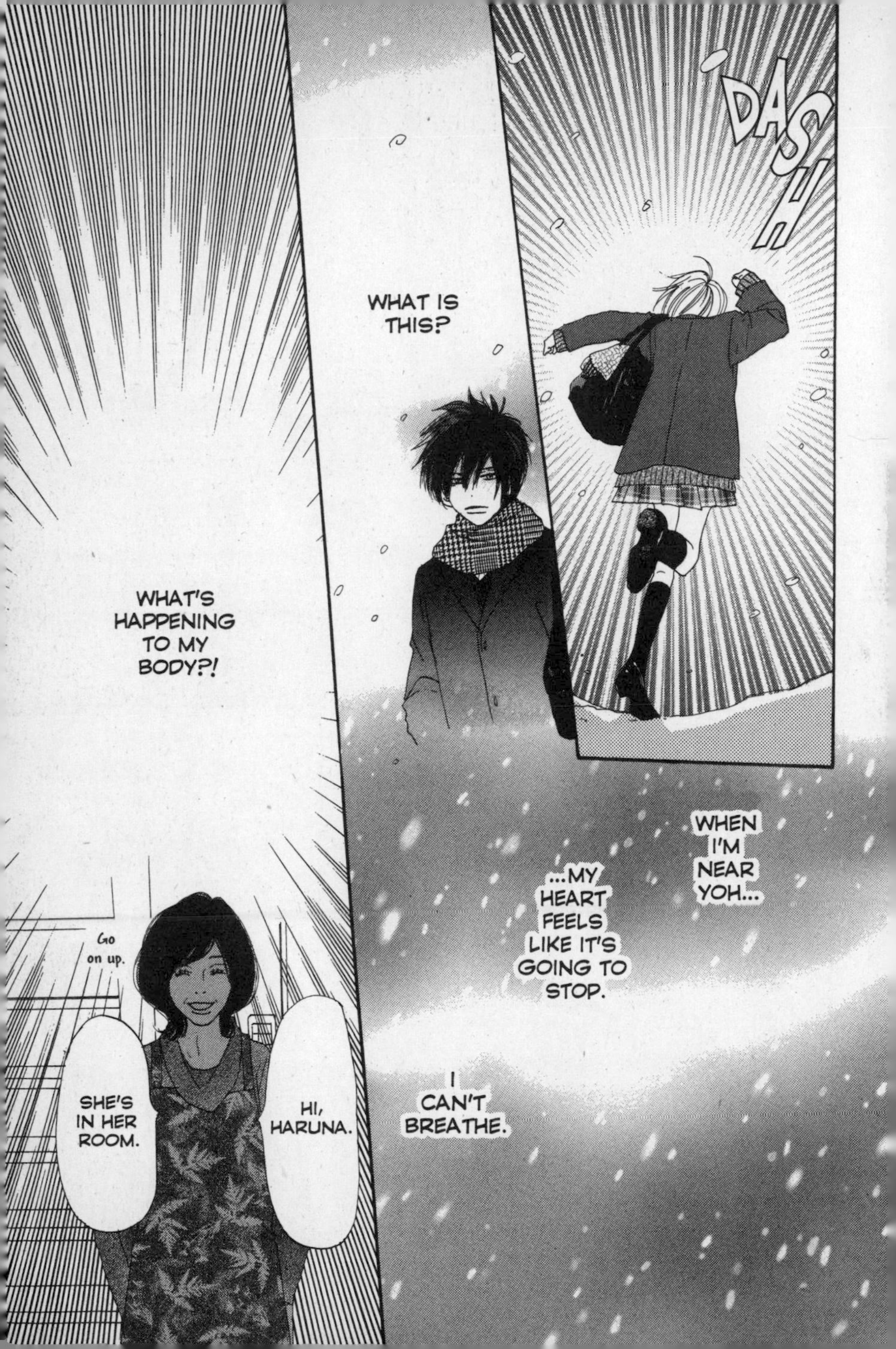
DASH
WHAT IS THIS?
WHEN I'M NEAR YOH...
...MY HEART FEELS LIKE IT'S GOING TO STOP.
I CAN'T BREATHE.
WHAT'S HAPPENING TO MY BODY?!
HI, HARUNA.
SHE'S IN HER ROOM.
Go on up.

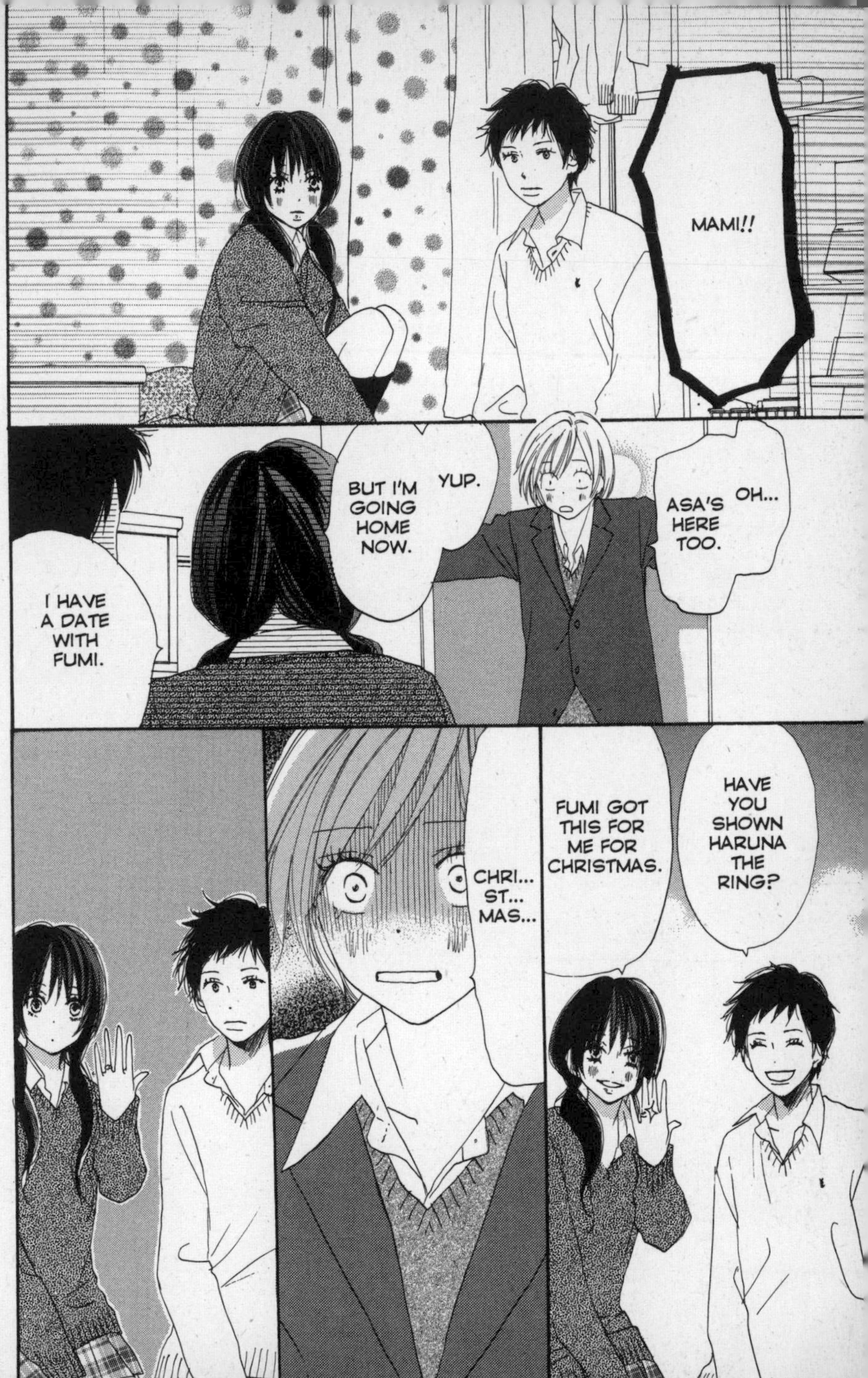
MAMI!!
OH... ASA'S HERE TOO.
YUP. BUT I'M GOING HOME NOW.
I HAVE A DATE WITH FUMI.
HAVE YOU SHOWN HARUNA THE RING?
FUMI GOT THIS FOR ME FOR CHRISTMAS.
CHRI... ST... MAS...

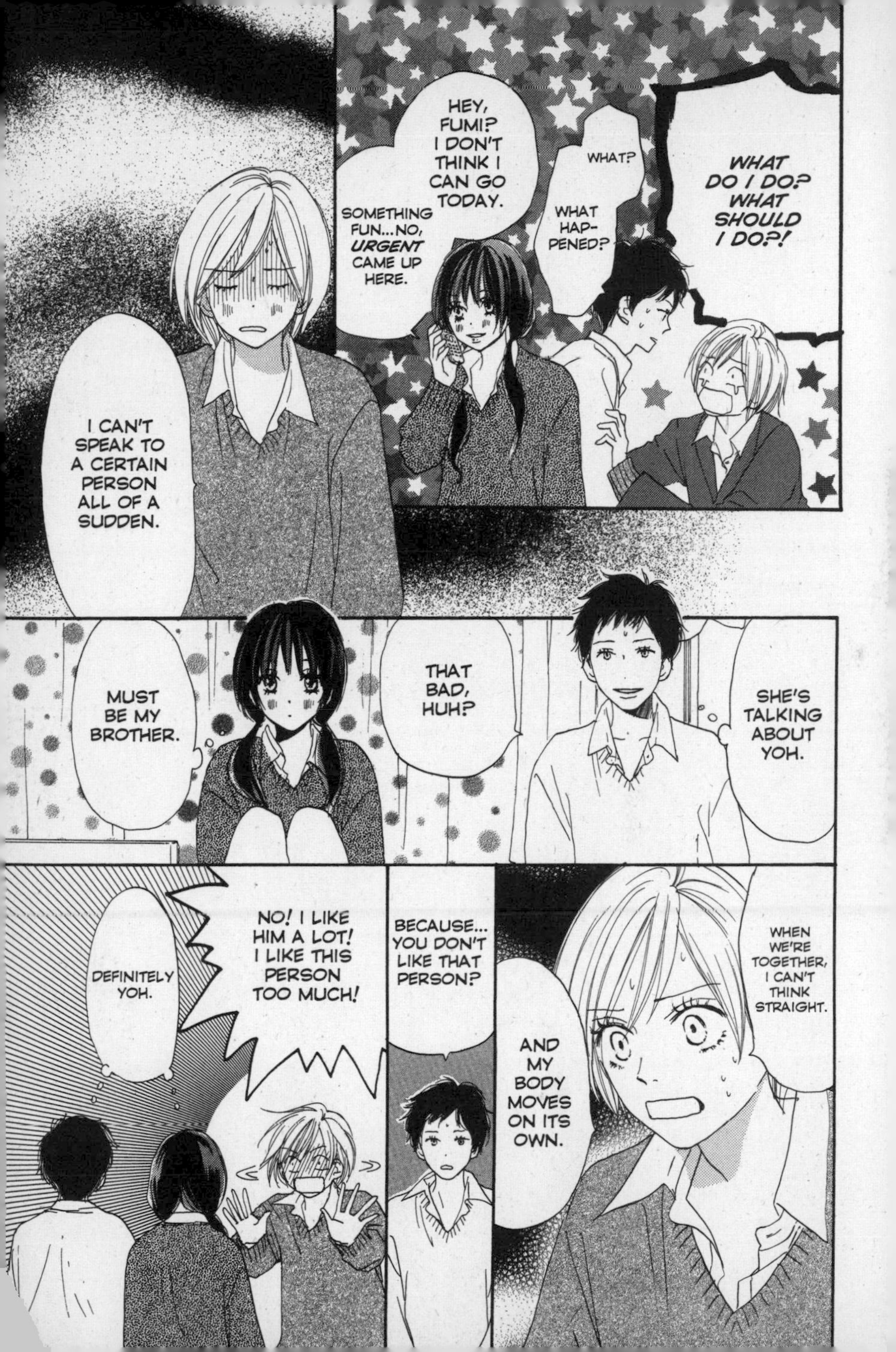
WHAT DO I DO? WHAT SHOULD I DO?!
WHAT?
WHAT HAPPENED?
HEY, FUMI? I DON'T THINK I CAN GO TODAY.
SOMETHING FUN...NO, URGENT CAME UP HERE.
I CAN'T SPEAK TO A CERTAIN PERSON ALL OF A SUDDEN.
SHE'S TALKING ABOUT YOH.
THAT BAD, HUH?
MUST BE MY BROTHER.
WHEN WE'RE TOGETHER, I CAN'T THINK STRAIGHT.
AND MY BODY MOVES ON ITS OWN.
BECAUSE... YOU DON'T LIKE THAT PERSON?
NO! I LIKE HIM A LOT! I LIKE THIS PERSON TOO MUCH!
DEFINITELY YOH.

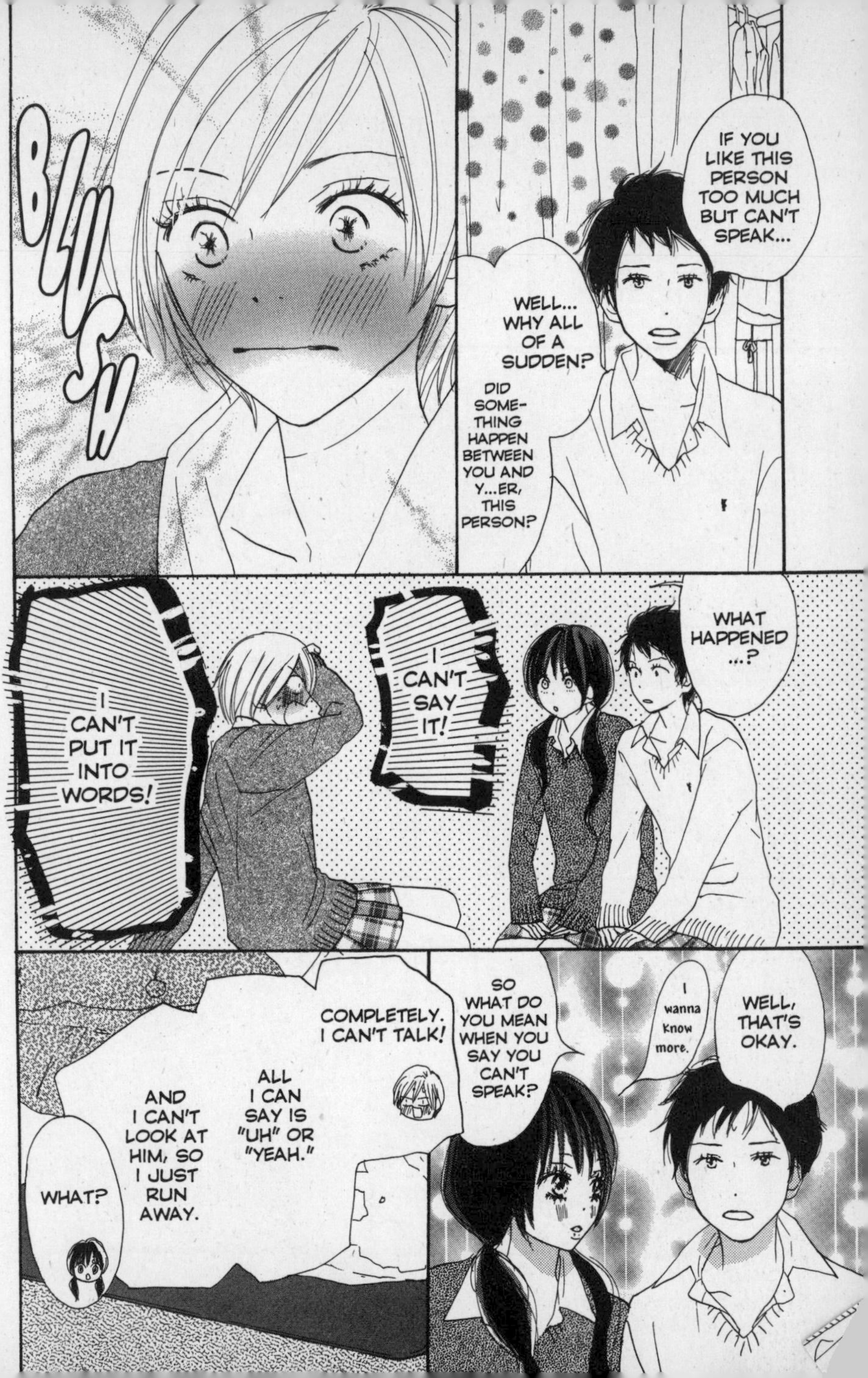
IF YOU LIKE THIS PERSON TOO MUCH BUT CAN'T SPEAK...
WELL... WHY ALL OF A SUDDEN?
DID SOMETHING HAPPEN BETWEEN YOU AND Y...ER, THIS PERSON?
BLUSH
WHAT HAPPENED ...?
I CAN'T SAY IT!
I CAN'T PUT IT INTO WORDS!
WELL, THAT'S OKAY.
I wanna know more.
SO WHAT DO YOU MEAN WHEN YOU SAY YOU CAN'T SPEAK?
COMPLETELY. I CAN'T TALK!
ALL I CAN SAY IS "UH" OR "YEAH."
AND I CAN'T LOOK AT HIM, SO I JUST RUN AWAY.
WHAT?

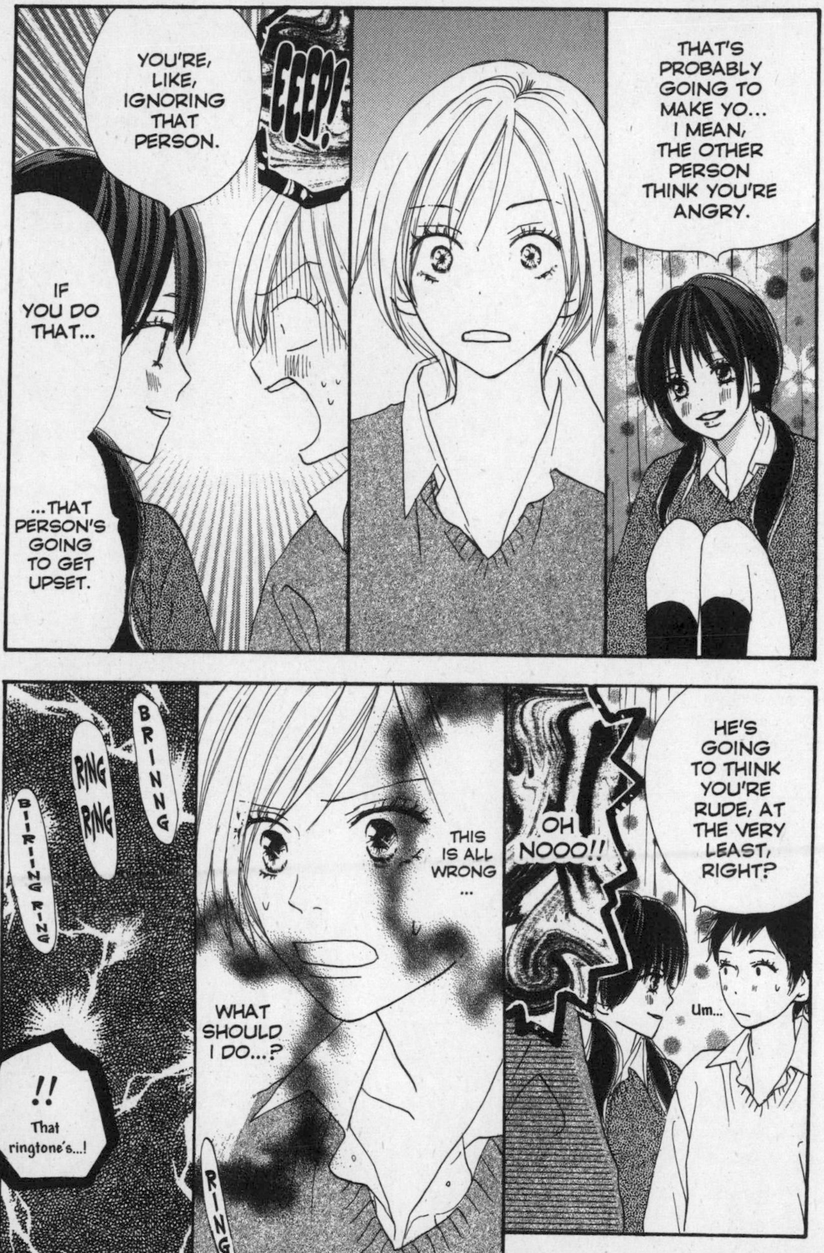
THAT'S PROBABLY GOING TO MAKE YO... I MEAN, THE OTHER PERSON THINK YOU'RE ANGRY.
EEEP!
YOU'RE, LIKE, IGNORING THAT PERSON.
IF YOU DO THAT...
...THAT PERSON'S GOING TO GET UPSET.
HE'S GOING TO THINK YOU'RE RUDE, AT THE VERY LEAST, RIGHT?
OH NOOO!!
Um...
THIS IS ALL WRONG ...
WHAT SHOULD I DO...?
RING
BRINNG
RING RING
BIRIIING RING
!! That ringtone's...!

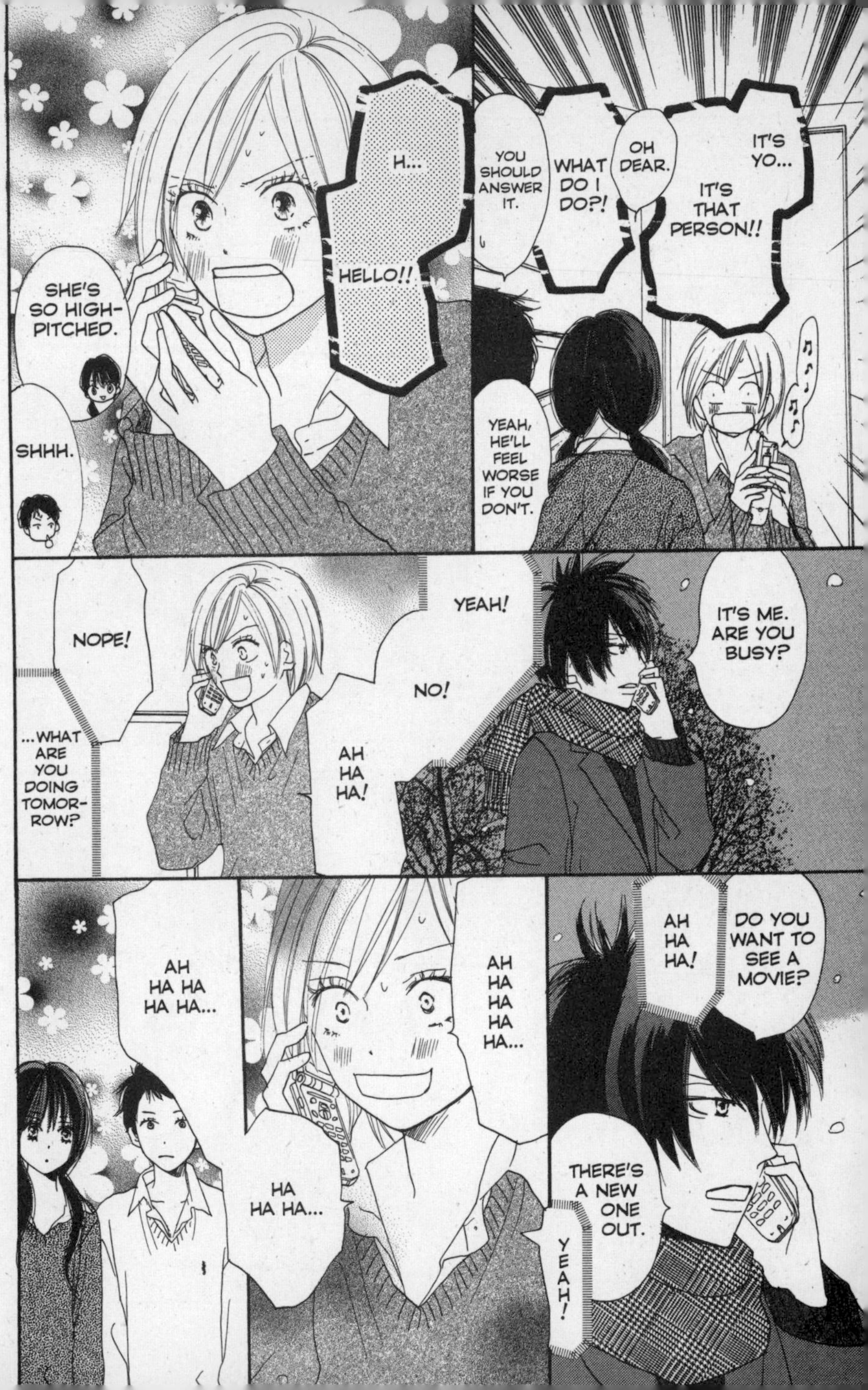
IT'S YO... IT'S THAT PERSON!!
OH DEAR.
WHAT DO I DO?!
YOU SHOULD ANSWER IT.
YEAH, HE'LL FEEL WORSE IF YOU DON'T.
H... HELLO!!
SHE'S SO HIGH-PITCHED.
SHHH.
IT'S ME. ARE YOU BUSY?
YEAH!
NOPE!
NO!
AH HA HA!
...WHAT ARE YOU DOING TOMORROW?
DO YOU WANT TO SEE A MOVIE?
AH HA HA!
THERE'S A NEW ONE OUT.
YEAH!
AH HA HA HA HA...
AH HA HA HA...
HA HA HA...

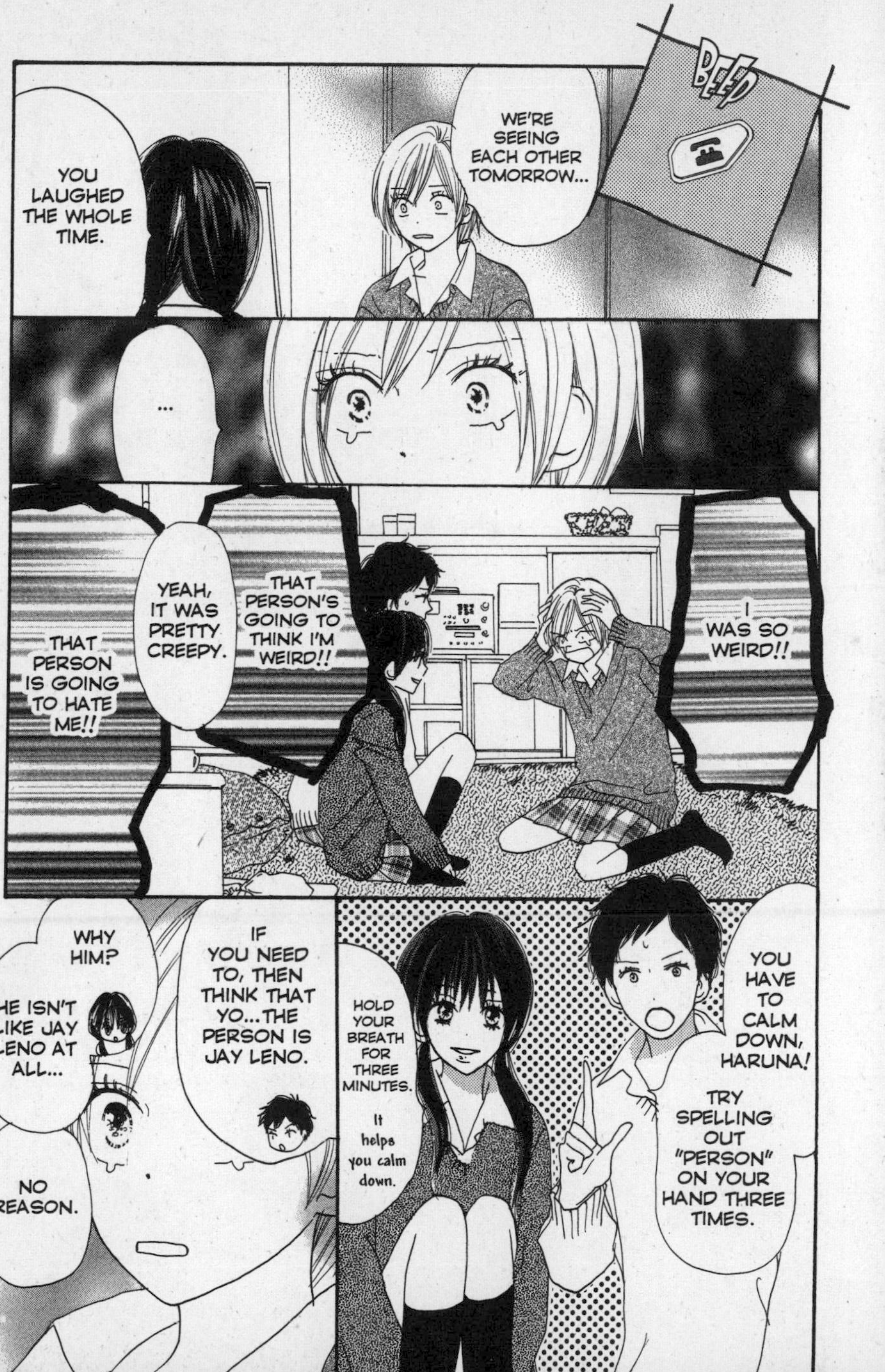
BEEP
WE'RE SEEING EACH OTHER TOMORROW...
YOU LAUGHED THE WHOLE TIME.
...
I WAS SO WEIRD!!
THAT PERSON'S GOING TO THINK I'M WEIRD!!
YEAH, IT WAS PRETTY CREEPY.
THAT PERSON IS GOING TO HATE ME!!
YOU HAVE TO CALM DOWN, HARUNA!
TRY SPELLING OUT "PERSON" ON YOUR HAND THREE TIMES.
HOLD YOUR BREATH FOR THREE MINUTES.
It helps you calm down.
IF YOU NEED TO, THEN THINK THAT YO...THE PERSON IS JAY LENO.
WHY HIM?
HE ISN'T LIKE JAY LENO AT ALL...
NO REASON.

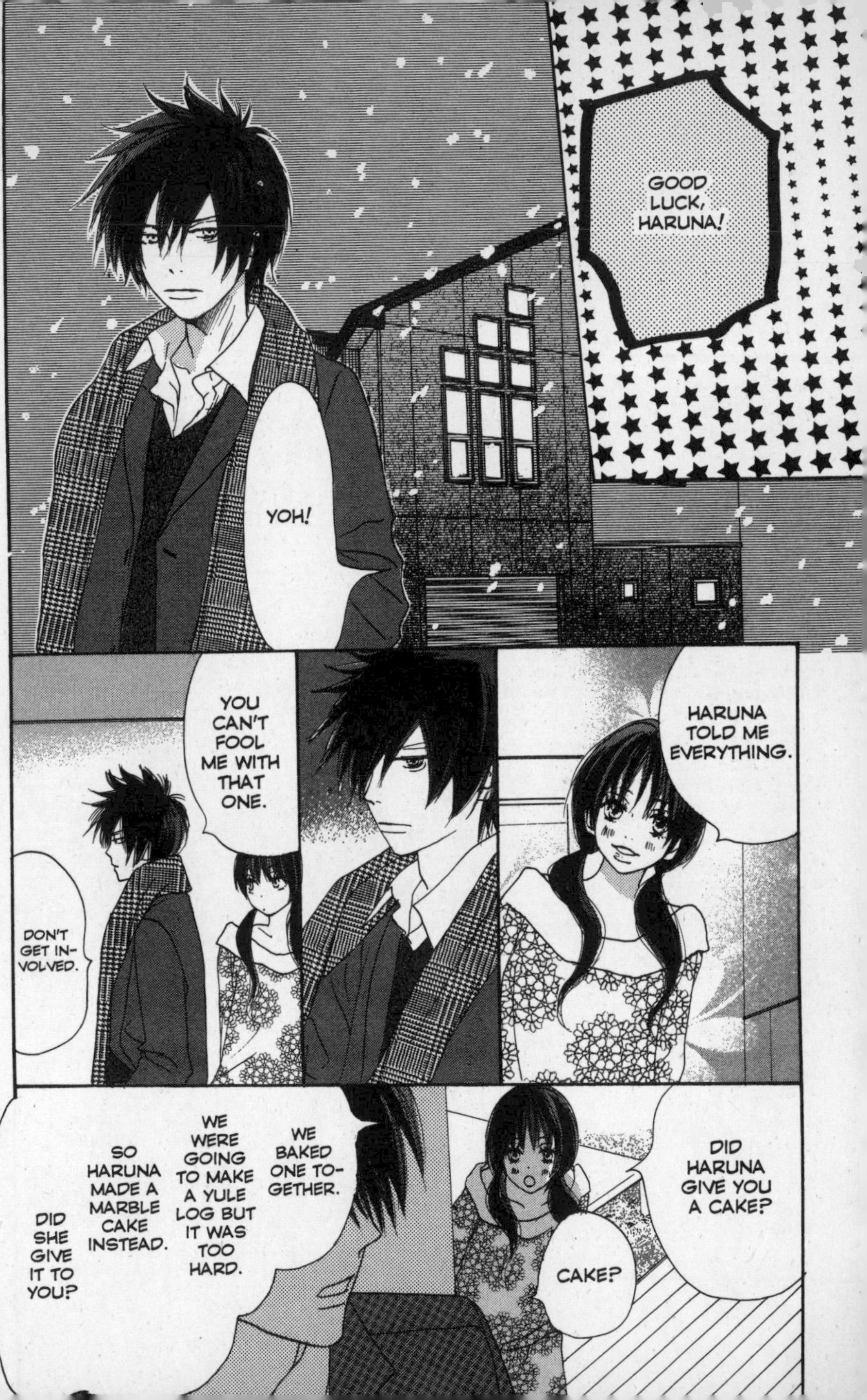
GOOD LUCK, HARUNA!
YOH!
HARUNA TOLD ME EVERYTHING.
YOU CAN'T FOOL ME WITH THAT ONE.
DON'T GET INVOLVED.
DID HARUNA GIVE YOU A CAKE?
CAKE?
WE BAKED ONE TOGETHER.
WE WERE GOING TO MAKE A YULE LOG BUT IT WAS TOO HARD.
SO HARUNA MADE A MARBLE CAKE INSTEAD.
DID SHE GIVE IT TO YOU?

3

I really love *The Lord of the Rings.*

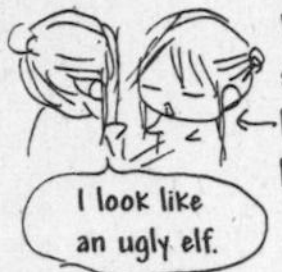

I look like an ugly elf.

When some hair is loose...

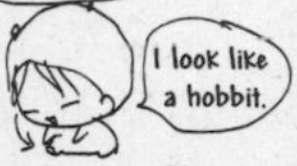

I look like a hobbit.

When I see hair on my feet...

Etc.

But I'm not a hobbit or an elf, so I should probably take better care of my appearance.

I wanted a complete collection, so I bought both the normal and the director's versions. The collector's cards that came in the director's edition of "Two Towers" were both of Gandalf. For a moment, I wondered if all the cards would be him. Gandalf... I mean, I don't have a favorite character, but I don't want two of him...

Changing the topic...The beauty salon that Haruna goes to is modeled after an actual one. My cousin works there, so if you know it, please try it! (^__^)

Well, see you in the next volume!

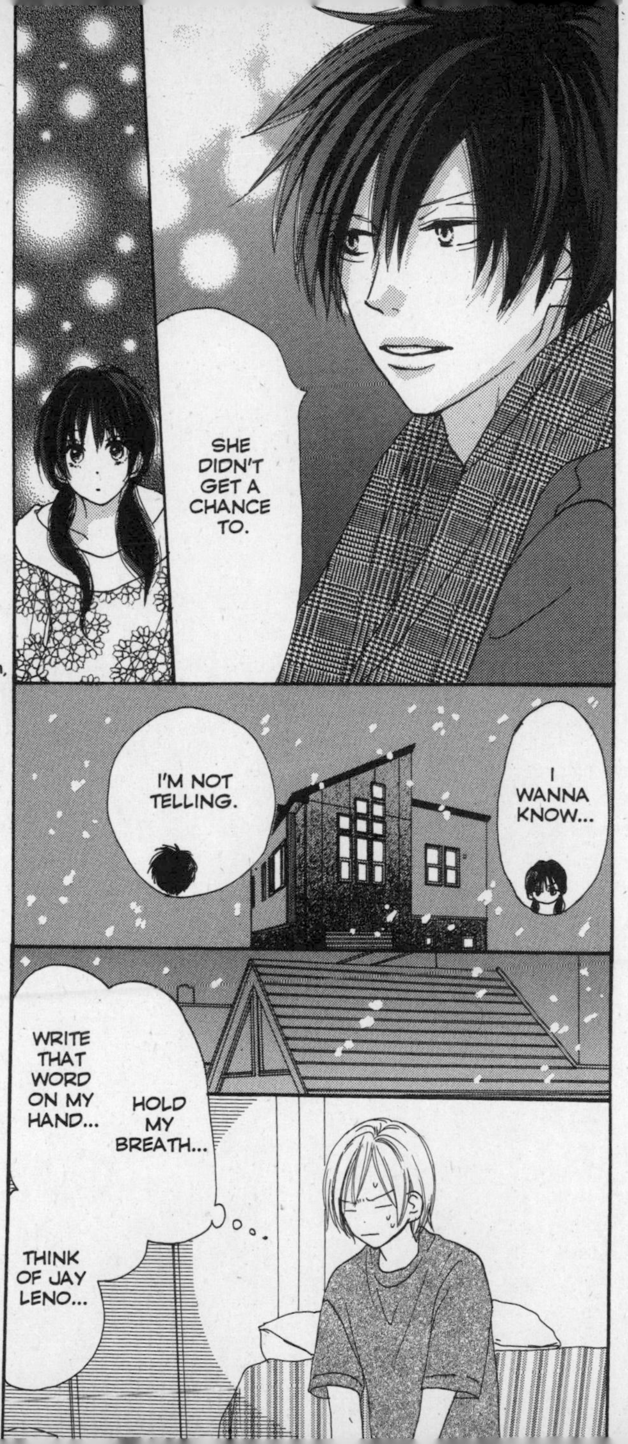

SHE DIDN'T GET A CHANCE TO.
I WANNA KNOW...
I'M NOT TELLING.
WRITE THAT WORD ON MY HAND...
HOLD MY BREATH...
THINK OF JAY LENO...

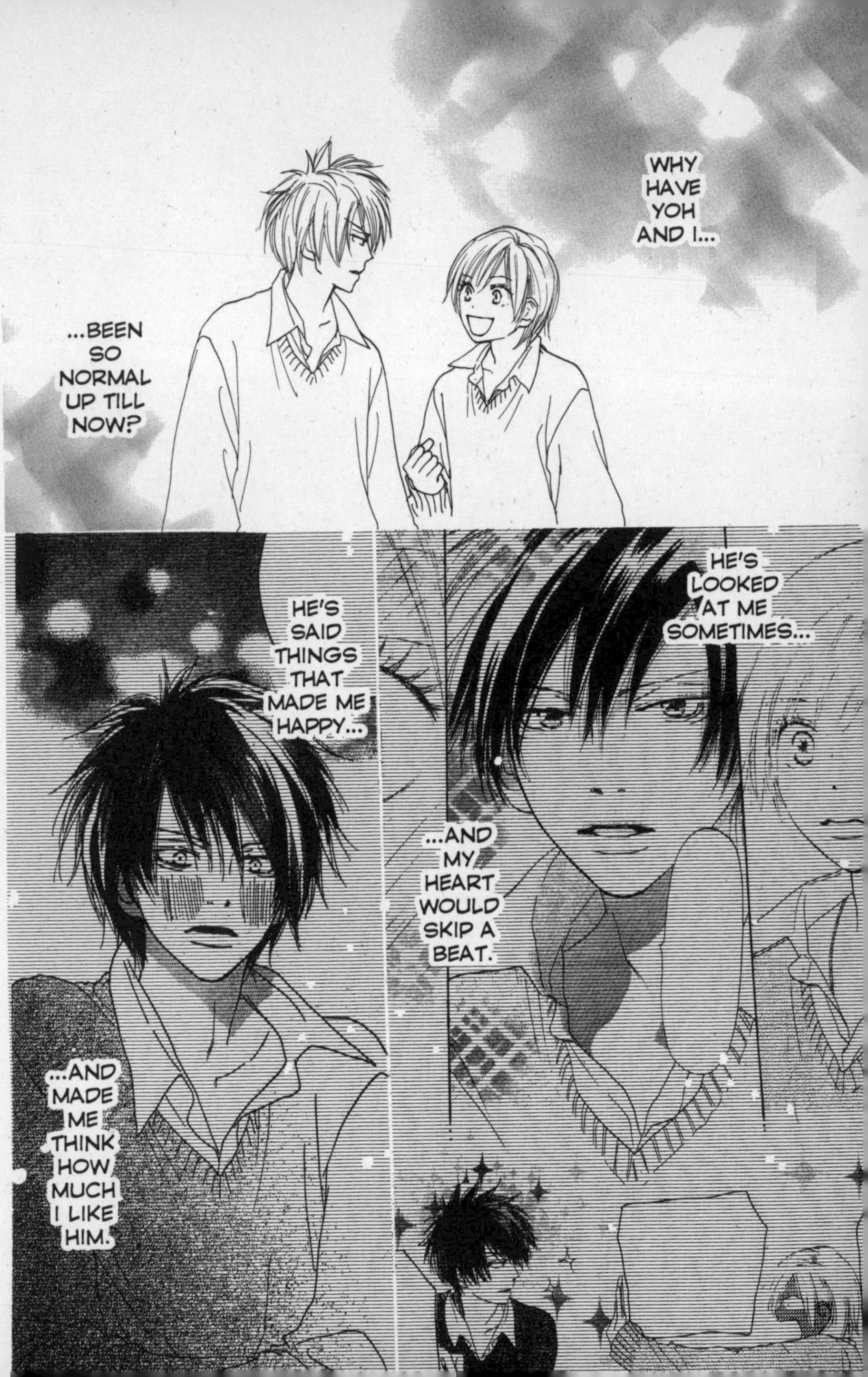
WHY HAVE YOH AND I...
...BEEN SO NORMAL UP TILL NOW?
HE'S LOOKED AT ME SOMETIMES...
...AND MY HEART WOULD SKIP A BEAT.
HE'S SAID THINGS THAT MADE ME HAPPY...
...AND MADE ME THINK HOW MUCH I LIKE HIM.

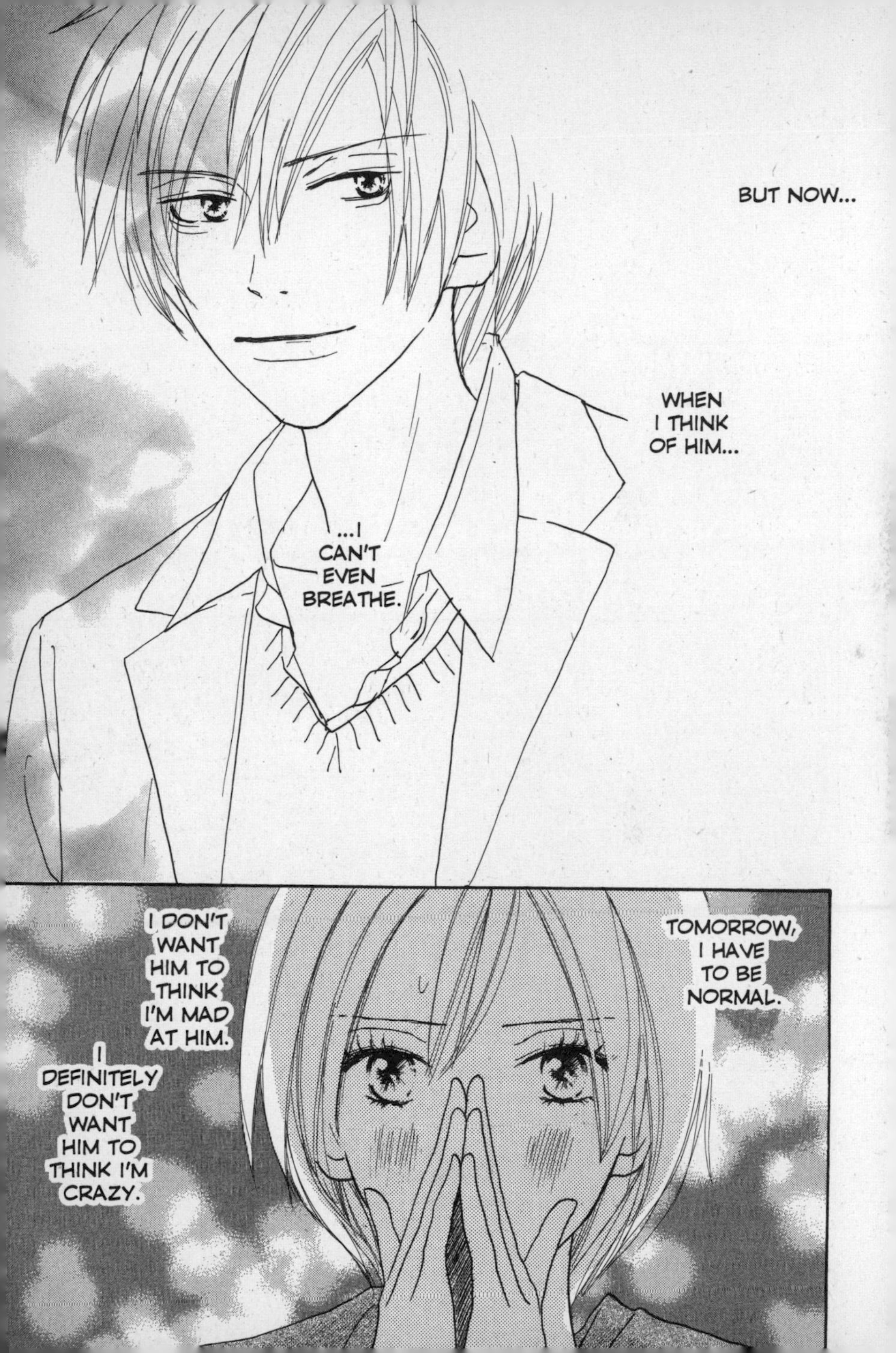
BUT NOW...
WHEN I THINK OF HIM...
...I CAN'T EVEN BREATHE.
TOMORROW, I HAVE TO BE NORMAL.
I DON'T WANT HIM TO THINK I'M MAD AT HIM.
I DEFINITELY DON'T WANT HIM TO THINK I'M CRAZY.

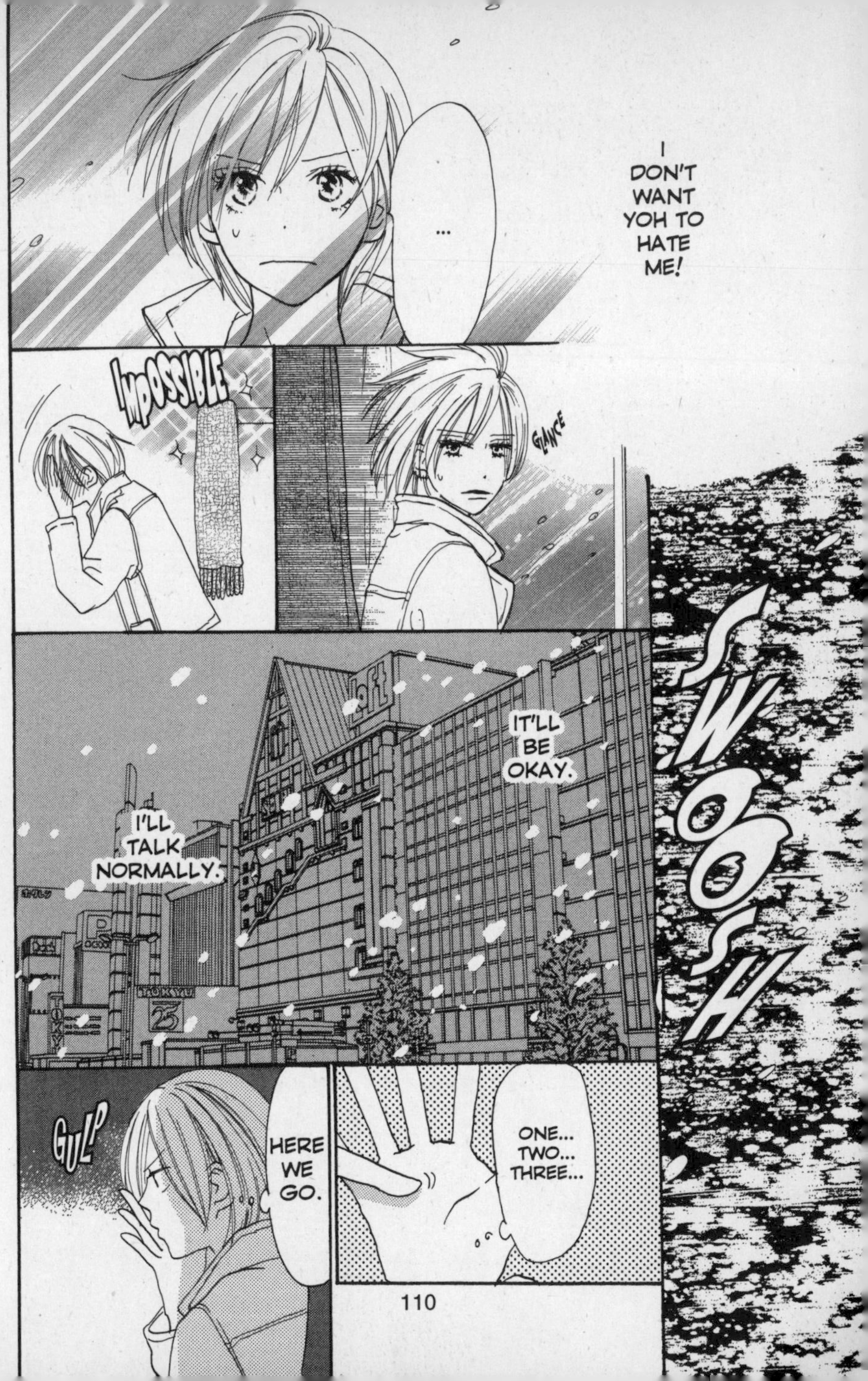
I DON'T WANT YOH TO HATE ME!
...
SWOOSH
GLANCE
IMPOSSIBLE
IT'LL BE OKAY.
I'LL TALK NORMALLY.
ONE... TWO... THREE...
HERE WE GO.
GULP

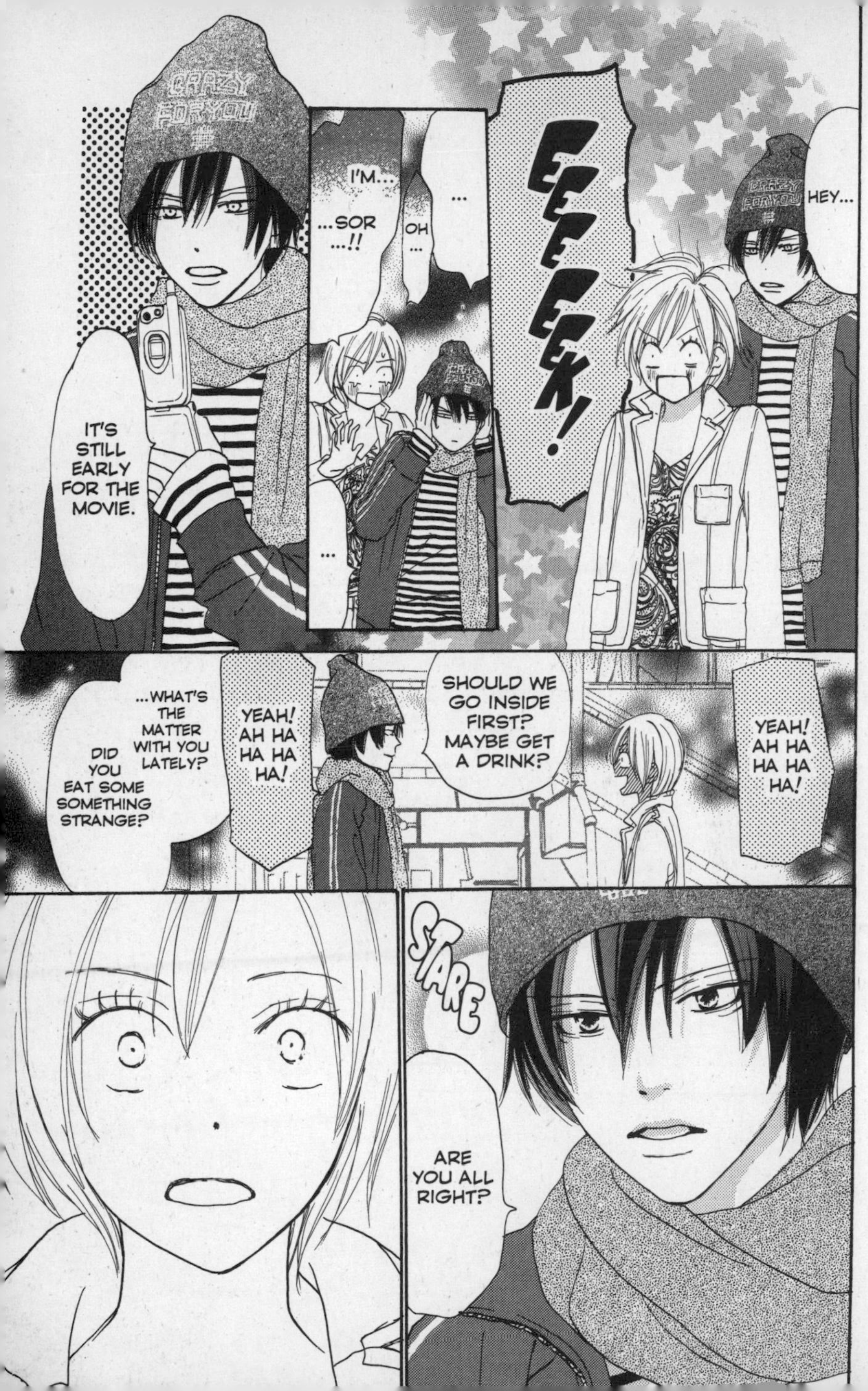
HEY...
EEEEEEK!
...
OH ...
I'M...
...SOR ...!!
...
IT'S STILL EARLY FOR THE MOVIE.
YEAH! AH HA HA HA HA!
SHOULD WE GO INSIDE FIRST? MAYBE GET A DRINK?
YEAH! AH HA HA HA HA!
...WHAT'S THE MATTER WITH YOU LATELY?
DID YOU EAT SOME SOMETHING STRANGE?
STARE
ARE YOU ALL RIGHT?

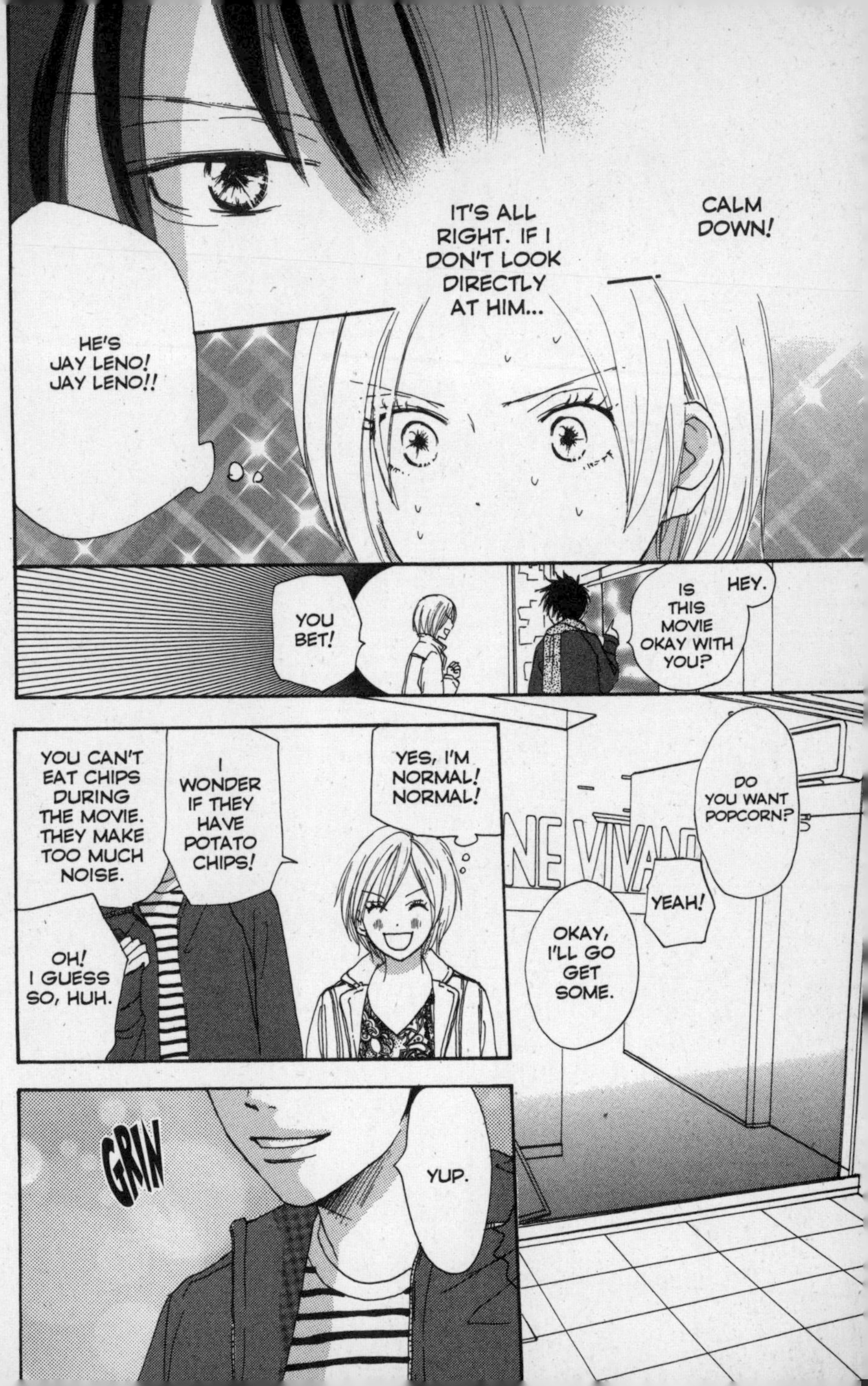
CALM DOWN!
IT'S ALL RIGHT. IF I DON'T LOOK DIRECTLY AT HIM...
HE'S JAY LENO! JAY LENO!!
HEY.
IS THIS MOVIE OKAY WITH YOU?
YOU BET!
DO YOU WANT POPCORN?
YEAH!
OKAY, I'LL GO GET SOME.
YES, I'M NORMAL! NORMAL!
I WONDER IF THEY HAVE POTATO CHIPS!
YOU CAN'T EAT CHIPS DURING THE MOVIE. THEY MAKE TOO MUCH NOISE.
OH! I GUESS SO, HUH.
YUP.
GRIN

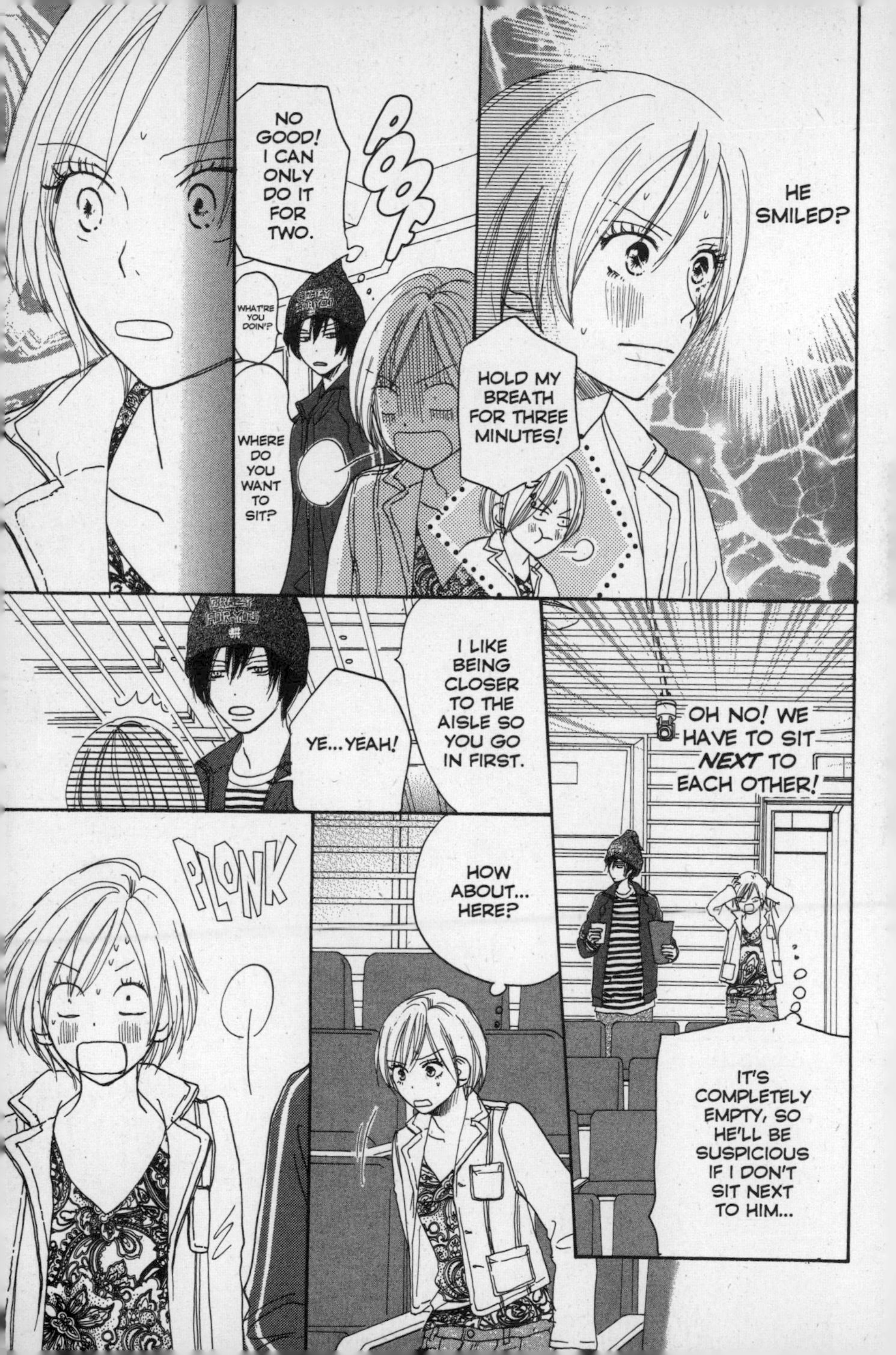
HE SMILED?
HOLD MY BREATH FOR THREE MINUTES!
NO GOOD! I CAN ONLY DO IT FOR TWO.
POOF
WHAT'RE YOU DOIN'?
WHERE DO YOU WANT TO SIT?
OH NO! WE HAVE TO SIT *NEXT* TO EACH OTHER!
I LIKE BEING CLOSER TO THE AISLE SO YOU GO IN FIRST.
YE...YEAH!
IT'S COMPLETELY EMPTY, SO HE'LL BE SUSPICIOUS IF I DON'T SIT NEXT TO HIM...
HOW ABOUT... HERE?
PLONK

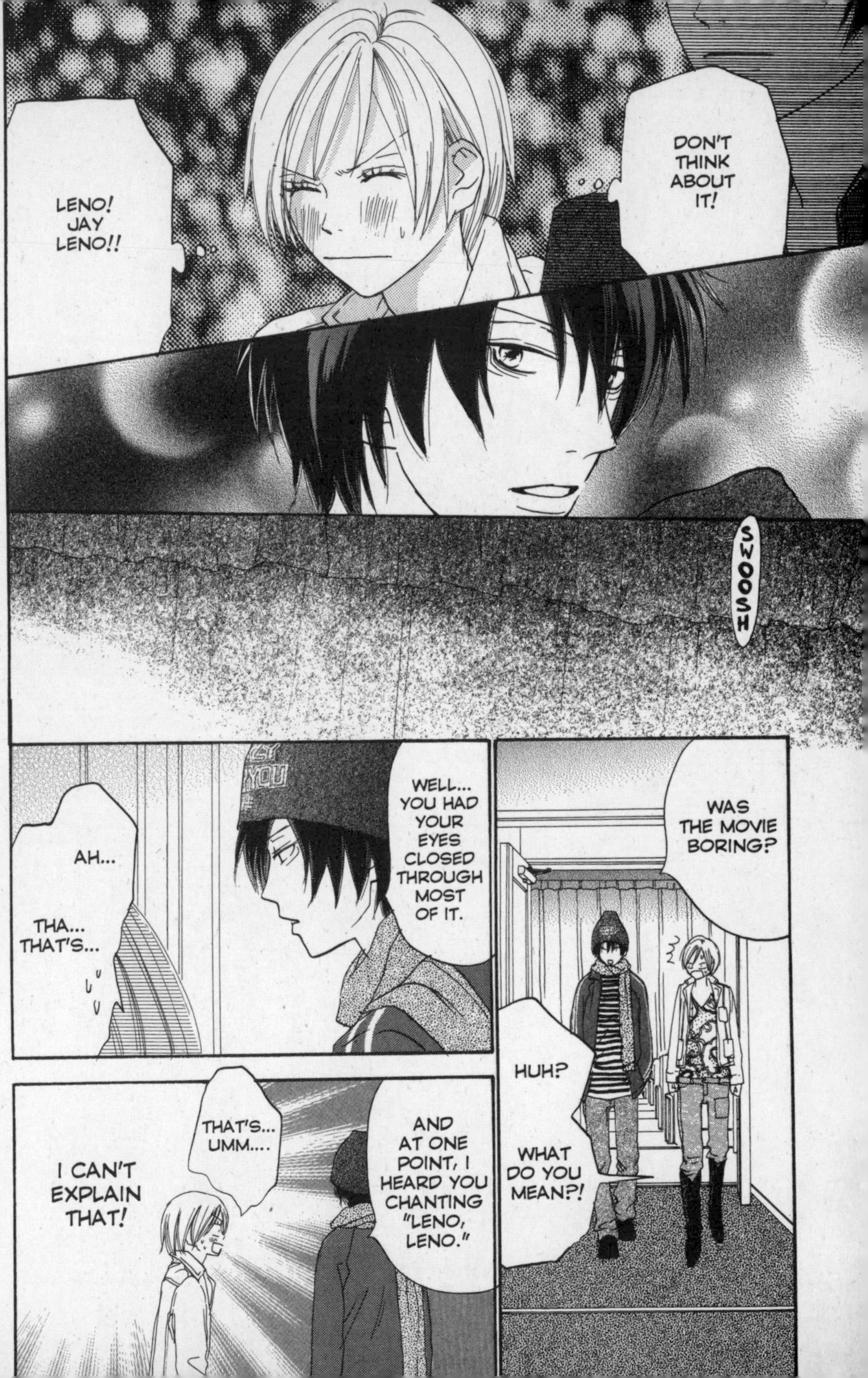
DON'T THINK ABOUT IT!
LENO! JAY LENO!!
SWOOSH
WAS THE MOVIE BORING?
HUH?
WHAT DO YOU MEAN?!
WELL... YOU HAD YOUR EYES CLOSED THROUGH MOST OF IT.
AH...
THA... THAT'S...
AND AT ONE POINT, I HEARD YOU CHANTING "LENO, LENO."
THAT'S... UMM....
I CAN'T EXPLAIN THAT!

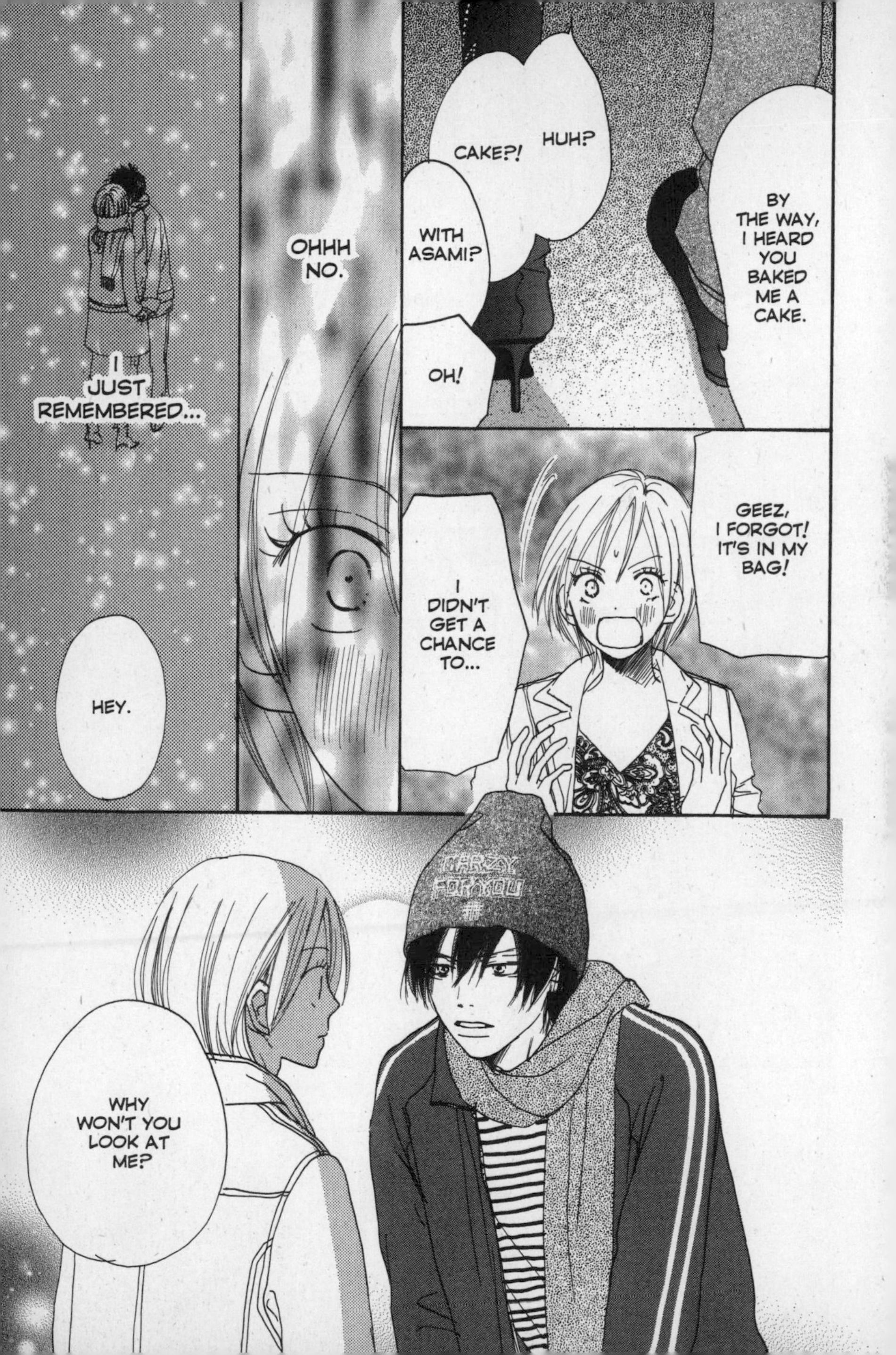
BY THE WAY, I HEARD YOU BAKED ME A CAKE.
HUH?
CAKE?!
WITH ASAMI?
OH!
GEEZ, I FORGOT! IT'S IN MY BAG!
I DIDN'T GET A CHANCE TO...
OHHH NO.
I JUST REMEMBERED...
HEY.
CRAZY FOR YOU
WHY WON'T YOU LOOK AT ME?

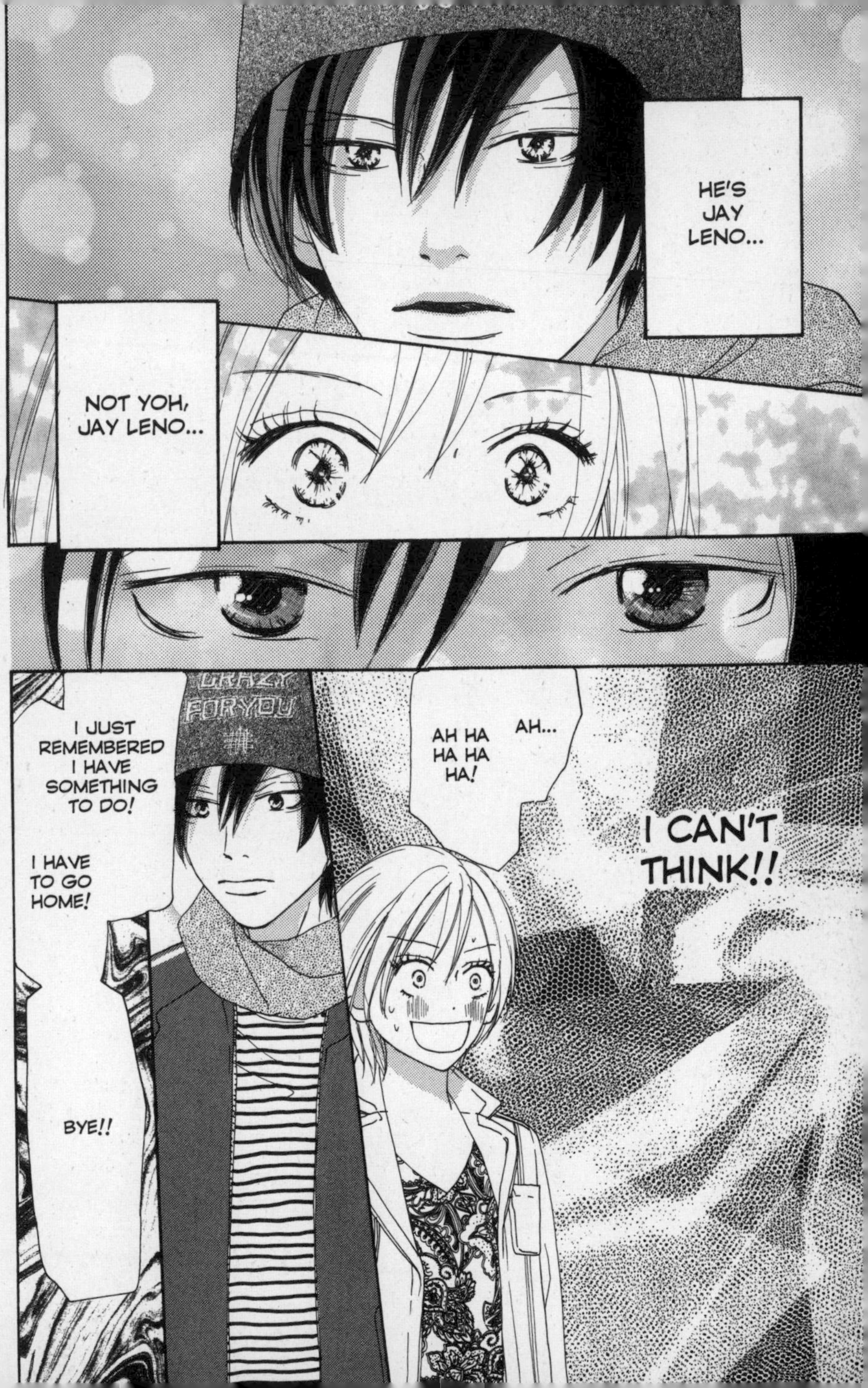
HE'S JAY LENO...
NOT YOH, JAY LENO...
I CAN'T THINK!!
AH...
AH HA HA HA HA!
CRAZY FORYOU
I JUST REMEMBERED I HAVE SOMETHING TO DO!
I HAVE TO GO HOME!
BYE!!

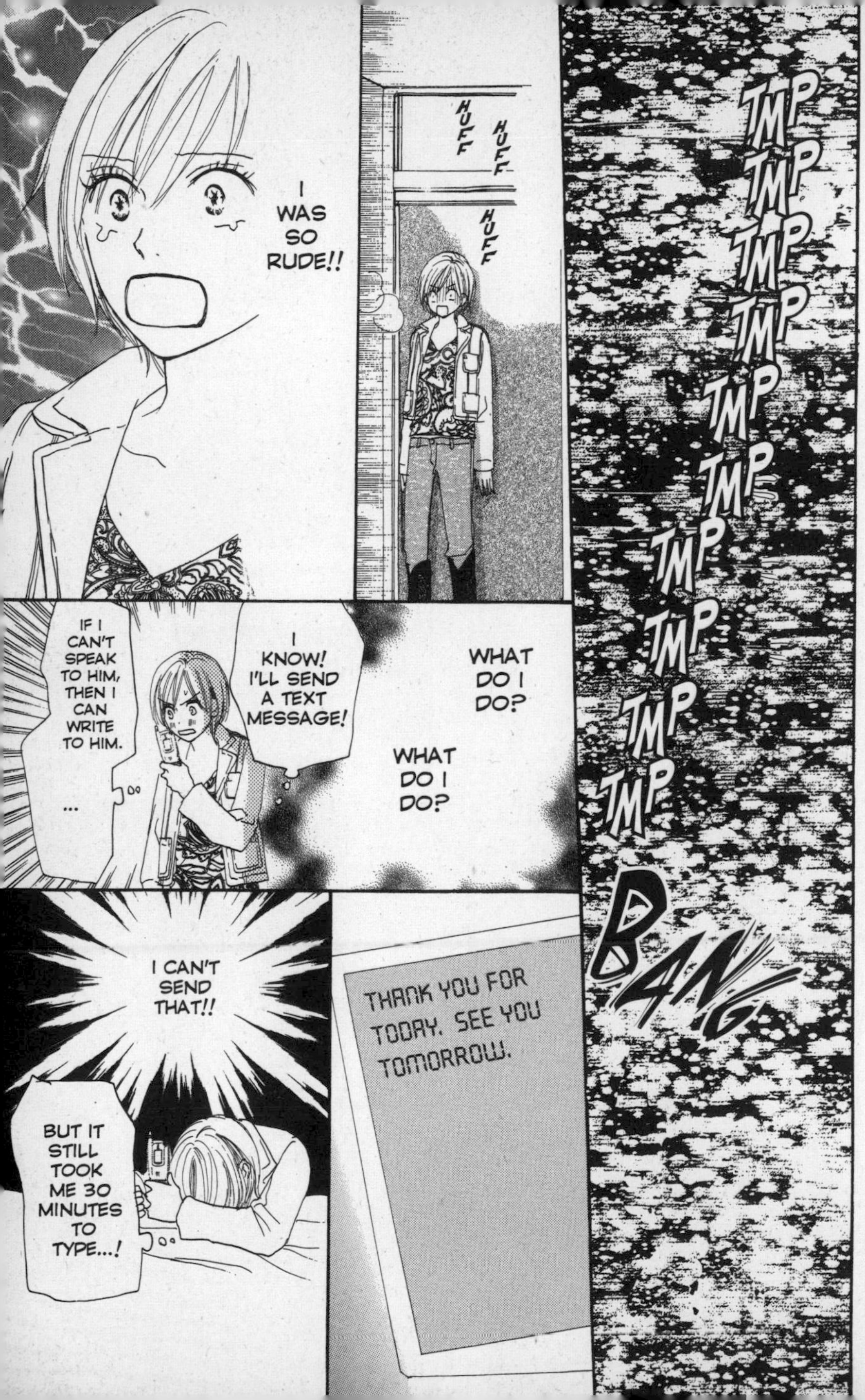
TMP TMP TMP TMP TMP TMP TMP TMP TMP TMP TMP TMP
BANG
HUFF HUFF HUFF
I WAS SO RUDE!!
WHAT DO I DO?
WHAT DO I DO?
I KNOW! I'LL SEND A TEXT MESSAGE!
IF I CAN'T SPEAK TO HIM, THEN I CAN WRITE TO HIM.
...
THANK YOU FOR TODAY. SEE YOU TOMORROW.
I CAN'T SEND THAT!!
BUT IT STILL TOOK ME 30 MINUTES TO TYPE...!

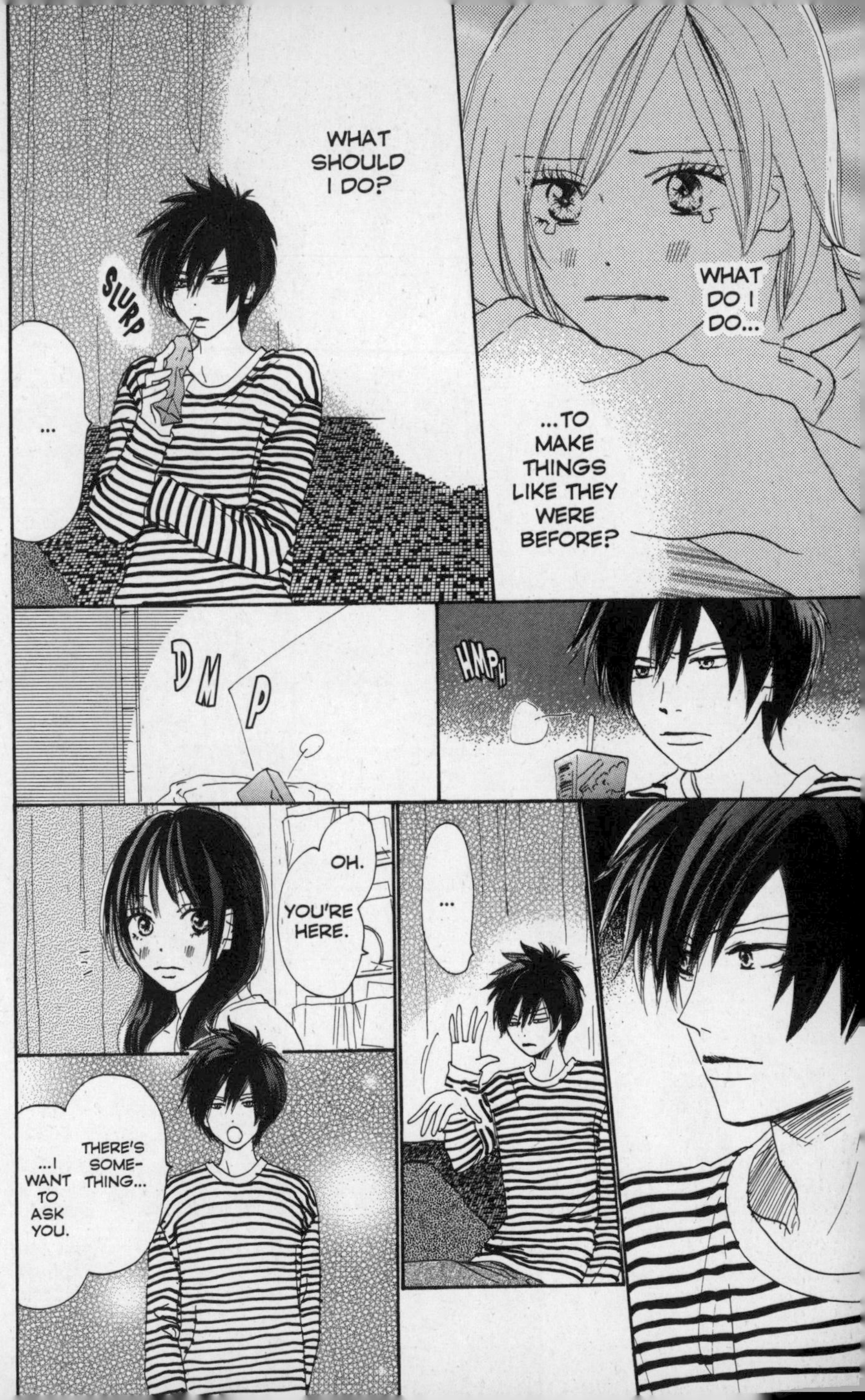
WHAT DO I DO...
...TO MAKE THINGS LIKE THEY WERE BEFORE?
WHAT SHOULD I DO?
SLURP
...
HMPH
DMP
...
OH.
YOU'RE HERE.
THERE'S SOMETHING...
...I WANT TO ASK YOU.

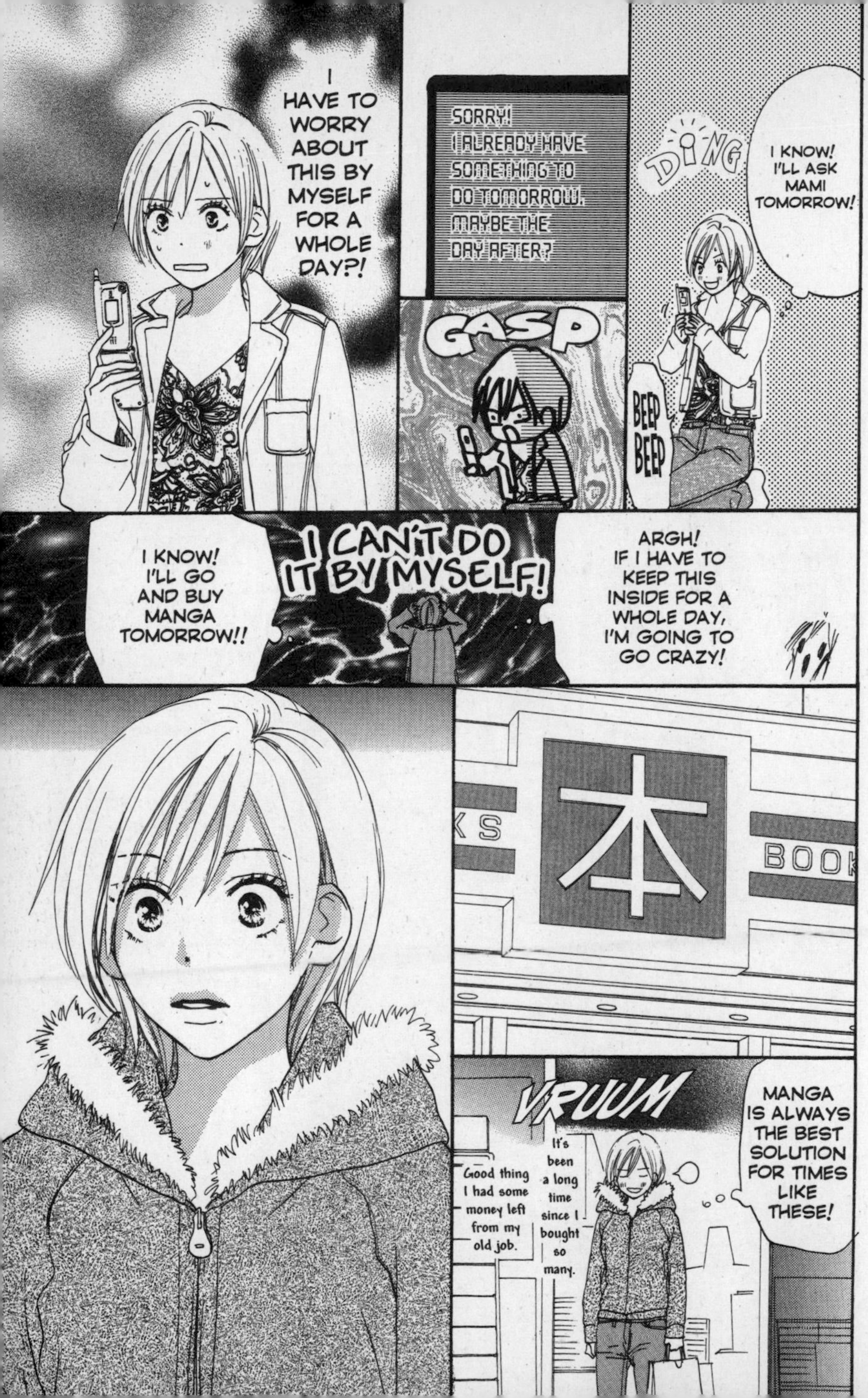
DING
I KNOW! I'LL ASK MAMI TOMORROW!
BEEP BEEP
SORRY! I ALREADY HAVE SOMETHING TO DO TOMORROW. MAYBE THE DAY AFTER?
GASP
I HAVE TO WORRY ABOUT THIS BY MYSELF FOR A WHOLE DAY?!
ARGH! IF I HAVE TO KEEP THIS INSIDE FOR A WHOLE DAY, I'M GOING TO GO CRAZY!
I CAN'T DO IT BY MYSELF!
I KNOW! I'LL GO AND BUY MANGA TOMORROW!!
BOOK
本
KS
VRUUM
MANGA IS ALWAYS THE BEST SOLUTION FOR TIMES LIKE THESE!
It's been a long time since I bought so many.
Good thing I had some money left from my old job.

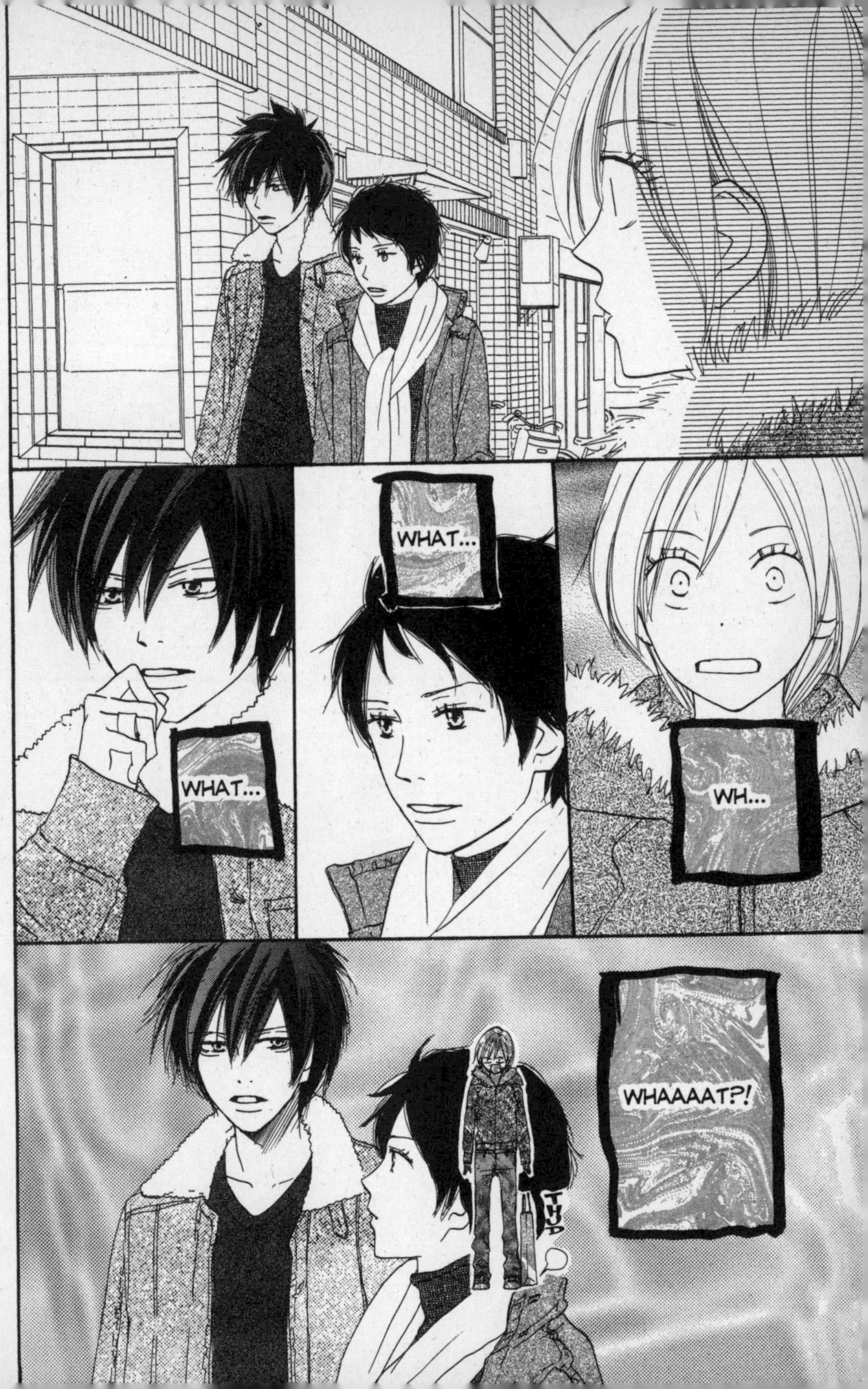
WH...
WHAT...
WHAT...
WHAAAAT?!
THUD

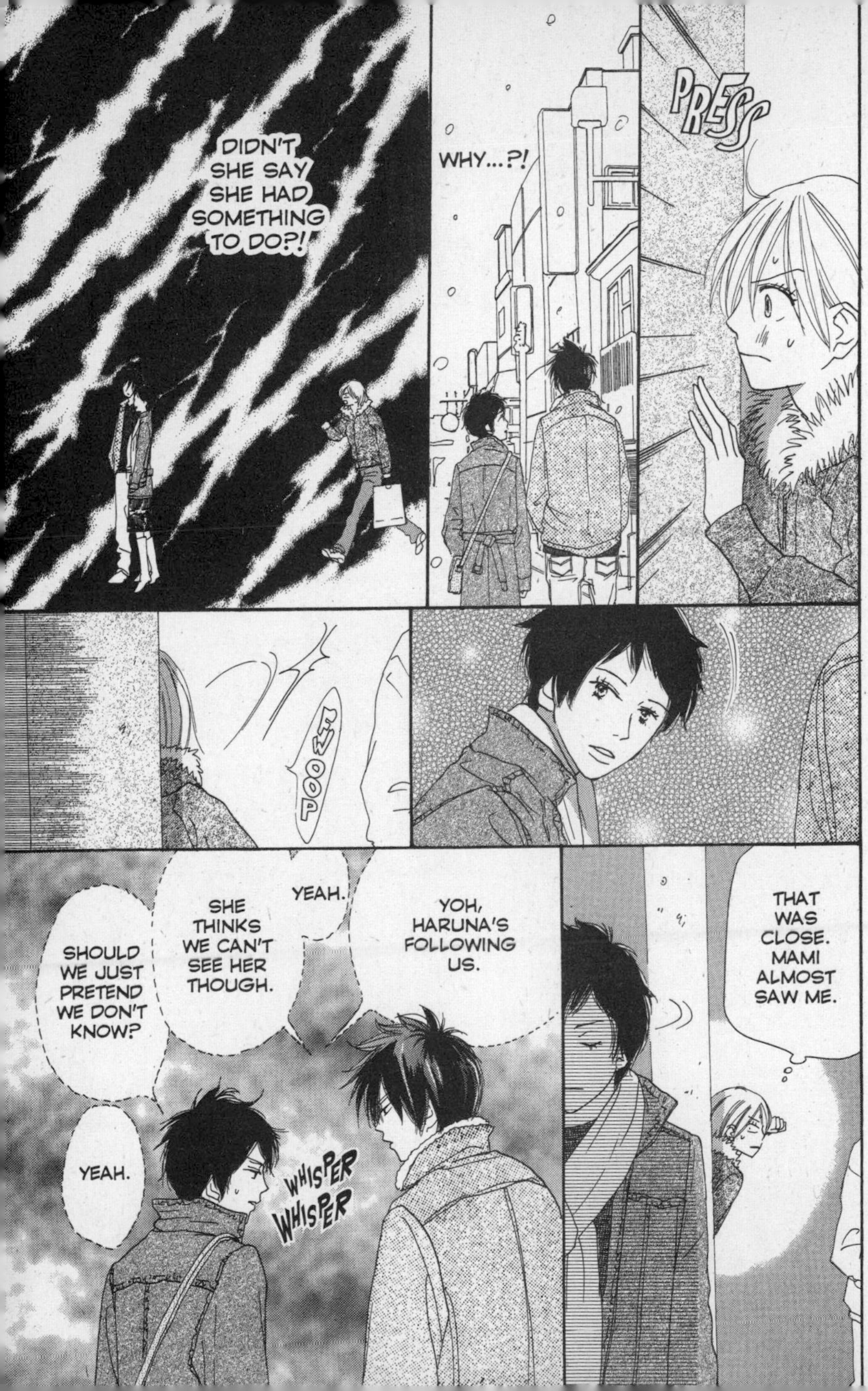
PRESS
WHY...?!
DIDN'T SHE SAY SHE HAD SOMETHING TO DO?!
FWOOP
THAT WAS CLOSE. MAMI ALMOST SAW ME.
YOH, HARUNA'S FOLLOWING US.
YEAH.
SHE THINKS WE CAN'T SEE HER THOUGH.
SHOULD WE JUST PRETEND WE DON'T KNOW?
WHISPER WHISPER
YEAH.

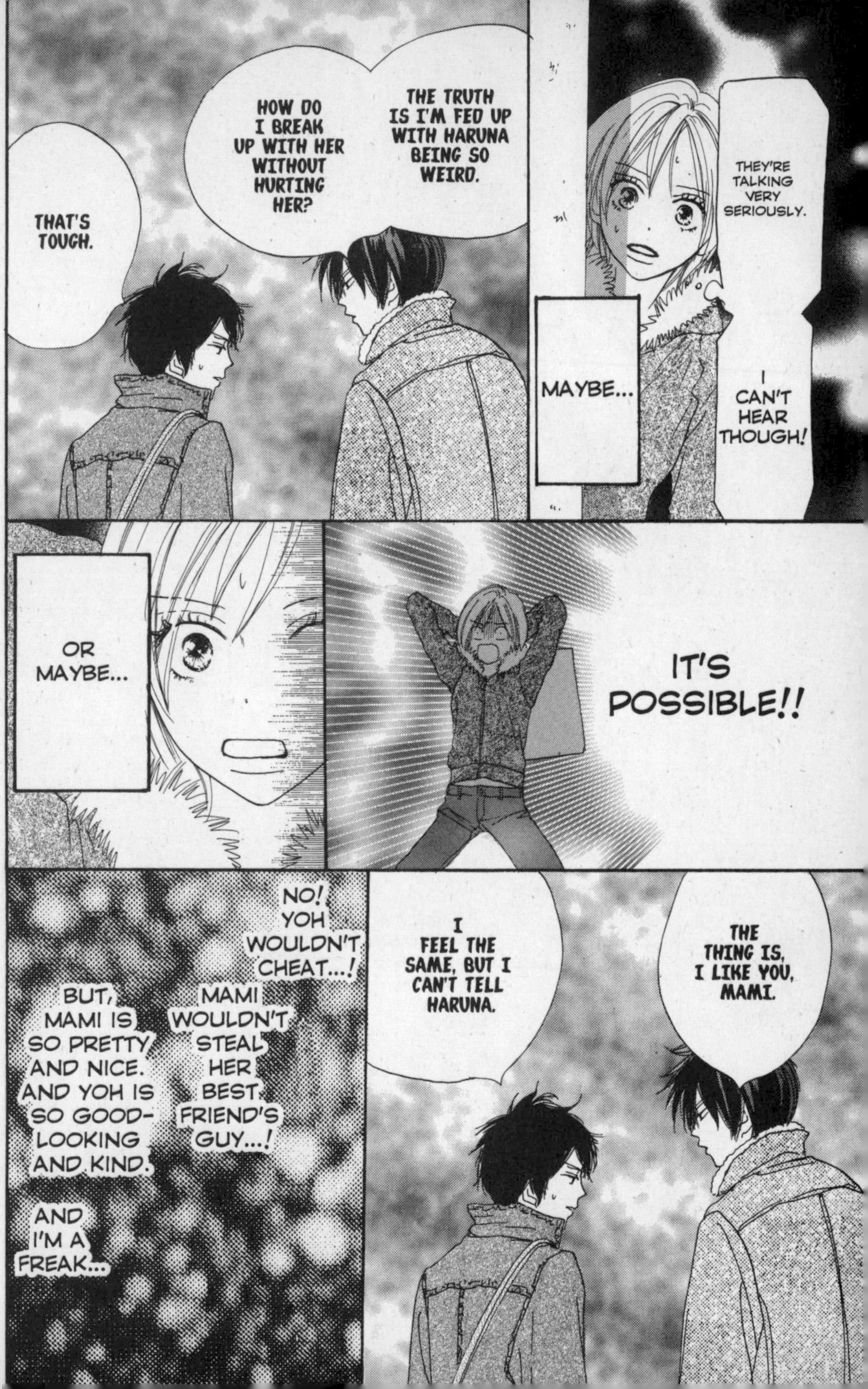

THEY'RE TALKING VERY SERIOUSLY.
I CAN'T HEAR THOUGH!
MAYBE...
THE TRUTH IS I'M FED UP WITH HARUNA BEING SO WEIRD.
HOW DO I BREAK UP WITH HER WITHOUT HURTING HER?
THAT'S TOUGH.
IT'S POSSIBLE!!
OR MAYBE...
THE THING IS, I LIKE YOU, MAMI.
I FEEL THE SAME, BUT I CAN'T TELL HARUNA.
NO! YOH WOULDN'T CHEAT...!
MAMI WOULDN'T STEAL HER BEST FRIEND'S GUY...!
BUT, MAMI IS SO PRETTY AND NICE. AND YOH IS SO GOOD-LOOKING AND KIND.
AND I'M A FREAK...

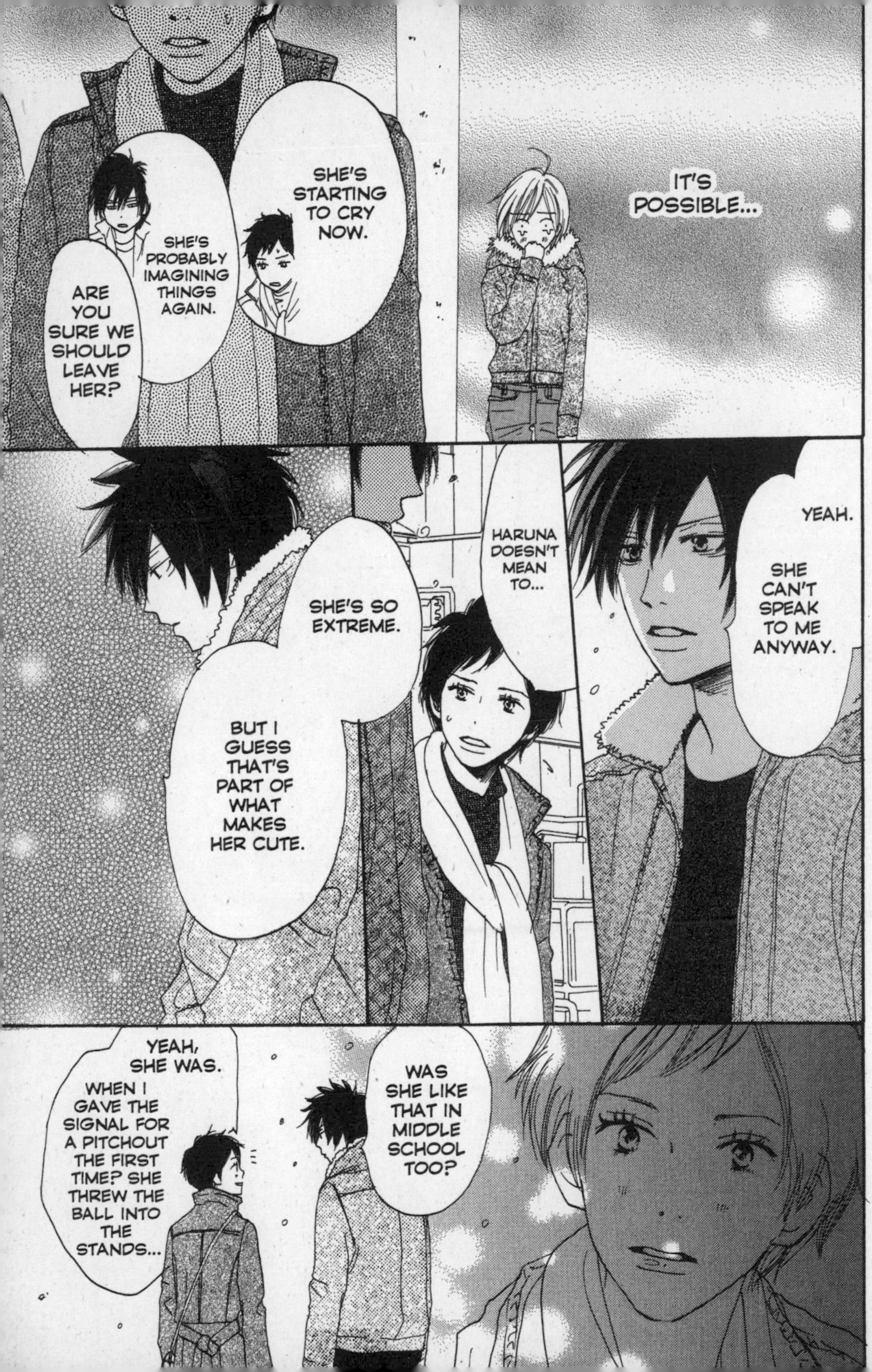
IT'S POSSIBLE...
SHE'S STARTING TO CRY NOW.
SHE'S PROBABLY IMAGINING THINGS AGAIN.
ARE YOU SURE WE SHOULD LEAVE HER?
YEAH.
SHE CAN'T SPEAK TO ME ANYWAY.
HARUNA DOESN'T MEAN TO...
SHE'S SO EXTREME.
BUT I GUESS THAT'S PART OF WHAT MAKES HER CUTE.
WAS SHE LIKE THAT IN MIDDLE SCHOOL TOO?
YEAH, SHE WAS.
WHEN I GAVE THE SIGNAL FOR A PITCHOUT THE FIRST TIME? SHE THREW THE BALL INTO THE STANDS...

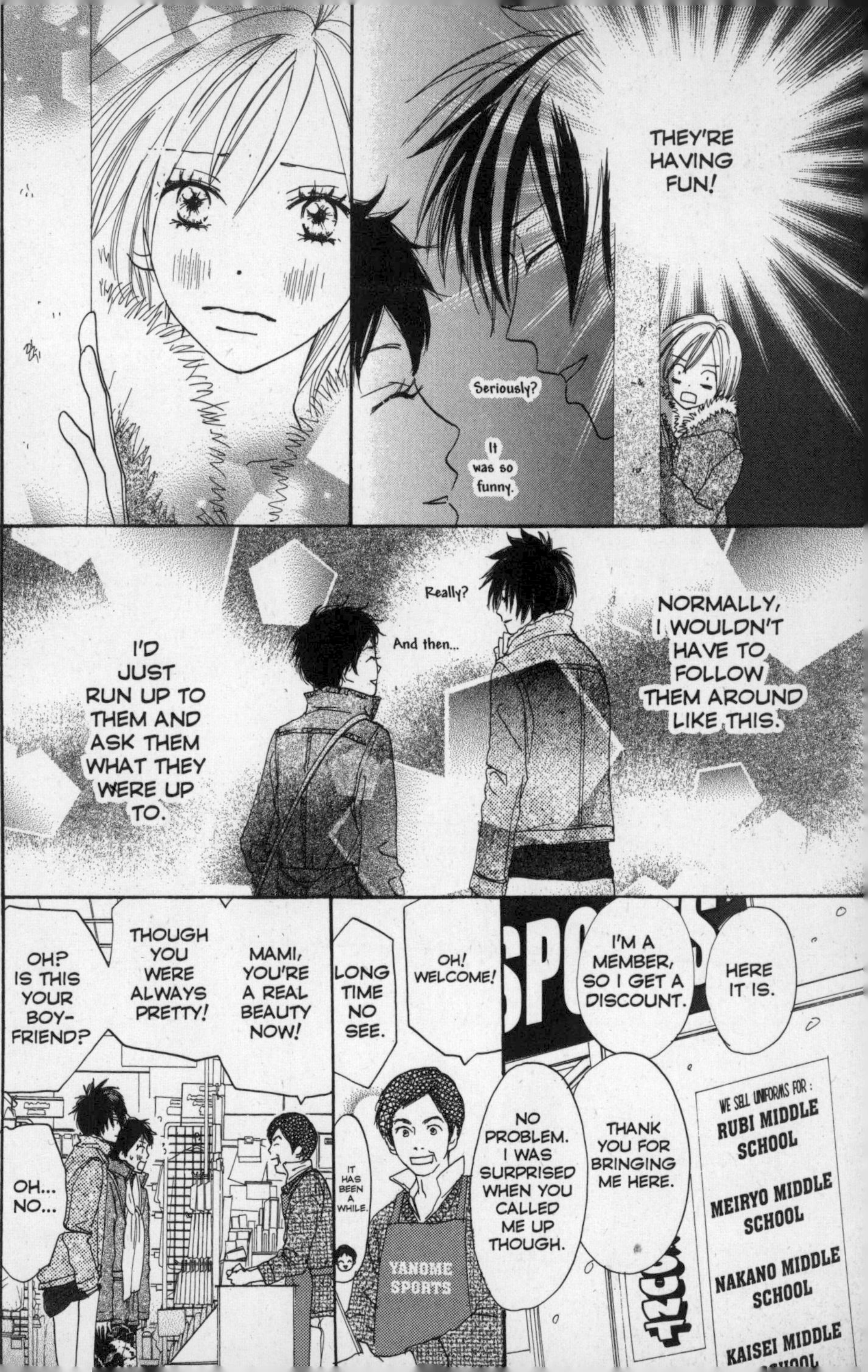
THEY'RE HAVING FUN!
Seriously?
It was so funny.
NORMALLY, I WOULDN'T HAVE TO FOLLOW THEM AROUND LIKE THIS.
Really?
And then...
I'D JUST RUN UP TO THEM AND ASK THEM WHAT THEY WERE UP TO.
SPORTS
HERE IT IS.
I'M A MEMBER, SO I GET A DISCOUNT.
THANK YOU FOR BRINGING ME HERE.
NO PROBLEM. I WAS SURPRISED WHEN YOU CALLED ME UP THOUGH.
WE SELL UNIFORMS FOR:
RUBI MIDDLE SCHOOL
MEIRYO MIDDLE SCHOOL
NAKANO MIDDLE SCHOOL
KAISEI MIDDLE SCHOOL
OH! WELCOME!
LONG TIME NO SEE.
IT HAS BEEN A WHILE.
YANOME SPORTS
MAMI, YOU'RE A REAL BEAUTY NOW!
THOUGH YOU WERE ALWAYS PRETTY!
OH? IS THIS YOUR BOY-FRIEND?
OH... NO...

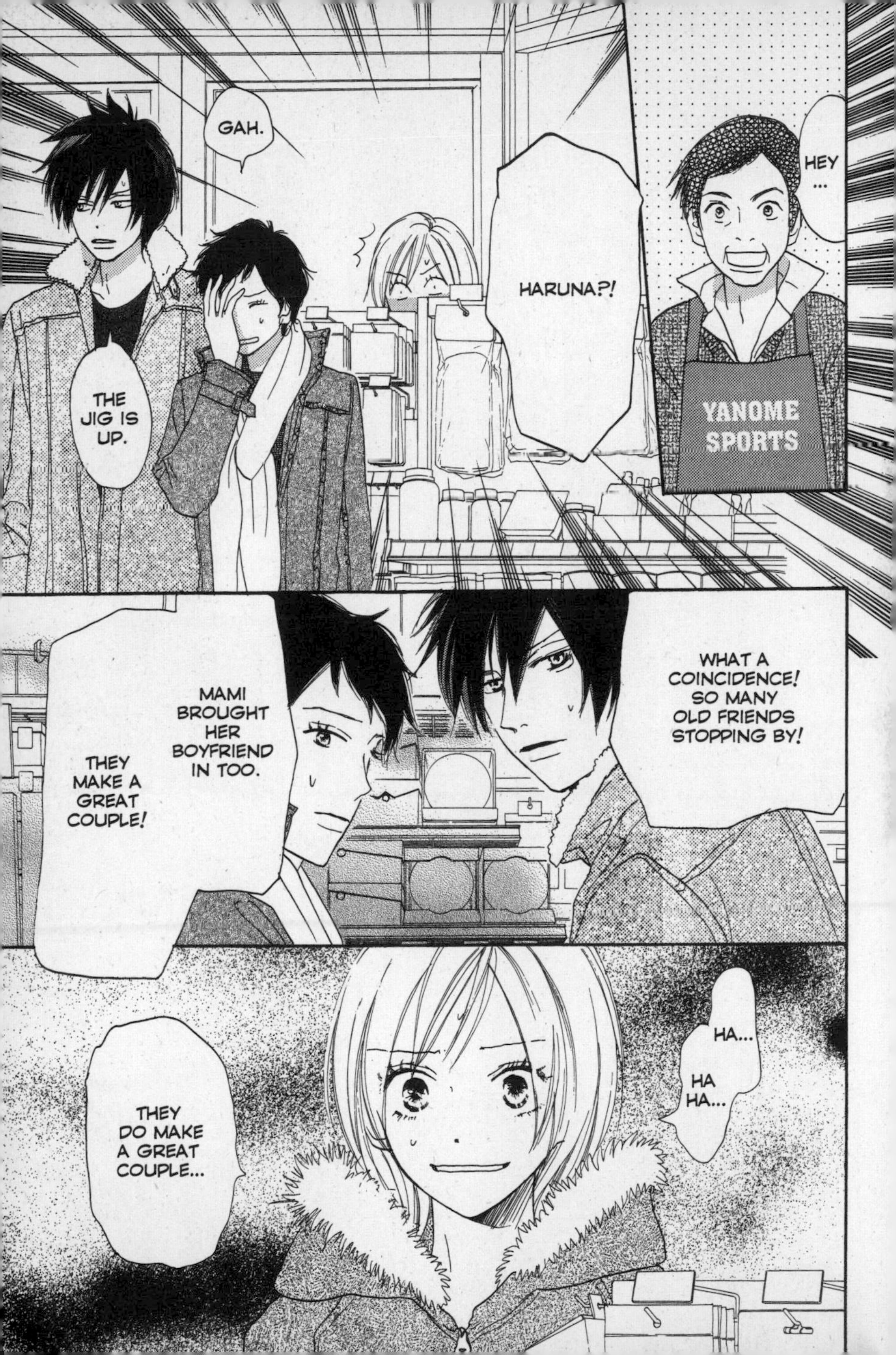
HEY ...
HARUNA?!
YANOME SPORTS
GAH.
THE JIG IS UP.
WHAT A COINCIDENCE! SO MANY OLD FRIENDS STOPPING BY!
MAMI BROUGHT HER BOYFRIEND IN TOO.
THEY MAKE A GREAT COUPLE!
HA... HA HA...
THEY DO MAKE A GREAT COUPLE...

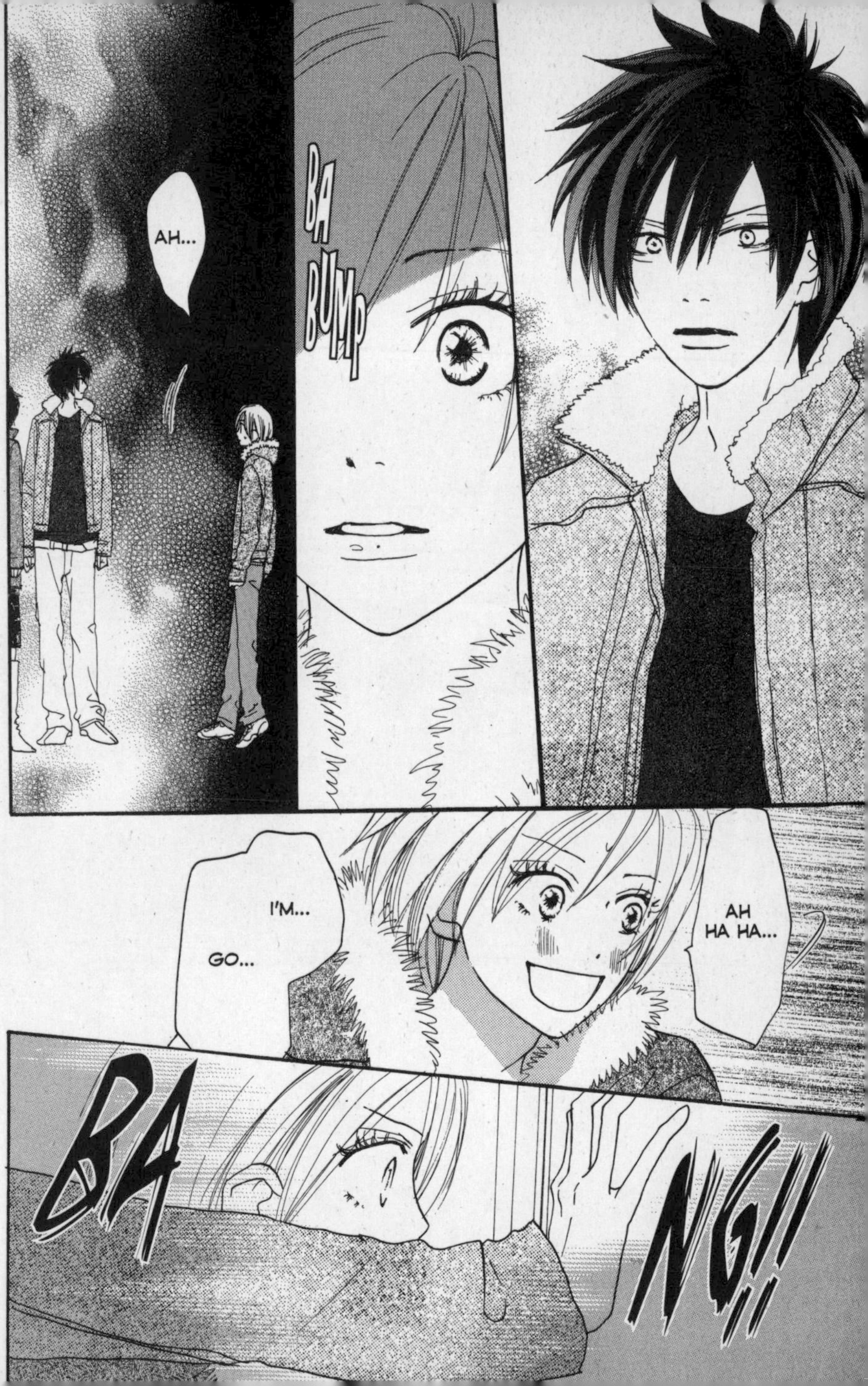
BA BUMP
AH...
AH HA HA...
I'M... GO...
BANG!!

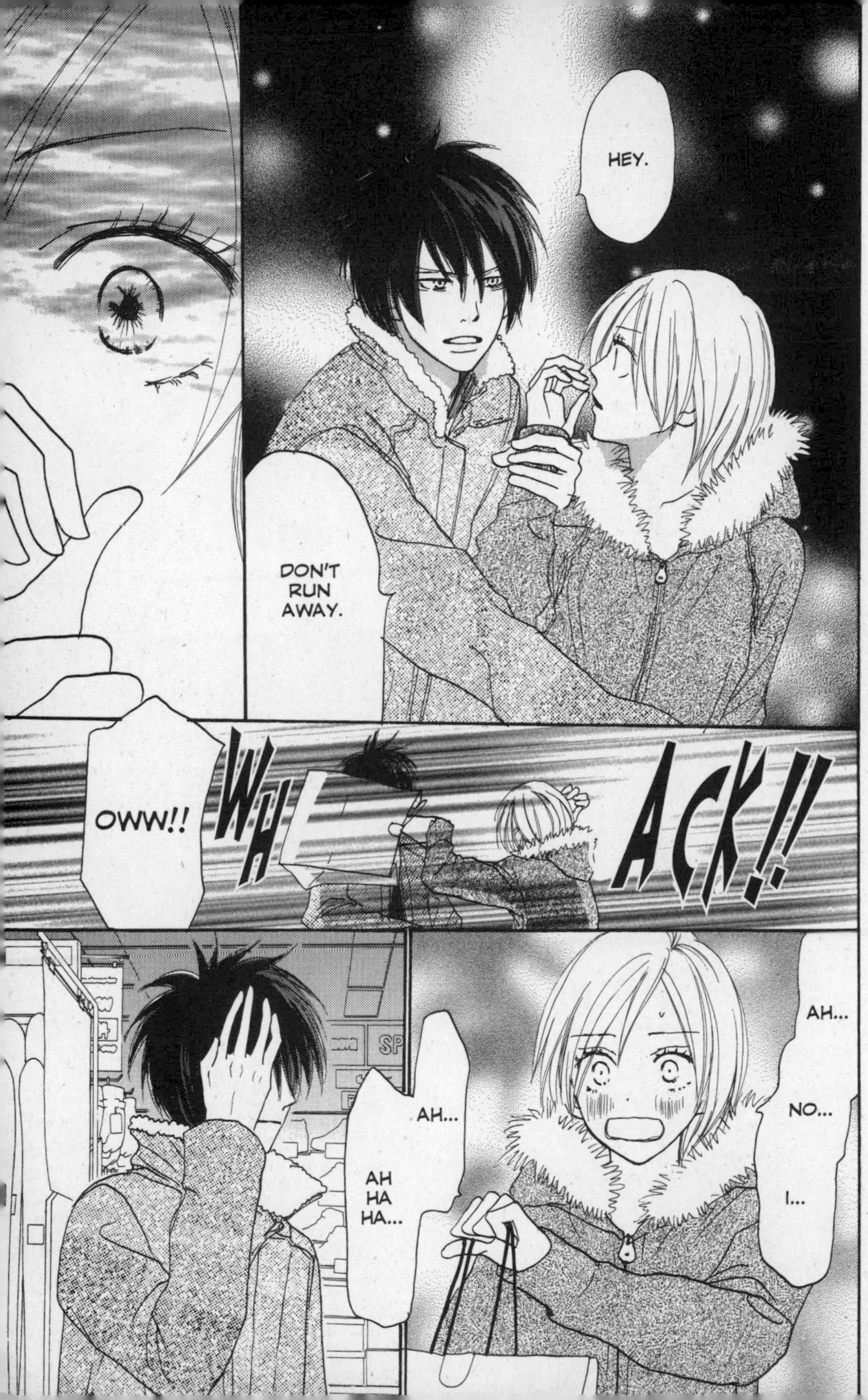
HEY.
DON'T RUN AWAY.
WHACK!!
OWW!!
AH...
NO...
I...
AH...
AH HA HA...

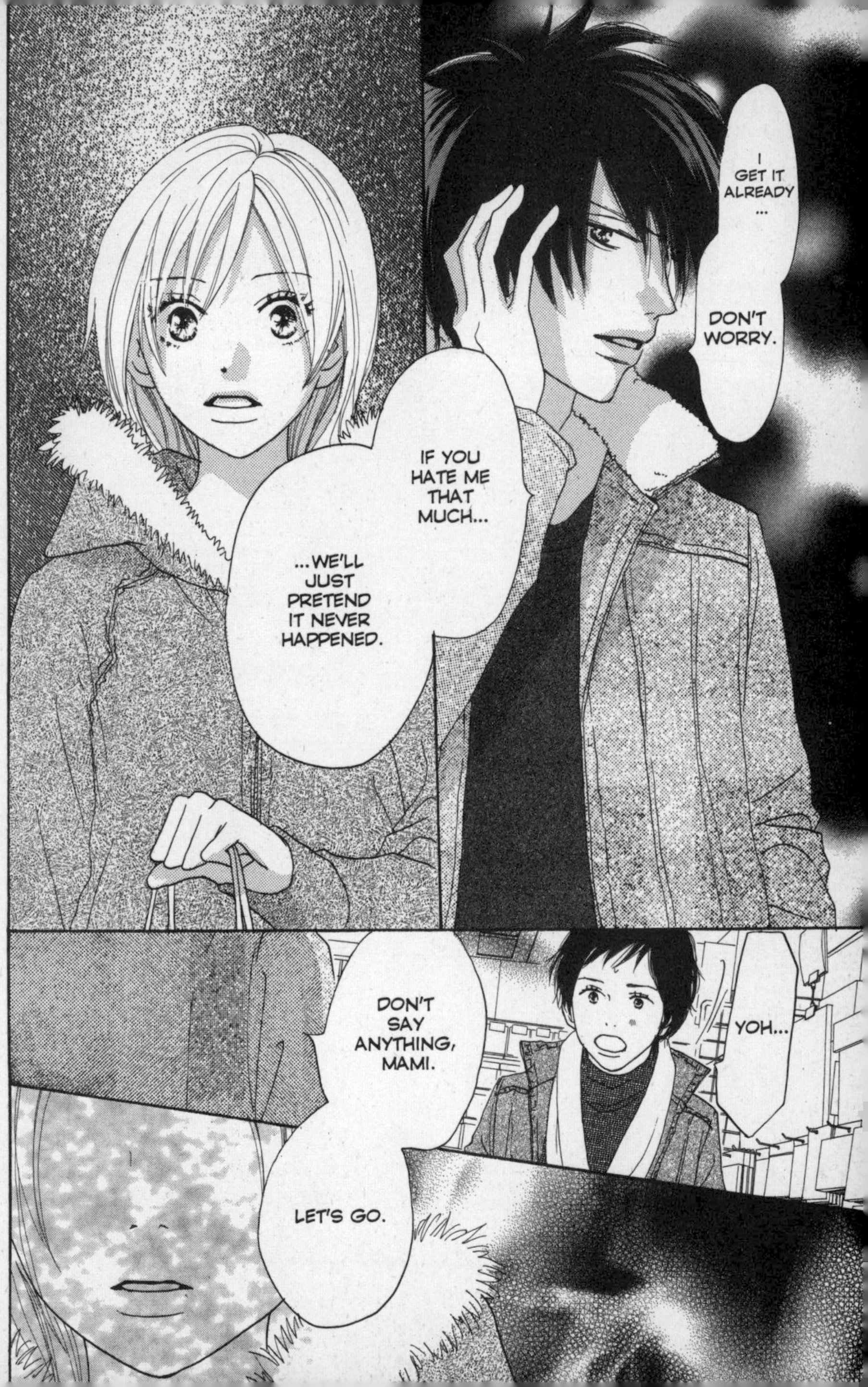
I GET IT ALREADY ...
DON'T WORRY.
IF YOU HATE ME THAT MUCH...
...WE'LL JUST PRETEND IT NEVER HAPPENED.
YOH...
DON'T SAY ANYTHING, MAMI.
LET'S GO.

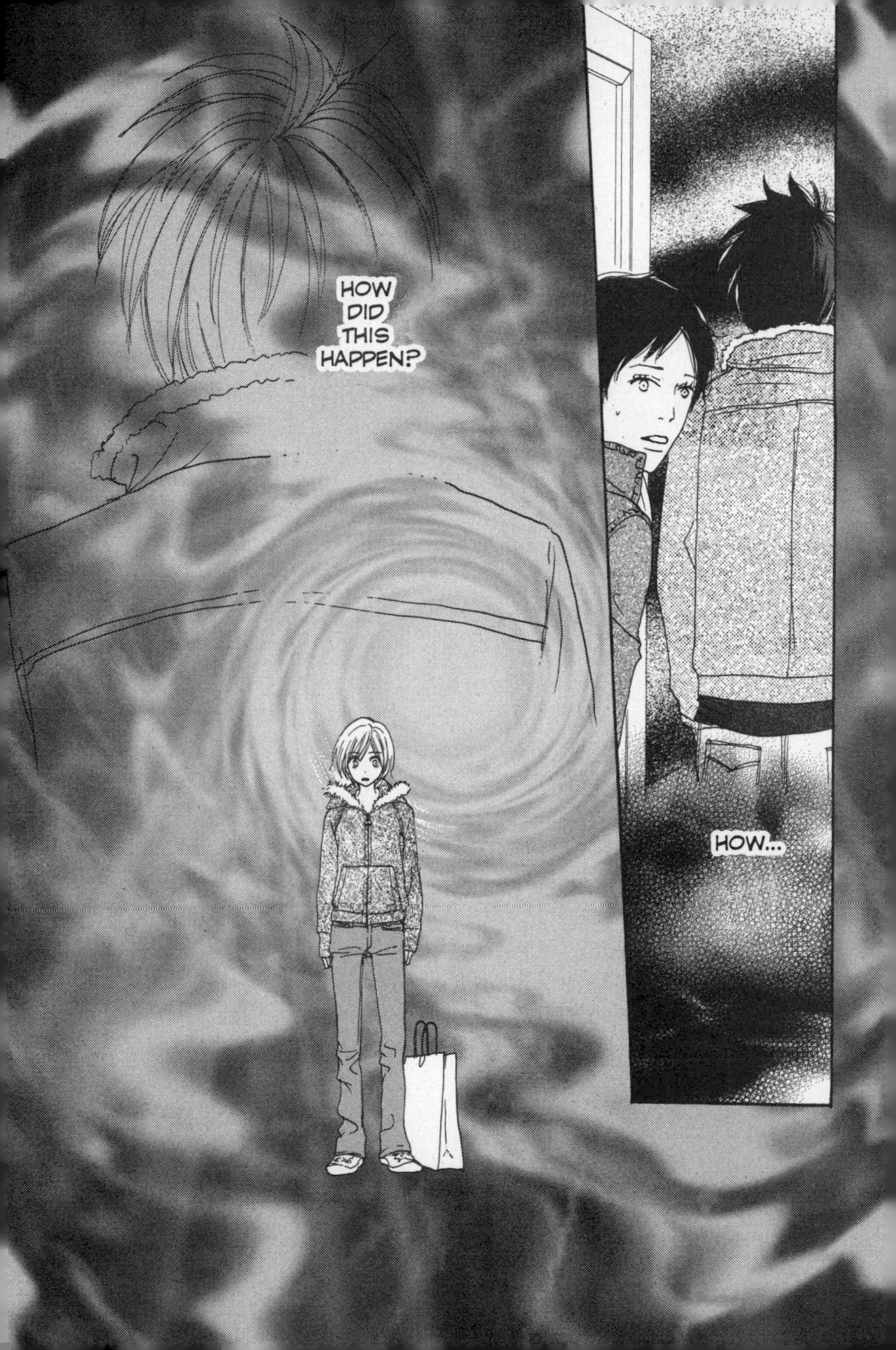
HOW...
HOW DID THIS HAPPEN?

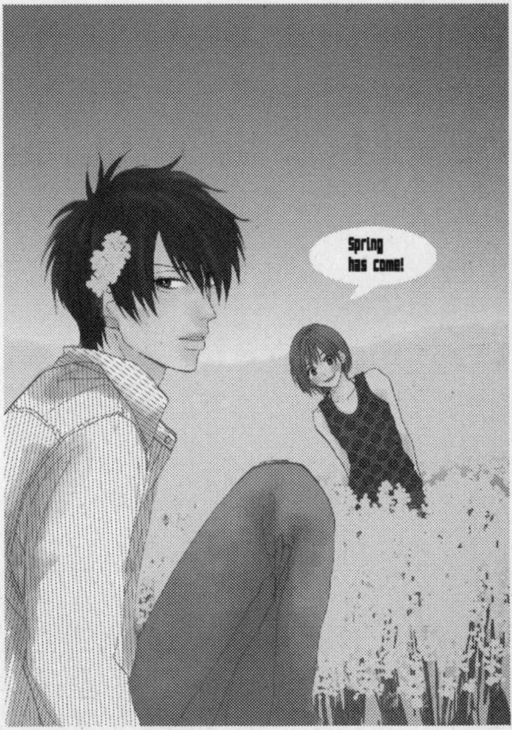
Spring
has come!

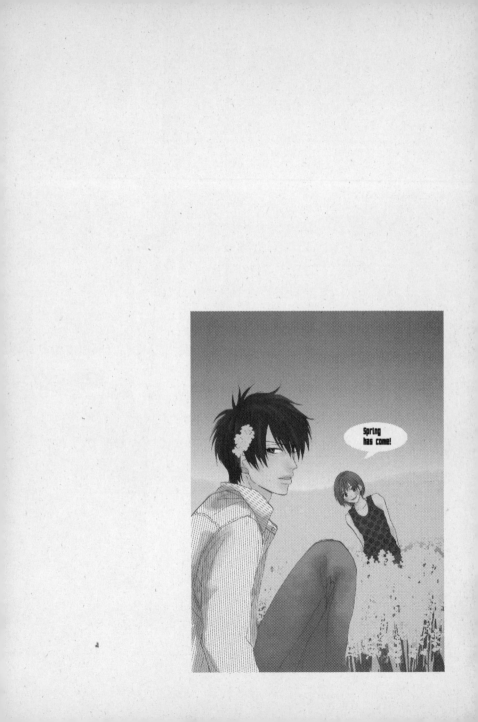

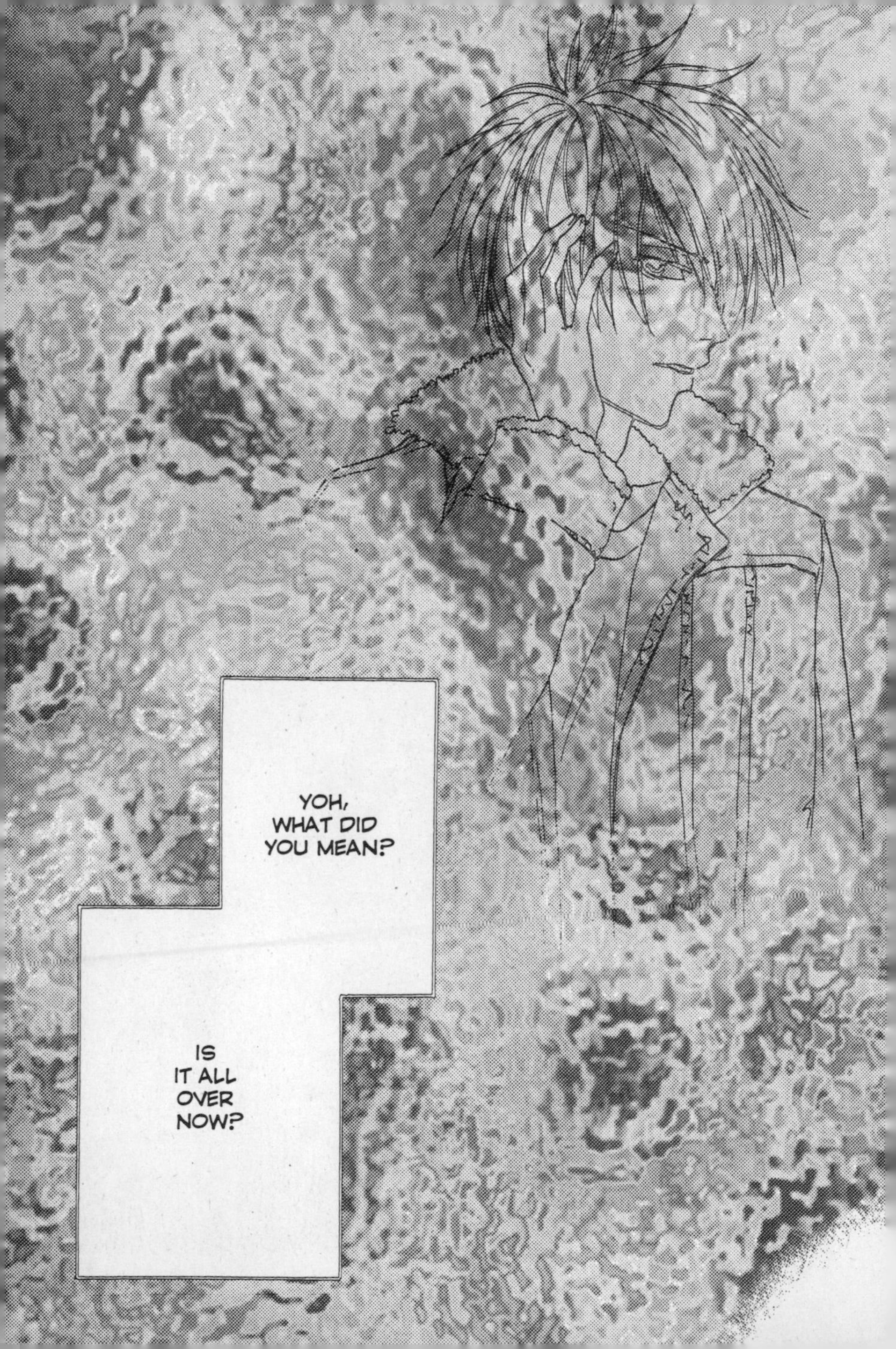
YOH, WHAT DID YOU MEAN?
IS IT ALL OVER NOW?

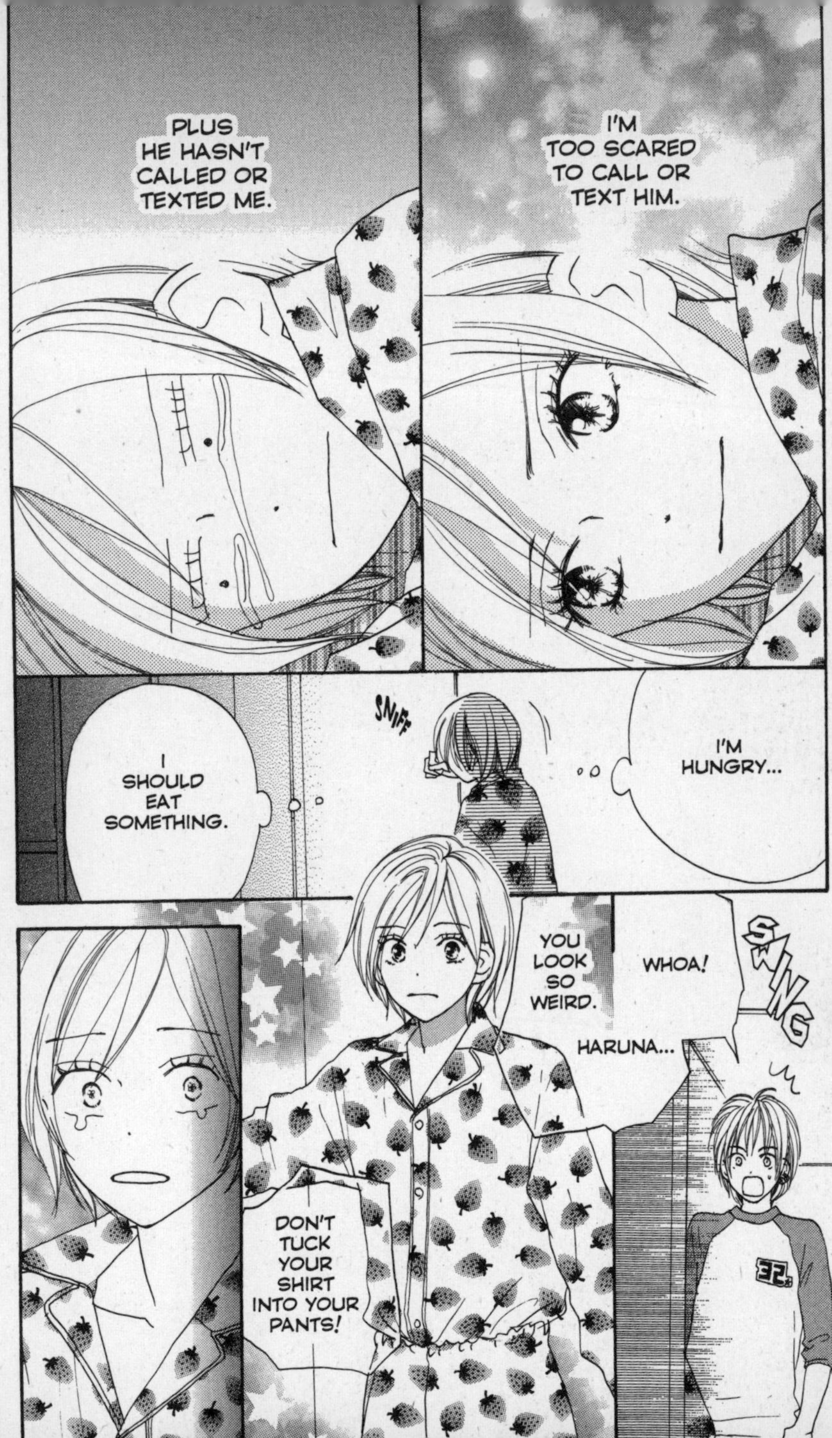
I'M TOO SCARED TO CALL OR TEXT HIM.
PLUS HE HASN'T CALLED OR TEXTED ME.
I'M HUNGRY...
SNIFF
I SHOULD EAT SOMETHING.
SWING
WHOA!
HARUNA...
YOU LOOK SO WEIRD.
DON'T TUCK YOUR SHIRT INTO YOUR PANTS!

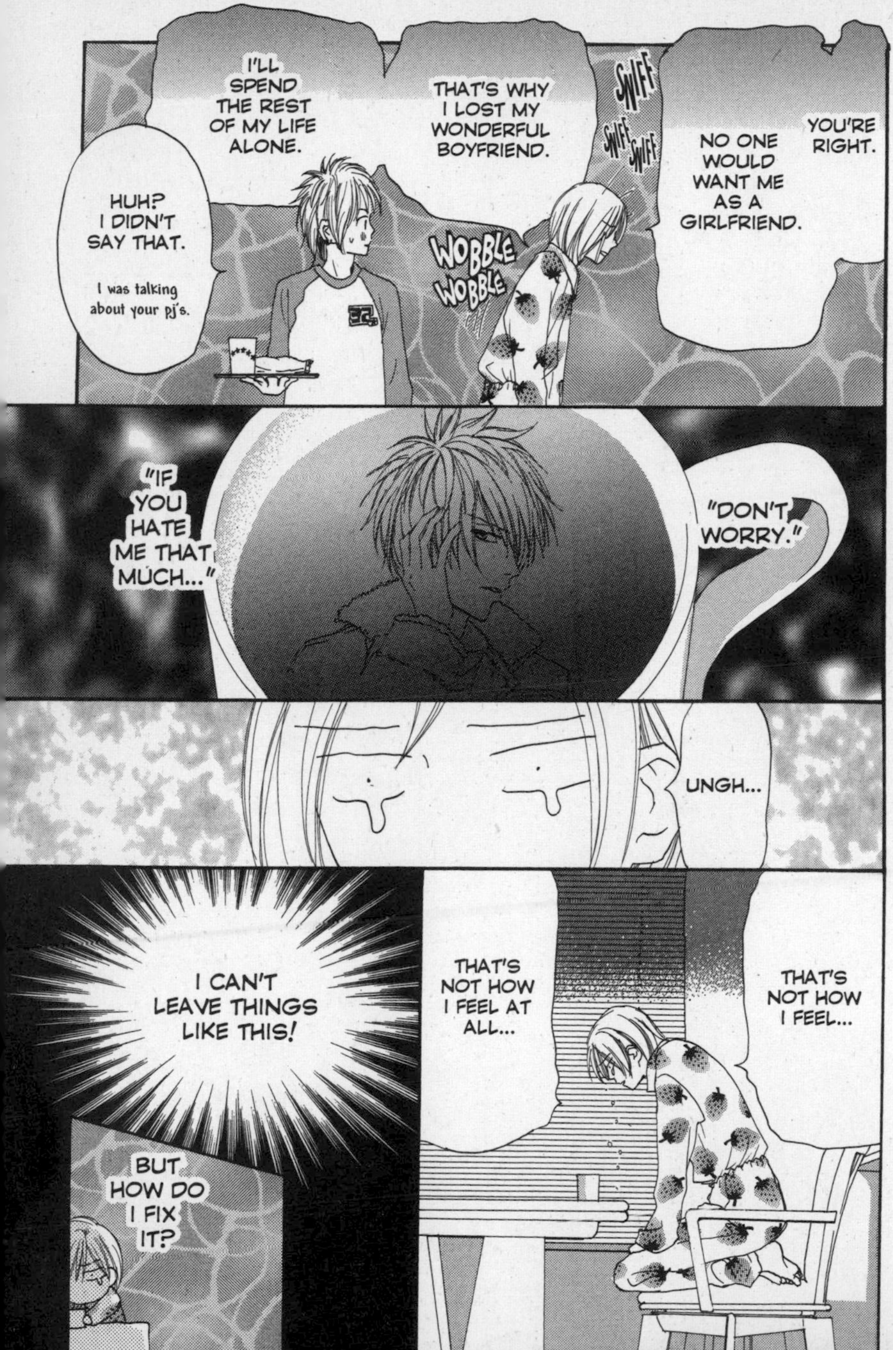
YOU'RE RIGHT.
NO ONE WOULD WANT ME AS A GIRLFRIEND.
SNIFF SNIFF SNIFF
THAT'S WHY I LOST MY WONDERFUL BOYFRIEND.
I'LL SPEND THE REST OF MY LIFE ALONE.
WOBBLE WOBBLE
HUH? I DIDN'T SAY THAT.
I was talking about your pj's.
"DON'T WORRY."
"IF YOU HATE ME THAT MUCH..."
UNGH...
THAT'S NOT HOW I FEEL...
THAT'S NOT HOW I FEEL AT ALL...
I CAN'T LEAVE THINGS LIKE THIS!
BUT HOW DO I FIX IT?

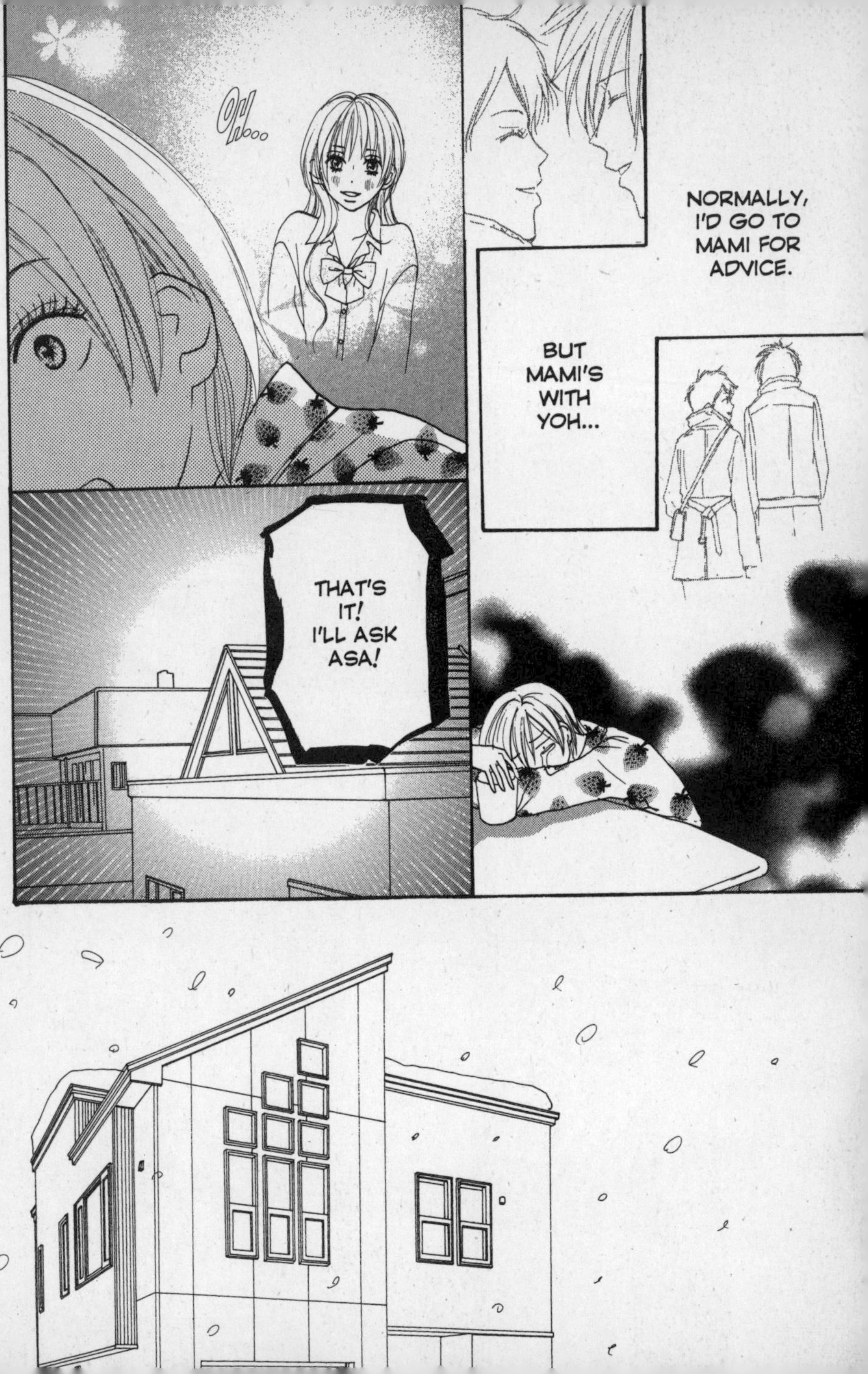
NORMALLY, I'D GO TO MAMI FOR ADVICE.
BUT MAMI'S WITH YOH...
OH...
THAT'S IT! I'LL ASK ASA!

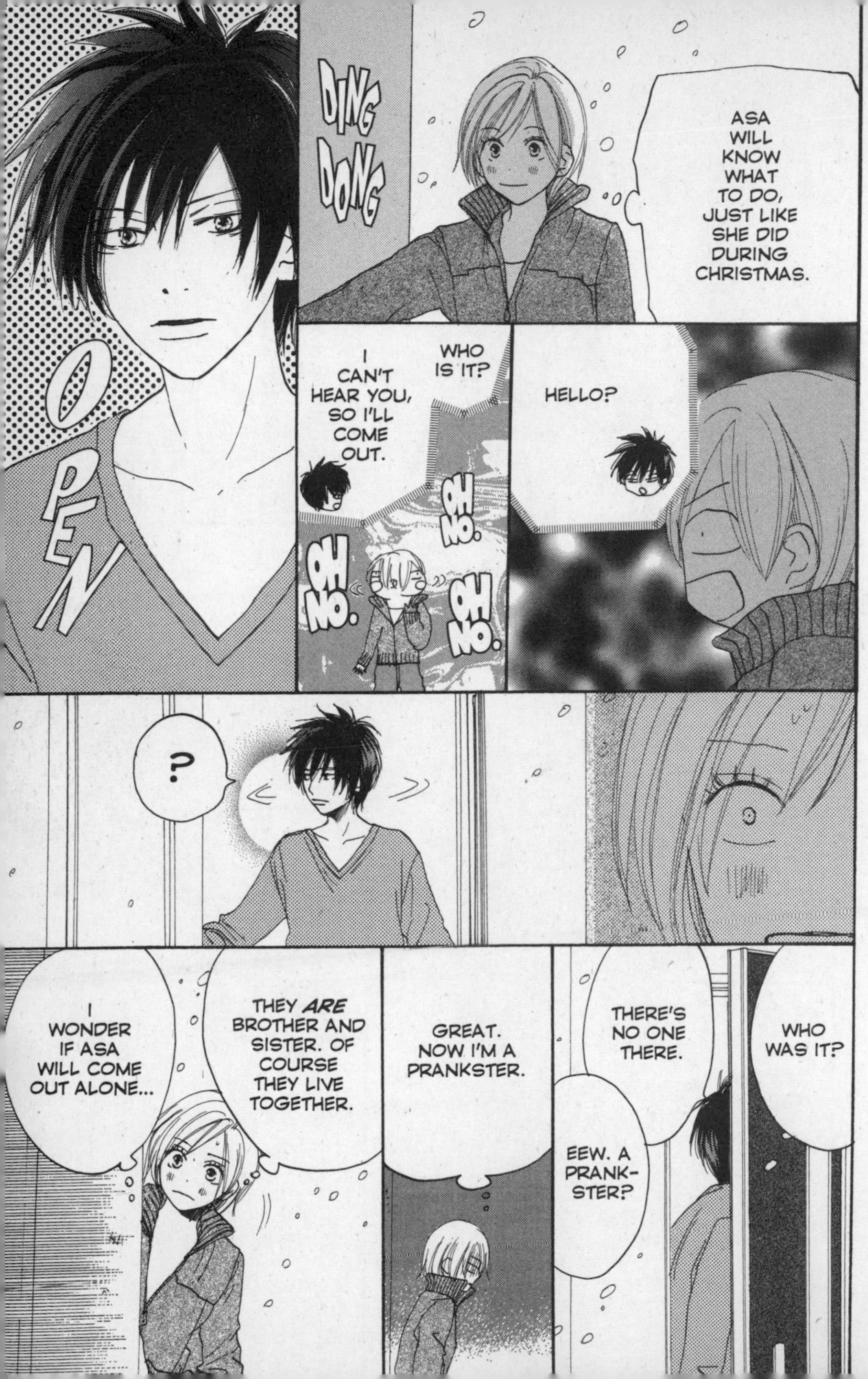
ASA WILL KNOW WHAT TO DO, JUST LIKE SHE DID DURING CHRISTMAS.
DING DONG
HELLO?
WHO IS IT?
I CAN'T HEAR YOU, SO I'LL COME OUT.
OH NO.
OH NO.
OH NO.
OPEN
?
WHO WAS IT?
THERE'S NO ONE THERE.
EEW. A PRANKSTER?
GREAT. NOW I'M A PRANKSTER.
THEY *ARE* BROTHER AND SISTER. OF COURSE THEY LIVE TOGETHER.
I WONDER IF ASA WILL COME OUT ALONE...

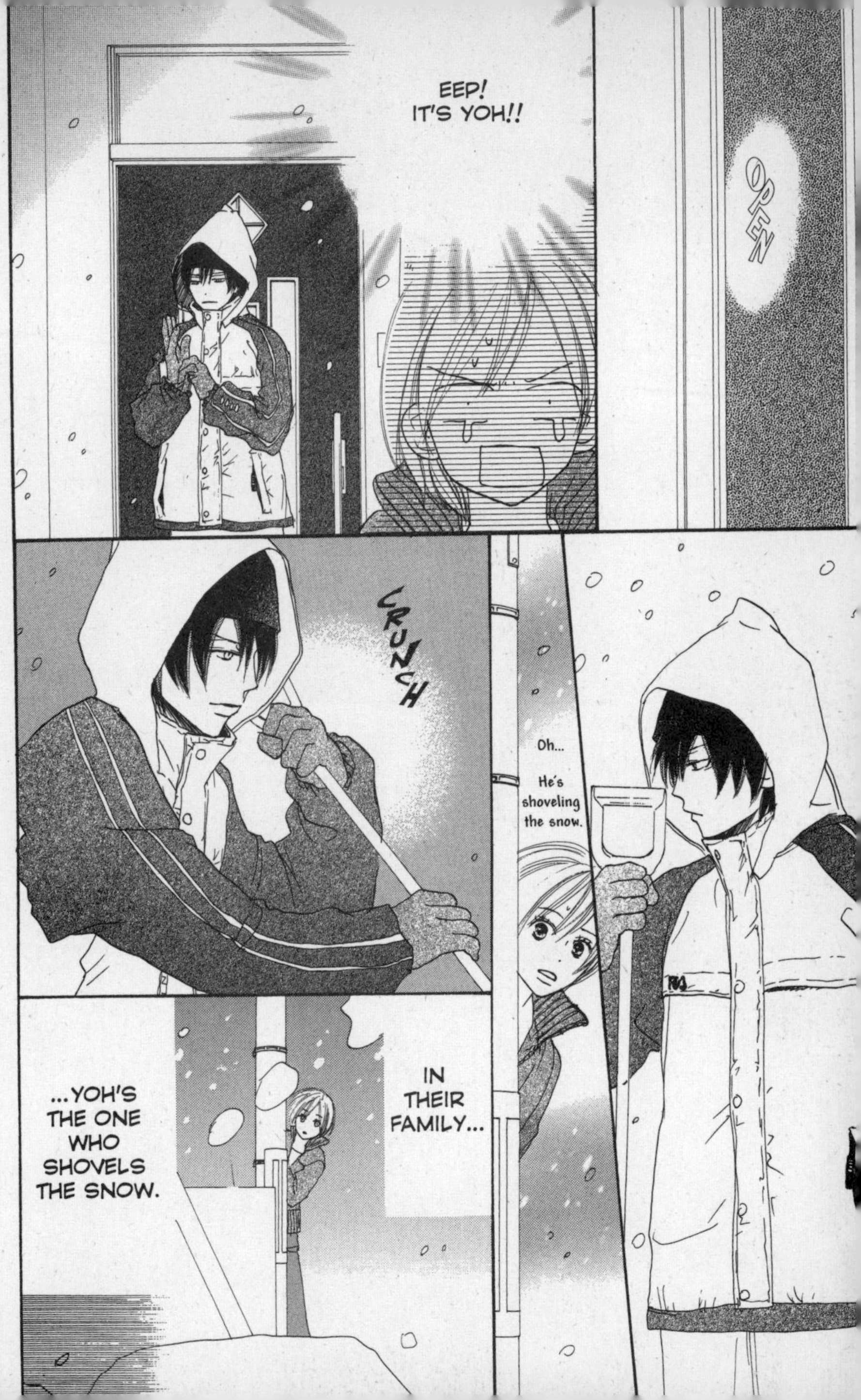
EEP! IT'S YOH!!
OPEN
Oh...
He's shoveling the snow.
CRUNCH
IN THEIR FAMILY...
...YOH'S THE ONE WHO SHOVELS THE SNOW.

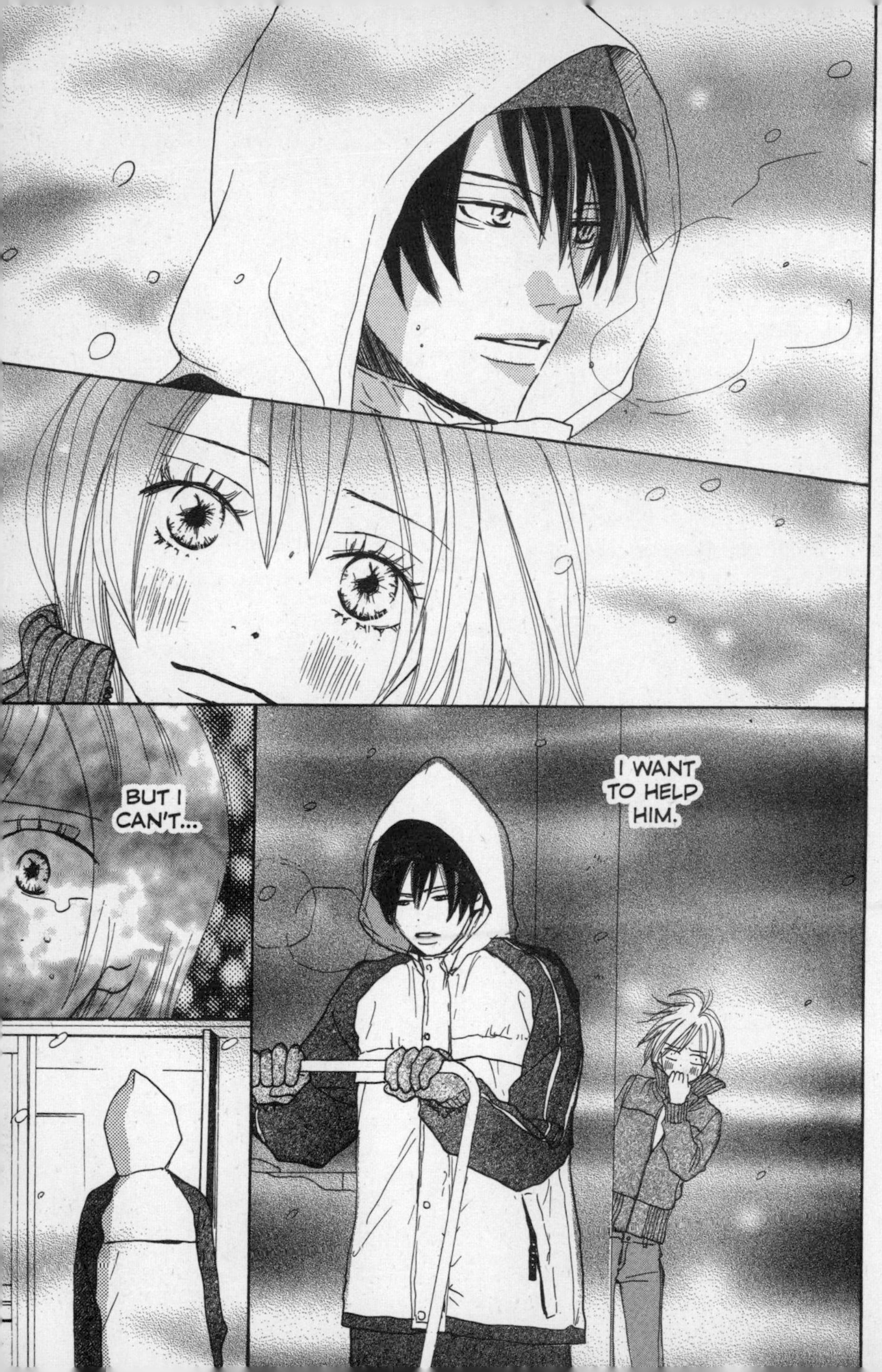
I WANT TO HELP HIM.
BUT I CAN'T...

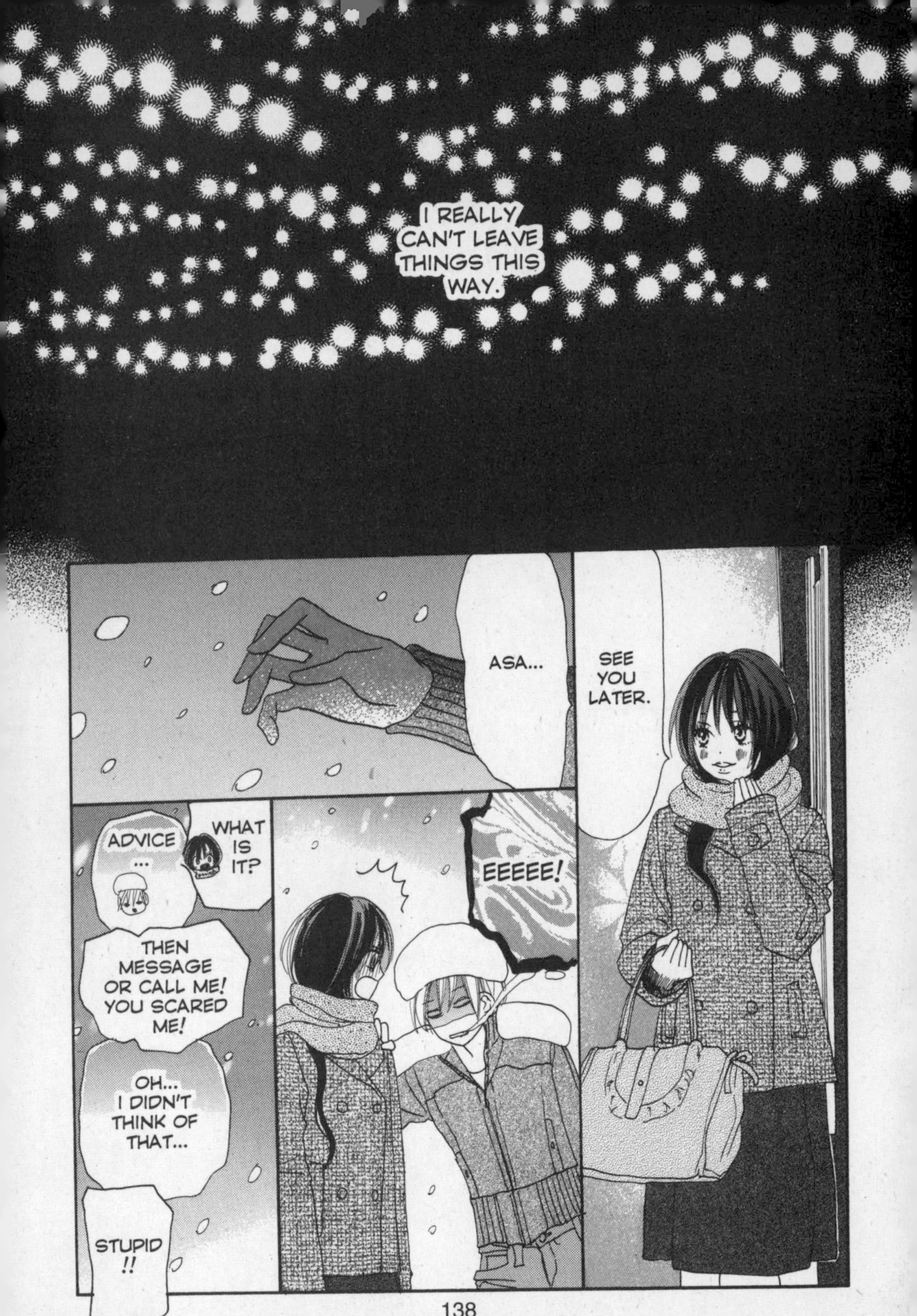
I REALLY CAN'T LEAVE THINGS THIS WAY.
SEE YOU LATER.
ASA...
EEEEE!
WHAT IS IT?
ADVICE ...
THEN MESSAGE OR CALL ME! YOU SCARED ME!
OH... I DIDN'T THINK OF THAT...
STUPID !!

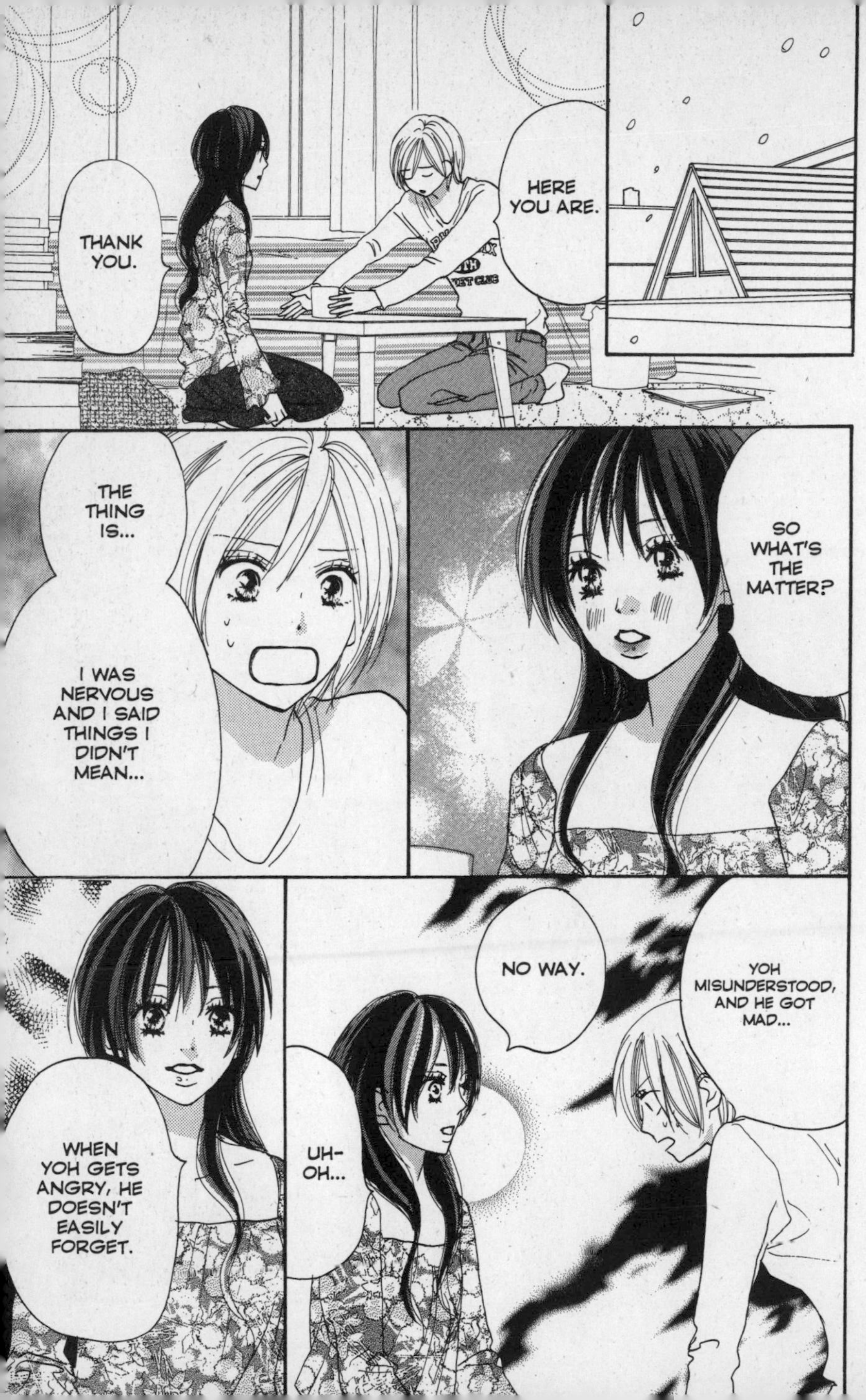
HERE YOU ARE.
THANK YOU.
SO WHAT'S THE MATTER?
THE THING IS...
I WAS NERVOUS AND I SAID THINGS I DIDN'T MEAN...
YOH MISUNDERSTOOD, AND HE GOT MAD...
NO WAY.
UH-OH...
WHEN YOH GETS ANGRY, HE DOESN'T EASILY FORGET.

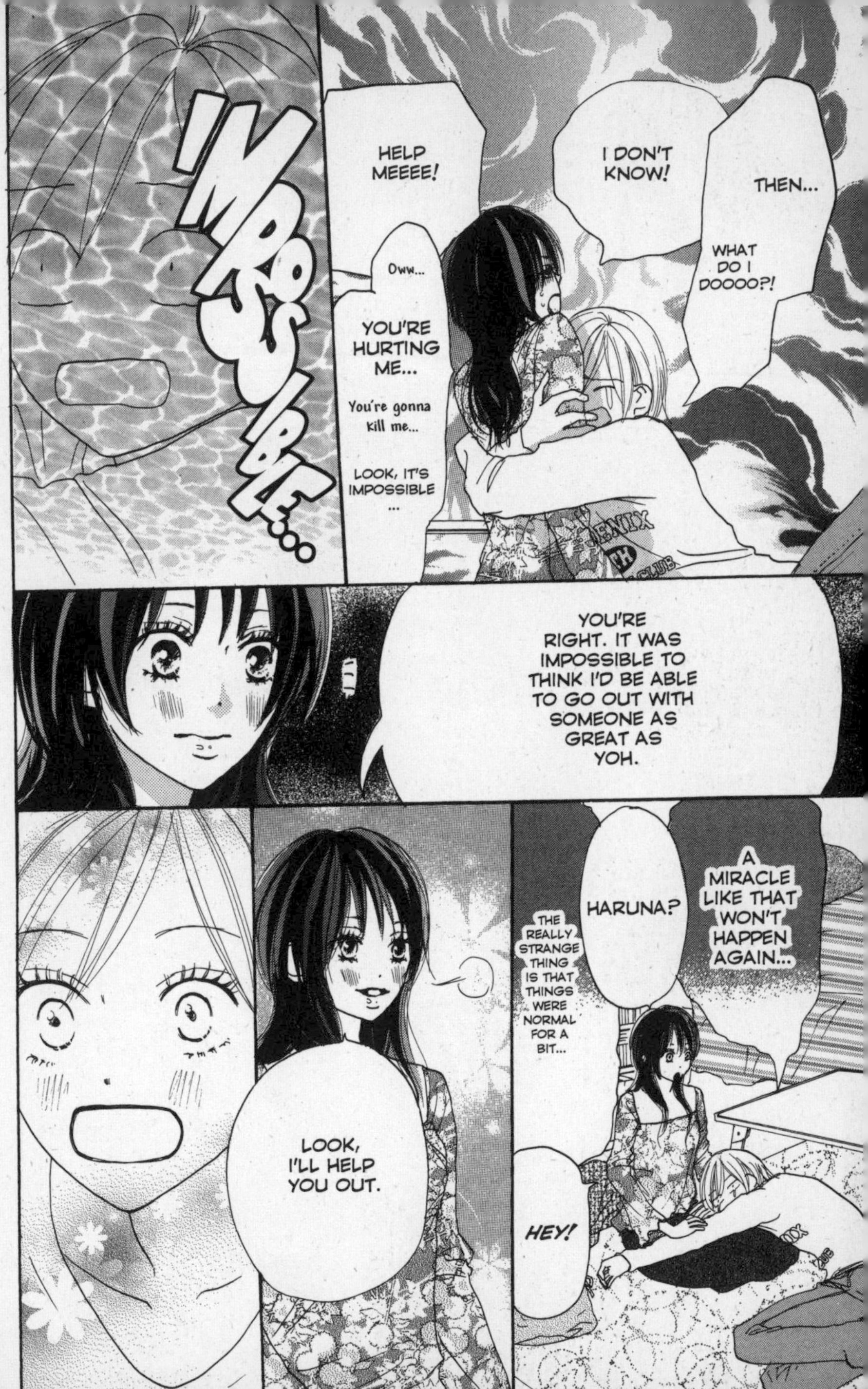
THEN... WHAT DO I DOOOO?!
I DON'T KNOW!
HELP MEEEE!
Oww...
YOU'RE HURTING ME...
You're gonna kill me...
LOOK, IT'S IMPOSSIBLE ...
IMPOSSIBLE...
YOU'RE RIGHT. IT WAS IMPOSSIBLE TO THINK I'D BE ABLE TO GO OUT WITH SOMEONE AS GREAT AS YOH.
A MIRACLE LIKE THAT WON'T HAPPEN AGAIN...
HARUNA?
THE REALLY STRANGE THING IS THAT THINGS WERE NORMAL FOR A BIT...
HEY!
LOOK, I'LL HELP YOU OUT.

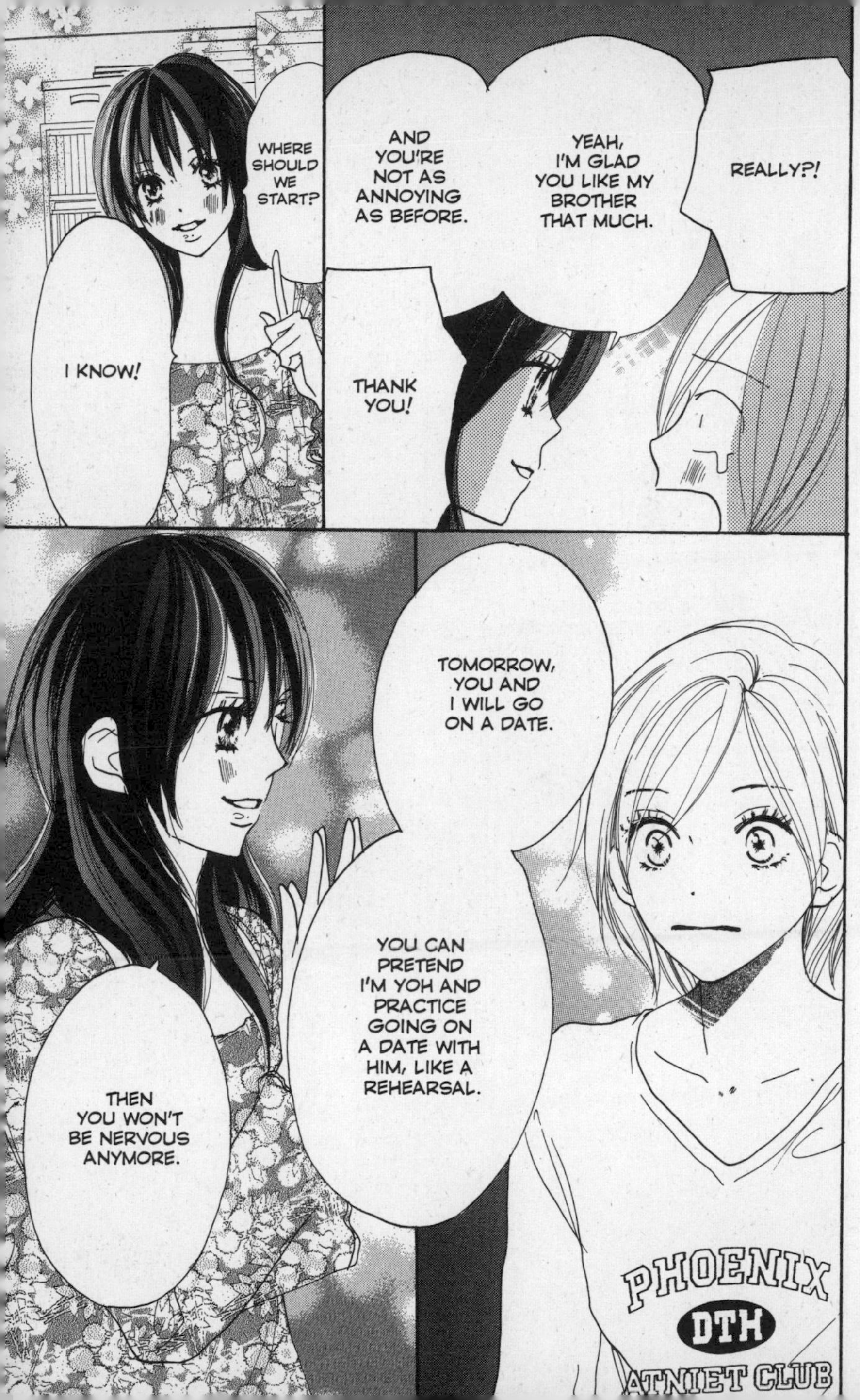
REALLY?!
YEAH, I'M GLAD YOU LIKE MY BROTHER THAT MUCH.
AND YOU'RE NOT AS ANNOYING AS BEFORE.
THANK YOU!
WHERE SHOULD WE START?
I KNOW!
TOMORROW, YOU AND I WILL GO ON A DATE.
YOU CAN PRETEND I'M YOH AND PRACTICE GOING ON A DATE WITH HIM, LIKE A REHEARSAL.
PHOENIX
DTH
ATNIET CLUB
THEN YOU WON'T BE NERVOUS ANYMORE.

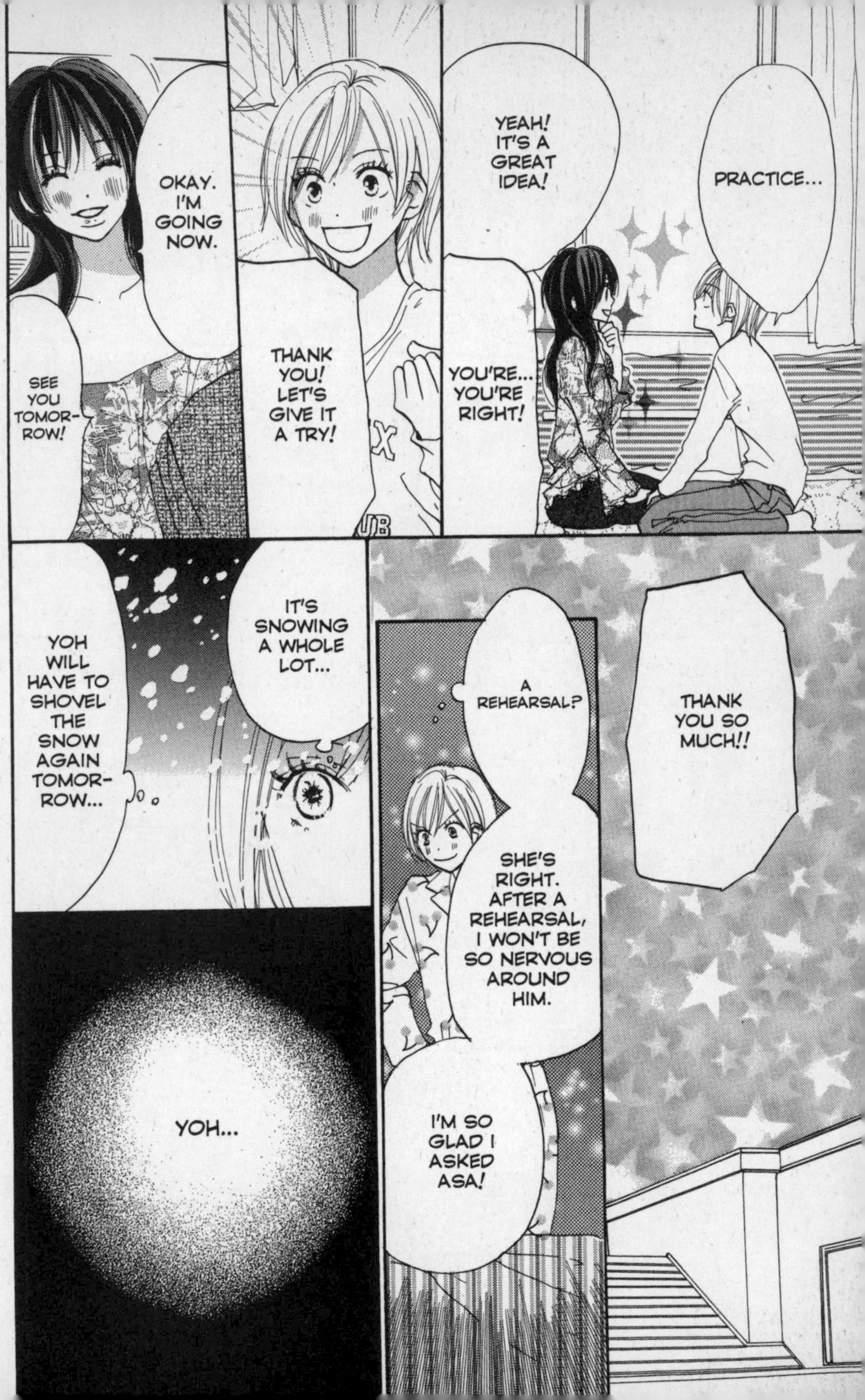
PRACTICE...
YEAH! IT'S A GREAT IDEA!
YOU'RE... YOU'RE RIGHT!
THANK YOU! LET'S GIVE IT A TRY!
OKAY. I'M GOING NOW.
SEE YOU TOMORROW!
THANK YOU SO MUCH!!
A REHEARSAL?
SHE'S RIGHT. AFTER A REHEARSAL, I WON'T BE SO NERVOUS AROUND HIM.
I'M SO GLAD I ASKED ASA!
IT'S SNOWING A WHOLE LOT...
YOH WILL HAVE TO SHOVEL THE SNOW AGAIN TOMORROW...
YOH...

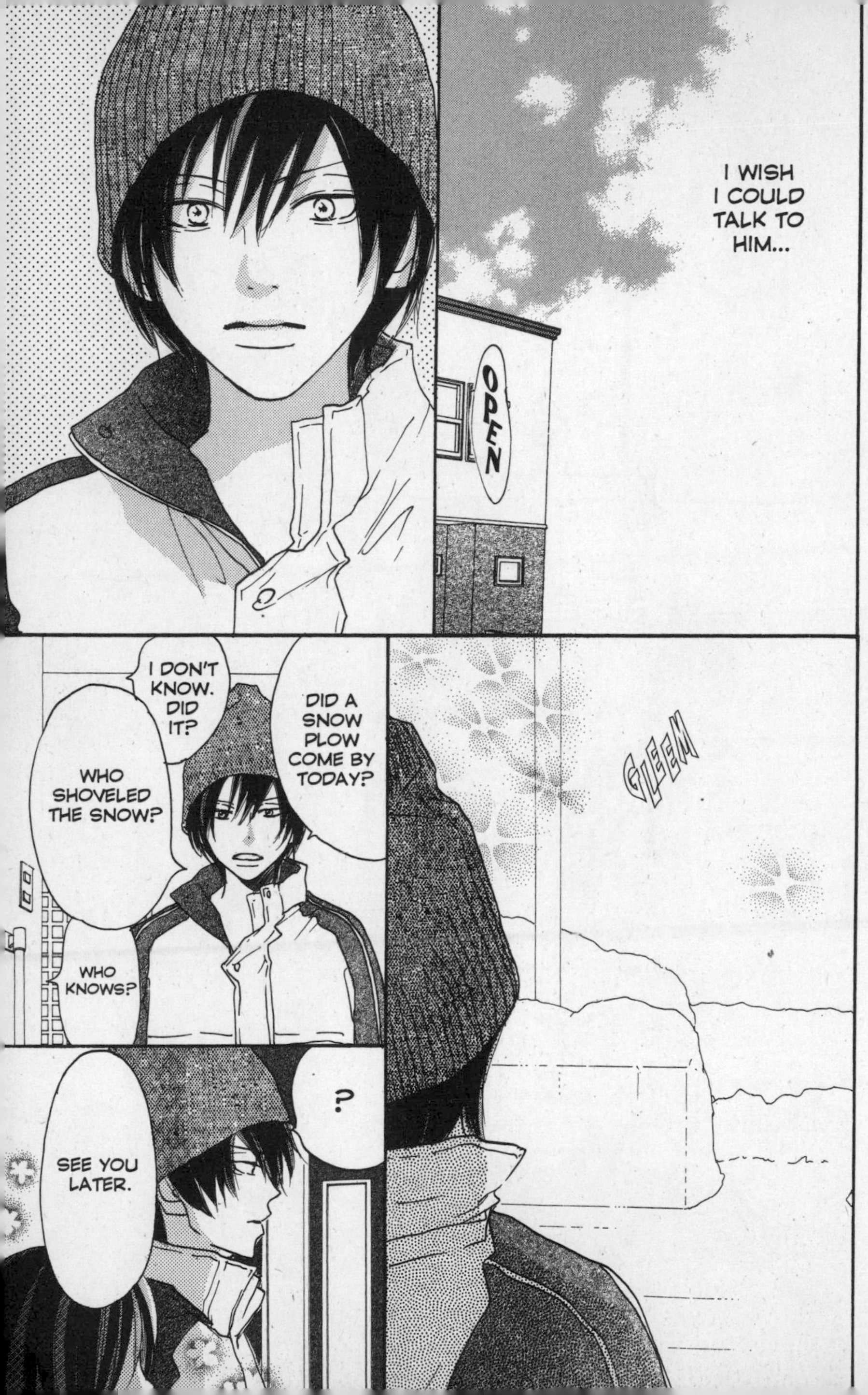
I WISH I COULD TALK TO HIM...
OPEN
GLEEM
DID A SNOW PLOW COME BY TODAY?
I DON'T KNOW. DID IT?
WHO SHOVELED THE SNOW?
WHO KNOWS?
?
SEE YOU LATER.

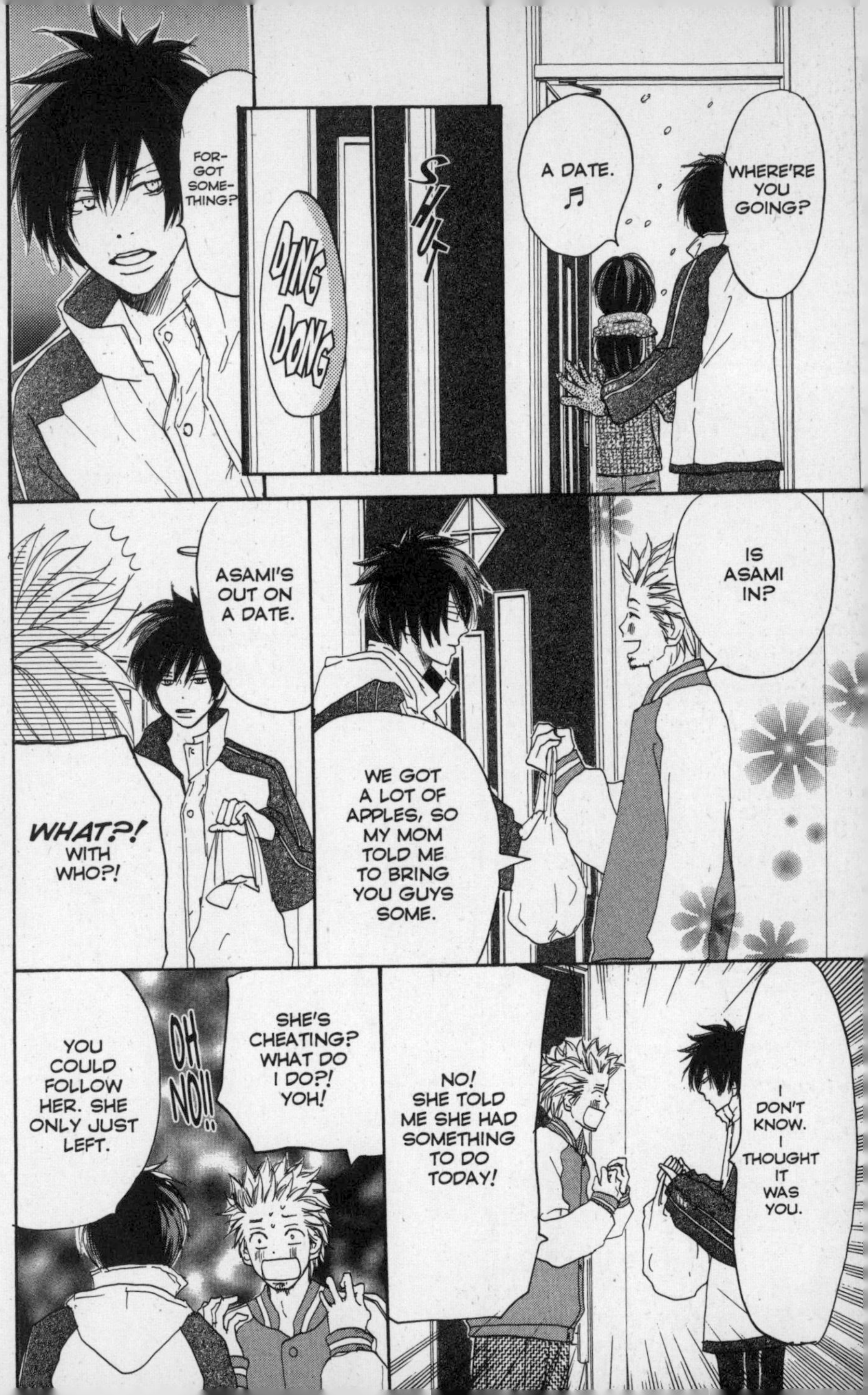
WHERE'RE YOU GOING?
A DATE. ♬
SHUT
DING DONG
FOR-GOT SOME-THING?
IS ASAMI IN?
WE GOT A LOT OF APPLES, SO MY MOM TOLD ME TO BRING YOU GUYS SOME.
ASAMI'S OUT ON A DATE.
WHAT?! WITH WHO?!
I DON'T KNOW. I THOUGHT IT WAS YOU.
NO! SHE TOLD ME SHE HAD SOMETHING TO DO TODAY!
SHE'S CHEATING? WHAT DO I DO?! YOH!
OH NO!!
YOU COULD FOLLOW HER. SHE ONLY JUST LEFT.

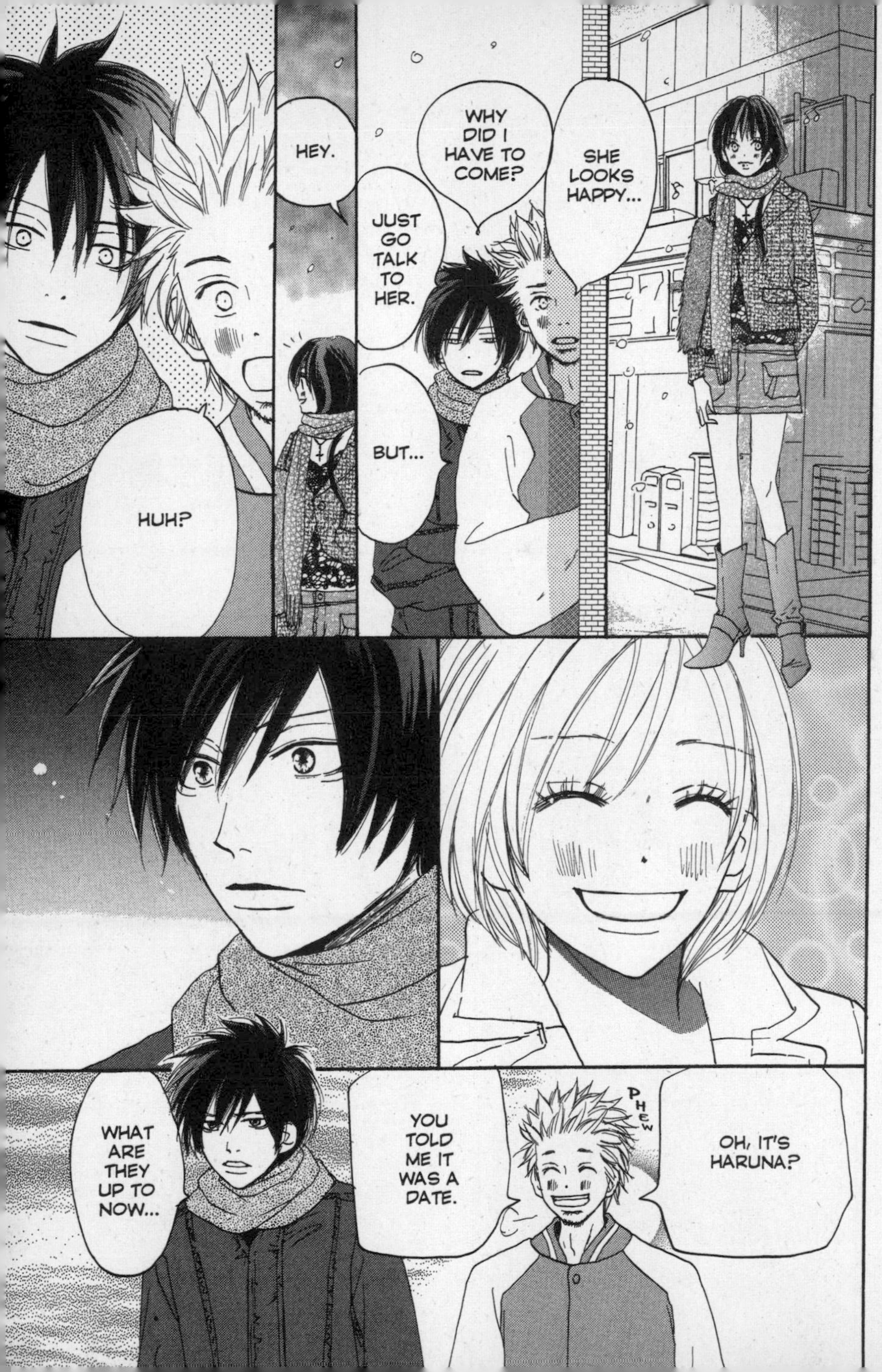
SHE LOOKS HAPPY...
WHY DID I HAVE TO COME?
JUST GO TALK TO HER.
BUT...
HEY.
HUH?
OH, IT'S HARUNA?
PHEW
YOU TOLD ME IT WAS A DATE.
WHAT ARE THEY UP TO NOW...

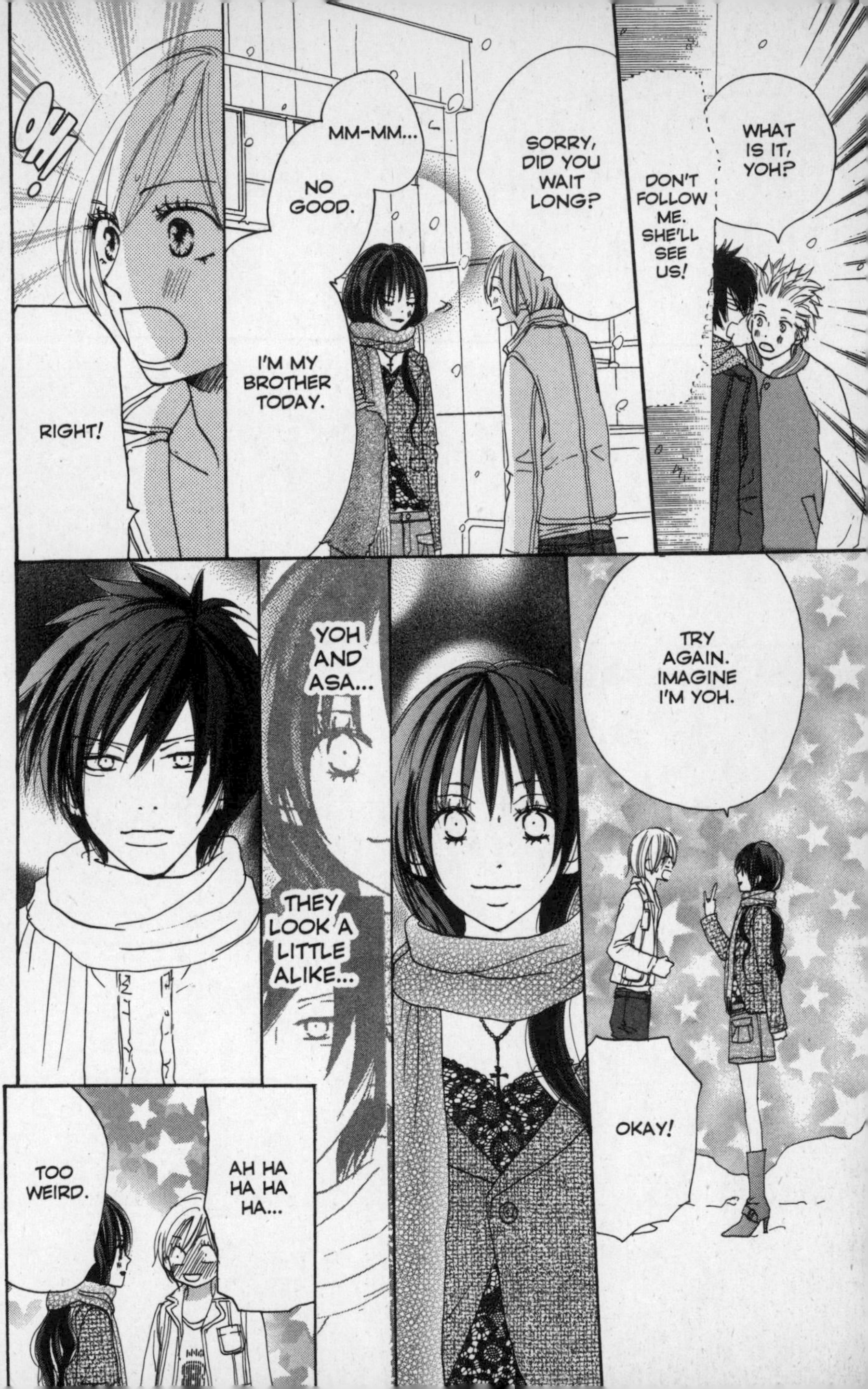
WHAT IS IT, YOH?
DON'T FOLLOW ME. SHE'LL SEE US!
SORRY, DID YOU WAIT LONG?
MM-MM...
NO GOOD.
I'M MY BROTHER TODAY.
OH!
RIGHT!
TRY AGAIN. IMAGINE I'M YOH.
OKAY!
YOH AND ASA...
THEY LOOK A LITTLE ALIKE...
AH HA HA HA HA...
TOO WEIRD.

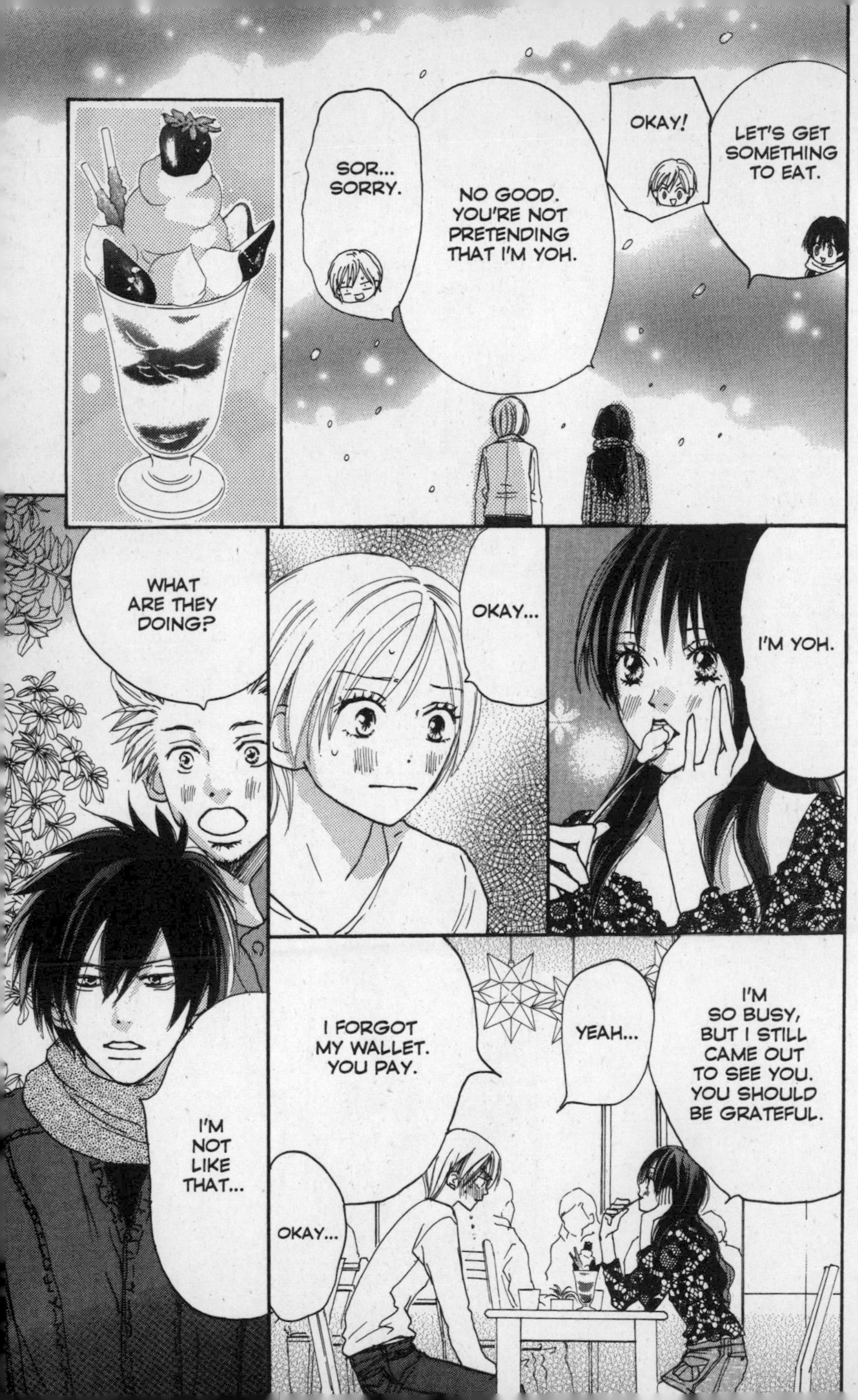
LET'S GET SOMETHING TO EAT.
OKAY!
NO GOOD. YOU'RE NOT PRETENDING THAT I'M YOH.
SOR... SORRY.
I'M YOH.
OKAY...
I'M SO BUSY, BUT I STILL CAME OUT TO SEE YOU. YOU SHOULD BE GRATEFUL.
YEAH...
I FORGOT MY WALLET. YOU PAY.
OKAY...
WHAT ARE THEY DOING?
I'M NOT LIKE THAT...

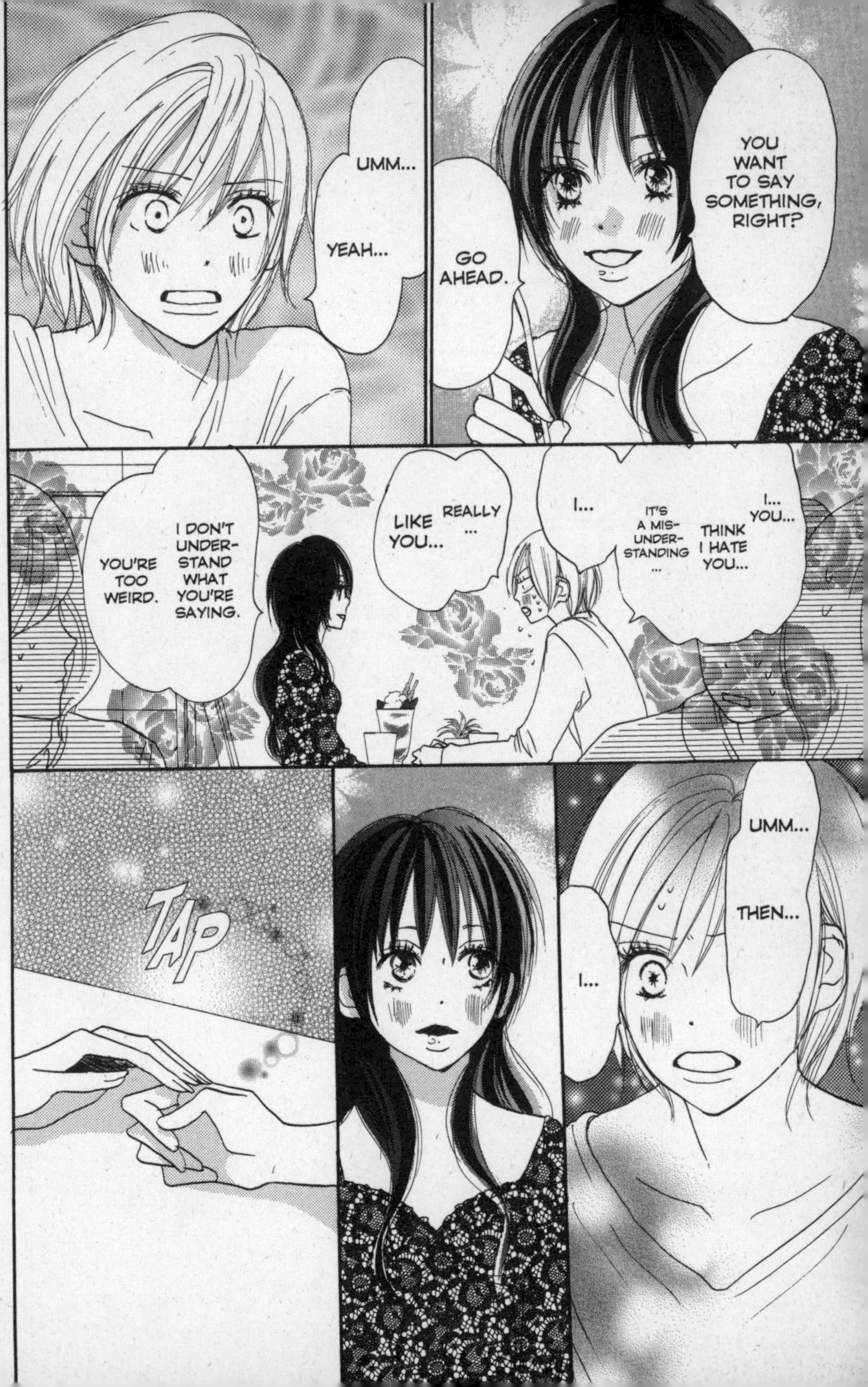
YOU WANT TO SAY SOMETHING, RIGHT?
GO AHEAD.
UMM...
YEAH...
I... YOU...
THINK I HATE YOU...
IT'S A MIS-UNDER-STANDING...
I...
REALLY...
LIKE YOU...
I DON'T UNDER-STAND WHAT YOU'RE SAYING.
YOU'RE TOO WEIRD.
UMM...
THEN...
I...
TAP

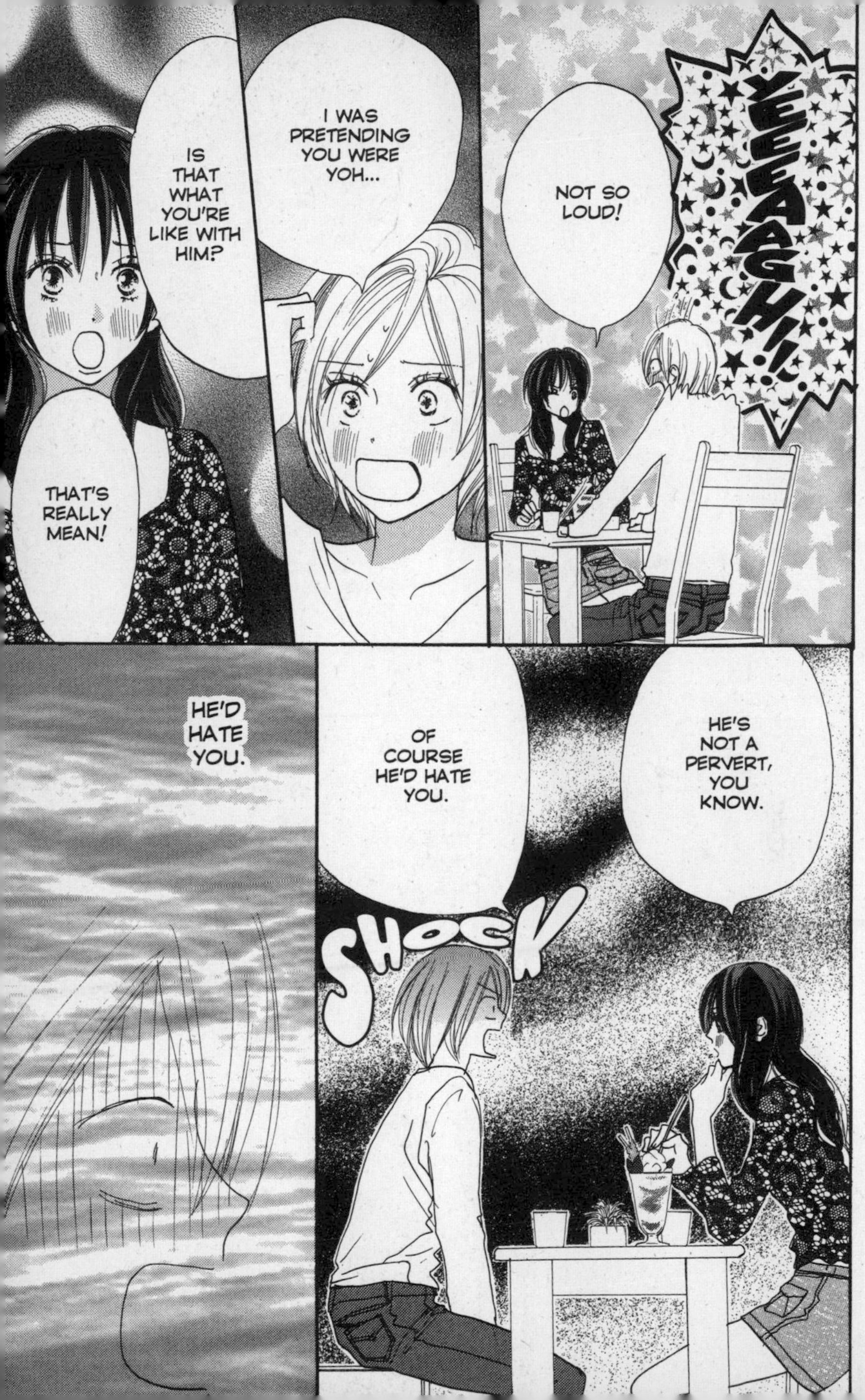
YEEEAAGH!!!
NOT SO LOUD!
I WAS PRETENDING YOU WERE YOH...
IS THAT WHAT YOU'RE LIKE WITH HIM?
THAT'S REALLY MEAN!
HE'S NOT A PERVERT, YOU KNOW.
OF COURSE HE'D HATE YOU.
SHOCK
HE'D HATE YOU.

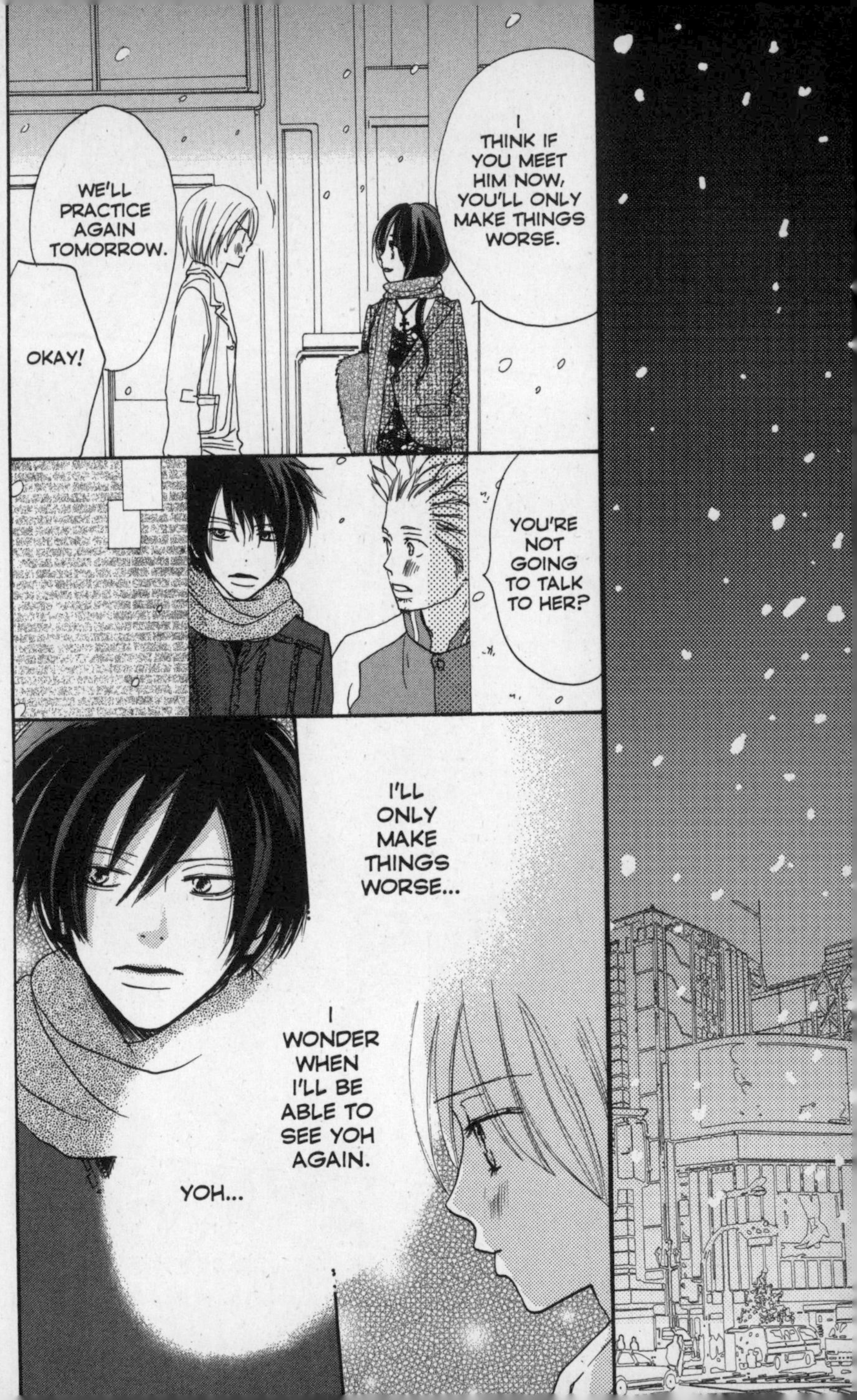

I THINK IF YOU MEET HIM NOW, YOU'LL ONLY MAKE THINGS WORSE.
WE'LL PRACTICE AGAIN TOMORROW.
OKAY!
YOU'RE NOT GOING TO TALK TO HER?
I'LL ONLY MAKE THINGS WORSE...
I WONDER WHEN I'LL BE ABLE TO SEE YOH AGAIN.
YOH...

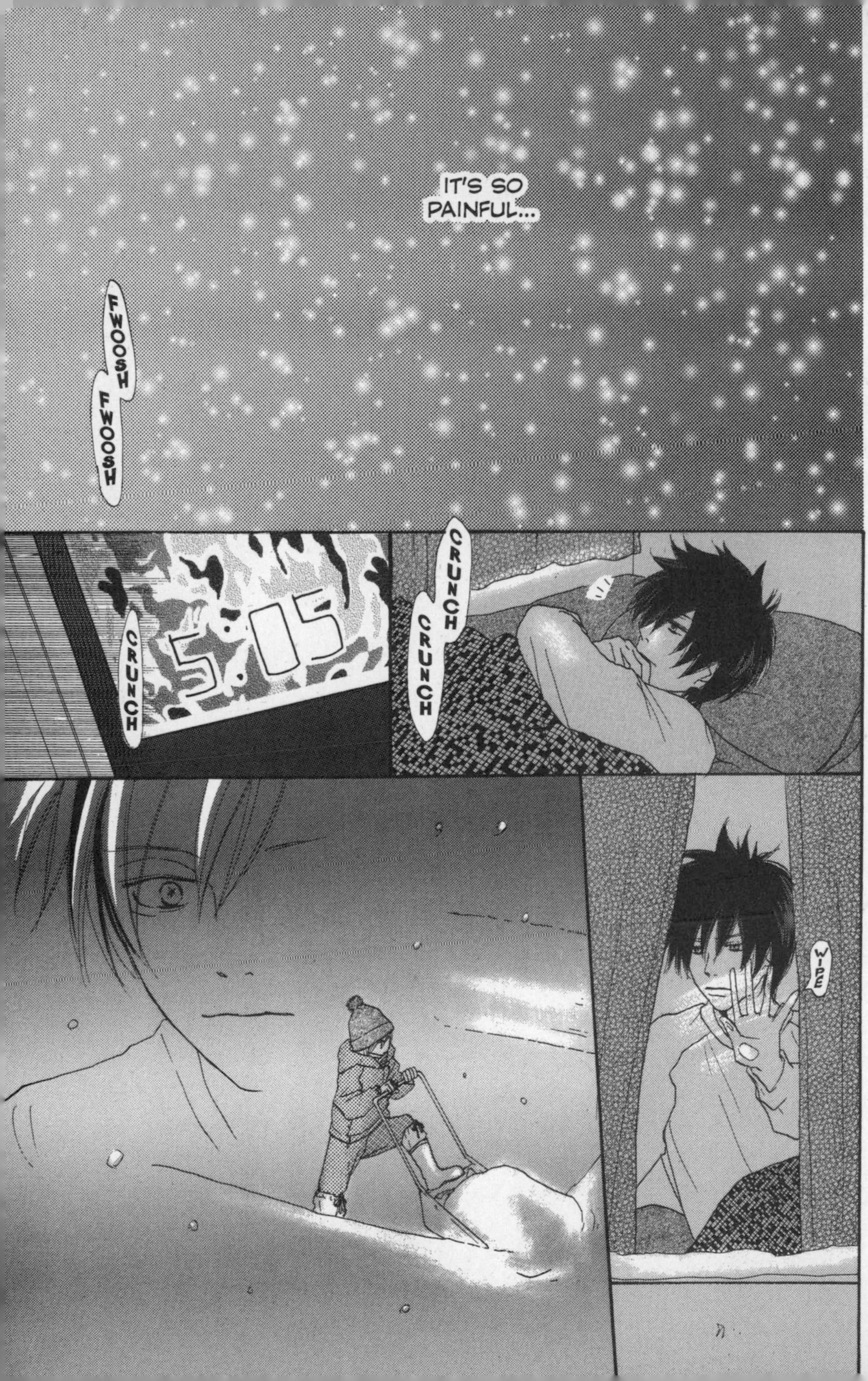
IT'S SO PAINFUL...
FWOOSH FWOOSH
CRUNCH CRUNCH
CRUNCH
WIPE

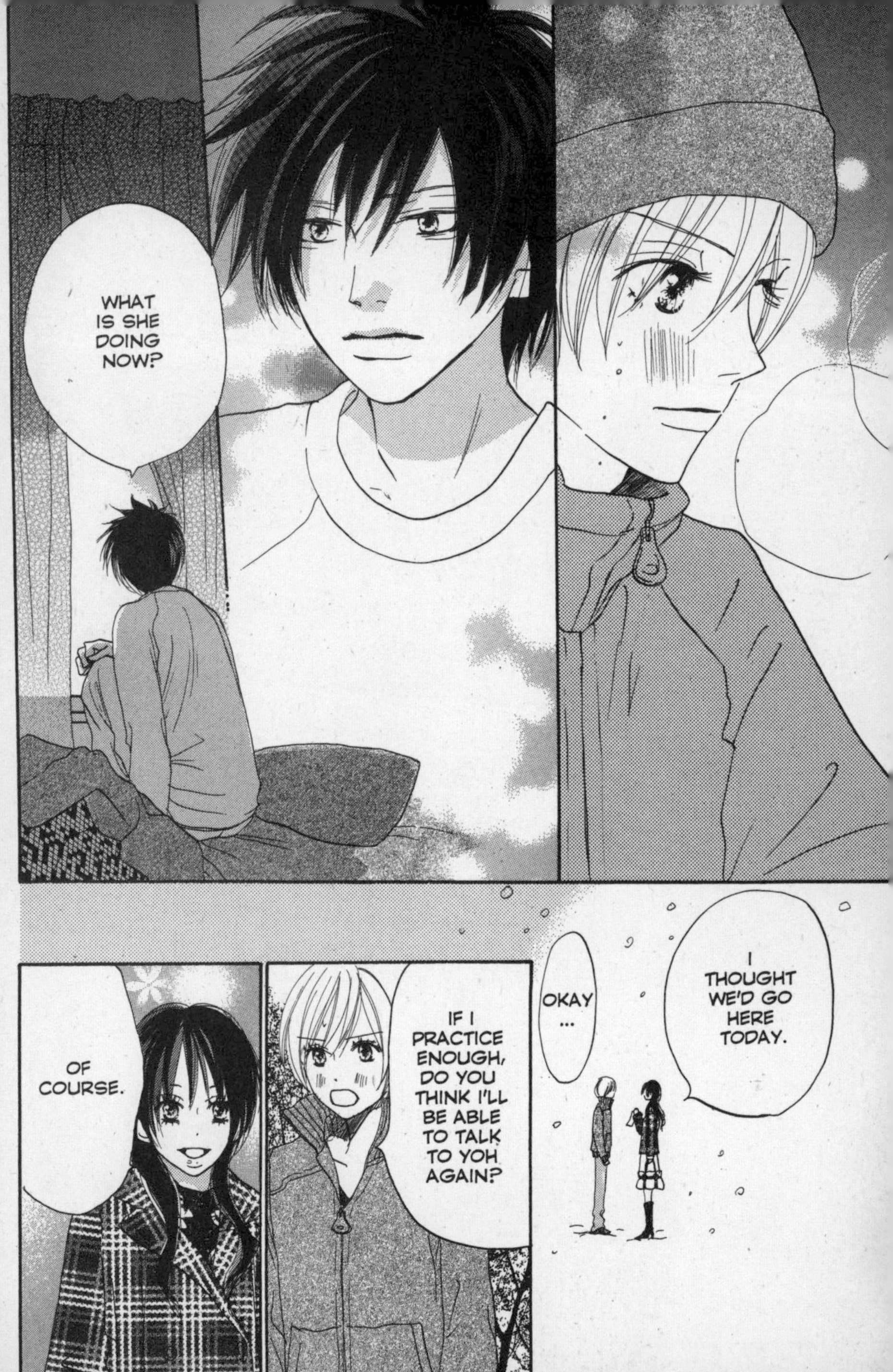
WHAT IS SHE DOING NOW?
I THOUGHT WE'D GO HERE TODAY.
OKAY...
IF I PRACTICE ENOUGH, DO YOU THINK I'LL BE ABLE TO TALK TO YOH AGAIN?
OF COURSE.

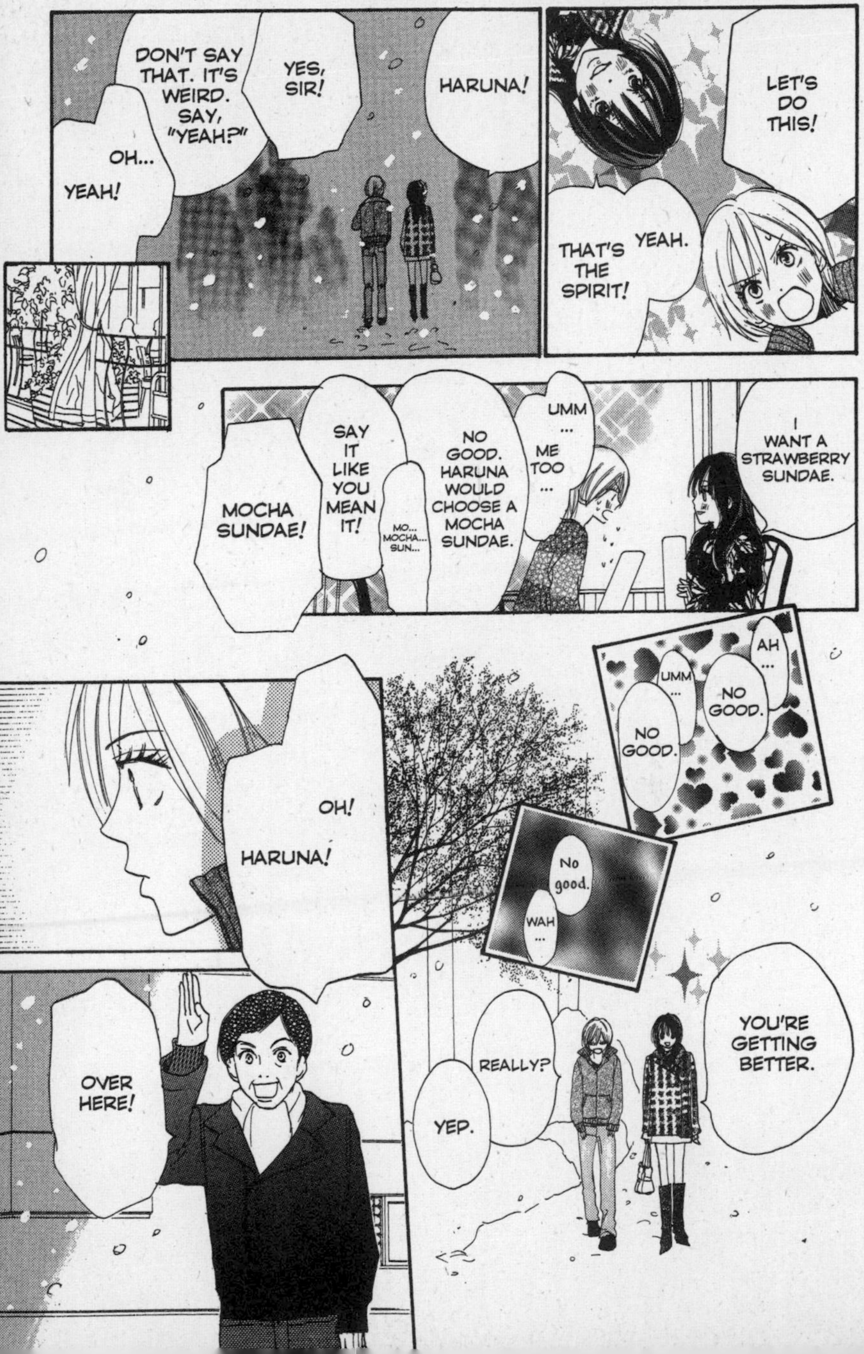
LET'S DO THIS!
YEAH.
THAT'S THE SPIRIT!
HARUNA!
YES, SIR!
DON'T SAY THAT. IT'S WEIRD. SAY, "YEAH?"
OH...
YEAH!
I WANT A STRAWBERRY SUNDAE.
UMM... ME TOO...
NO GOOD. HARUNA WOULD CHOOSE A MOCHA SUNDAE.
MO... MOCHA... SUN...
SAY IT LIKE YOU MEAN IT!
MOCHA SUNDAE!
AH...
NO GOOD.
UMM...
NO GOOD.
No good.
WAH...
YOU'RE GETTING BETTER.
REALLY?
YEP.
OH!
HARUNA!
OVER HERE!

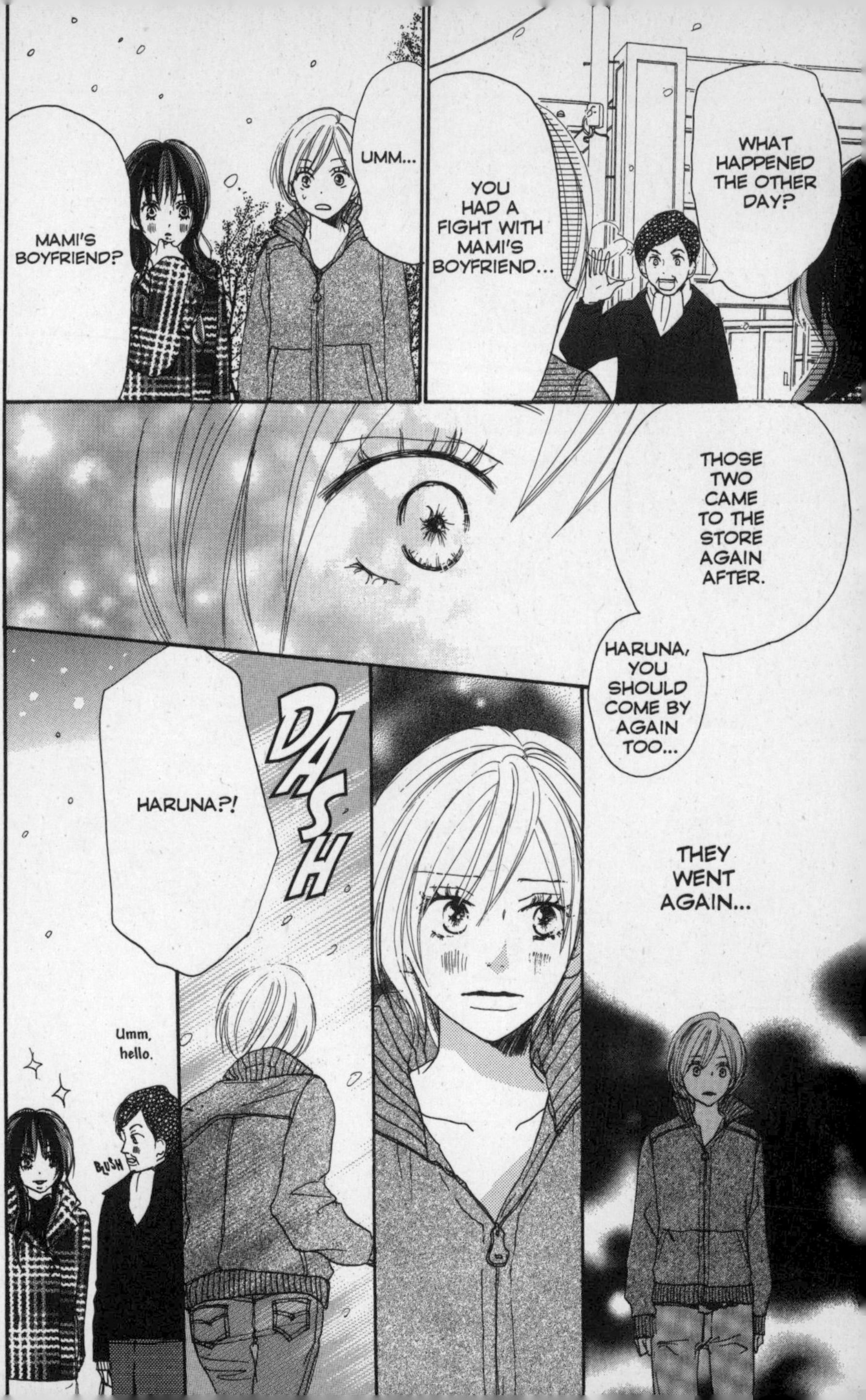
WHAT HAPPENED THE OTHER DAY?
YOU HAD A FIGHT WITH MAMI'S BOYFRIEND...
UMM...
MAMI'S BOYFRIEND?
THOSE TWO CAME TO THE STORE AGAIN AFTER.
HARUNA, YOU SHOULD COME BY AGAIN TOO...
THEY WENT AGAIN...
DASH
HARUNA?!
Umm, hello.
BLUSH

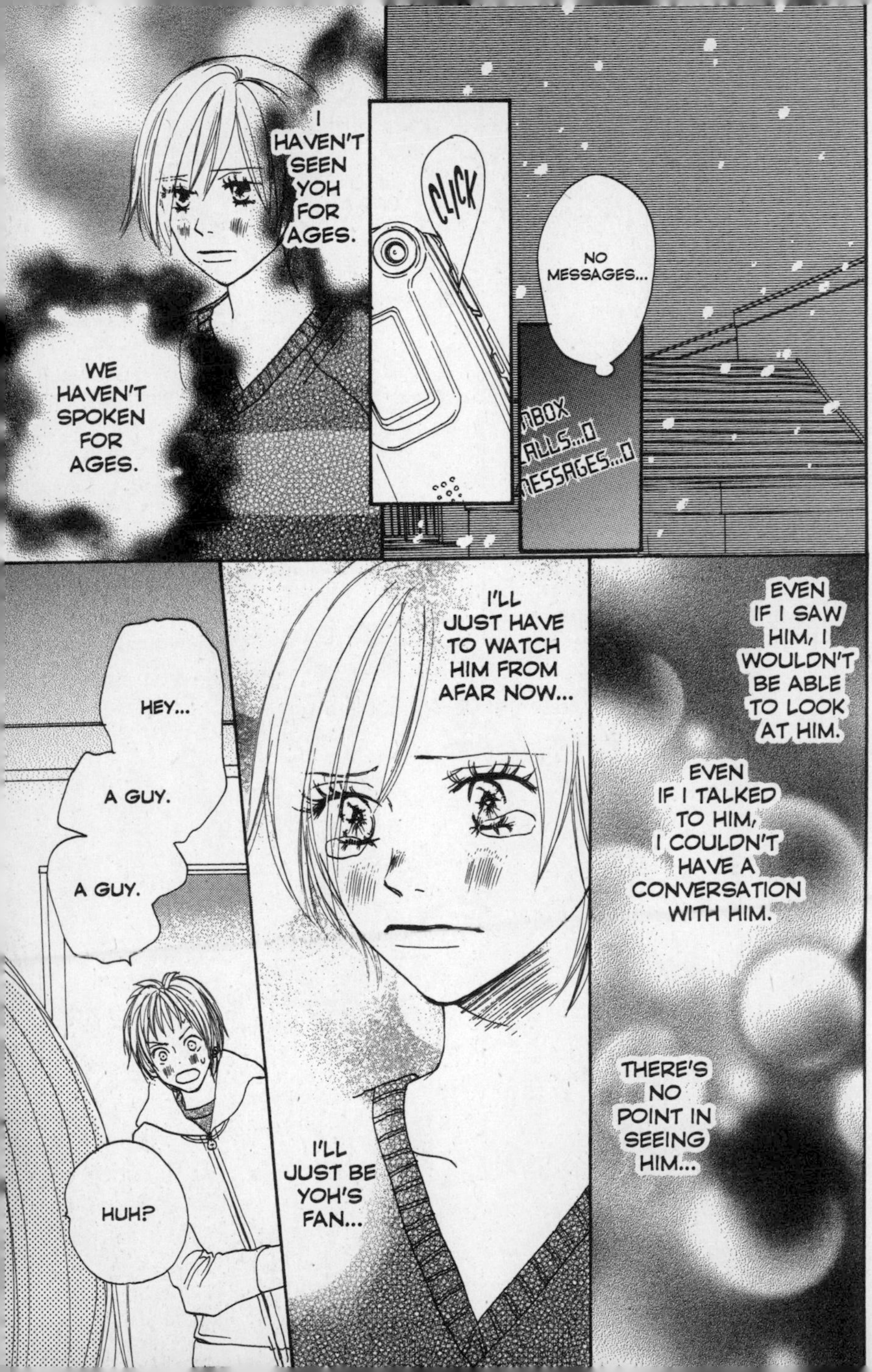
NO MESSAGES...
CLICK
I HAVEN'T SEEN YOH FOR AGES.
WE HAVEN'T SPOKEN FOR AGES.
EVEN IF I SAW HIM, I WOULDN'T BE ABLE TO LOOK AT HIM.
EVEN IF I TALKED TO HIM, I COULDN'T HAVE A CONVERSATION WITH HIM.
THERE'S NO POINT IN SEEING HIM...
I'LL JUST HAVE TO WATCH HIM FROM AFAR NOW...
I'LL JUST BE YOH'S FAN...
HEY...
A GUY.
A GUY.
HUH?

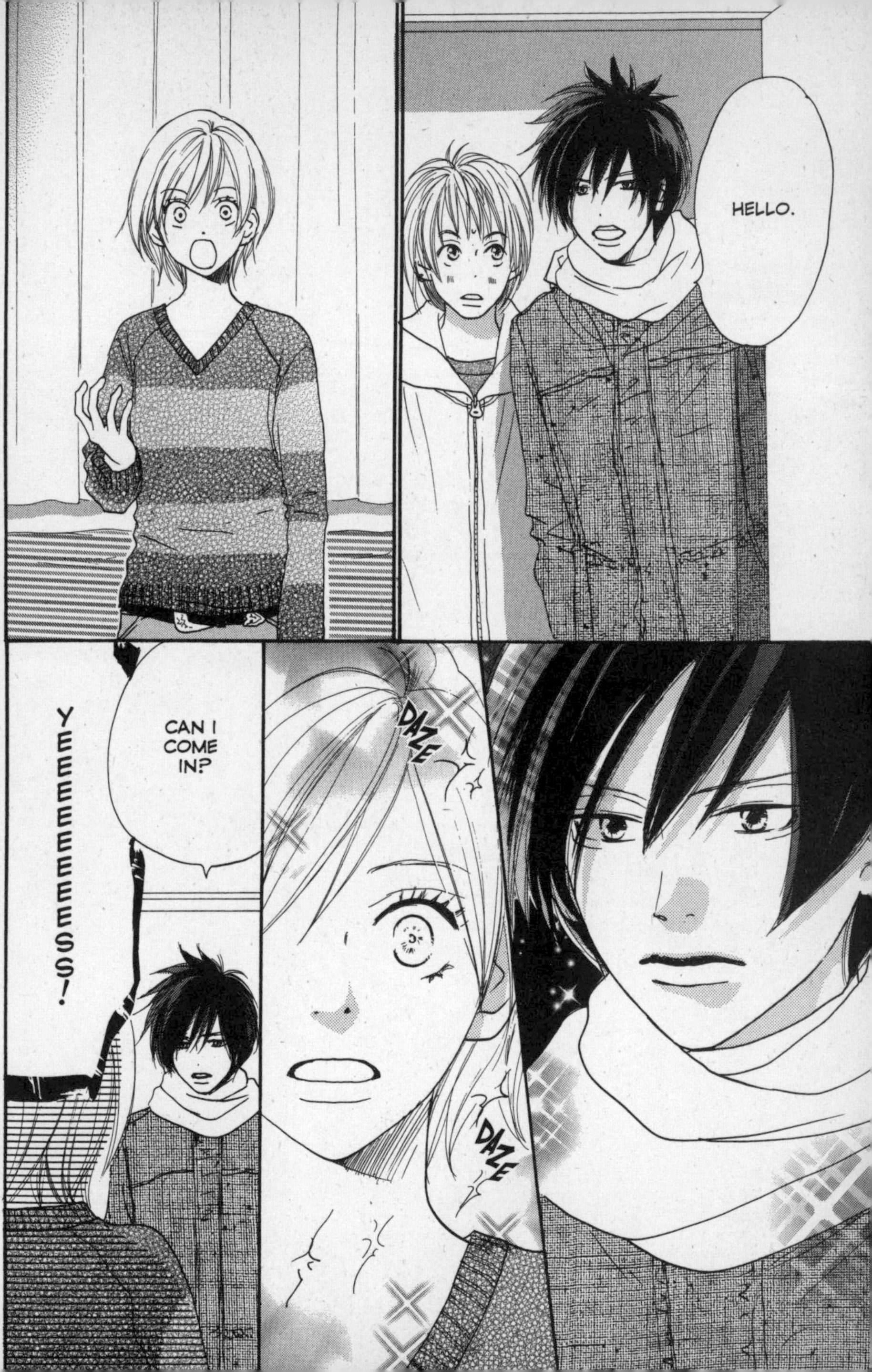
HELLO.
DAZE
DAZE
CAN I COME IN?
YEEEEEEEESS!

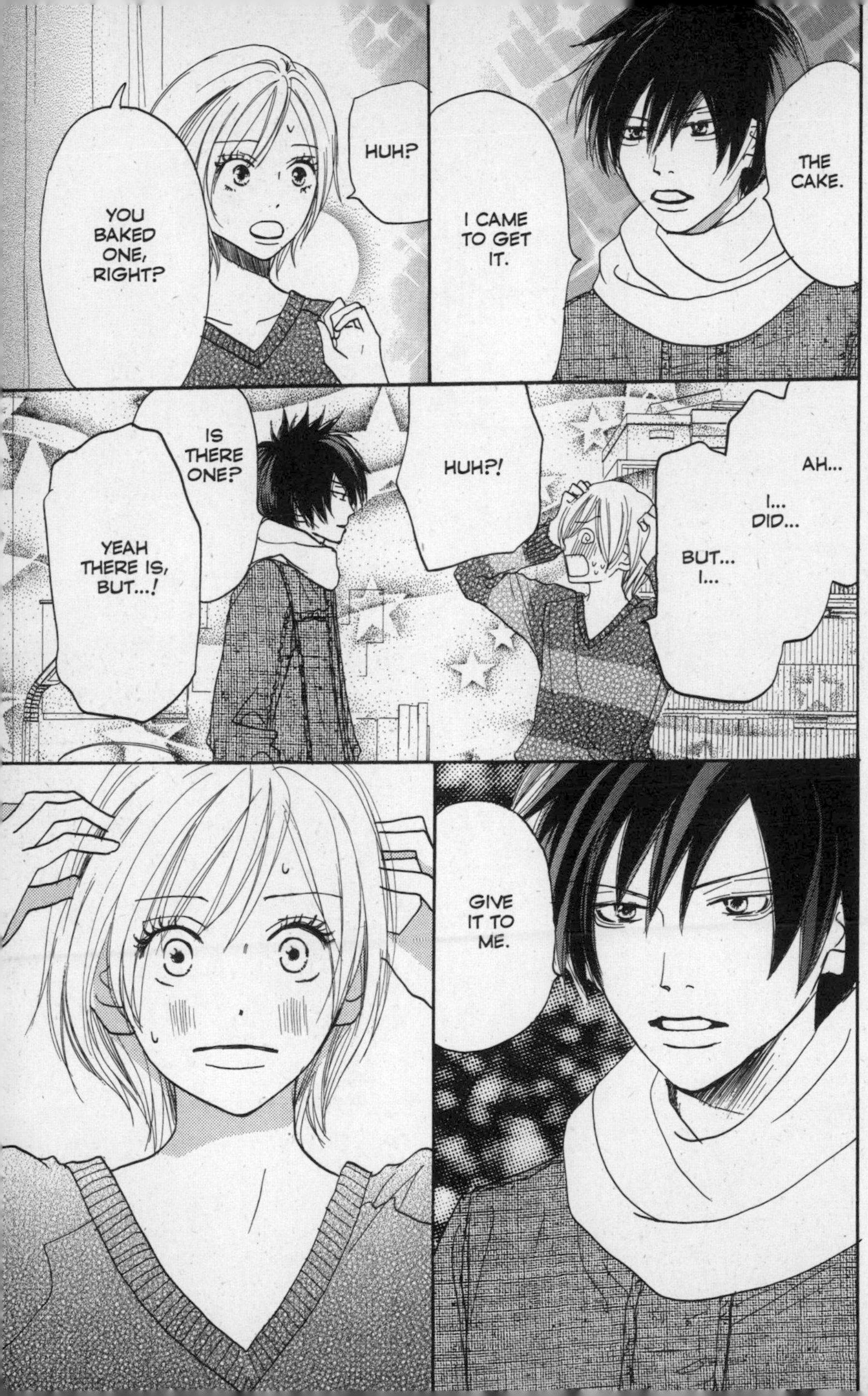
THE CAKE.
I CAME TO GET IT.
HUH?
YOU BAKED ONE, RIGHT?
HUH?!
AH...
I... DID...
BUT... I...
IS THERE ONE?
YEAH THERE IS, BUT...!
GIVE IT TO ME.

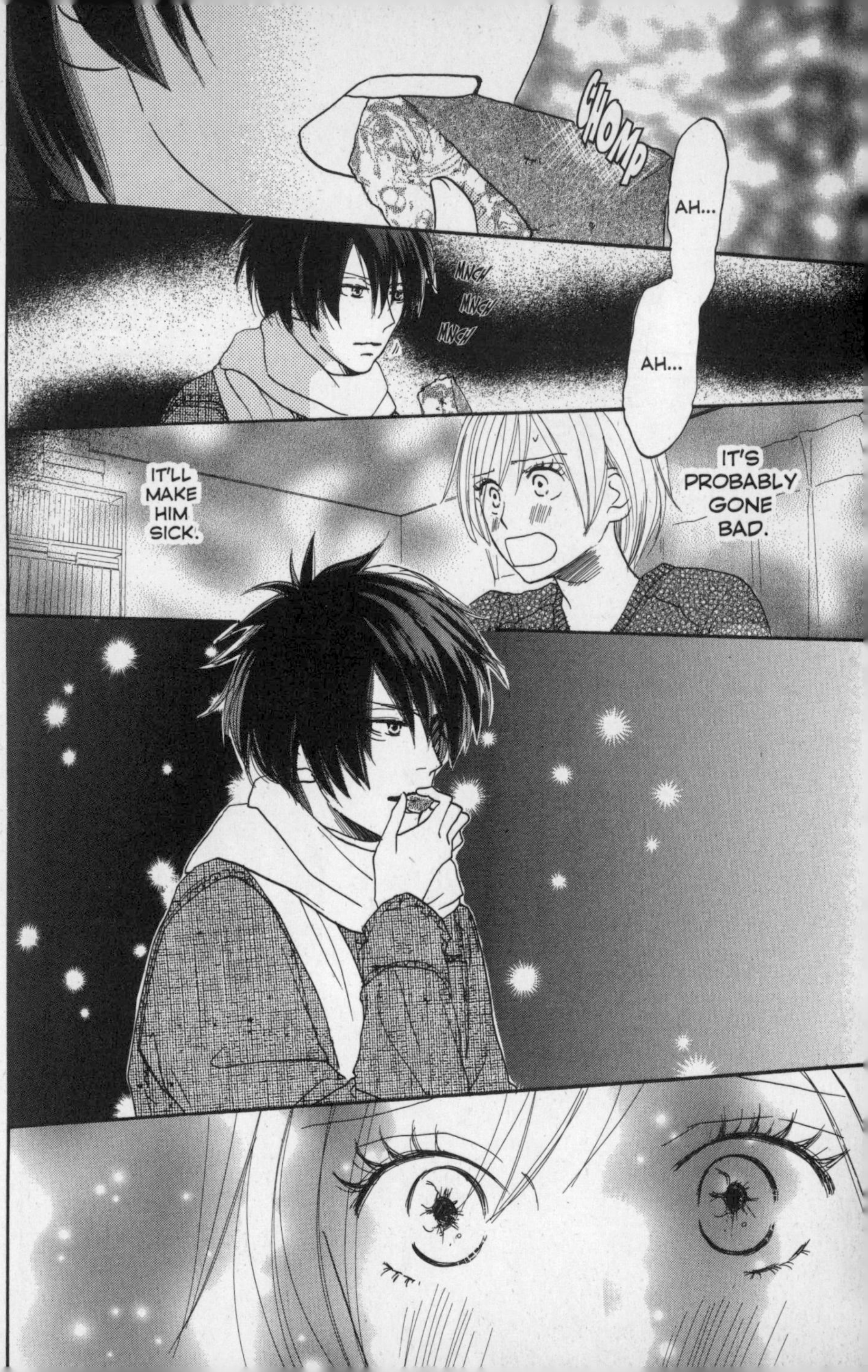
CHOMP
AH...
MNCH
MNCH
MNCH
AH...
IT'S PROBABLY GONE BAD.
IT'LL MAKE HIM SICK.

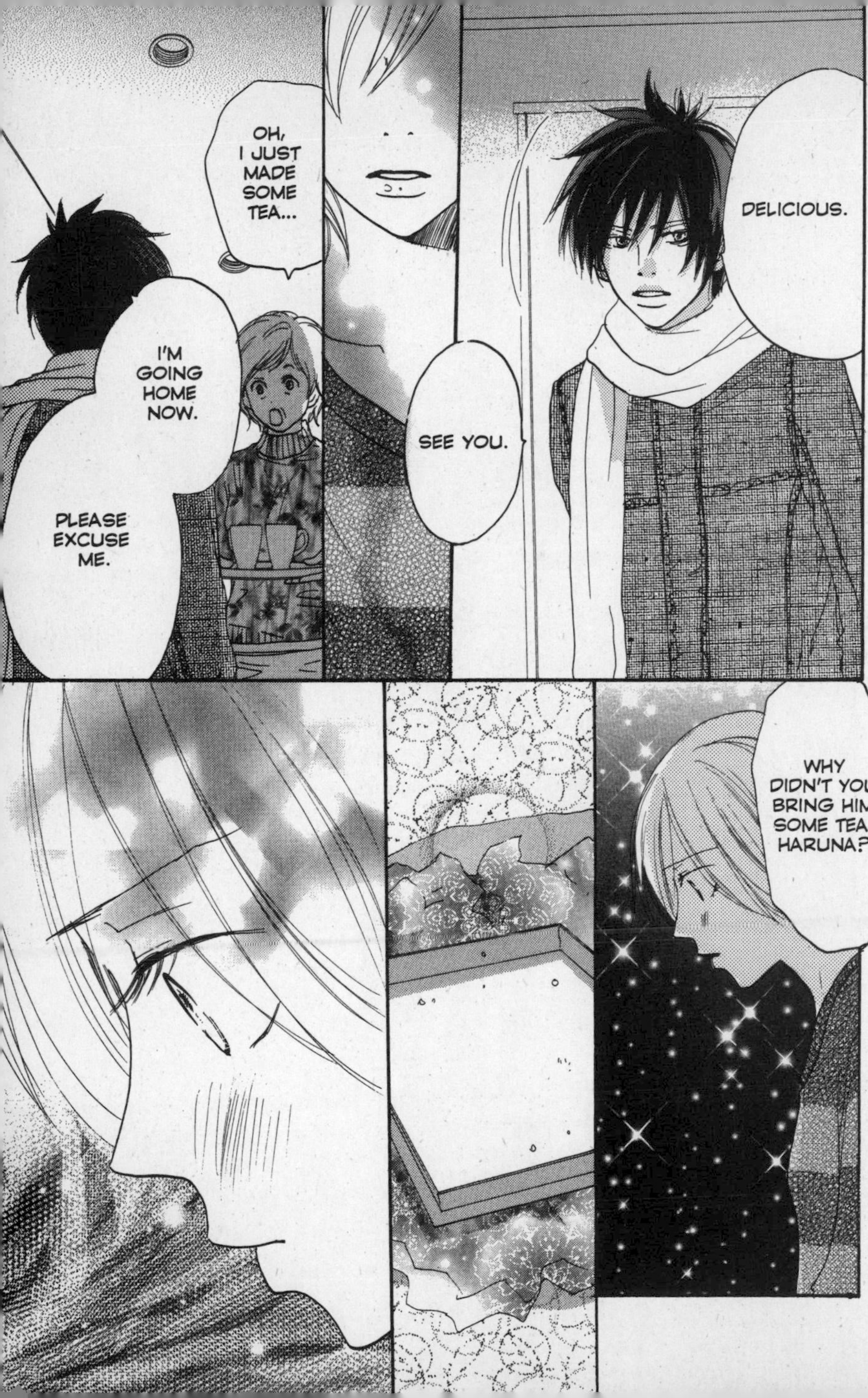
DELICIOUS.
SEE YOU.
OH, I JUST MADE SOME TEA...
I'M GOING HOME NOW.
PLEASE EXCUSE ME.
WHY DIDN'T YOU BRING HIM SOME TEA, HARUNA?

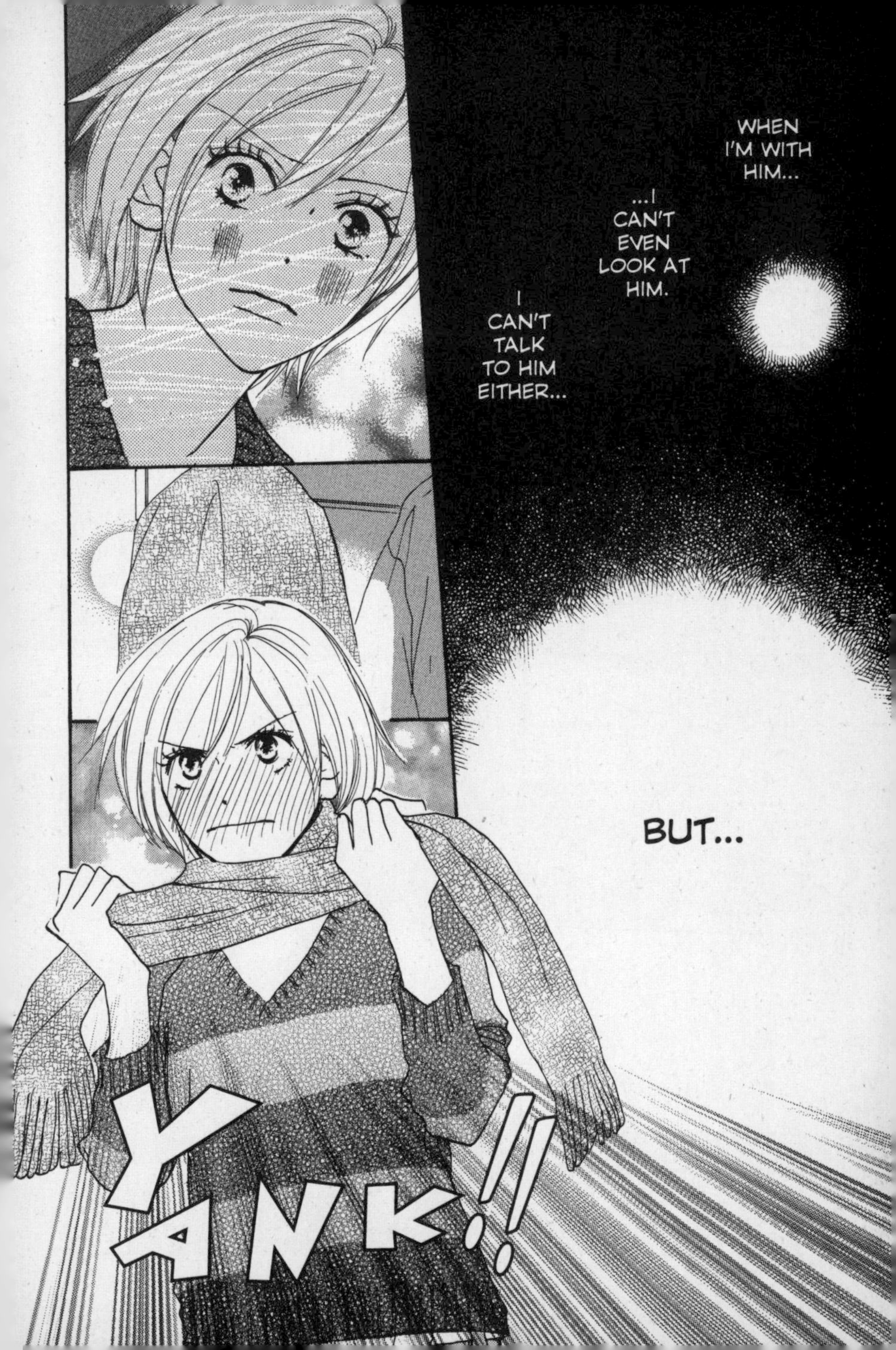
WHEN I'M WITH HIM...
...I CAN'T EVEN LOOK AT HIM.
I CAN'T TALK TO HIM EITHER...
BUT...
YANK!!

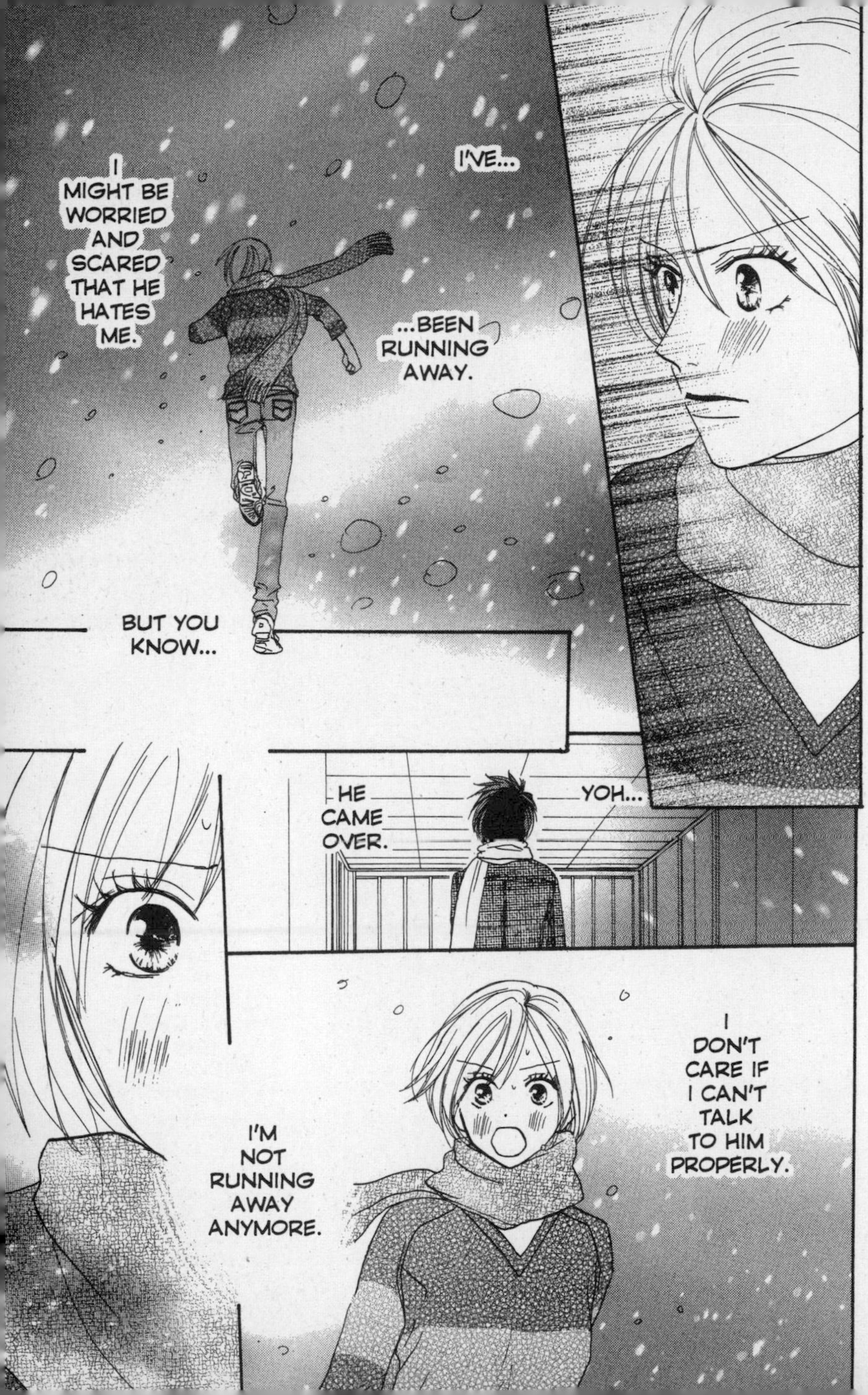
I'VE...
...BEEN RUNNING AWAY.
I MIGHT BE WORRIED AND SCARED THAT HE HATES ME.
BUT YOU KNOW...
YOH...
HE CAME OVER.
I DON'T CARE IF I CAN'T TALK TO HIM PROPERLY.
I'M NOT RUNNING AWAY ANYMORE.

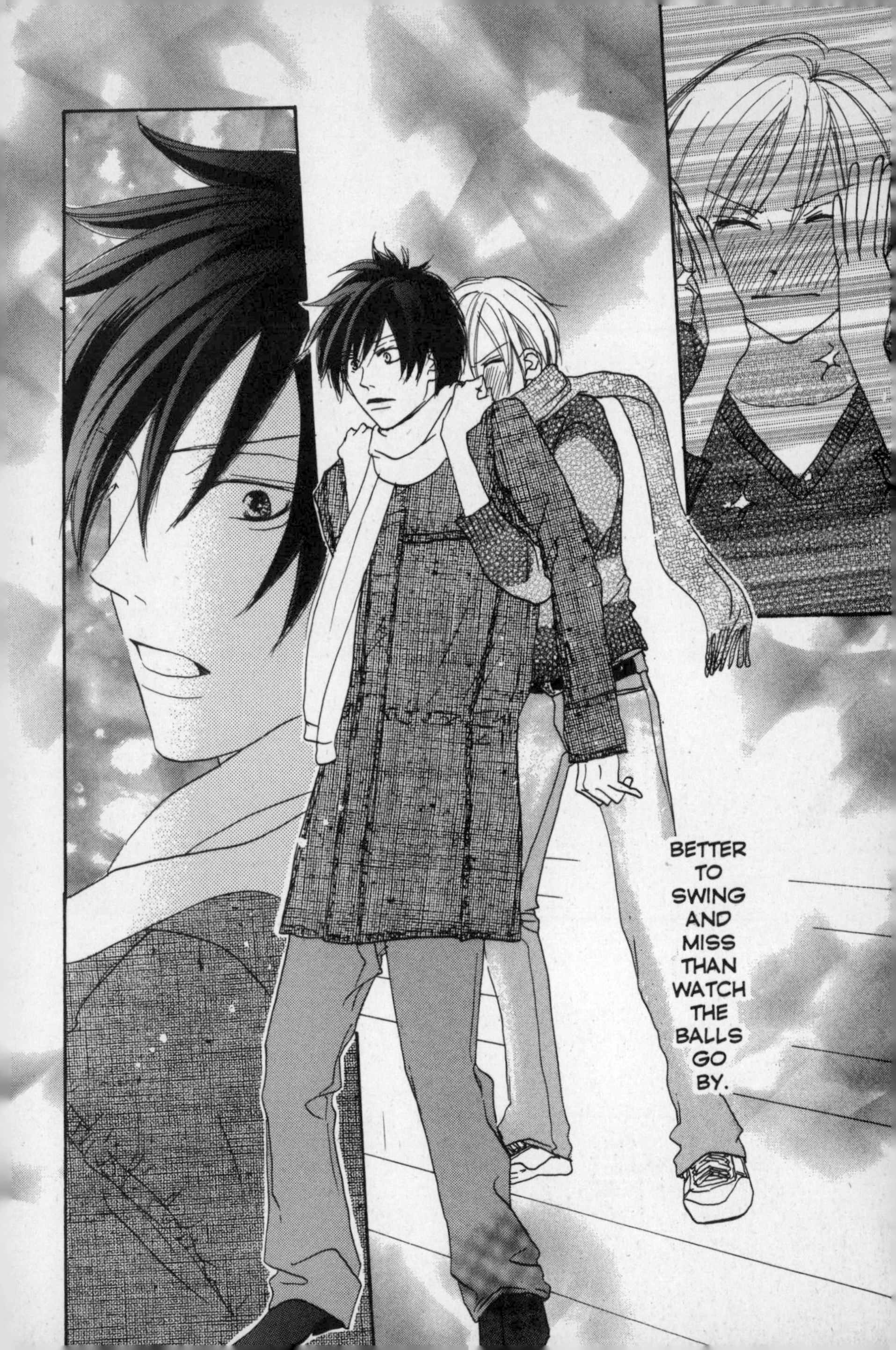
BETTER TO SWING AND MISS THAN WATCH THE BALLS GO BY.

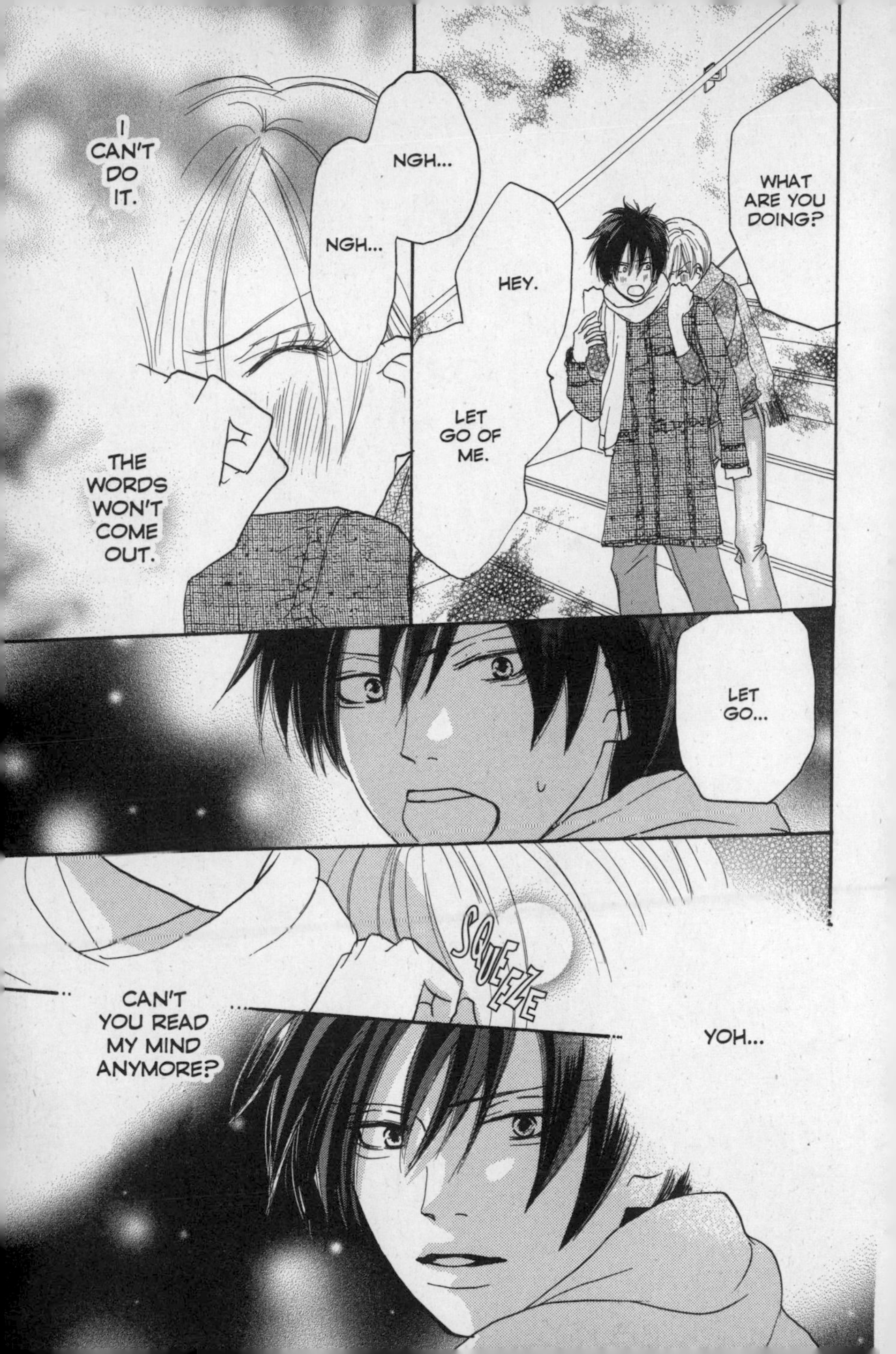
WHAT ARE YOU DOING?
HEY.
LET GO OF ME.
NGH...
NGH...
I CAN'T DO IT.
THE WORDS WON'T COME OUT.
LET GO...
YOH...
SQUEEZE
—...CAN'T YOU READ MY MIND ANYMORE?

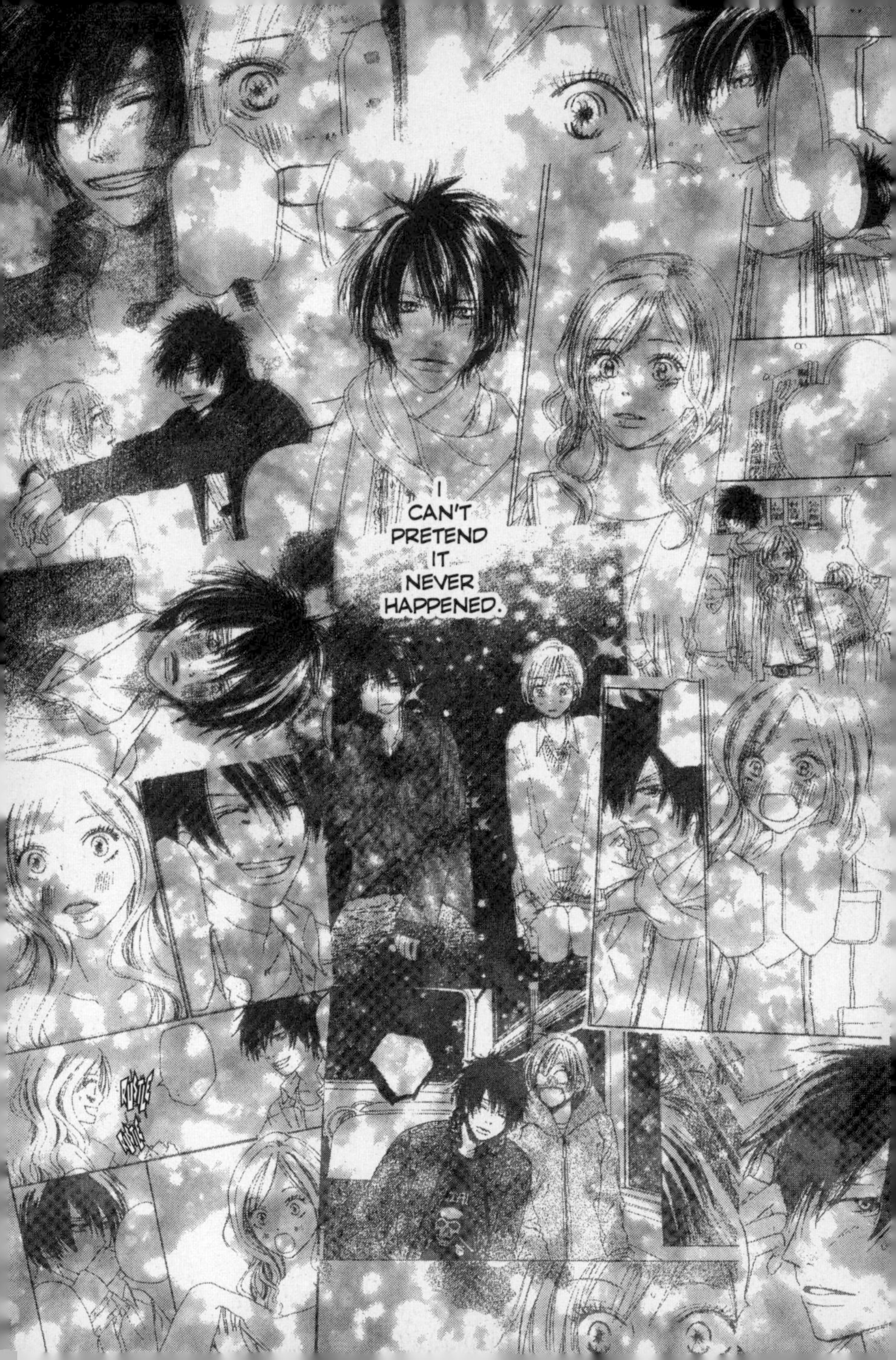
I CAN'T PRETEND IT NEVER HAPPENED.
RUSTLE
RUSTLE

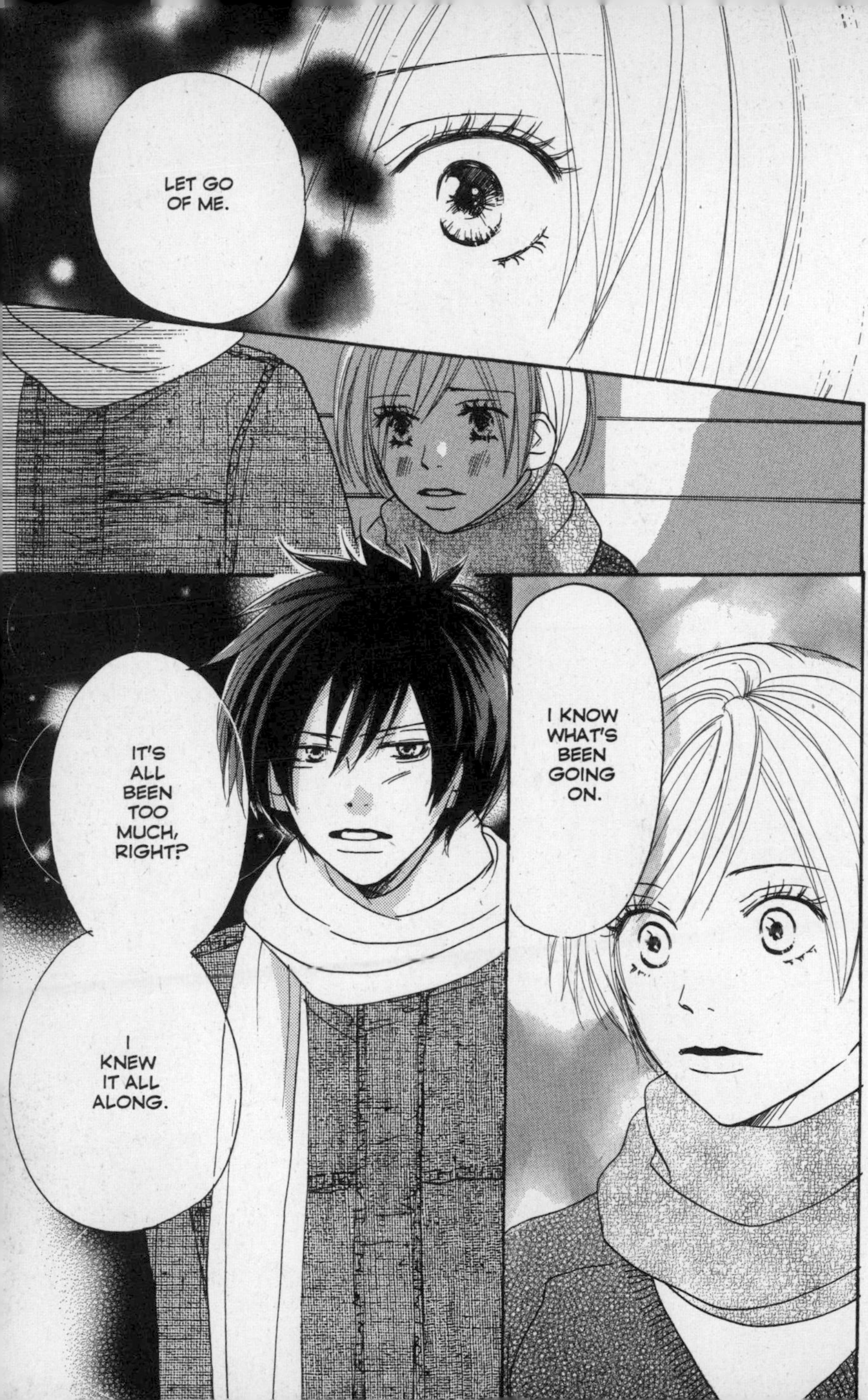
LET GO OF ME.
I KNOW WHAT'S BEEN GOING ON.
IT'S ALL BEEN TOO MUCH, RIGHT?
I KNEW IT ALL ALONG.

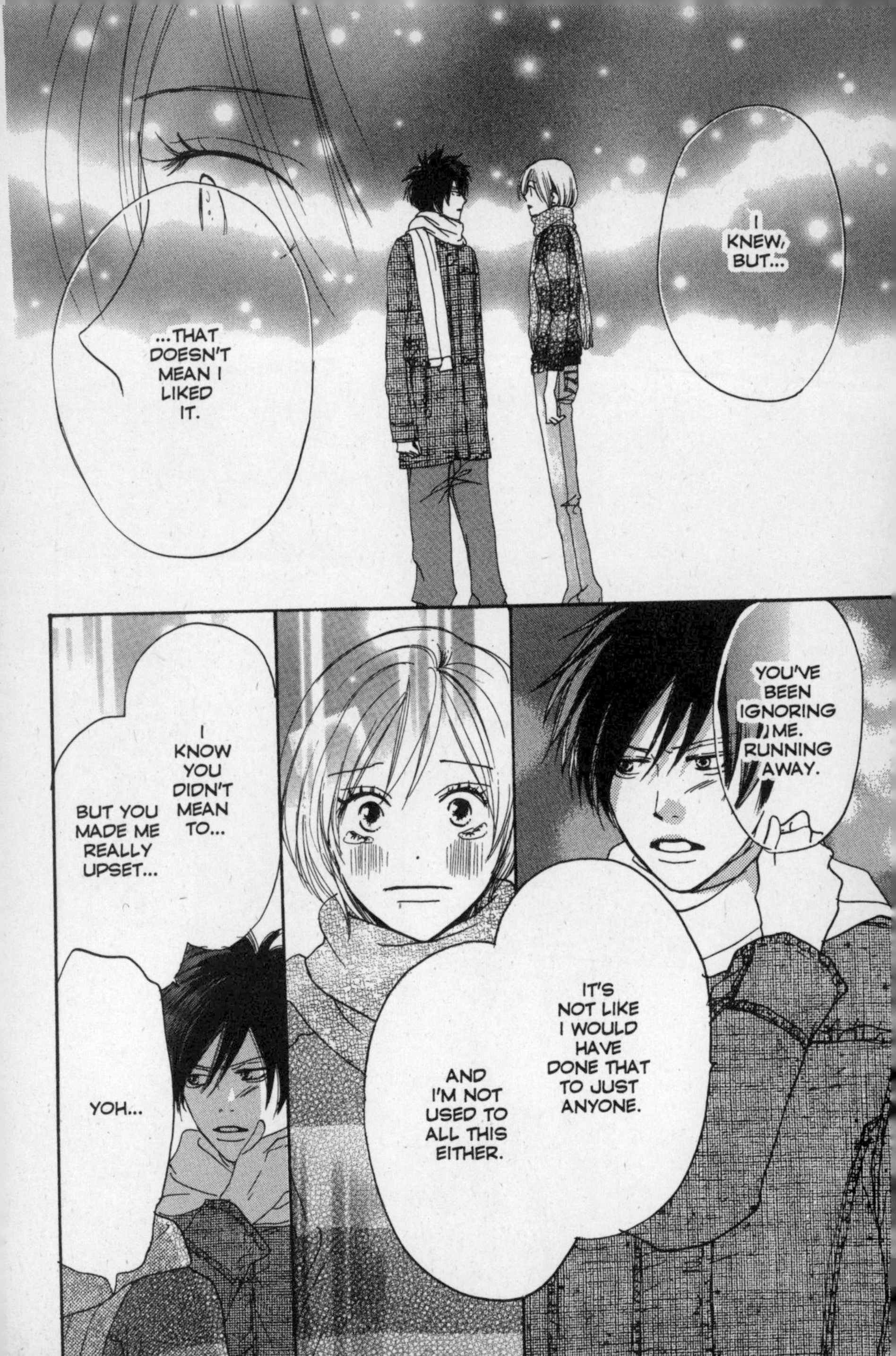
I KNEW, BUT...
...THAT DOESN'T MEAN I LIKED IT.
YOU'VE BEEN IGNORING ME. RUNNING AWAY.
IT'S NOT LIKE I WOULD HAVE DONE THAT TO JUST ANYONE.
AND I'M NOT USED TO ALL THIS EITHER.
I KNOW YOU DIDN'T MEAN TO...
BUT YOU MADE ME REALLY UPSET...
YOH...

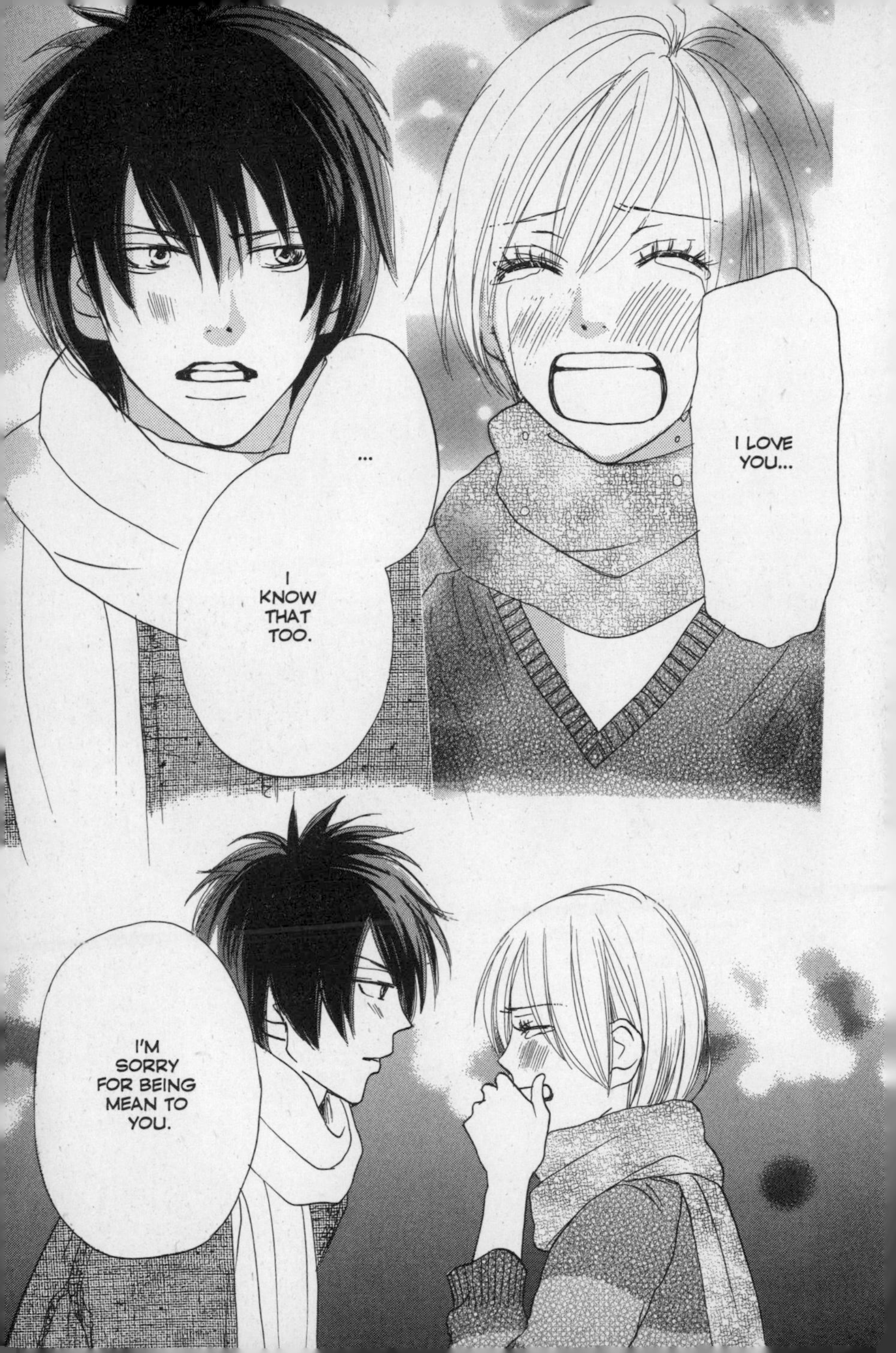
I LOVE YOU...
...
I KNOW THAT TOO.
I'M SORRY FOR BEING MEAN TO YOU.

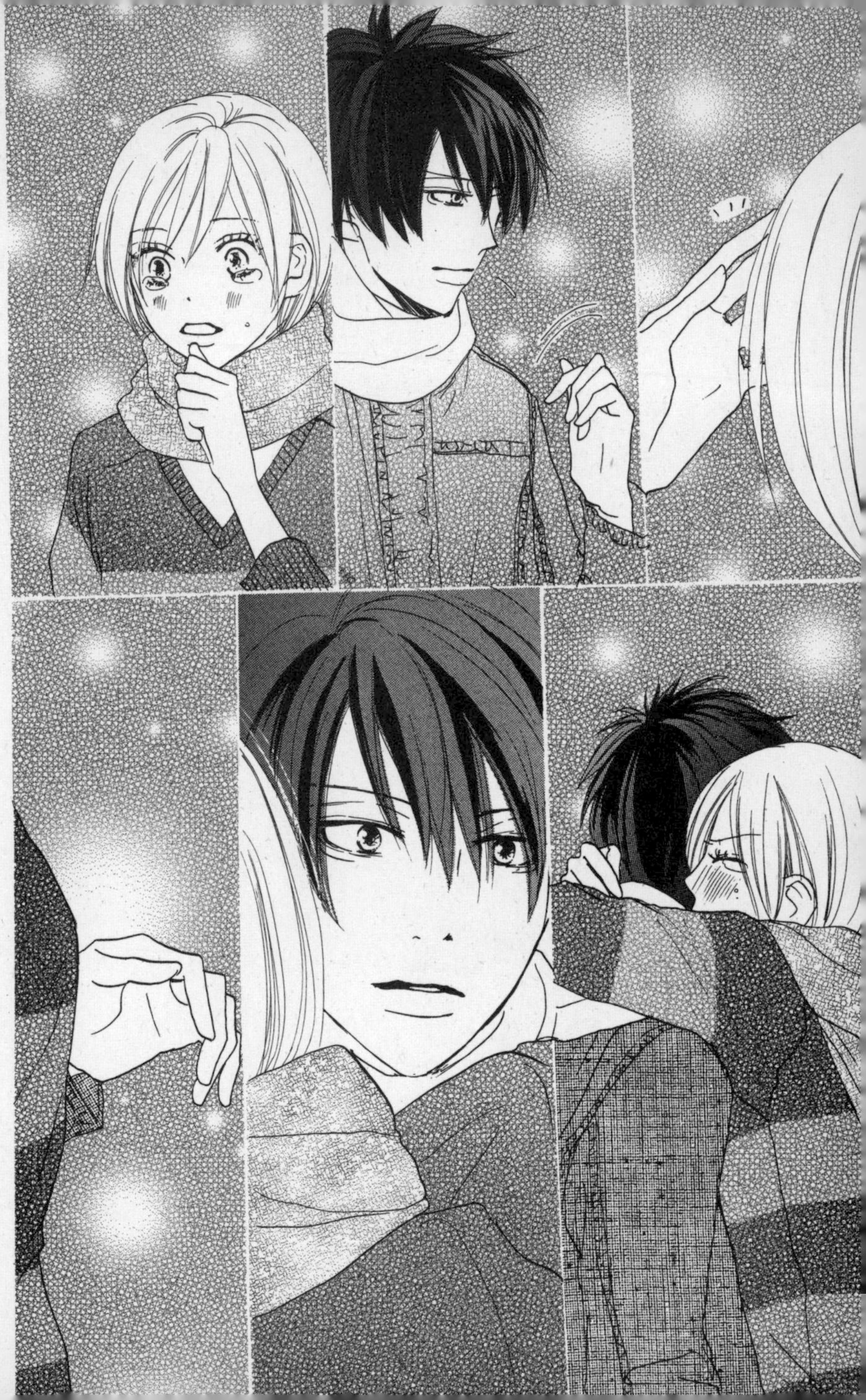

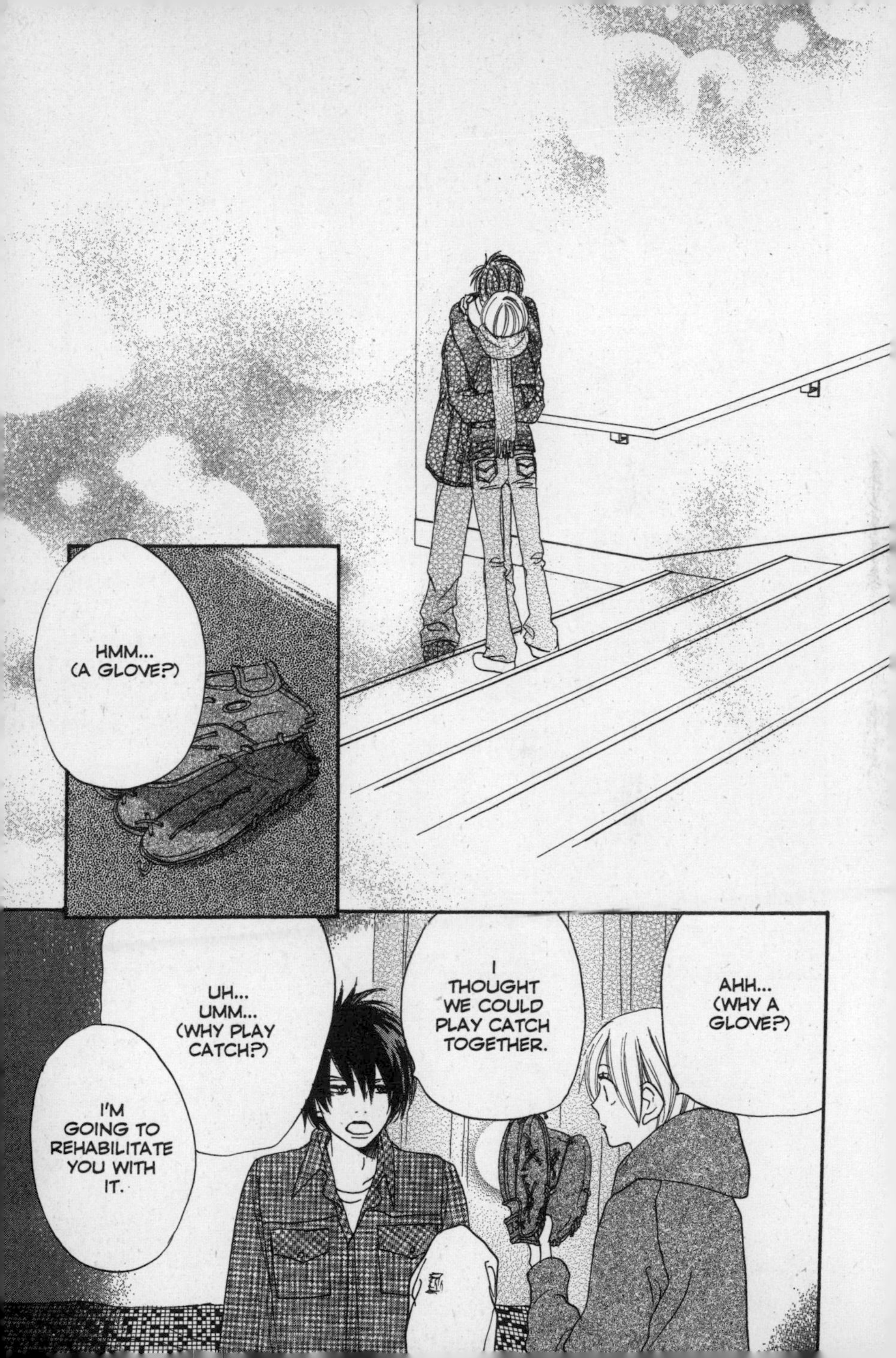
HMM... (A GLOVE?)
AHH... (WHY A GLOVE?)
I THOUGHT WE COULD PLAY CATCH TOGETHER.
UH... UMM... (WHY PLAY CATCH?)
I'M GOING TO REHABILITATE YOU WITH IT.

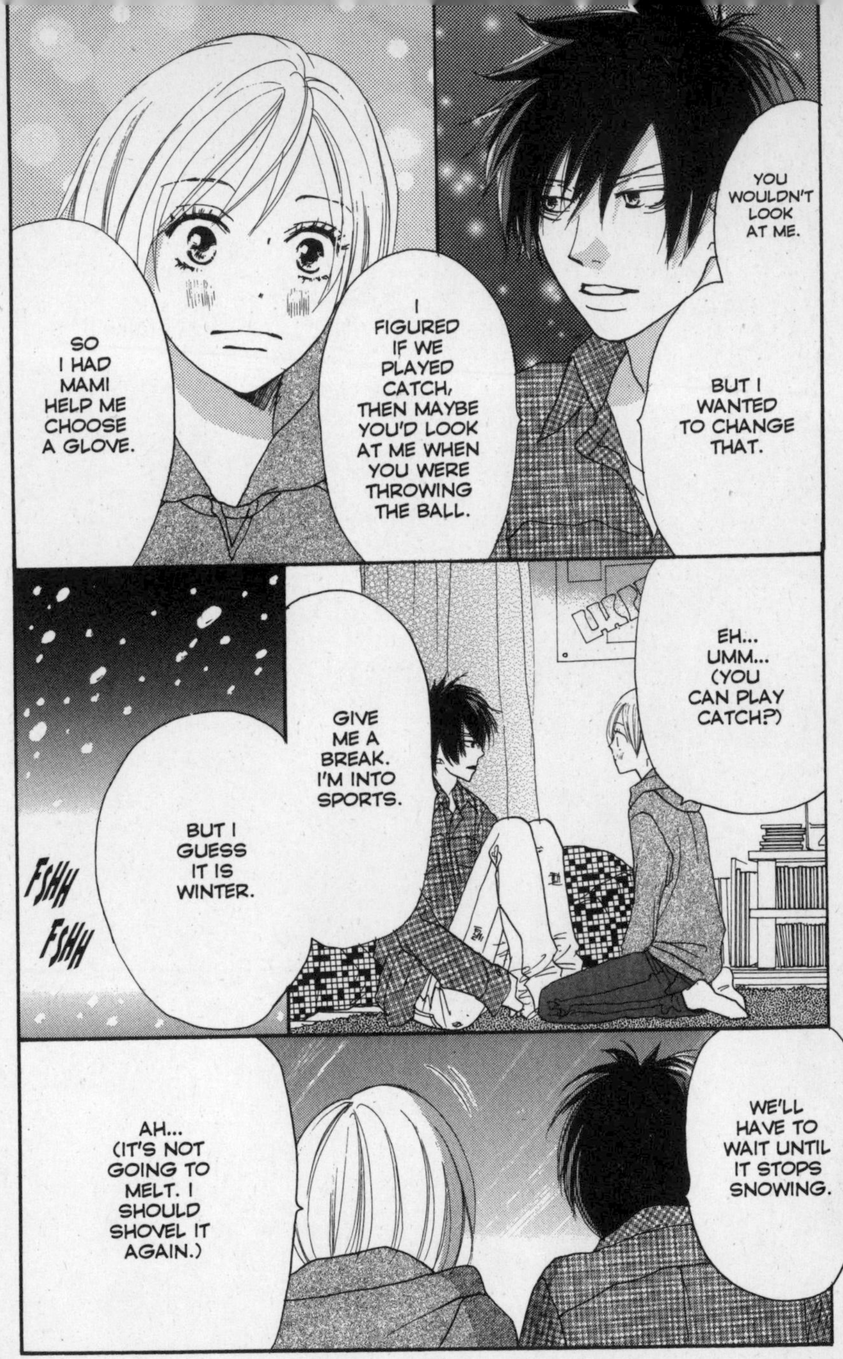
YOU WOULDN'T LOOK AT ME.
BUT I WANTED TO CHANGE THAT.
I FIGURED IF WE PLAYED CATCH, THEN MAYBE YOU'D LOOK AT ME WHEN YOU WERE THROWING THE BALL.
SO I HAD MAMI HELP ME CHOOSE A GLOVE.
EH... UMM... (YOU CAN PLAY CATCH?)
GIVE ME A BREAK. I'M INTO SPORTS.
BUT I GUESS IT IS WINTER.
FSHH
FSHH
WE'LL HAVE TO WAIT UNTIL IT STOPS SNOWING.
AH... (IT'S NOT GOING TO MELT. I SHOULD SHOVEL IT AGAIN.)

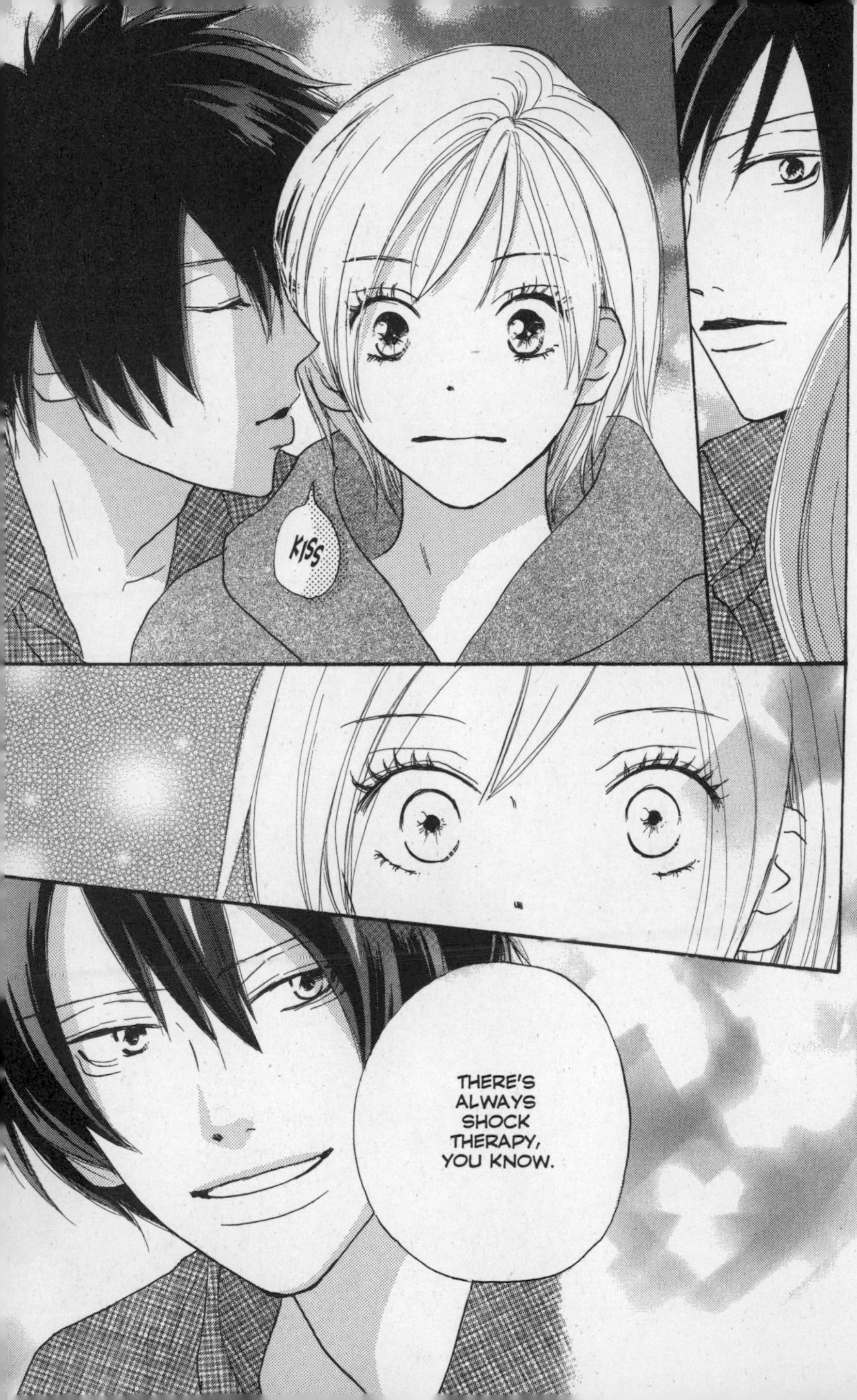
KISS
THERE'S ALWAYS SHOCK THERAPY, YOU KNOW.

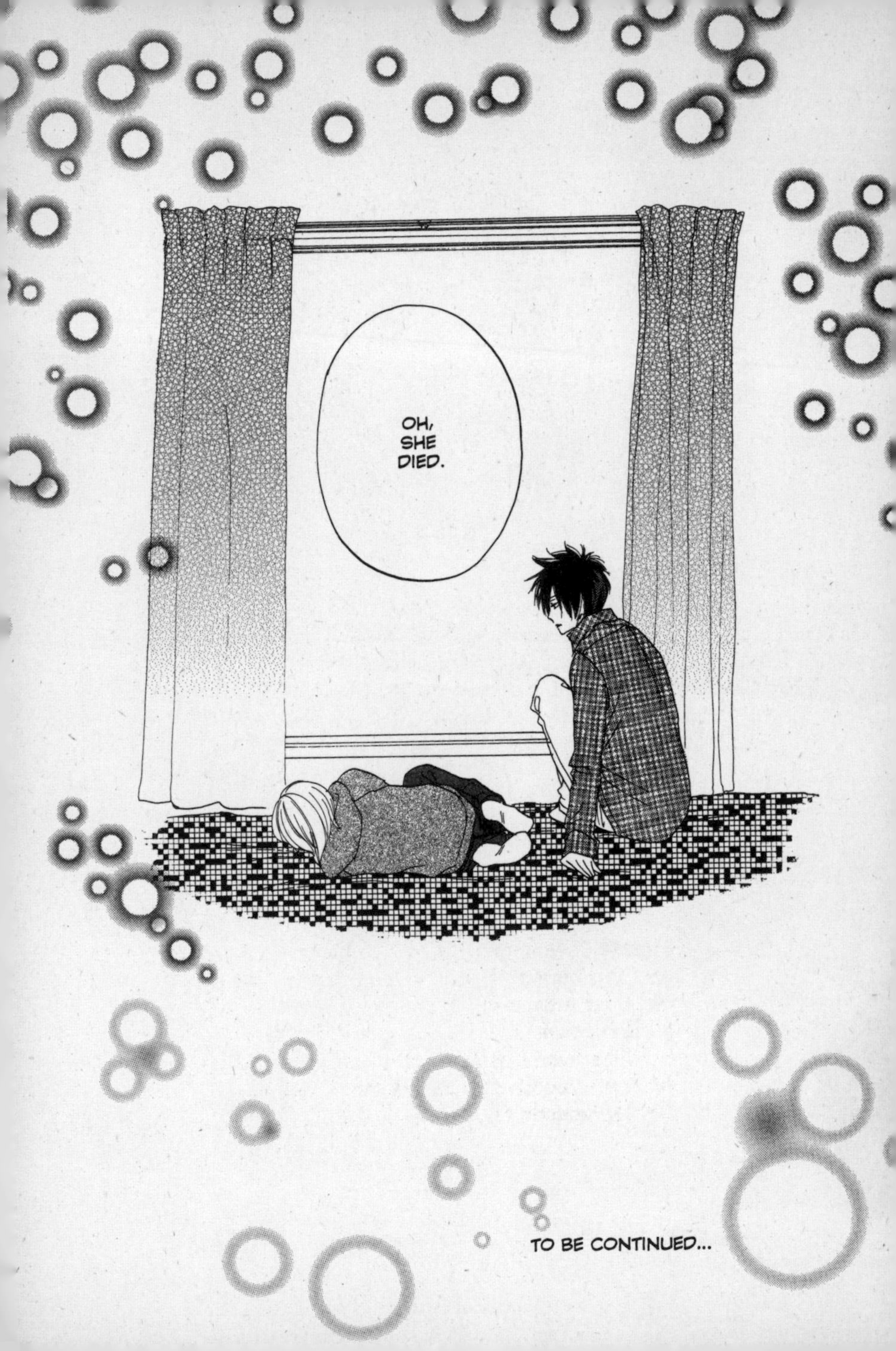
OH, SHE DIED.
TO BE CONTINUED...

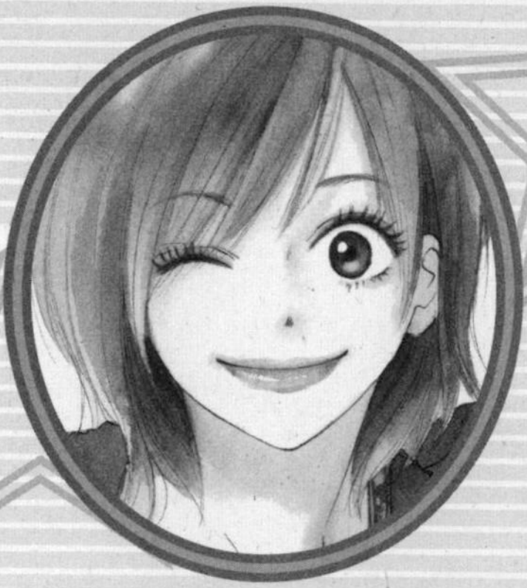

I bought a bread-making machine. Now I can bake bread in my own home. Bread is so yummy. I bought a mochi maker. Now I can make mochi in my own home. Mochi is so yummy. They're all I eat.

– Kazune Kawahara

Kazune Kawahara is from Hokkaido prefecture and was born on March 11th (a Pisces!). She made her manga debut at age 18 with *Kare no Ichiban Sukina Hito* (His Most Favorite Person). Her other works include *Sensei!*, serialized in *Bessatsu Margaret* magazine. Her hobby is interior redecorating.

HIGH SCHOOL DEBUT
VOL. 4
Shojo Beat Edition

STORY & ART BY
KAZUNE KAWAHARA

Translation & Adaptation/Gemma Collinge
Touch-up Art & Lettering/Mark Griffin
Design/Izumi Hirayama
Editor/Amy Yu

KOKO DEBUT © 2003 by Kazune Kawahara
All rights reserved.
First published in Japan in 2003 by SHUEISHA Inc., Tokyo.
English translation rights arranged by SHUEISHA Inc.

The stories, characters and incidents mentioned in this publication are
entirely fictional.

Printed in the U.S.A.

Published by VIZ Media, LLC
P.O. Box 77010
San Francisco, CA 94107

10 9 8 7 6 5 4 3
First printing, July 2008
Third printing, October 2011

www.viz.com   www.shojobeat.com

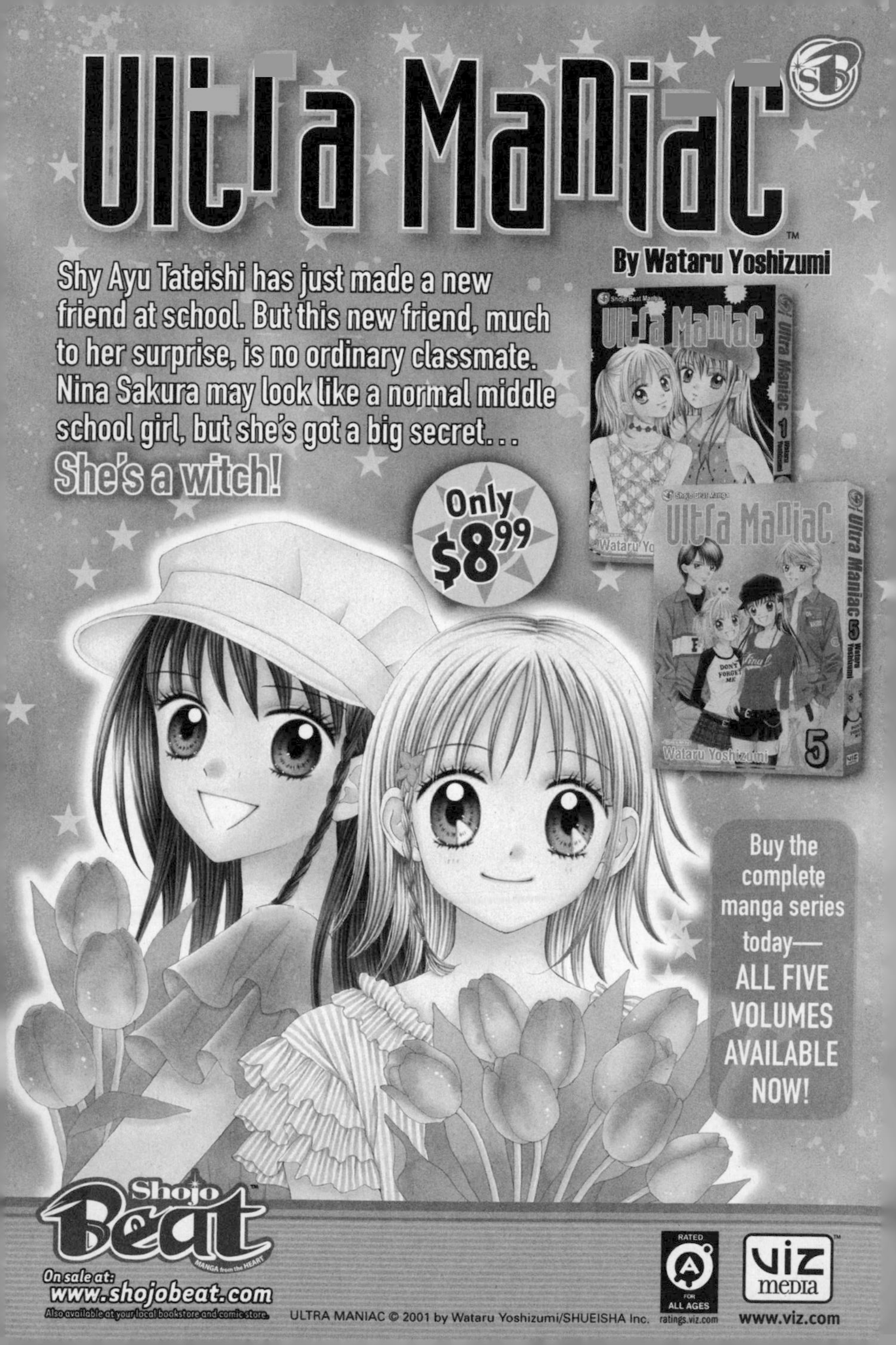
Ultra Maniac™
By Wataru Yoshizumi
Shy Ayu Tateishi has just made a new friend at school. But this new friend, much to her surprise, is no ordinary classmate. Nina Sakura may look like a normal middle school girl, but she's got a big secret...
She's a witch!
Only $8.99
Buy the complete manga series today— ALL FIVE VOLUMES AVAILABLE NOW!
Shojo Beat
MANGA from the HEART
On sale at:
www.shojobeat.com
Also available at your local bookstore and comic store.
ULTRA MANIAC © 2001 by Wataru Yoshizumi/SHUEISHA Inc.
RATED
FOR ALL AGES
ratings.viz.com
VIZ media
www.viz.com

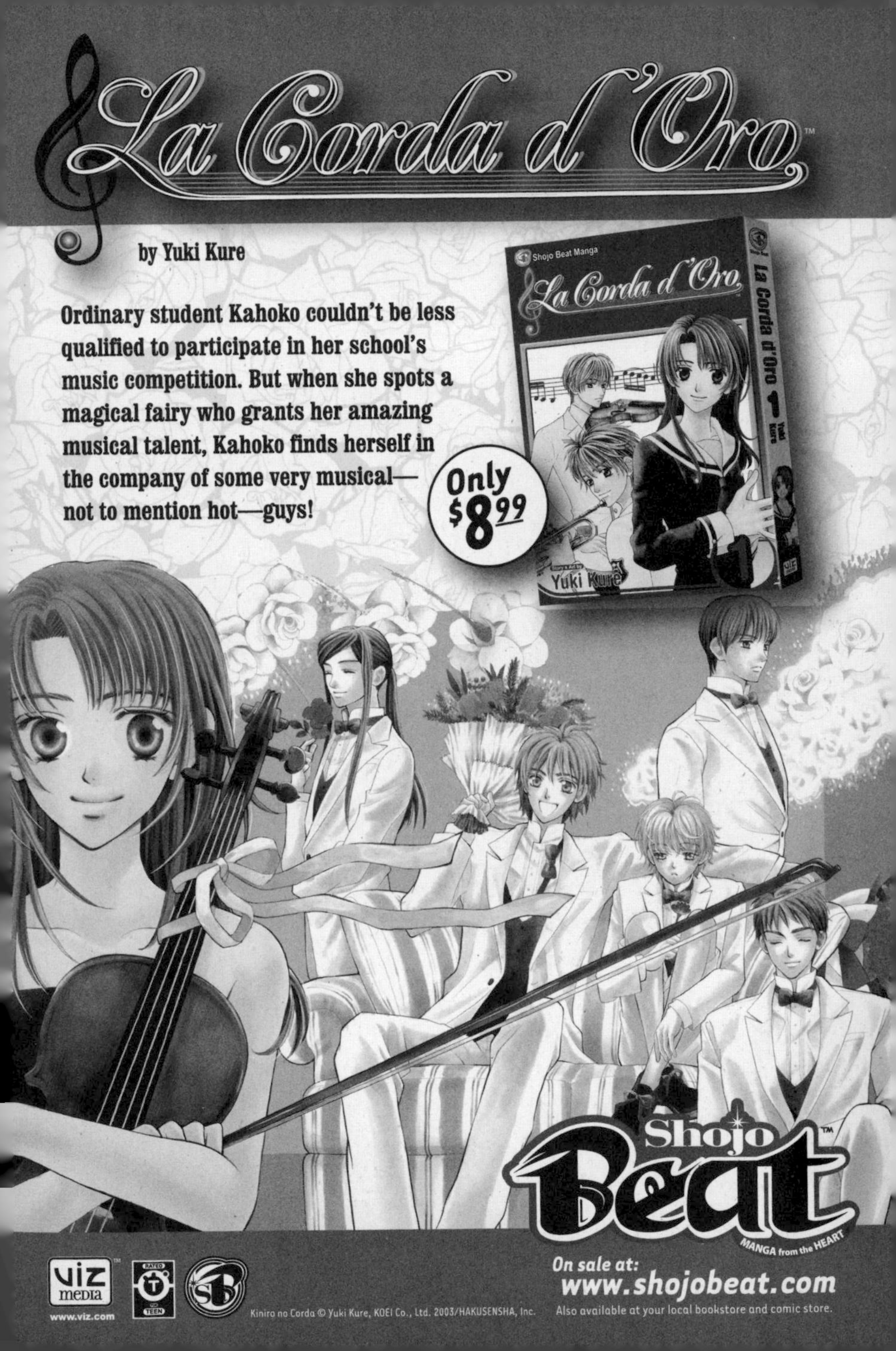

La Corda d'Oro™
by Yuki Kure
Ordinary student Kahoko couldn't be less qualified to participate in her school's music competition. But when she spots a magical fairy who grants her amazing musical talent, Kahoko finds herself in the company of some very musical—not to mention hot—guys!
Only $8.99
Shojo Beat Manga
La Corda d'Oro
La Corda d'Oro 1
Yuki Kure
Shojo Beat™
MANGA from the HEART
On sale at:
www.shojobeat.com
Also available at your local bookstore and comic store.
viz media™
www.viz.com
RATED T TEEN
Kiniro no Corda © Yuki Kure, KOEI Co., Ltd. 2003/HAKUSENSHA, Inc.

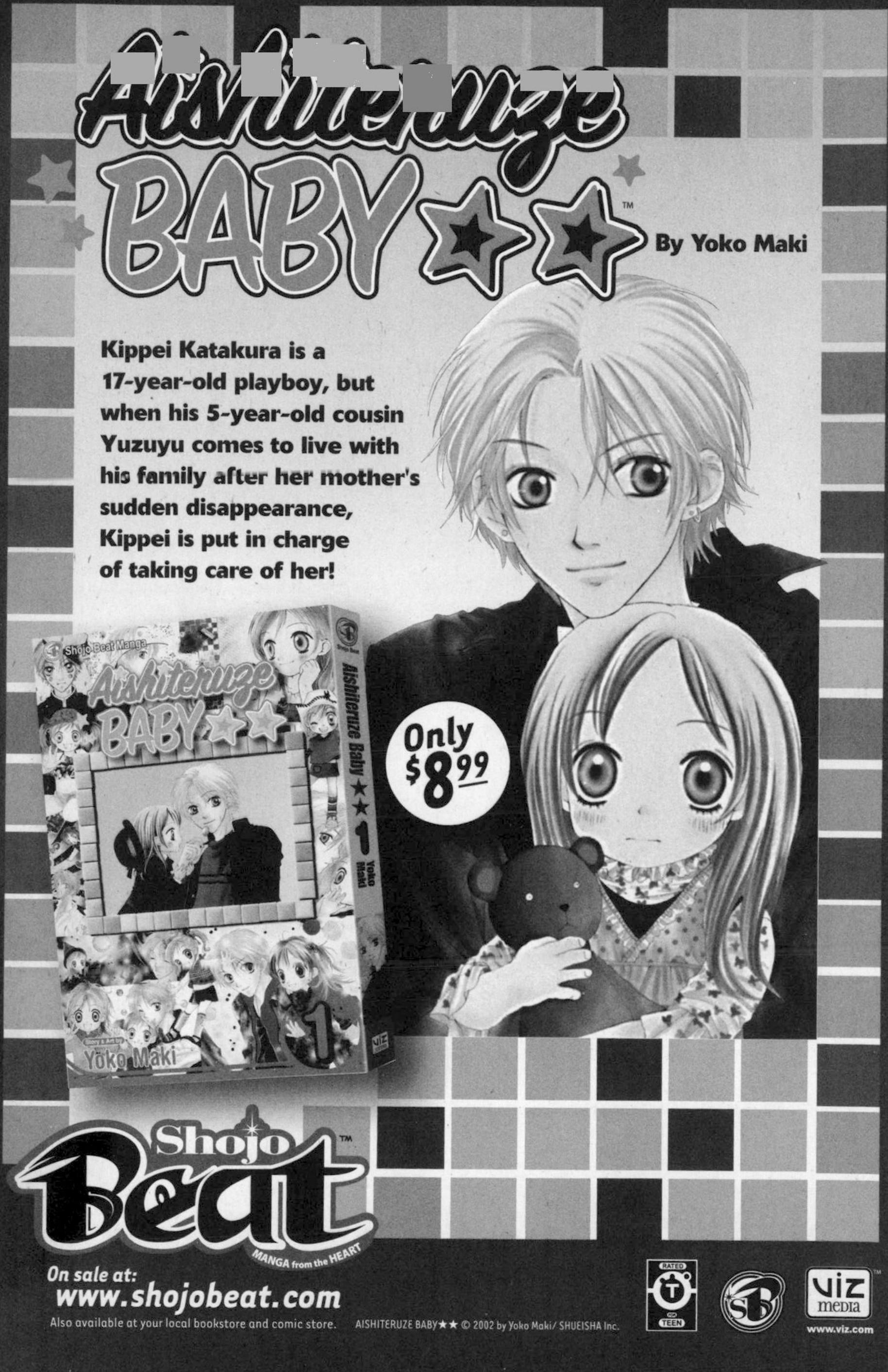
Aishiteruze BABY★★™
By Yoko Maki
Kippei Katakura is a 17-year-old playboy, but when his 5-year-old cousin Yuzuyu comes to live with his family after her mother's sudden disappearance, Kippei is put in charge of taking care of her!
Shojo Beat Manga
Aishiteruze BABY★★
Aishiteruze Baby ★★ 1 Yoko Maki
Story & Art by Yoko Maki
Only $8.99
Shojo Beat™
MANGA from the HEART
On sale at:
www.shojobeat.com
Also available at your local bookstore and comic store.
AISHITERUZE BABY★★ © 2002 by Yoko Maki/ SHUEISHA Inc.
RATED T FOR TEEN
VIZ MEDIA
www.viz.com

BY ARINA TANEMURA, CREATOR OF *FULL MOON* AND *THE GENTLEMEN'S ALLIANCE* †

Ion Tsuburagi is a normal junior high girl with normal junior high problems. But when a mysterious substance grants her telekinetic powers, she finds herself struggling to keep everything together! Are her new abilities a blessing...or a curse?

Find out in *I•O•N*—manga on sale now!

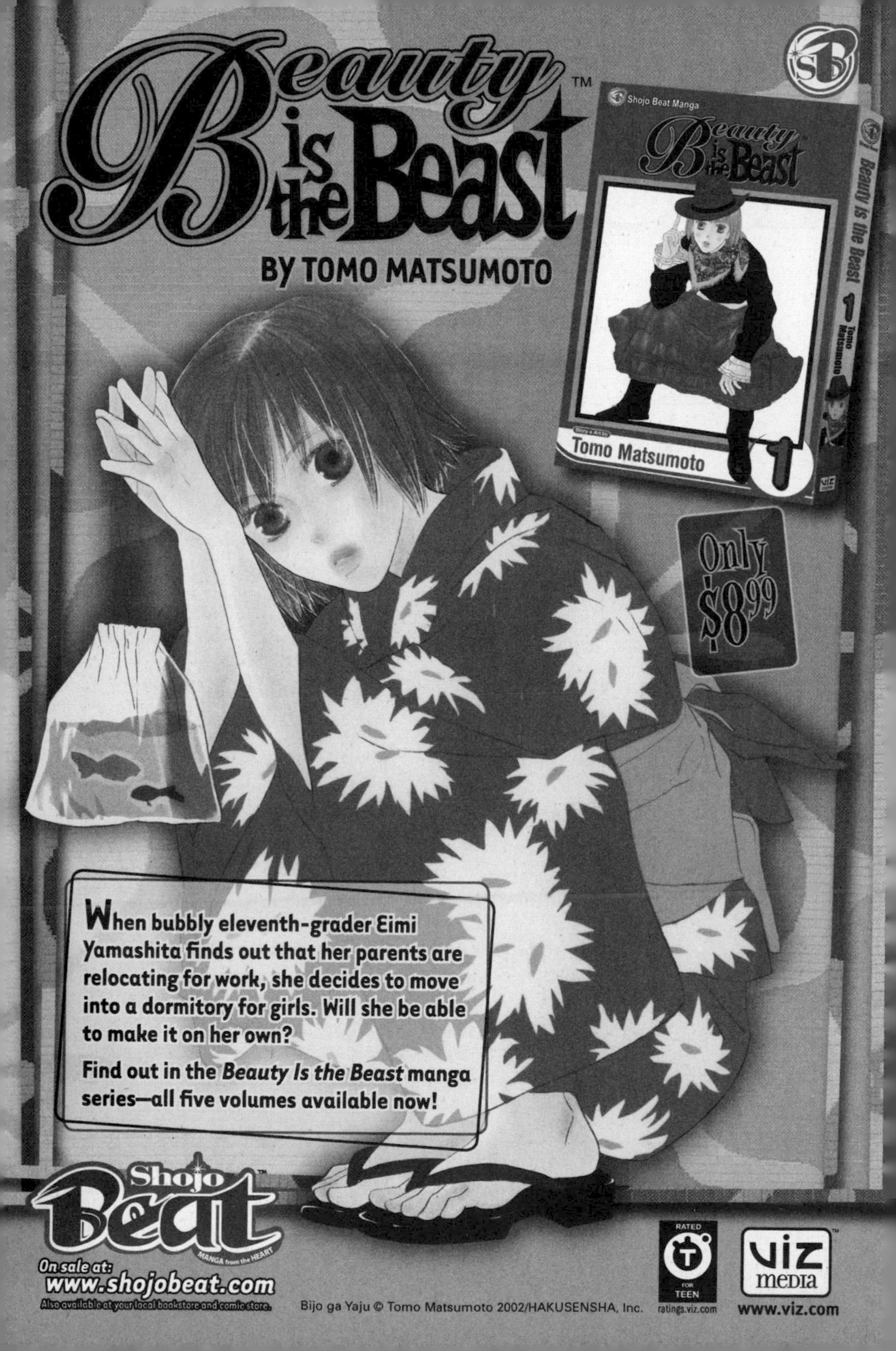
Beauty is the Beast™
BY TOMO MATSUMOTO
Shojo Beat Manga
Beauty is the Beast
Tomo Matsumoto
1
Only $8.99
When bubbly eleventh-grader Eimi Yamashita finds out that her parents are relocating for work, she decides to move into a dormitory for girls. Will she be able to make it on her own?
Find out in the Beauty Is the Beast manga series—all five volumes available now!
Shojo Beat™
MANGA from the HEART
On sale at:
www.shojobeat.com
Also available at your local bookstore and comic store.
Bijo ga Yaju © Tomo Matsumoto 2002/HAKUSENSHA, Inc.
RATED T FOR TEEN
ratings.viz.com
VIZ MEDIA
www.viz.com

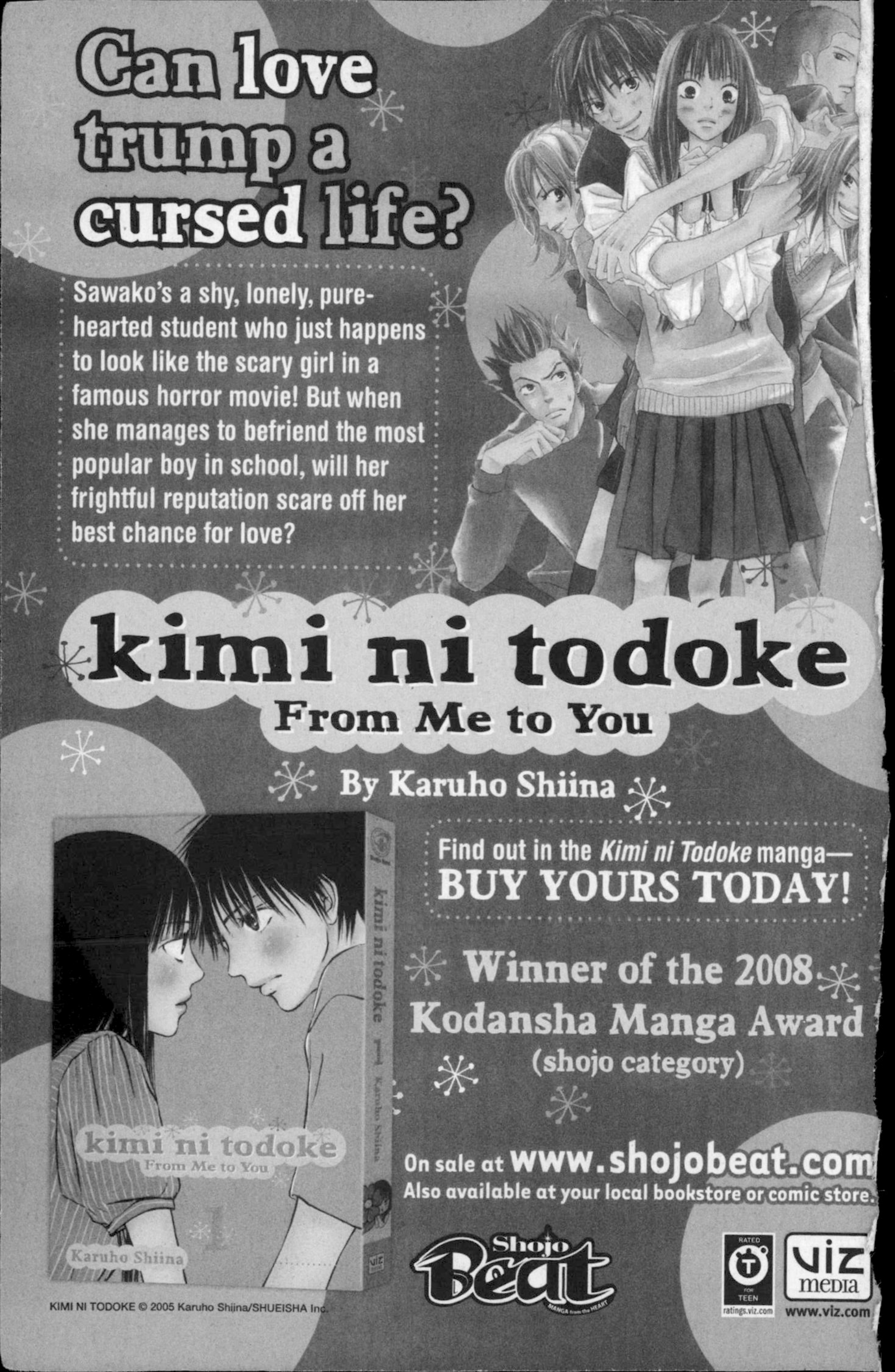
Can love trump a cursed life?
Sawako's a shy, lonely, pure-hearted student who just happens to look like the scary girl in a famous horror movie! But when she manages to befriend the most popular boy in school, will her frightful reputation scare off her best chance for love?
kimi ni todoke
From Me to You
By Karuho Shiina
kimi ni todoke
From Me to You
Karuho Shiina
Find out in the *Kimi ni Todoke* manga—
BUY YOURS TODAY!
Winner of the 2008
Kodansha Manga Award
(shojo category)
On sale at www.shojobeat.com
Also available at your local bookstore or comic store.
Shojo Beat
RATED T FOR TEEN
ratings.viz.com
viz media
www.viz.com
KIMI NI TODOKE © 2005 Karuho Shiina/SHUEISHA Inc.